A Consumer's Dictionary of Cosmetic Ingredients

ALSO BY THE AUTHOR

Poisons in Your Food
Beware of the Food You Eat
How to Reduce Your Medical Bills
A Consumer's Dictionary of Food Additives
Ageless Aging
Cancer-Causing Agents

A Consumer's Dictionary of Cosmetic Ingredients

NEW, THIRD REVISED EDITION

Ruth Winter, M.S.

Crown Publishers, Inc. New York

Published by Crown Publishers, Inc., 201 East 50th Street,
New York, New York 10022
Manufactured in the United States of America
CROWN is a trademark of Crown Publishers, Inc.
Library of Congress Cataloging-in-Publication Data
Winter, Ruth, 1930—
A consumer's dictionary of cosmetic ingredients.
Includes bibliographical references.
I. Cosmetics—Dictionaries. I. Title
TP983,W54 1989 668'.55'0321 83-23197
ISBN 0-517-57263-X

10 9 8 7 6 5 4 3 2 1

Third Revised Edition

A Consumer's Dictionary of Cosmetic Ingredients

INTRODUCTION

Like the alchemists and medicine men of old, cosmetic companies promise beauty and youth in a bottle. "Rub this into your face and your wrinkles will disappear" they say or "put this on your skin and you will be irresistible."

If you feel more attractive or more youthful after using cosmetics, what's the harm? So you pay $50 for five cents worth of ingredients. Maybe it is worth it psychologically.

The problem is that cosmetics may cost you more than you want to pay.

Cosmetics have received and still receive the lowest priority in the offices of the Food and Drug Administration. The agency spends less than half of one percent of its budget on cosmetic safety surveillance. In its cosmetics division in Washington, there are 60 toxicologists that not only have to evaluate cosmetics but food products as well. There are 373 inspectors who must cover the national and international multibillion dollar food and cosmetic industries. Cosmetics alone is a 17 billion dollar a year industry producing more than twenty thousand different products.

Cosmetics have traditionally received little attention because it has been wrongly assumed that such products do not really affect our health and safety. The skin was believed to be a nearly perfect barrier that prevented chemicals applied to it from penetrating into the body. This belief went unchallenged until the 1960s when the much-heralded—but unmarketed—miracle drug DMSO proved its ability to carry substances with it through the skin and into the body's tissue and blood stream. Until it was shown that rabbits' eyes were adversely affected by the drug, DMSO was being promoted as a through-the-skin carrier of all sorts of medication. In fact, an increasingly popular new way to deliver drugs today is "transdermally." Medications to prevent seasickness or to treat angina (chest pains) and hormonal deficiencies are placed in an adhesive disk for delivery through the skin.

It has now been accepted that all chemicals penetrate the skin to some extent, and many do so in significant amounts. What degree of absorption is there when a cosmetic is left on the face (as a makeup base might be for twelve hours) or spread over the entire body (as suntan lotions may be)? What is the effect of exposure to ingredients that may be used over a number of years?

Most consumers and the cosmetic companies are concerned with allergic reactions and skin irritations, but what of systemic absorption, toxicity, and chronic effects?

If you take a drug that may cause side effects, the risk may be worth it because you may need the drug to regain or maintain your health. But although they may be rewarding psychologically, are cosmetics worth any risk?

In September 1980, the National Toxicology Program (NTP) contracted with the National Research Council (NRC) and the National Academy of Sciences for a study with two principal charges:

1. To determine toxicity-testing needs for substances to which humans are exposed so that the federal agencies responsible for the protection of public health will have the information needed to assess the toxicity of such substances.

2. To develop and validate uniformly applicable and wide-ranging criteria by which to set priorities for research on substances with potentially adverse public-health impact.

The NRC considered 65,725 substances of possible concern, among them 8,627 food additives and 3,410 cosmetic ingredients approved for use. Through a random sample program, 100 of these substances were selected by screening for the presence of *at least* some toxicity information. An in-depth examination of this subsample led to the conclusion that on the great majority of the substances, data considered to be essential for conducting a health hazard assessment are lacking. In 1984, the NRC published their findings:[1]

• When judged against current standards for toxicity testing, 92 percent of the tests in the subsample were inadequate.

• Of 18 standard tests, only one—the oral administration in rodents—was judged to be adequate. The other 17 tests necessary according to the standards needed repetition or were not done at all on 33 to 80 percent of the cosmetic ingredients.

• In general, chronic studies, inhalation studies and more complex studies such as neurotoxicity, genetic toxicity, and effects on the fetus are most frequently needed. The greatest need for cosmetic ingredient testing was found to be for subchronic eye toxicity and subchronic neurotoxicity.

The experts who participated in the vast government study concluded: "This report shows that, of tens of thousands of commercially important chemicals, only a few have been subjected to extensive toxicity testing and most have scarcely been tested at all."

[1] *Toxicity Testing: Strategies to Determine Needs and Priorities*. Washington, D.C.: National Research Council (U.S.), National Academy Press, 1984.

There is no toxicity information available for 56 percent of the cosmetic ingredients and 28 percent have less than minimal information and only 2 percent have complete health hazard assessment possible.

Fewer than 4 percent of the manufacturers and packagers and distributors file injury reports. Reports that filter in from emergency rooms deal mainly with abuse of products rather than use—broken bottles, accidental ingestion, etc. If consumers do develop a skin, hair, or eye reaction, they may just stop using the product and not report it. Frequently, neither the consumer nor the consumer's doctor associates a physical problem, particularly a systemic one, with the use of a cosmetic.[2]

In an effort to determine what kind of reactions might occur, a study was done by the North American Contact Dermatitis Group between 1977 and 1980.[3] Among 8,093 patients, 487 cases were found to be cosmetic-related. In about half those cases, it was found that neither the patient nor his or her doctor at first linked the problem to a cosmetic. Eighty percent of the cosmetic related cases of contact dermatitis were allergic, 16 percent due to irritation, and the rest caused by photoallergy, phototoxicity, and other skin reactions.

The most frequent cosmetic culprits were fragrances, preservatives, lanolin, and its derivatives, *p*-phenylenediamine and propylene glycol (*see all*).[4]

The most difficult issue in the identification of ingredients and contaminants in cosmetics concerns cancer-causing agents. A number of cosmetic ingredients now in use have been shown to be carcinogenic in animals or to cause genetic breaks in cells. Testing for mutagenicity—breaks in the genetic material of bacteria—can screen many chemicals inexpensively and rapidly. Almost all chemicals known to be carcinogenic in humans have been shown to be mutagens in these systems. However, not all mutagens are necessarily carcinogenic. Thus animal studies—which cost approximately $300,000 to thoroughly test an ingredient—are needed.

All agents that cause cancer in humans cause cancer in rats and mice with the exception of trivalent arsenic. Whether all chemicals that cause cancer in animals also cause cancer in humans is not known, but many scientists in the cancer field believe they do.

In 1978 there was a great outcry when it was shown that ingredients

[2] Zeona W. Mally, *What United States FDA Cosmetic Regulations Meant to Physicians and Consumers, Principles of Cosmetics for Dermatologists.* St. Louis: C. V. Mosby Co., 1982.

[3] "Prospective Study of Cosmetic Reactions, 1977–1980, North American Contact Dermatitis Group," *Journal of the American Academy of Dermatology,* Vol. 6, No. 5, May 1982.

[4] Ibid.

in hair dyes caused cancer in animals. The FDA has no power over hair dyes because coal tar colors, which were incriminated, are exempted from the Cosmetic Act. The FDA was unsuccessful in requiring a warning label on hair coloring products, and women returned to coloring their hair at the rate of $450 million a year. In the meantime, questions about hair dye ingredients remain.

The University of California researchers studying more than 58,000 hairdressers, manicurists, and cosmetologists found that they developed multiple myeloma at four times the rate of the general population. Multiple myeloma is a malignant tumor of the bone marrow. Women aged twenty to sixty-five residing in the Los Angeles area were studied. In 1982 Dr. John Peters and two coauthors said in *The American Journal of Industrial Medicine* that among the suspect substances are hair dyes, shampoos, hair conditioners, relaxers, permanent wave solutions, detergents, nail antiseptics, fungi, and bacteria.[5]

In another study, it was reported that women who color their hair do show greater chromosomal damage than women who have never colored their hair. They said the damage to the genetic material in women caused by hair dyes supports laboratory studies that suggest that hair dyes may have mutagenic and carcinogenic properties.[6]

Another common cosmetic ingredient has also been cited several times as a possible carcinogen—talcum powder. In 1972 a study by the Office of Product Technology of the FDA showed that of forty cosmetic talcum powder samples tested, thirty-nine contained one percent asbestos or less. Asbestos is a proven human carcinogen. The manufacturers maintain that they have solved the problem of contamination. However, asbestos and talc fibers are similar in composition. Cancer of the ovary was linked to talc use in an article in the journal *Cancer* in 1982. Daniel Cramer, M.D., an obstetrician and gynecologist, found in a study of 215 Boston area women with ovarian cancer that thirty-two had used talcum powder on their genitals and sanitary napkins, and when compared to a group of women without cancer, women who used talc had 328 times the risk of ovarian cancer. In the 1960s granulomas of the internal organs had been associated with the talc used on surgeon's gloves during operations.

A simple product that could be either a drug or a cosmetic, mouthwash, was also tied to cancer in 1983. Two reports in the February *Journal of the National Cancer Institute* linked daily use of mouthwash with cancer of the mouth and throat among women usually

[5] John Peters, M.D., et al., in *American Journal of Industrial Medicine*, September 1982.

[6] D. J. Kirland, M.D. et al., "Hair Dye Genotoxicity," *American Heart Association Journal*, Vol. 98, No. 6, December 1979.

considered a low risk for cancers because they did not smoke or drink alcohol. The association between mouthwash and cancer may be an artifact or it may be significant. How will we know? The fact is that we must rely on the cosmetic companies themselves to protect us and to test thoroughly their products before putting them on the market. The Cosmetic, Toiletries and Fragrance Association, in fact, has established its own safety assessment system. Since 1976 a panel of seven scientists has been conducting an independent review to assess the safety data concerning ingredients. The Cosmetic Ingredient Review panel recommendations are publicly announced without any private review of comment, according to the CTFA. Members have questioned the safety of several ingredients thus far, such as 6-methyl coumarin and musk ambrette, and those substances have been voluntarily removed by CTFA member companies. The CTFA claims that 90 percent of the cosmetics produced are produced by its members.

New federal rules require that cosmetic manufacturers put a label on untested products that have not been substantiated as safe. To date, the manufacturers have not complied, and since there is no law mandating such action, they probably will not.

We should be grateful that there are scientists testing ingredients for us. However, the cosmetic companies are politically astute. Such self-testing and efforts at self-regulation fend off potential outside regulation by government agencies. And the cosmetics manufacturers contribute heavily to political campaigns, including the presidential.[7]

It is in their own interest, of course, to avoid using an ingredient that might be found at some later date to be potentially harmful. Adverse publicity can instantly kill a product in which millions of dollars have been invested. Cosmetic companies also do not want the price of their ingredients publicized. If you read labels, you'll see that water and alcohol are two of the most commonly used ingredients.

One French perfumer was asked, for example, how much the ingredients in a perfume selling for $230 per ounce in a department store really cost. His answer: "Four to six dollars."

Cosmetics are big business. Skin care alone is a $2 billion category, women's fragrances, $3 billion, and men's cosmetics, the fastest growing toiletries category, is $1,300,000,000. Women's hair products sell $3,200,000,000 worth a year. About 500 new cosmetic products are introduced annually.[8]

In the cosmetic business, image is everything. Large cosmetic

[7] "Panel's Plan for '84 Election," *Women's Wear Daily*, February 25, 1983.
[8] *Advertising Age*, March 28, 1988, p. S-18.

companies are reluctant, for example, to distribute franchise lines in heavily trafficked drugstores because they want to maintain a "fashion image," which is fostered by department stores and drug stores; however, the drugstore item is blister-packaged, whereas the department store outlet items are sold in a pretty box.

The most effective skin sealants—they keep the moisture in the skin from evaporating—are petrolatum and lanolin. Most moisturizers contain one or both of them. If you check the moisturizers found in a drugstore or a variety store, you'll see that a jar of popular cream sells for $2.79 for six ounces. If you check department or specialty stores, you'll see that a fancy moisturizer sells for $18.50 or more for an ounce. *Look at* the ingredients on the respective labels and you'll discover that they are identical; only the packaging is different.

Advertising is one of the major costs in cosmetics. For most cosmetics, there is a 500 percent to 1,000 percent spread between costs and sale prices. This margin is needed, according to manufacturers, to meet heavy promotional costs. The industry is the largest advertiser on TV and in magazines. Cosmetic advertising can make Barnum look like an introvert. For example, if a cosmetologist has discovered a cream that can eliminate wrinkles and prevent aging, he or she should at least receive the Nobel Prize in medicine.

Dr. Christiaan Barnard, who might have received the Nobel Prize for his pioneering heart transplant surgery, was enlisted by a Swiss producer of anti-aging cream. The advertising proclaimed that Dr. Barnard "and his team of cell biologists" discovered "a molecule called glycosphingolipids (GSL)." The promotion quoted Dr. Barnard as saying: "The changes we observe in the human body which we identify with aging are largely due to damage inflicted on the various skin cells by environmental factors . . . When environmental damage is repaired, many of the normal functions of the cells will return, allowing the skin to look younger . . . Hence, I believe the GSL ingredient represents an important scientific breakthrough . . ."

The prestige of the pioneer heart surgeon helped sell the tiny jars of cream for more than $90 a smidgeon. Soon, other cosmetic manufacturers jumped on the wagon and we had "Fresh Cell Therapy" from Forelle "to challenge the inevitability of aging skin" and Milopa Cell Support Treatment for "a new elasticity for your skin."

Medical reports that a derivative of Vitamin A, Retin-A, could, indeed, reverse some sun damage and fade wrinkles, fueled a whirlwind of promotion.

Now, by definition, cosmetics are:

"(1) Articles intended to be rubbed, poured, sprinkled or sprayed on, introduced into, or otherwise applied to the human body or any part thereof for cleansing, beautifying, promoting attractiveness, or altering the appearance and (2) Articles intended for use as a component of any such articles, except that such terms should not include soap."

To the United States government, a cosmetic improves appearance, while a drug diagnoses, relieves, or cures a disease.

A wrinkle cream, such as Retin-A, if it does not alter or treat aging skin, is a drug, not a cosmetic.

In 1987, the FDA sent a letter to 23 cosmetic firms warning them that they are in serious violation of the Food, Drug and Cosmetic Act if they do not correct the violation. The FDA did not object to the products, just to the claims.

The Cosmetic companies continued promoting wrinkle creams. In March 1988, the FDA issued another regulatory letter to the companies involved.

Finally, the FDA shifted enforcement of skincare claim cases from the Bureau of Drug Labeling to its Health Fraud Branch where, as of this writing, it remains.

However, as Heinz Eiermann said in an interview, the FDA is there to enforce the rules, not to make them. The representatives in Congress and the regulators at the FDA are there to carry out the wishes of the people. If there is not sufficient desire for stronger cosmetic laws, there won't be stronger laws.

If you believe a cream can take away wrinkles or a mascara can make you alluring, what's the harm? It may be worth it to you to pay for the emotional lift you receive. On the other hand, if a cosmetic ingredient may cause an allergic reaction or contribute to the cancer burden, that's quite another matter.

Until the time the public demands tighter controls over cosmetics, your greatest protection is your own knowledge. The cosmetic companies are very sensitive to consumer desires, and both the industry and the FDA will respond to reports of untoward effects from a cosmetic. But they can't if no one tells them about it.

The purpose of this dictionary is to enable you to look up any cosmetic ingredient under its alphabetical listing to determine if a product is safe or not. Thereby you can choose among products on the basis of what is in them, whether or not they do what the advertising claims they do, and at the same time avoid any unnecessary injury to your health. The dictionary includes most of the cosmetic ingredients in common use, a large percentage of which have been kept secret. For the sake of clarity and ease of use, their many functions are grouped under the following broad categories:

PRESERVATIVES

A preservative used in cosmetics is required to offer protection against infection under conditions of use and prevent the decomposition of the product due to microbial multiplication. For example, many kinds of yeast, fungi, and bacteria have been identified in cosmetics. Just the presence of water and various organic components, such as lanolin or cocoa butter, provides an excellent environment for the growth of germs. Furthermore, as consumers, we are constantly introducing new germs into open jars, bottles, and boxes. In many instances a product may not show evidence of contamination and yet contain germs that, when in contact with the skin or eyes, may cause infection.

A cosmetic preservative should be active at low concentration, against a wide range of microorganisms, and over a wide acidity/alkalinity range. According to cosmetic chemists, it must also be compatible with other ingredients in the formulation, be nontoxic, nonirritating, and nonsensitizing. It should also be colorless, odorless, and stable, as well as economically feasible and easily incorporated into the product.

Parabens and quaternary ammonium compounds (*see both*) are widely used today as preservatives. So are the various alcohols such as ethyl and isopropyl, and so are the phenols such as *p*-chloro-*m*-cresol. Essential oils, such as citrus and menthol, have been used for hundreds of years as preservatives.

An additional use for preservatives is for fatty products in cosmetic creams and lotions. Such substances are called antioxidants. They prevent the production of off-colors and off-odors. Examples are benzoic acid, BHA, and tocopherols (Vitamin E).

ACIDS, ALKALIES, BUFFERS, NEUTRALIZERS

The degree of acidity or alkalinity (known as the pH) of a product is important in cosmetics because too little or too much of either may irritate the skin. Furthermore, the formulation of a product is dependent upon properly maintaining the intended pH. Citric acid, widely used as the acid, and ammonium carbonate, an alkali, are frequently found in cosmetic formulations. Buffers and neutralizing agents are chemicals added to cosmetic formulas to control acidity or alkalinity in the same way that acids and alkalies might be added directly. Some common chemicals in this class are ammonium bicarbonate, calcium carbonate, and tartaric acid.

MOISTURE CONTENT CONTROLS

Humectants are necessary to keep many cosmetics from drying out. An open jar of cream, for instance, may stiffen and crumble without a humectant to keep it soft and pliable. Substances used for this purpose include glycerin and propylene glycol, which keep cleansing lotions and moisturizing creams smooth and spreadable. On the other hand, chemicals may be necessary to keep cosmetics from absorbing moisture from the air and becoming sticky or cakey. Calcium silicate, for instance, is used in powders to prevent moisture absorption.

COLORING AGENTS

These colors, of course, are extremely important to cosmetics. Without pleasing hues, lipsticks, rouges, and eye makeup would remain on store shelves. Colors of both natural and synthetic origin are extensively employed in cosmetics. However, indiscriminate use of color can cause adverse reactions when applied in a cosmetic. For example, coal tar colors are subject to government regulations—although they are exempted from the Cosmetic Act because they were determined to be irreplaceable. Each batch must be certified by the FDA as "harmless and suitable for use." The World Health Organization, in delineating some 140 different kinds of colorants, found many to be unsafe. Some of the colors originally listed as "harmless" were found to produce injury when fed to animals and were removed from the list. In 1960, the federal government required manufacturers to retest all artificial colors to determine safety. At present, there are nine colors permanently listed as safe. Among them FD & C Blue No. 1 and FD & C Citrus Red No. 2 have been shown to cause tumors at the site of injection in animals. But the FDA does not consider this significant because the experiment concerned injection by needle and not by ingestion in food or application on the skin. FD & C Red No. 40, one of the most widely used colorings, is also being questioned because it is made from a base known to be carcinogenic and because many scientists feel that it should not have been given permanent listing based solely on the manufacturer's tests.

Almost all cosmetics are colored, but until recently it was frequently impossible for FDA scientists to detect specific colors and quantities employed. Now, with newly developed techniques, FDA scientists are able to analyze finished products and determine the colors and quantities used.

Among the natural colors widely used in cosmetics are alkanet, annatto, carotene, chlorophyll, cochineal, saffron, and turmeric.

FLAVORINGS

A wide variety of spices, natural extractives, oleoresins, and essential oils are used in cosmetics. In fact, of the 3,000 additives known to be available for use in food, cosmetics, and drugs, 2,000 are flavorings to replace the flavors lost during processing. Of these flavorings, some five hundred are natural—that is, they are derived from a wide variety of spices, plant extracts, and essential oils. The balance are synthetics such as amyl acetate, benzaldehyde, and ethyl acetate. Cosmetic products in which flavorings are important include lipsticks, dentifrices, and mouthwashes. Flavorings are employed in amounts ranging from a few parts to three hundred parts per million.

FRAGRANCES

In the entire cosmetic industry perhaps the greatest number of creative people are employed in the production of fragrances. It is an ancient art and the formulas are closely guarded. Even the federal labeling regulations recognize this and require that only the words *perfume* or *fragrance* be added to the label. There may be more than two hundred ingredients in a scent. Pleasant aromas are derived from a spectacular number of substances, including plant materials and synthetic chemicals. Perfumers can even improve on nature. Certain natural flower scents, for instance, cannot be extracted, yet the experts, using various chemicals, can reproduce the same aroma we smell from the actual blossom. Because of the complexity of perfume formulas, it is difficult but possible for competitors to break them down and reproduce them. Since fragrances are intended to vaporize, and they do contain plant and floral derivatives as well as many other chemicals, they frequently cause allergic reactions. A less frequent side effect of perfume is a skin pigmentation called berloque dermatitis (*see under its alphabetical listing*). With new awareness that chemicals can be delivered to the body not only by ingestion and absorption through the skin but by inhalation of scent, federal and industrial scientists are concerned that some of the volatile ingredients in cosmetics may have an adverse systemic effect. In fact, the fixative AETT was voluntarily removed after it was shown to be a nerve toxin in animals.

PROCESSING AIDS

Many cosmetic ingredients fall into this category. One of the most frequently used groups of ingredients includes surfactants (*see*), compounds that reduce the work between two surfaces. A large subdivision of surface-active agents consists of emulsifiers and emulsion stabilizers. Such ingredients help maintain a mixture and ensure consistency. They also influence smoothness, volume, and uniformity. Sodium lauryl sulfate and alumina gel are examples used in moisture creams and lauryl sulfate and alumina gel are examples used in moisture creams and lotions. Another division of surfactants includes solubilizers and texturizers. Solubilizers mix oil and water. Sodium sulfonate, for instance, is used to disperse oils in shampoos. Texturizers are added to products to give them a desired feel and appearance. An emulsifier may be a texturizer, but a texturizer is not necessarily an emulsifier. For example, acacia is used in hairdressings to thicken them and also to help them hold unruly hair in place. Clarifying and chelating agents are other processing aids that remove extraneous matter from liquids. Tannin, for instance, is used for removing extraneous matter from liquids. Ethylenediamine tetraacetic acid is used to remove calcium, magnesium, and iron soaps from shampoo solutions. Opacifiers, on the other hand, are added to liquids to darken them. The higher alcohols, such as stearyl and cetyl, are frequently used in shampoos for this purpose. Foaming agents, such as dodecylbenzene sulfonic acid, are added to make shampoos foamy.

Texturizers or stabilizers are added to products to give them "body" and maintain a desired texture. For instance, calcium chloride or some other calcium salt is added to canned tomatoes and canned potatoes to keep them from falling apart. Sodium nitrate and sodium nitrite are used in curing meats to develop and stabilize the pink color. Nitrogen, carbon dioxide, and nitrous oxide are employed in pressure-packed containers of certain foods to act as whipping agents or as propellants. The texture of ice cream and other frozen desserts is dependent on the size of the ice crystals in the product. By addition of agar-agar, gelatin, cellulose gum, or some other gum, the size of the ice crystals is stabilized. Texturizer gums are also used in chocolate milk to increase the viscosity of the product and to prevent the settling of cocoa particles to the bottom of the container. Gelatin, pectin, and starch are used in confectionary products to give a desired texture. Artificially sweetened beverages also need products to give a desired texture. Artificially sweetened beverages also need bodying agents because they do not contain the "thickness" normally contributed by sugar. The thickeners employed include such natural gums as sodium alginate and pectins. The foaming properties of brewed beer can also be improved by the addition of texturizers.

For further ease of use, the dictionary also lists products alphabetically by general use. For example, you can look up eye shadow, mascara, lipstick, eyebrow pencils, and any appearance-improving products to see what is in them. Or you may be interested in grooming products, such as dentifrices, mouthwash, nail polish, perfume, eyewashes, and after-shave lotions, deodorants, depilatories, hair bleach, and so on. Anyone looking for treatment aids would check under cleansing creams, emollients, astringents, hand creams, permanent waves, hair straighteners, skin bleaches, and any other corrective treatment products. In addition, all terms used in this dictionary that might be unfamiliar are also listed alphabetically, such as polymer, reagent, and so on.

While unique in content, this dictionary follows the format of most dictionaries. The following are examples of entries with any explanatory notes that may be necessary.

ABIETIC ACID • **Sylvic Acid.** Chiefly a texturizer in the making of soaps. A widely available natural acid, water-insoluble, prepared from pine rosin, usually yellow, and composed of either glassy or crystalline particles. Used also in the manufacture of vinyls, lacquers, and plastics. Little is known about abietic acid toxicity; it is harmless when injected into mice but causes paralysis in frogs and is slightly irritating to human skin and mucous membranes. May cause allergic reactions.

We have learned that abietic acid is also known as sylvic acid, that it is a naturally occurring rosin acid, which as a texturizer maintains a consistency in soaps, and we discovered its noncosmetic uses and its known toxicity. Source material for the comments on toxicity is indicated in the notes at the end of the dictionary.

ALLANTOIN • Used in cold creams, hand lotions, hair lotions, after-shave lotions, and other skin-soothing cosmetics because of its ability to help heal wounds and skin ulcers and to stimulate the growth of healthy tissue. Composed of colorless crystals, soluble in hot water, it is prepared synthetically by the oxidation of uric acid (*see*) or by heating uric acid with dichloroacetic acid. It is nontoxic.

Allantoin, we can see, is a synthetic product, derived from uric acid. By looking up uric acid, we learn that it derives from urine and is used in sunburn preventatives.

WHAT TO DO IF YOU HAVE AN ADVERSE RESPONSE TO A COSMETIC

• Before using any cosmetic, read the label carefully and follow directions exactly. This is especially important when using antiperspirants, depilatories, hair dyes, and colorings, home permanents, freckle creams, and skin packs.

• To determine whether you are allergic to a cosmetic, apply a small amount on the inside of your forearm. Leave it on for twenty-four hours. If you see any adverse effects, such as redness, blisters, or itching, don't use it again.

• If a cosmetic causes any adverse effect—burning, breaking out, stinging, or itching—stop using it. If you are not sure whether it was a cosmetic that gave you the problem or which of several cosmetics it was that affected you adversely, stop the use of all cosmetics. Shampoo your hair with a bland soap in order to remove all hair preparations. Stop the use of all creams, including cleansing creams, foundation creams, and cold creams. Wash your face with unscented soap. Remove all nail polish.

• If the condition does not clear up or is very uncomfortable, bring the offending or suspected cosmetic to your physician for testing. This includes cosmetic sponges and powder puffs used to apply cosmetics.

• If you have recently visited a beauty parlor and have had an adverse reaction, return to the shop and obtain the name of the brands used and samples of them.

• If the lips are not involved, the use of lipstick may be continued.

• The cosmetic responsible for your problem may be a relatively new one or it may be one that you have used for years. The fact that all cosmetics have been applied for a long time does not rule out an adverse reaction from any one of them. The development of allergic hypersensitivity may occur at any time. Also, some ingredients in the product may have been changed by the manufacturer.

• Do not let children play with cosmetics. As you will read within this dictionary, some ingredients are toxic, and although some might not hurt an adult, they might harm children.

• Be especially careful in the use of eye cosmetics to avoid possible chemical and mechanical damage to the eyes.

• Report any adverse effects from cosmetics to the manufacturer of the products, to the FDA, and to the store where you purchased them. Look up the local Food and Drug Administration office under "United States" in your telephone directory. If you cannot find a local office, write directly to the FDA, Parklawn Building, 5600 Fishers Lane, Rockville, MD 20857.

Terminology generally has been kept to a middle road between what is understandable to the technician and to the average interested consumer, while at the same time avoiding oversimplification of data. Once again, if in doubt, look up alphabetically any term listed that seems unfamiliar or whose meaning has been blunted by overuse, such as *isolate, extract, demulcent, emollient,* or even *shampoo.*

With a *Consumer's Dictionary of Cosmetic Ingredients,* you will be able to work with current and future labels to determine the purpose and desirability or toxicity of the ingredients listed. For the first time you will have the knowledge to choose the best cosmetics for you. By checking on a product's ingredients, as listed on the label, you can eliminate many products and choose those that are harmless, even beneficial, and you save money and reward those manufacturers who deserve your purchases. For the first time, with the aid of this book, you will really know what is in the cosmetics you have been using.

A

ABIETIC ACID • **Sylvic Acid.** Chiefly a texturizer in the making of soaps. A widely available natural acid, water-insoluble, prepared from pine rosin, usually yellow and comprised of either glassy or crystalline particles. Used also in the manufacture of vinyls, lacquers, and plastics. Little is known about abietic acid toxicity; it is harmless when injected into mice but causes paralysis in frogs and is slightly irritating to human skin and mucous membranes. May cause allergic reactions.
ABIETYL ALCOHOL • See Abietic Acid.
ABITOL • **Dihydroabietyl Alcohol.** Used in cosmetics, plastics, and adhesive. See Abietic Acid.
ABSOLUTE • The term refers to a plant-extracted material that has been concentrated, but that remains essentially unchanged in its original taste and odor. For example, see Jasmine Absolute. Often called "natural perfume materials" because they are not subjected to heat and water as are distilled products. See Distilled.
ABSORPTION BASES • Compounds used to improve the water-absorbing capacity and stability of creams, lotions, and hairdressings. Lanolin-type absorption bases are made of mixtures of lanolin alcohols, mineral oil, and petrolatum (*see all*). Also used as bases are cholesterol and beeswax (*see both.*)
ACACIA • **Gum Arabic. Catechu.** Acacia is the odorless, colorless, tasteless dried exudate from the stem of the acacia tree grown in Africa, the Near East, India, and the southern United States. Its most distinguishing quality among the natural gums is its ability to dissolve rapidly in water. The use of acacia dates back 4,000 years when the Egyptians employed it in paints. Its principal use in the confectionery industry is to retard sugar crystallization and as a thickener for candies, jellies, glazes, and chewing gum. As a stabilizer, it prevents chemical breakdown in food mixtures. Gum acacia is a foam stabilizer in soft drink and brewing industries. Other uses are for mucilage, and the gum gives form and shape to tablets. Medically, it is used as a demulcent to soothe irritations, particularly of the mucous membranes. It can cause allergic reactions such as skin rash and asthmatic attacks. Oral toxicity is low. See also Vegetable Gums and Catechu Black.
ACEROLA • Used as an antioxidant. Derived from the ripe fruit of the West Indian or Barbados cherry grown in Central America and the West Indies. A rich source of ascorbic acid. Used in Vitamin C. No known toxicity.
ACETAL • A volatile liquid derived from acetaldehyde (*see*) and alcohol and used as a solvent in synthetic perfumes such as jasmine. Also used in fruit flavorings (it has a nutlike aftertaste) and as a

hypnotic in medicine. It is a central nervous system depressant, similar in action to paraldehyde but more toxic. Paraldehyde is a hypnotic and sedative whose side effects are respiratory depression, cardiovascular collapse, and possible high blood pressure reactions. No known skin toxicity.

ACETALDEHYDE • **Ethanal.** An intermediate (*see*) and solvent in the manufacture of perfumes. A flammable, colorless liquid, with a characteristic odor, occurring naturally in apples, broccoli, cheese, coffee, grapefruit, and other vegetables and fruit. Also used in the manufacture of synthetic rubber and in the silvering of mirrors. It is irritating to the mucous membranes, and ingestion of large doses may cause death by respiratory paralysis. Inhalation, usually limited by intense irritation of lungs, can also be toxic. Skin toxicity not identified.

ACETAMIDE MEA • **N-Acetyl Acid Amide. N-Acetyl Ethanolamine.** Used as a solvent, plasticizer, and stabilizer (*see all*). Crystals absorb water. Odorless when pure but can have a mousy scent. A mild skin irritant with low toxicity. Has caused liver cancer when given orally to rats in doses of 5,000 milligrams per kilogram of body weight.

ACETANILID • **Acetanilide.** A solvent in nail polishes and used in liquid powders to give an opaque matte finish. Usually made from aniline and acetic acid (*see both*), it is of historic interest because it was the first coal tar analgesic and antifever agent introduced into medicine. It is a precursor of penicillin, and is used as an antiseptic. It is sometimes still used in medicines but is frowned upon by the American Medical Association since there are other related products with less toxicity. It can cause a depletion of oxygen in the blood upon ingestion and eczema when applied to the skin. It caused tumors when given orally to rats in doses of 3,500 milligrams per kilogram of body weight.

ACETARSOL • **Acetarsone.** Used in mouthwashes, toothpaste, and vaginal suppositories. Thick white crystals with slight acid taste. Soluble in water. The lethal dose in mice is only 4 mg per kilogram of body weight. May cause sensitization.

ACETATE • Salt of acetic acid (*see*) used in perfumery and as a flavoring. No known toxicity.

ACETIC ACID • Solvent for gums, resins, and volatile oils. Styptic (stops bleeding) and a rubefacient (*see*). A clear colorless liquid with a pungent odor, it is used in freckle-bleaching lotions, hand lotions, and hair dyes. It occurs naturally in apples, cheese, cocoa, coffee, grapes, skimmed milk, oranges, peaches, pineapples, strawberries, and a variety of other fruits and plants. Vinegar is about 4 to 6 percent acetic acid and essence of vinegar is about 14 percent. In its glacial form (without much water) it is highly corrosive and its vapors are capable of producing lung obstruction. Less than 5 percent acetic acid in solution is mildly irritating to the skin. GRAS for packaging only. It caused cancer in rats and mice when given orally or by injection.

ACETIC ANHYDRIDE • **Acetyl Oxide; Acetic Oxide.** Colorless liquid with a strong odor, it is derived from oxidation of acetaldehyde (*see*). It is used as a dehydrating and acetylating agent (*see both*) and in the production of dyes, perfumes, plastics, food starch, and aspirin. It is a strong irritant and may cause burns and eye damage.

ACETOIN • **Acetyl Methyl Carbinol.** A flavoring agent and aroma carrier used in perfumery, it occurs naturally in broccoli, grapes, pears, cultured dairy products, cooked beef, and cooked chicken. As a product of fermentation and of cream ripened for churning, it is a colorless or pale yellow liquid or a white powder, it has a buttery odor and must be stored in a light-resistant container. No known toxicity.

ACETOLAMIDE • **N-Acetyl Ethanolamine.** Used in hair-waving solutions and in emulsifiers. See Ethanolamines.

ACETONE • A colorless ethereal liquid derived by oxidation or fermentation and used as a solvent in nail polish removers and nail finishes. It is obtained by fermentation and is frequently used as a solvent for airplane dope, fats, oils, and waxes. It can cause peeling and splitting of the nails, skin rashes on the fingers and elsewhere, and nail brittleness. Inhalation may irritate the lungs, and in large amounts it is narcotic, causing symptoms of drunkenness similar to ethanol (*see*).

ACETOPHENONE • A synthetic agent derived from coal tar, with an odor of bitter almonds, used in strawberry, floral, fruit, cherry, almond, walnut, tobacco, vanilla, and tonka bean flavorings for beverages, ice creams, ices, candy, baked goods, gelatin desserts, and chewing gum. It occurs naturally in strawberries and tea and may cause allergic reactions.

ACETYL HEXAMETHYL TETRALIN • Used in perfumes. It is closely related to acetyl ethyl tetramethyl tetralin, which was voluntarily removed from perfumes when it was reported it caused nerve damage in animals. The "hexyl" component was inserted to make the fragrances less volatile and less allergenic.

ACETYL TRIBUTYL CITRATE • See Citric Acid.

ACETYL TRIETHYL CITRATE • A clear oily, essentially odorless liquid used as a solvent. See Citric Acid.

ACETYL TRIOCTYL CITRATE • Salt of Citric Acid. See Citric Acid.

ACETYL TRIOCTYL CITRATE PECTIN • **Citrus Pectin.** A jelly-forming powder obtained from citrus peel and used as a texturizer and thickening agent to form gels with sugars and acids. Light in color. It has no known toxicity.

ACETYLATED • Any organic compound that has been heated with acetic anhydride or acetyl chloride to remove its water. Acetylated lanolins are used in hand creams and lotions, for instance. Acetic anhydride produces irritation and necrosis of tissues in vapor state and carries a warning against contact with skin and eyes.

ACETYLATED CASTOR OIL • See Acetylated and Castor Oil.

ACETYLATED GLYCOL STEARATE • See Acetylated and Glycols.

ACETYLATED HYDROGENATED COTTONSEED GLYCERIDE • See Cottonseed Oil.

ACETYLATED HYDROGENATED LARD GLYCERIDE • See Lard.

ACETYLATED HYDROGENATED VEGETABLE GLYCERIDE • See Vegetable Oils.

ACETYLATED LANOLIN • Repels water better than plain lanolin and does not form emulsions. It is used as a water-resistant film when applied to the skin and reduces water loss through the skin. It is used as an emollient and gives that "velvety feel" to baby products, to skin, hair, bath preparations and skin preparations such as creams, lotions, powders, and sprays. See Lanolin.

ACETYLATED LANOLIN ALCOHOL. • See Acetylated Lanolin.

ACETYLATED LANOLIN RICINOLEATE • The acetyl ester (*see*) of lanolin (*see*) and Ricinoleate (*see*), a substance found in castor oil and used to make soaps. No known toxicity.

ACETYLATED SUCROSE DISTEARATE • The acetyl ester of sucrose distearate (*see both*).

ACETYLATED TALLOW • See Acetylated and Tallow.

ACETYLBENZOYL PEROXIDE • **Benzo-benzone.** White crystals that decompose slowly. It is an active germicide and disinfectant and is used for bleaching flour. It is toxic by ingestion, a strong irritant to the skin and mucous membranes.

ACETYLISOEUGENOL • **Isoeugenol acetate.** White crystals with a spicy, clovelike odor, it is used in perfumery, especially for carnation-type odors and for flavoring.

ACETYLMETHYLCARBINOL • See Acetoin.

ACID • An acid can be liquid, solid or gas. Though there are a great many varieties of acids there are certain properties which are common to most of them. When dissolved, acids taste sour, they neutralize bases, react with metals to form salts and water, turn blue litmus paper red, and they can conduct electric current. An acid aqueous solution is one that has a pH (*see*) of less than 7. Citric acid (*see*) is an example of a widely used acid in cosmetics.

ACID AMMONIUM SULFATE • See Quaternary Ammonium Compounds.

ACID BLACK 58 • **Irgalan Grey B1®.** A commercial color. See Acid Black 131 and Colors.

ACID BLACK 107 • **Lanamid Black BL®.** Classed chemically as a monoazo color (*see*).

ACID BLACK 131 • **Nigrosine.** It is a greenish-blue-black. Acid colors are made by adding acids such as adipic (*see*) and tartaric to obtain various shades. Toxicity depends upon ingredients used. See Colors and Acid Dyes.

ACID BLUE 9 AMMONIUM SALT • A color classed chemically as a triphenylmethane (*see*). The CTFA adopted name for certified (*see*) batches of this color is FD & C Blue No. 4 (*see*).

ACID BLUE 62 • Classed chemically as an anthraquinone color (*see*).

ACID BROWN 46 • See Acid Dyes.

ACID BROWN 48 • See Acid Dyes.

ACID DYES • The ability of these dyes to color and to remain fast during washing and exposure to light varies greatly. The ones that give the best water and light fastness are the compounds that are combined with metals. They are widely used in inexpensive dyes for plastics, varnishes, and some pigments.

ACID FUCHSIN • See Azo Dyes.

ACID GREEN 25 • Classed chemically as an anthraquinone color (*see*), the name can be applied only to batches of uncertified colors. The CTFA adopted name for certified (*see*) batches of this dye is D & C Green No. 5 (*see*).

ACID ORANGE 7 • A color classed as a monoazo (*see*). The name can be used only when applied to uncertified batches of this dye. The CTFA adopted name for certified (*see*) batches is D & C Orange No. 4 (*see*).

ACID ORANGE 24 • A diazo color (*see*), the name can be applied only to uncertified batches of this color. The CTFA adopted name for certified batches is D & C Brown No. 1 (*see*).

ACID RED 33 • A monoazo color (*see*), the name can be applied only to uncertified batches. The CTFA adopted name for certified (*see*) batches is D & C Red No. 33 (*see*).

ACID RED 35 • A monoazo color (*see*), it is the disodium salt of napthalenedisulfonic acid. It is very soluble. Determined by NIOSH to be a positive animal carcinogen.

ACID RED 51 • A xanthene color (*see*), the name can be applied only to uncertified batches of color. The CTFA adopted name for certified (*see*) batches is FD & C Red No. 3 (*see*).

ACID RED 52 • A xanthene color (*see*).

ACID RED 87 • A xanthene color (*see*), it is the sodium salt of Solvent Red 43. The name can be used only when applied to uncertified batches of this dye. The CTFA adopted name for certified (*see*) batches is D & C Red No. 22 (*see*).

ACID RED 92 • A xanthene color (*see*), it is the sodium salt of Solvent Red 48. The name can be applied only to uncertified batches of this dye. The CTFA adopted name for certified (*see*) batches of color is D & C Red No. 28 (*see*).

ACID RED 95 • A xanthene color (*see*), it is the sodium salt of Solvent Red 73. The name can be applied only to uncertified batches of this dye. The CTFA adopted name for certified (*see*) batches is D & C Orange No. 11 (*see*).

ACID VIOLET 43 • An anthraquinone color (*see*), the name can be applied only to uncertified batches of this dye. The CTFA adopted name for the certified (*see*) batches of this color is Ext. D & C Violet No. 2 (*see*).

ACID YELLOW 1 • A nitro color, the name can be applied only to uncertified batches of this dye. The CTFA adopted name for the certified (*see*) batches of this color is Ext. D & C Yellow No. 7 (*see*).

ACID YELLOW 3 • A mixture of the disodium salts of the mono- and disulfonic acids of indanedione, a class of indirect-acting anticoagulants. The name can be applied only to uncertified batches of this dye. The CTFA adopted name for the certified (*see*) batches of this color is D & C Yellow No. 10 (*see*).

ACID YELLOW 23 • A pyrazole color (*see*), the name can be applied only to uncertified batches of this dye. The CTFA adopted name for the certified (*see*) batches of this color is FD & C Yellow No. 5 (*see*).

ACID YELLOW 73 • Classified as a coal tar dye, the name can be applied only to uncertified batches of this dye. The CTFA adopted name for certified (*see*) batches of this color is D & C Yellow No. 7 (*see*).

ACID YELLOW 73 SODIUM SALT • A fluoran color, the name can be applied only to uncertified batches of this dye. The CTFA adopted name for the certified (*see*) batches of this color is D & C Yellow No. 8 (*see*).

ACINTOL • See Tall Oil.

ACRYL GLUTAMATE • A surfactant. See Acrylic Acid and Glutamate.

ACRYLAMIDE • Colorless, odorless crystals soluble in water and derived from acrylonitrile and sulfuric acid. It is used in the manufacture of dyes, adhesives, and in permanent-press fabrics, nail enamels, and face masks. It is toxic by skin absorption.

ACRYLAMIDE/SODIUM ACRYLATE • A polymer of acrylamide and sodium acrylate monomers. See Acrylamide and Acrylates.

ACRYLAMIDE COPOLYMER • **Polytrap FLM 203 R.** A polymer (*see*) of two or more monomers (*see*) consisting of acrylamide and/or its simple alkyl derivatives. See Acrylamide.

ACRYLATE/ACRYLAMIDE COPOLYMER • Provides a continuous film for nail enamels or controls film formation in hair sprays. See Acrylates.

ACRYLATES • Salts or esters of acrylic acid used as thickening agents and as constituents of nail polishes. Strong irritants. See Acrylic Monomer.

ACRYLIC MONOMER • A tough rubbery material first used in fake nails in the cosmetic industry. They were once used as fillings for teeth. Fake nails usually consist of acrylates, a catalyst such as peroxide, and a plasticizer (*see all*). The compound to be effective must be stiff at room temperature. The acrylates if inhaled can cause allergic reactions in humans. Lethal to rats when inhaled. Can penetrate rubber gloves. May contain hydroquinone benzoyl peroxide and tertiary amines (*see both*).

ACRYLIC RESINS • Polymers (*see*) of acrylics. Used in waxy oils, base coats, protective coatings, and waterproofing. Acrylates (*see*), if inhaled, can cause allergic reactions in humans.

ACRYLINOLEIC ACID • **C29–70 Carboxylic Acid.** Thickening, suspending, dispersing, and emulsifying agent in cosmetics. No known toxicity.

ADENOSINE • White crystalline powder with mild saline or bitter taste. It is isolated by the hydrolysis of yeast nucleic acid.

ADENOSINE PHOSPHATE • See Adenosine Triphosphate.

ADENOSINE TRIPHOSPHATE • **Adenylic Acid.** An organic compound that is derived from adenosine (*see*). A fundamental unit of nucleic acid, it serves as source of energy for biochemical transformation in plants, photosynthesis, and also for many chemical reactions in the body, especially those associated with muscular activity.

ADIPIC ACID • **Hexanedoic Acid.** Colorless needlelike formations fairly insoluble in water; found in beets. A buffering and neutralizing agent impervious to humidity. Used in hair color rinses, nylon manufacture, and plasticizers. Lethal to rats in large oral doses. No known human toxicity.

ADIPIC ACID/EPOXYUPROPOYL DIETHYLENETRIAMINE COPOLYMER • A "bodying" agent and film-former that combines chemically with the amino acid cysteine to give "body" to hair. Shampooing removes it.

ADIPIC ACID DIHYDRAZIDE • See Adipic Acid.

AEROSOL • Small particles of material suspended in gas.

AEROSOL SHAVING CREAMS • See Shaving Creams.

AEROSOLS • Many cosmetic sprays, particularly hair and fragrances are in aerosol containers. The first aerosol patent was actually issued in 1899 but was not used until 1940 when insecticides were first packaged in self-dispensing gas-pressurized containers. Freon, the most commonly used group among aerosol gases, is a lung irritant, central nervous system depressant and in high concentrations can cause coma. More than 100 people, mostly young Americans, have died from sniffing aerosol gases for "kicks." These gases can cause severe irregular heartbeats. In addition to Freon, hair sprays contain PVP (Polyvinyl pyrrolidone—*see*), or shellac. PVP is believed to be cancer-causing. In addition, thesaurosis, a condition in which there are foreign bodies in the lungs, has been found in persons subjected to repeated inhalation of hair sprays. The aerosol container can become a lethal weapon; a flame thrower if near a fire and a shrapnel bomb when heated. It has been known to explode when placed too near a radiator or heater. Also, aerosol gases turn into toxic gases: fluorine, chlorine, hydrogen fluoride, and chloride or even phosgene, a military poison gas. Aerosol hair dyes and "hot" shave creams were made possible by compartmentalization of the container. However, in the case of the hot shave cream, there was unreliable mixing of the chemicals and skin rashes resulted. In powder products, the inhalation of powder, or the silicones, can damage the lungs. In 1972 the Society of Cosmetic Chemists reported that powder aerosols evidenced a high particle retention in the lungs and profound pulmonary effects. Tests showed large powder particles in 23 separate areas of the lungs. In addition, *Freon*, the propellant, cannot be considered inert, that is, lacking in chemical activity or in an expected biologic or pharmacologic effect. Many products have been placed in hand pump containers because of the concern about aerosols.

AFTERBATH LOTIONS • See Cologne.

AFTER-SHAVE LOTIONS • See Shaving Lotions.

AGAR • **Japanese Isinglass.** Used as an emulsifier and emollient in cosmetics and as a substitute for gelatin in foods. Extracted from various seaweeds found in the Pacific and Indian oceans and the Sea of Japan. It is also used as a bulk laxative. It is an occasional allergen.

AGAVE LECHUGUILLA • **American Aloe.** Native to the warm part of the United States, and known by its heavy stiff leaf and tall panicle or spike of candelabralike flowers. The leaves are used for juice employed in cosmetics as an adhesive and in medicines as a diuretic. The fermented juice is popular in Mexico for its distilled spirit (mescal). Some species are cultivated for their fibers, which are used in thread and rope. No known skin toxicity.

AGE SPOTS • See Skin Bleach.

AGRIMONY EXTRACT • An extract of *Agrimonia eupatoria*, an herb found in north temperate regions. It has yellow flowers and bristly fruit.

ALANINE • Colorless crystals derived from protein. Believed to be a nonessential amino acid. It is used in microbiological research and as a dietary supplement in the L and DL forms. The FDA has asked for supplementary information. It is now GRAS for addition to food. It caused cancer of the skin in mice and tumors when injected into their abdomens.

ALBUMEN • See Albumin.

ALBUMIN • A group of simple proteins composed of nitrogen, carbon, hydrogen, oxygen, and sulfur that are soluble in water. Albumin is usually derived from egg white and employed as an emulsifier in foods and cosmetics. May cause a reaction to those allergic to eggs.

ALCLOXA • **Aluminum Chlorhydroxy Allantoinate.** See Allantoin.

ALCOHOL • **Ethyl Alcohol. Ethanol.** Alcohol as a solvent is widely used in the cosmetic field; many cosmetics consist largely of alcohol: after-shave lotions, bubble baths, colognes, cold cream, deodorants, freckle lotions, face packs, hair lacquers, hair tonics, liquid face powders, mouthwashes, nail polish removers, perfumes, preshaving lotions, shampoos, shaving creams, skin lotions, spray deodorants, suntan lotions and oils, and toilet waters. Alcohol is manufactured by the fermentation of starch, sugar, and other carbohydrates. It is clear, colorless, and flammable, with somewhat pleasant odor and a burning taste. Medicinally used externally as an antiseptic and internally as a stimulant and hypnotic. *Absolute Alcohol* is ethyl alcohol to which a substance has been added to make it unfit for drinking. *Rubbing Alcohol* contains not less than 68.5 percent and not more than 71.5 percent by volume of absolute alcohol and a remainder of denaturants, such as perfume oils. Since it is a fat solvent, alcohol can dry the hair and skin when used in excess. Toxic in large doses.

ALDEHYDE, ALPHATIC • A class of organic chemical compounds intermediate between acids and alcohols. Aldehyde contains less oxygen than acids and less hydrogen than alcohols. Formaldehyde (*see*), a preservative, is an example of an aldehyde widely used in cosmetics. Benzaldehyde and cinnamic aldehydes are used to scent perfumes. Most are irritating to the skin and gastrointestinal tract.

ALDIOXA • **Aluminum Dihydroxy Allantoinate.** Astringent, antiperspirant prepared with the skin-healing salts of aluminum chlorhydroxy allantoinate (*see*). Used as astringents, keratolytics, tissue stimulants, and buffers in cosmetics. Nonsensitizing and nonirritating.

ALDOL • Made from acetaldehyde, which occurs naturally in apples, broccoli, cheese, coffee, grapefruit, and other vegetables and fruits. It is a colorless thick liquid, used in the manufacture of rubber and in perfumes. It has also been used as a sedative and hypnotic in medicine. May cause contact dermatitis.

ALFALFA EXTRACT • **Lucerne.** Extract of *Medicago sativa.* A natural cola, liquor, and maple flavoring agent for beverages and cordials. Alfalfa is widely cultivated for forage and is a commercial source of chlorophyll. No known toxicity.

ALGAE • From seaweed and pond scum. Algae is claimed to prevent wrinkles and to moisturize the skin, but the American Medical Association denies any validity for algae's therapeutic benefits. However, seaweed products are widely used in cosmetics for many purposes. Nontoxic. See Alginates.

ALGIN • The sodium salt of alginic acid (*see*).

ALGINATES • All derivatives of alginic acid are designated "algin" (ammonium, calcium, potassium, and sodium). Gelatinous substances obtained from certain seaweeds and used as emulsifiers in hand lotions and creams, as thickening agents in shampoos, wave sets, and lotions. They are also used as barrier agents (*see*) in hand creams and lotions, in the manufacture of celluloid, as an emulsifier in mineral oil, and in mucilage. Sodium alginate from brown seaweed is used as a thickener in dentifrices, but the FDA is testing the sodium form (largest use in ice cream) for short-term mutagenic birth-deforming, reproduction, and subacute effects. Alginates are also used as stabilizers and water retainers in many foods. No known toxicity on skin.

ALGINIC ACID • A stabilizer in cosmetics, it is obtained as a highly gelatinous precipitate. The sodium carbonate (*see*) extracts of brown dried seaweeds are treated with acid to achieve the result. Resembles albumin or gelatin (*see both*). Alginic acid is slowly soluble in water, forming a very thick liquid. No known toxicity.

ALIZARIN • **Turkey Red.** Occurs in the root of the madder plant and was known and used in Ancient Egypt, Persia, and India. Today, it is produced synthetically from anthracene, a coal tar. It yields different colors depending upon the metals mixed with it. Colors used in cosmetics are Turkey red, blue, orange, red, rose, black, violet, lilac, yellow, and dark brown. It is also used to dye wool. Can cause contact dermatitis.

ALKALI • The term originally covered the caustic and mild forms of potash and soda. Now a substance is regarded as an alkali if it gives hydroxyl ions in solution. An alkaline aqueous solution is one with a pH (*see*) greater than 7. Sodium bicarbonate is an example of an alkali that is used to neutralize excess acidity in cosmetics.

ALKALOID • A vegetable substance with an organic nitrogen base capable of combining with acids to form crystalline salts. Alkaloids exert a powerful response, even in small amounts. Chemical alkaloids end in *-ine* such as Betaine from beets.

ALKANET ROOT • A red coloring obtained from extraction of the herblike tree root grown in Asia Minor and the Mediterranean. Used as a copper or blue coloring (when combined with metals) for hair oils and other cosmetics. It is also used as a coloring for wines, inks, and sausage casings. May be mixed with synthetic dyes for color tints. Formerly used as an astringent. No known toxicity.

ALKANNIN • A red powder and the principal ingredient of alkanet root (*see*). Used as an astringent in cosmetics and to color cosmetics and food.

ALKANOLAMINES • Compounds used in cold creams and eyeliners as a solvent and comprised of alcohols from alkene (a saturated fatty hydrocarbon) and amines (from ammonia). These compounds are viscous, colorless liquids that form soaps from fatty acids (*see*). No known toxicity.

ALKYL • Meaning "from alcohol", usually derived from alkane. Any one of a series of saturated hydrocarbons such as methane. The introduction of one or more alkyls into a compound is for the purpose of making the product more soluble. The mixture is usually employed with surfactants (*see*), which have a tendency to float when not alkylated.

ALKYL ARYLPOLYETHYLENE GLYCOL ETHER • A dispersant for preshave lotions, but basically a wetting agent. It rarely sensitizes or irritates human skin.

ALKYL BENZENE SULFONATES • A detergent used in bubble baths and for shampoos. Prolonged feeding to animals showed no evidence of toxicity but such agents are known to be defatting and therefore drying to the skin.

ALKYL SODIUM SULFATES • Used in shampoos because they have cleaning power and wash out of the hair easier than soap. A basic alkyl sulfate shampoo formula: sodium lauryl sulfate, 15 percent; behenic acid, 3.5 percent (*see both*); water, 81.5 percent. These sulfates were developed by the Germans when vegetable fats and oils were scarce. A large number have been made. They are prepared from primary alcohols by treatment with chlorosulfuric or sulfuric acid. The alcohols are usually prepared from fatty acids (*see*). For example, lauric acid makes a soap effective in hard water. If it is reduced to lauryl alcohol and sulfated, it makes sodium lauryl sulfate, a widely used detergent. The alcohol (alkyl) sulfates are low in acute and chronic toxicity but they may cause skin irritation.

ALKYL SULFATES • Used in detergents to thicken and improve foaming. Can be irritating.

ALKYLARYLSUFONATE • A detergent. See Bubble Baths.

ALLANTOIN • Used in cold creams, hand lotions, hair lotions, after-shave lotions, and other skin-soothing cosmetics because of its ability to help heal wounds and skin ulcers and to stimulate the growth of healthy tissue. Colorless crystals, soluble in hot water, it is prepared synthetically by the oxidation of uric acid (*see*) or by heating uric acid with dichloroacetic acid. It is nontoxic.

ALLANTOIN ACETYL METHIONINE • See Allantoin.

ALLANTOIN ASCORBATE • Allantoin (*see*) with Ascorbic Acid (*see*) salt.

ALLANTOIN BIOTIN • Allantoin (*see*) with B-Complex Vitamin.

ALLANTOIN CALCIUM PANTOTHENATE • Allantoin (*see*) with calcium and a B-Complex Vitamin. A combination of the salt of the B-complex vitamin and the healing agent allantoin (*see*). Used to soothe the skin in emollients. Nontoxic.

ALLANTOIN GALACTURONIC ACID • Allantoin (*see*) and galacturonic acid which is derived from plant pectin (*see*).

ALLANTOIN GLYCYRRHETINIC ACID • See Allantoin and the derivative of licorice root, Glycyrrhetinic Acid.

ALLANTOIN POLYGALACTURONIC ACID • See Allantoin and Galacturonic Acid.

ALLANTOINATE • A salt of Allantoin (*see*).

ALLERGEN • A substance that provokes an allergic reaction in the susceptible person but does not normally affect other people. Plant pollens, fungi spores, and animal danders are some of the common allergens.

ALLERGIC CONTACT DERMATITIS • **ACD.** Skin rash caused by direct contact with a substance to which the skin is sensitive. Symptoms include a red rash, swelling, and intense itching. Blisters may develop and break open, forming a crust. In severe cases, the rash and blisters may spread all over the body. A variety of substances can cause the condition. The most common is poison ivy (*see*). Others include industrial chemicals, metals, cosmetics, deodorants, mouthwashes, dyes, certain types of textiles, medicines, as well as local treatments with ointments and local application of antibiotics. ACD may develop at any age. Its precise prevalence is unknown but is thought to affect a significant percentage of the population. The disease may be acute or chronic. It is less common than skin rashes caused by irritants but more serious because relapses commonly occur and may force a person to change jobs. Symptoms may appear 7 to 10 days after the first exposure to an allergen. More often, the allergic reaction doesn't develop for many years, and may require many repeated low-level exposures. Once the sensitivity does develop, however, contact with the triggering allergen will produce symptoms within 24 to 48 hours. An attack builds in severity from one to seven days. Even without treatment, healing often occurs in one or two weeks, although it may take a month or longer.

The rash does not spread on one's body nor can it be spread to another person. The extension of the rash is caused by renewed contact with whatever triggered the initial outbreak.

Some substances such as film developers, rubber chemicals, and beryllium, can cause symptoms other than the classic red rash and blisters. In some cases, ACD may look like hives. Detailed questioning about the work and leisure activities and the pattern of the rash often reveal its source. Patch tests (*see*) may confirm the diagnosis.

ALLERGIC REACTION • An adverse immune response following repeated contact with otherwise harmless substances such as pollens, molds, foods, cosmetics, and drugs.

ALLERGY • An adverse immune response following repeated contact with otherwise harmless substances such as pollens, molds, foods, cosmetics and drugs. See Allergic Contact Dermatitis.

4-ALLYL-2-METHOXYPHENOL • See Eugenol.

ALLYL PELARGONATE • Liquid, fruity odor, used in flavors and perfumes.

ALMOND MEAL • A powder obtained by pulverizing blanched almonds and used in various cosmetics and perfumes for its soothing properties. See Bitter Almond Oil for toxicity.

ALMOND MILK • A creamy mixture of blanched almonds, acacia (*see*), sugar, and water blended to a smooth paste and sieved. Used as a demulcent, especially in organic cosmetics. See Bitter Almond Oil.

ALMOND OIL • Used in brilliantines and spice flavorings. See Bitter Almond Oil.

ALMOND PASTE • A favorite early European cleanser. Made from the dried ripe seeds of the sweet almond. See Bitter Almond Oil for toxicity.

ALOE VERA • An anthraquinone (*see*) compound expressed from the aloe plant leaf from a South African lilylike plant. Used for supposed softening benefits in skin creams. It contains 99.5 percent water, with the remaining 0.5 percent composed of some 20 amino acids (*see*) and carbohydrates. There is no scientific evidence that aloe vera in cosmetics has any benefits according to the American Medical Association. Used in bitters, vermouth, and spice flavorings for beverages and alcoholic drinks. It has been used as a cathartic but was found to cause severe intestinal cramps and sometimes kidney damage. Crossreacts with benzoin and Balsam Peru in those who are allergic to these ingredients.

ALOE VERA GEL • See Aloe Vera.

ALPHA OLEFIN SULFONATE • See Sulfonated Oils.

ALPHA TOCOPHEROL • See Tocopherols and Vitamin E.

ALPHATIC ALDEHYDE • See Aldehyde.

ALTHEA ROOT • **Marshmallow Root.** A natural flavoring substance from a plant grown in Europe, Asia, and the United States. The dried root is used in strawberry, cherry, and root beer flavorings for beverages. The boiled root is used as a demulcent in ointments to soothe mucous membranes. The roots, flowers, and leaves are used externally as a poultice. Nontoxic.

ALUM • **Potash Alum. Aluminum Ammonium. Potassium Sulfate.** A colorless, odorless, crystalline, water-soluble solid used in astringent lotions, after-shave lotions, and as a styptic (stops bleeding). Also used to prevent aluminum chloride (*see*) from causing skin irritation in antiperspirants. In concentrated solutions alum has produced gum damage and fatal intestinal hemorrhages. It has a low toxicity in experimental animals but ingestion of 30 grams (an ounce) has killed an adult human. It is also known to cause kidney damage. Concentrated doses have damaged gums. No specific harmful effects reported in cosmetics.

ALUMINA • A natural or synthetic oxide of aluminum occurring in nature as bauxite and corundum. The aluminum hydroxide (*see*) formed is washed, dried, and used as an extender for cosmetic colors in which opacity is not desired. High concentrations of alumina may be irritating to the respiratory tract, and lung problems have been reported in alumina workers. No known skin toxicity.

ALUMINUM HYDRATE • White coloring for cosmetics. See Alumina and Colors.

ALUMINUM ACETATE • **Burow's Solution.** A mixture including acetic acid and boric acid, with astringent and antiseptic properties used in astringent lotions, antiperspirants, deodorants, and protective creams. It is also used as a fur dye, in fabric finishes, waterproofing, and as a disinfectant by embalmers. Ingestion of large doses can cause nausea and vomiting, diarrhea, and bleeding. Prolonged and continuous exposure can produce severe sloughing of the skin. It also causes skin rashes in some persons.

ALUMINUM BEHENATE • The aluminum (*see*) salt of behenic acid (*see*).

ALUMINUM BROMOHYDRATE • **Aluminum Bromide.** White, yellowish, deliquescent crystals derived by passing bromine over heated aluminum. The waterless form is highly corrosive to the skin. It is used in bromation, alkylation, and isomerization.

ALUMINUM CAPRYLATE • See Aluminum Salts.

ALUMINUM CHLORHYDROXIDE • See Aluminum Chlorohydrate.

ALUMINUM CHLORHYDROXY ALLANTOINATE • Used in aftershave lotions and other astringents. Also used as a buffer. Nonsensitizing and nonirritating. See Allantoin.

ALUMINUM CHLORIDE • The first antiperspirant salt to be used for commercial antiperspirant products and still the strongest available in effectiveness. It is also antiseptic but can be irritating to sensitive skin and it does cause allergic reactions in susceptible people. Lethal to mammals upon ingestion of large doses.

ALUMINUM CHLOROHYDRATE • The most frequently used antiperspirant in the United States. Causes occasional infections of the hair follicles. May be irritating to abraded skin and may also cause allergic reactions, but it is considered by cosmetic manufacturers as one of the least irritating of the aluminum salts.

ALUMINUM CHLOROHYDRATE COMPLEX • See Aluminum Chlorohydrate.

ALUMINUM CHLOROHYDREX • A derivative of aluminum chlorohydrate (*see*) combined with propylene glycol making it soluble in alcohol. It is used in deodorants and in antiperspirants. See Aluminum Salts.

ALUMINUM CITRATE • The salt of aluminum hydroxide and citric acid. See Aluminum Salts.

ALUMINUM DIACETATE • See Aluminum Salts.

ALUMINUM DICHLOROHYDREX PEG AND PG • Aluminum dichlorate and propylene glycol in which some of the water molecules have been replaced by the propylene glycol. See Aluminum Salts.

ALUMINUM DIMERATE • The aluminum salt of dimer acid. See Aluminum Salts.

ALUMINUM DISTEARATE • A binder that holds loose powders together when compressed into a solid cake form. See Aluminum Stearates.

ALUMINUM FORMATE • Used as an antiperspirant to make other aluminum salts less acid and corrosive to fabrics. See Aluminum Salts and Formic Acid.

ALUMINUM GLYCINATE • See Aluminum Salts.

ALUMINUM HYDRATE • **Gloss White.** Usually obtained as a white bulky amorphous powder. Practically insoluble in water but soluble in alkaline solution. Used as an adsorbent, emulsifier, and alkali in detergents, antiperspirants, and dentifrices. Used medicinally as a gastric antacid. No known toxicity.

ALUMINUM HYDROXIDE • Mild astringent and alkali used in antiperspirants, dentifrices, and dusting powders. A white gelatinous mass used as a drying agent, catalyst, adsorbent, and coloring agent in many cosmetic processes. A leavening agent in the production of baked goods, as well as a gastric antacid in medicine. Practically insoluble in water but not in alkaline solutions. Aluminum hydroxide has a low toxicity but may cause constipation if ingested. No known skin toxicity. See Aluminum Salts and Deodorants.

ALUMINUM ISOSTEARATES/LAURATES/STEARATES • The aluminum salt of a mixture of isostearic acid, lauric acid, and stearic acid (*see all*). Used as a gelling agent. No known toxicity.

ALUMINUM ISOSTEARATES/MYRISTATES • Myristates is the aluminum salt of a mixture of isostearic acid and myristic acid (*see both*). Used as a gelling agent. No known toxicity.

ALUMINUM ISOSTEARATES/PALMITATES • Palmitates is the aluminum salt of palmitic acid (*see*) and isostearic acid (*see*). Used as a gelling agent. No known toxicity.

ALUMINUM LACTATE • The aluminum salts of lactic acid (*see both*).

ALUMINUM LANOLATE • See Aluminum Salts.

ALUMINUM METHIONATE • See Aluminum Salts.

ALUMINUM MYRISTATES/PALMITATES • Myristates is the aluminum salt of a mixture of palmitic acid and isostearic acid (*see both*). Used as a gelling agent. No known toxicity.

ALUMINUM PALMITATE • White granules, insoluble in water, used as a lubricant and waterproofing material. Employed as an antiperspirant. See Aluminum Salts and Deodorants.

ALUMINUM PHENOSULFONATE • **Aluminum Sulfocarbolate.** Pink powder, soluble in water, used in preshave astringent-type lotions and spray deodorants for its antiseptic and detergent properties. It is also used in dusting powder. See Aluminum Sulfate for toxicity.

ALUMINUM PHOSPHATE • **Aluminum Orthophosphate.** White crystals insoluble in water. Used in ceramics, dental cements, and cosmetics as a gelling agent. Corrosive to tissue.

ALUMINUM POWDER • A color additive composed of finely divided particles of aluminum. Used in face powders and hair colorings. No known toxicity. Permanently listed by the FDA in 1977 for use as a coloring.

ALUMINUM SALTS • **Aluminum Acetate. Aluminum Caprylate. Aluminum Chloride. Aluminum Chlorohydrate. Aluminum Diacetate. Aluminum Distearate. Aluminum Glycinate. Aluminum Hydroxide. Aluminum Lanolate. Aluminum Methionate. Aluminum Phenolsulfonate. Aluminum Silicate. Aluminum Stearate. Aluminum Sulfate. Aluminum Tristearate.** These are both the strong and weak acids of aluminum used in antiperspirants to combat body odors. The smell of sweat is caused by bacterial action on the moisture. The salts are believed to prevent perspiration from reaching the skin by impeding the action of sweat and act as an antibacterial. The strong salts may cause skin irritation and damage fabrics, particularly linens and cottons. Therefore, buffering agents are added by cosmetic manufacturers to counteract such adverse effects. The salts are also styptic (*see*).

ALUMINUM SILICATE • A white mass, insoluble in water, obtained naturally from clay or synthesized, used as an anticaking and coloring agent in powders. Essentially harmless when given orally and when applied to skin. See Aluminum Salts.

ALUMINUM STARCH OCTENYLSUCCINATE • **Dry Flow®.** See Aluminum Phenosulfonate.

ALUMINUM STEARATES • Hard, plasticlike materials used in waterproofing fabrics, thickening lubricating oils, and as a chewing gum base component and a defoamer component used in processing beet sugar and yeast. Aluminum tristearate is a hard plastic material used as a thickener and coloring in cosmetics. No known toxicity.

ALUMINUM SULFATE • **Cake Alum.** Colorless crystals, soluble in water, used as an antiseptic, astringent, and detergent in antiperspirants, deodorants, and skin fresheners; also purifies water. It may cause pimples under the arm when in antiperspirants and/or allergic reactions in some people.

ALUMINUM TRIPALMITATE/TRIISOSTEARATE • See Aluminum Isostearates/Palmitates.

ALUMINUM TRIPALMITATE/TRIMYRISTATE • See Aluminum Myristates/Palmitates.

ALUMINUM TRISTEARATE • See Aluminum Stearates.

ALUMINUM ZIRCONIUM TRICHLOROHYDREX GLYC • Aluminum zirconium trichlorohydrate in which glycine is added to replace some of the water molecules that normally cling to metal. It is used in antiperspirants. See Aluminum Salts.

AMARANTH • See FD & C Blue No. 2.

AMBER OIL, RECTIFIED • A perfume ingredient distilled from amber, a fossil resin of vegetable origins, and purified. The oil is pale yellow to yellowish brown and volatile, with a penetrating odor and acrid taste. No known toxicity.

AMBERGRIS • Concretion from the intestinal tract of the sperm whale found in tropical seas. About 80 percent cholesterol, it is a gray to black waxy mass and is used for fixing delicate odors in perfumery. It is also used in a flavoring for food and beverages. No known toxicity.

AMBRETTOLID • Formed in ambrette-seed oil. Used as a flavoring, perfume fixative. No known toxicity.

"AMERACHOL"™ • A series of surface-active lanolin derivatives. Most are soft solids used as emulsifiers and stabilizers for water and oil systems. Emollients in cosmetics.

AMES TEST • Dr. Bruce Ames, a biochemist at the University of California, developed a simple, inexpensive test using bacteria that reveals whether a chemical is a mutagen. Almost all chemicals that are known carcinogens have also been shown to be mutagenic on the Ames Test. Whether the test can identify carcinogens is suill controversial.

AMIDE • Derived from ammonia. Used in cosmetics as thickeners, soil removers, and foam stabilizers. Also used as an anti-irritant to prevent "stinging" of other cosmetic ingredients. Cocoamide DEA (*see*) is an example.

AMIDO • Denoting a compound that contains ammonia. Quaternary ammonium compounds (*see*) are amines.

AMINE ACID SURFACTANTS • **Acyl Glutamate.** Used as an "anti-irritant" in cosmetics to prevent stinging of some cosmetic ingredients.

AMINE OXIDES • See Amine Acid Surfactants.

AMINO ACIDS • The body's building blocks, from which proteins are constructed. Of the twenty-two known amino acids, eight cannot be manufactured in the body in sufficient quantities to sustain growth health. These eight are called "essential" because they are necessary to maintain good health. A ninth, histidine, is thought to be necessary for growth only in childhood. Widely used in moisturizers and emollients because they are thought to help water penetrate the skin.

p-AMINOBENZOIC ACID • See Para-aminobenzoic Acid.

PARA-AMINOBENZOIC ACID • The colorless or yellowish acid found in the Vitamin B-complex. In an alcohol and water solution plus a little light perfume, it is sold under a wide variety of names as a sunscreen lotion to prevent skin damage from the sun. It is also used as a local anesthetic in sunburn products. It is used medicinally to treat arthritis. However, it can cause allergic eczema (*see*) and a sensitivity to light in susceptible people whose skin may react to sunlight by erupting with a rash, sloughing, and/or swelling.

6-AMINOCAPROIC ACID • See Amino Acids and Caproic Acid.

2-AMINO-6-CHLORO-4-NITROPHENOL • See Phenol.

AMINODIMETHICONE • Used as a skin protectant and in hair sprays. See Dimethicone.

AMINOETHYLACRYLATE PHOSPHATE/ACRYLATE COPOLYMER • See Acrylates.

4-AMINO-2-HYDROXYTOLUENE • Used in the manufacture of dyes. See Toluene.

AMINOMETHYL PROPANEDIOL • Crystals made from nitrogen compounds that are soluble in alcohol and mixable with water. Used as an emulsifying agent for cosmetic creams and lotions and in mineral oils. No known toxicity.

AMINOMETHYL PROPANOL • An alcohol made from nitrogen compounds; mixes with water. Soluble in alcohol and used as an emulsifying agent for cosmetic creams, lotions, and hair sprays. Used in medicines that reduce body water. Prolonged skin exposure may cause irritation due to alkalinity, but in most commercial products the alkalinity is neutralized.

2-AMINO-4-NITROPHENOL • See Hair Coloring.

2-AMINO-5-NITROPHENOL • See Aminophenol.

4-AMINO-2-NITROPHENOL • See Aminophenol.

AMINOPHENOL • **o-Aminophenol. p-Aminophenol. m-Aminophenol. 2-Amino-5-Nitrophenol. 4-Amino-2-Nitrophenol. 2-Amino-6-Chloro-4-Nitrophenol. p-Aminophenol HCL.** Aromatic, colorless crystals derived from phenol (*see*), used as intermediates (*see*) in orange red and medium brown hair dyes. Discovered in London in 1854, aminophenols are also used in the manufacture of sulfur and azo dyes (*see*). Can cause a lack of oxygen in the blood but is less toxic than aniline (*see*) in animals. Solutions on the skin have produced restlessness and convulsions in humans as well as skin irritations. May also cause skin rashes and sensitizations. Inhalation may cause asthma.

m-AMINOPHENOL • See Aminophenol.

p-AMINOPHENOL • See Aminophenol.

p-AMINOPHENOL HCL • See Aminophenol.

AMMONIA • Liquid used in permanent wave (cold) and hair bleaches. Obtained by blowing steam through incandescent coke. Ammonia is also used in the manufacture of explosives and synthetic fabrics. It is extremely toxic when inhaled in concentrated vapors, and is irritating to the eyes and mucous membranes. It may cause hair breakage when used in permanent waves and hair bleaches.

AMMONIA WATER • Ammonia gas dissolved in water. Used as an alkali (*see*) in metallic hair dyes, hair straighteners, and in protective skin creams. Colorless with a very pungent odor, it is irritating to the eyes and mucous membranes. In strong solution can cause burns and blistering.

AMMONIATED MERCURY • **Mercuric Chloride Ammoniated.** A white odorless powder with a metallic taste used in ointment form to combat skin infections and to treat eye disorders. All forms of mercury are poisonous. Topical application may lead to skin rash and other allergic manifestations. Prolonged use may cause skin pigmentation and when applied too vigorously, it can be absorbed and result in systemic poisoning. Absorption or ingestion may lead to kidney damage. Ingestion also causes stomach pains and vomiting. No longer permitted in cosmetics except in small amounts as a preservative.

AMMONIUM ACETATE • The ammonium salt of acetic acid (*see*).

AMMONIUM ACRYLATES COPOLYMER • See Acrylates.

AMMONIUM ALGINATE • See Alginates.

AMMONIUM ALUM • See Alum.

AMMONIUM BICARBONATE • Used as a buffer in thioglycolate cold permanent waving lotions. Occurs in the urine of alligators. Usually prepared by passing carbon dioxide gas through concentrated ammonia water. Shiny, hard, colorless or white crystals; faint odor of ammonia. Used in baking powder formulas, for cooling baths. Used medicinally as an expectorant and to break up intestinal gas. Also used in compost heaps to accelerate decomposition. See Ammonium Carbonate for toxicity.

AMMONIUM BROMIDE • Colorless crystals or white powder, it is derived by the action of an acid on ammonium hydroxide. It is used in hair conditioners and as an anticorrosive agent and fire retardant agent. See Bromides.

AMMONIUM C12-15 PARETH SULFATE • **Pareth-25-3 Sulfate.** The ammonium salt of a sulfated polyethylene glycol ether of a mixture of C12-15 fatty alcohols (*see*). See also Ammonium Sulfate.

AMMONIUM CARBONATE • A white solid alkali derived partly from ammonium bicarbonate (*see*) and used as a neutralizer and buffer in permanent wave solutions and creams. It decomposes when exposed to air. Also used in baking powders, for defatting woolens, in fire extinguishers, and as an expectorant. Ammonium carbonate can cause skin rashes on the scalp, forehead, or hands.

AMMONIUM CHLORIDE • Ammonium salts that occur naturally. Colorless, odorless crystals or white powder, saline in taste, and incompatible with alkalies. Used as an acidifier in permanent wave solutions, eye lotions, and as a cooling and stimulating skin wash. Industrially employed in freezing mixtures, batteries, dyes, safety explosives, and in medicine as a urinary acidifier and diuretic. Keeps snow from melting on ski slopes. If ingested, can cause nausea, vomiting, and acidosis. Lethal as an intramuscular dose in rats and guinea pigs. As with any ammonia compound, concentrated solutions can be irritating to the skin.

AMMONIUM CITRATE • See Citric Acid.

AMMONIUM COCOMONOGLYCERIDES • See Coconut Oil and Sulfated Oils.

AMMONIUM CUMENESULFONATE • **Benzenesulfonic Acid, Methylated Ammonium Salt.** Derived from coal tar or petroleum, it is used as a solvent. See Coal Tar.

AMMONIUM DICHROMATE • Orange needles used in dyeing red colors and in synthetic perfumes. Irritating to the eyes, skin, and a suspected carcinogen.

AMMONIUM DODECYLBENZENESULFONATE • **Ammonium Lauryl Benzene Sulfonate.** See Quaternary Ammonium Compounds and Surfactants.

AMMONIUM GLYCYRRHIZATE • The ammonium salt of glycyrrhizic acid (*see*). See also Quaternary Ammonium Compounds.

AMMONIUM HYDROLYZED ANIMAL PROTEIN • The ammonium salt of hydrolyzed animal protein. See Hydrolyzed Animal Protein and Surfactants.

AMMONIUM HYDROXIDE • **Ammonia Water.** A weak alkali formed when ammonia dissolves in water and exists only in solution. A clear colorless liquid with an extremely pungent odor. Used as an alkali (*see*) in metallic hair dyes, hair straighteners, and in protective skin creams. Also used in detergents and for removing stains. It is irritating to the eyes and mucous membranes. It may cause hair breakage.

AMMONIUM IODIDE • An ammonium salt prepared from ammonia and iodine. White odorless crystals with a sharp saline taste. The crystals become yellow and brown on exposure to air and light. Used in cosmetics as an antiseptic and preservative and in medicine as an expectorant. See Iodine for toxicity.

AMMONIUM ISOSTEARATE • The ammonium salts of isostearic acid (*see*). Also see Surfactants.

AMMONIUM LAURETH SULFATE • **Ammonium Lauryl Ether Sulfate.** A compound that breaks up and holds oils and soil so they can be easily removed from skin or hair. See Lauryl Alcohol.

AMMONIUM LAURYL SULFATE • The ammonium salt of lauryl sulfate derived from the natural coconut alcohols, it is a mild anionic surfactant (*see*) cleanser that is widely used at mild acidic pH values. See Lauryl Alcohol.

AMMONIUM MOLYBDATE • Colorless, green, or white crystalline salt. See Ammonia.

AMMONIUM MONOOLEAMIDO • See Ammonia.

AMMONIUM MYRETH SULFATE • See Sodium Lauryl Sulfate.

AMMONIUM MYRISTYL SULFATE • The ammonium salt of myristyl sulfate. See Myristic Acid.

AMMONIUM NONOXYNOL-4-SULFATE • Cleansing material that breaks up and holds oils and soil so that they may be removed easily from the skin or hair surface. See Ammonium Sulfate.

AMMONIUM OLEATE • The ammonium salt of oleic acid (*see*) used as an emulsifying agent.

AMMONIUM PERSULFATE • **Ammonium Salt.** Colorless crystals soluble in water, used as an oxidizer and bleach in dyes and skin lighteners. Also as a disinfectant, deodorant, and preservative. It may be irritating to the skin and mucous membranes. In cosmetics, may make hair brittle. Lethal to rats in large oral doses.

AMMONIUM PHENOSULFONATE • The ammonium salt of phenolsulfonic acid. See Quaternary Ammonium Compounds.

AMMONIUM PHOSPHATE • **Dibasic. Ammonium Salt.** An odorless, white or colorless crystalline powder with a cooling taste used in mouthwashes. It is also used in fireproofing textiles, paper, and wood. No known toxicity.

AMMONIUM STEARATE • **Stearic Acid. Ammonium Salt.** A yellowish white powder used as a texturizer in vanishing creams. No known toxicity.

AMMONIUM STYRENE/ACRYLATE COPOLYMER • The ammonium salt of a polymer of styrene and a monomer of acrylic acid and methyacrylic acid used as an opacifier. See Acrylates.

AMMONIUM SULFATE • **Ammonium Salt.** A neutralizer in permanent wave lotions, it is odorless and colorless, either white crystals or powder. Industrially used in freezing mixtures, fireproofing fabrics, and tanning. Used medicinally to prolong analgesia. No known toxicity when used cosmetically. Rats were killed when fed large doses.

AMMONIUM SULFIDE • A salt derived from sulfur and ammonium, it is used as a neutralizer in permanent wave lotions, as a depilatory, to apply patina to bronze, and in spice flavorings. It has been reported to have caused a death when ingested in a permanent-wave solution. Irritating to the skin when used in depilatories.

AMMONIUM SULFITE • Ammonium salt made with sulfuric acid. White, crystalline, soluble in water, almost insoluble in alcohol and acetone. Antiseptic. A preservative in cold permanent waves. See Ammonia for toxicity.

AMMONIUM TALLATE • The ammonium salt of tall oil fatty acids. See Quaternary Ammonium Compounds.

AMMONIUM THIOGLYCOLATE • The ammonium salt of thioglycolic acid, a liquid with a strong unpleasant odor that is readily oxidized by air. A hair straightener. It can cause severe burns and blistering of the skin. Large doses injected into the stomachs of mice killed them.

AMMONIUM VINYL ACETATE/ACRYLATES TERPOLYMER • See Acrylates.

AMMONIUM XYLENESULFONATE • Ammonium salt of xylene. A lacquer solvent used in nail polishes. Flammable, insoluble in water. It may be narcotic in high doses. Chronic toxicity or skin effects are not known.

AMNIOTIC FLUID • The fluid surrounding the cow embryo *in utero*.

AMODIMETHICONE • The silicone polymer with amino acids. See Amino Acids and Silicones.

AMP • The abbreviation for aminomethyl propanol (*see*).

AMPD • The abbreviation for aminomethyl propanediol (*see*).

AMPD ACRYLATES/DIACETONEACRYLAMIDE COPOLYMER • **Acrylic Acid, Methacrylic Acid,** and their simple esters. See Acrylates.

AMPD ISOSTERIC HYDROLYZED ANIMAL PROTEIN • The salt of isostearic hydrolyzed animal protein. See Hydrolyzed Animal Protein.

AMPHO- • Means "double" or "both."

AMPHOTERIC • A material that can display both acid and basic properties. Used primarily in surfactants (*see*), it contains betaines and imidazoles (*see both*).

AMPHOTERIC-2 • A cleansing compound that breaks up and holds oils and soil so that they may be removed easily from skin or hair surface. See Amphoteric.

AMSONIC ACID • Used in hair dyes and bleaching products. Manufactured from sulfonic acid. Yellow needles, slightly soluble in water, and forms salts with ammonia compounds. No known toxicity.

AMYL ACETATE • **Banana Oil. Pear Oil.** Obtained from amyl alcohol, with a strong fruity odor. Used in nail finishes and nail polish remover as a solvent, and as an artificial fruit essence in perfume. Also used in food and beverage flavoring and for perfuming shoe polish. Amyl acetate is a skin irritant and causes central nervous system depression when ingested. Exposure of 950 ppm for one hour has caused headache, fatigue, chest pain, and irritation of the mucous membranes.

AMYL ALCOHOL • A solvent used in nail lacquers. It occurs naturally in cocoa and oranges and smells like camphor. Highly toxic and narcotic, ingestion of as little as 30 milligrams has killed humans. Inhalation causes violent coughing.

AMYL BUTYRATE • Used in some perfume formulas for its apricot-like odor. It occurs naturally in cocoa and is colorless. Also used for synthetic flavorings. No known toxicity.

AMYL CINNAMIC ALCOHOL • A solvent used in nail polish removers, waterproofing and enamelware. See Cinnamic Acid.

AMYL CINNAMIC ALDEHYDE • Liquid with a strong floral odor suggesting jasmine. Used in perfumes and flavorings. See Cinnamic Acid.

AMYL DIMETHYL PABA • Used in sunscreens to absorb ultraviolet light from sun's rays to help prevent or lessen sunburn while allowing the skin to tan. See Para-Aminobenzoic Acid and Sunscreens.

AMYL GALLATE • An antioxidant obtained from nutgalls and from molds. No known toxicity.

AMYL PHENOL • Used in hair-grooming preparations. See Phenol.

AMYL PROPIONATE • Colorless liquid with applelike odor used in perfumes, flavors and in lacquers. No known toxicity.

AMYL SALICYLATE • Derived from salicylic acid. A pleasant-smelling liquid used in sunscreen lotions and perfumes. Insoluble in water. See Salicylates.

AMYLASE • Used as a texturizer in cosmetics, it is an enzyme prepared from hog pancreas used in flour to break down starch into smaller molecules. Used medicinally to combat inflammation. No known toxicity.

AMYLOPECTIN • **Amioca.** Derived from starch, it is the almost insoluble outer portion of the starch granule. The gel constituent of starch. Used as a texturizer in cosmetics. Obtained from corn. Gives a red color when mixed with iodine and does not gel when mixed with water. No known toxicity.

AMYLTRICRESOL • A phenolmercury compound used in mouthwashes. See Phenol.

ANETHOLE • A flavoring agent used in mouthwashes and toothpastes and a scent for perfumes. Obtained from anise (*see*) oil and other sources. Colorless or faintly yellow liquid with a sweet taste and a characteristic aniselike odor. Chief constituent of anise. Anethole is affected by light and caused irritation of the gums and throat when used in a denture cream. When applied to the skin, anethole may produce hives, scaling, and blisters.

ANGELICA • Used in inexpensive fragrances, toothpastes, and mouthwashes. Grown in Europe and Asia, the aromatic seeds, leaves, stems, and roots have been used in medicine for flatus (gas), to increase sweating and reduce body water. Also used as a flavoring in food. When perfume is applied, skin may break out with a rash and swell when exposed to sunlight. The bark is used medicinally as purgative and emetic.

ANHYDRIDE • A residue resulting from water being removed from a compound. An oxide—combination of oxygen and an element—that can combine with water to form an acid, or that is derived from an acid by the abstraction of water. Acetic acid (*see*) is an example.

ANHYDROUS • Describes a substance that contains no water.

ANILINE DYES • **Coal Tar Dyes.** Aniline is a colorless to brown liquid that darkens with age. Used in the manufacture of hair dyes, medicinals, resins, and perfumes. It is used in carbons, fur dyeing, rubber, photographics, inks, colored pencils, and crayons. Can cause contact dermatitis.

ANIMAL COLLAGEN AMINO ACIDS • The major protein of the white fibers of connective tissue, cartilage, and bone, that is insoluble in water, but easily altered to gelatins by boiling in water, dilute acids, or alkalies. See Hydrolyzed Animal Protein.

ANIMAL KERATIN AMINO ACIDS • A mixture of amino acids from the hydrolysis of keratin (*see*). See also Hydrolyzed Animal Keratin.

ANIMAL PROTEIN DERIVATIVE • Used in skin conditioners which attract water, thereby helping to maintain the skin's moisture balance. See Hydrolyzed Animal Protein.

ANIMAL TISSUE EXTRACT • The mixed extract of the skin, testes and ovaries of the pig, and the thymus, placentae, and udder of the cow. Also called Epiderm Oil R, it is used in moisturizers and other creams.

ANIONIC SURFACTANTS • A class of synthetic compounds used as emulsifiers in about 75 percent of all hand creams, shampoos, and lotions. An anion is a negatively charged ion that is "surface active."

These detergents usually consist of an alkali or ammonium salt of a strong acid plus an inorganic salt. Irritation of the skin by anionics depends on the alkalinity of the detergent. Some anionics used in shampoos such as triethanolamine (TEA) Coco Hydrolyzed Animal Protein, are not even irritating to the eyes, while Sodium Laureth Sulfate is. See Emulsifiers and Ammonia Water.

ANISE • **Anise Seed.** Dried ripe fruit of Asia, Europe, and the United States. Used in licorice, anise, pepperoni sausage, spice, and vanilla flavorings for beverages, ice cream, ices, candy, baked goods, condiments, and meats. The oil is used for butter, caramel, licorice, anise, rum, sausage, nut, root beer, sarsaparilla, spice, vanilla, wintergreen, and birch beer flavorings for the same foods as above excepting condiments but including chewing gum and liquors. Sometimes used to break up intestinal gas. Used in masculine-type perfumes, cleaners, and shampoos. Can cause contact dermatitis.

ANISIDINE o-ANISIDINE. p-ANISIDINE • Derived from anisole (*see*). Colorless needles. Used in the manufacture of azo dyes (*see*). Can be absorbed through the skin. It is an irritant and sensitizer.

ANISYL FORMATE • Used in perfumery and flavoring. See Formic Acid.

ANISYLACETATE • Colorless liquid with a lilac odor used in perfumery. See Anise.

ANNATTO • A vegetable dye from a tropical tree, yellow to pink, it is used in dairy products, baked goods, margarine, and breakfast cereals. No known toxicity. Permanently listed as a coloring in 1977.

ANTHRANILIC ACID • **o-Aminobenzoic Acid.** Yellowish crystals with a sweet taste used in dyes and perfumes. See Benzoic Acid.

ANTHRAQUINONE • A coal tar color produced industrially from phthalic anhydride and benzene (*see both*). Light yellow slender prisms, which are insoluble in water, it is widely used as a starter for the manufacture of vat dyes. May cause skin irritation and allergic reactions. It is also used as an organic inhibitor to prevent growth of cells and a repellent to protect seeds from being eaten by birds. Caused tumors when given orally to rats in doses of 72 milligrams per kilogram of body weight. It can also cause contact dermatitis (*see*).

ANTIBODY • Protein in blood, formed in response to invasion by a germ, virus, or other foreign body. In sensitive individuals, a special antibody, IgE is responsible for the allergic reaction.

ANTIGEN • Any substance that provokes an immune response when introduced into the body.

ANTIMONY COMPOUNDS • **Antimony Potassium Tartrate. Tartar Emetic.** Used in hair dyes. Obtained from ore mined in China,

Mexico, and Bolivia, this silver-white, brittle metal can cause contact dermatitis, eye and nose irritation, and ulceration by contact, fumes or dust. It is used medicinally as an emetic and in the manufacture of bullets and metal bearings, and to combat worms.

ANTIOXIDANTS • Preservatives that prevent fats from spoiling. Tocopherols and BHA are examples (*see both*).

ANTIPERSPIRANT • Any substance having a mild astringent action that tends to reduce the size of skin pores and thus restrain the passage of moisture on local body areas. The most commonly used antiperspirant compound is aluminum chlorohydrate. Use of zirconium compounds in antiperspirant sprays has been virtually discontinued because of their suspected carcinogens though they are permissible in creams. Antiperspirants exert neutralizing action which gives them deodorant properties. The FDA classified them as drugs rather than as cosmetics.

APPLE BLOSSOM • Used in perfumes and colognes, it is the essence of the flowers from a species of apple tree. No known toxicity.

APRICOT • **Fruit and Oil.** The tart orange-colored fruit. The oil is used in brilliantine and the crushed fruit as a facial mask to soften the skin. For a do-it-yourself facial mask, a cup of dried apricots is soaked in water until softened and mixed with a small bunch of grapes and 3 tablespoons of skimmed milk powder. The concoction is mixed in a blender and patted on the neck and face and allowed to remain for 15 minutes, followed by a rinse of cool water. No known toxicity.

APRICOT EXTRACT • See Apricot.

ARABIC GUM • See Acacia.

ARACHIDIC ACID • A fatty acid, also called eicosanoic acid, that is widely distributed in peanut oil fats and related compounds. It is used in lubricants, greases, waxes, and plastics. No known toxicity.

ARACHIDONIC ACID • A liquid unsaturated fatty acid that occurs in liver, brain, glands, and fat of animals and humans. The acid is generally isolated from animal liver. Used essentially for nutrition and to soothe eczema and rashes in skin creams and lotions. No known toxicity.

ARACHIDYL PROPIONATE • The ester of arachidyl alcohol and *N*-propionic acid used as a wax. See Arachidic Acid.

ARBITRARY FIXATIVE • An odorous substance that lends a particular note to a perfume throughout all stages of evaporation but does not really influence the evaporation of the perfume materials in the compound. Oakmoss is an example. See Fixative and Oakmoss.

ARBUTUS EXTRACT • From the leaves of the evergreen shrub

Arbutus, found in southern Europe and western North America. It has a white or pink flower.

ARGININE • An essential amino acid (*see*), strongly alkaline. The FDA has asked for further information on the nutrient, which plays an important rǫle in the production of urea (*see*) excretion. It has been used for the treatment of liver disease.

ARMENIAN BOLE • A soft claylike red earth. The pigment is found chiefly in Armenia and Tuscany and used as a coloring material in face powder. No known toxicity.

ARNICA • **Wolf's Bane.** Skin fresheners may contain this herb found in the Northern Hemisphere. The dried flowerhead has long been used as an astringent and to treat skin disorders, especially in tinctures. It has been used externally to treat bruises and sprains. Ingestion leads to severe intestinal upset, nervous disturbances, irregular heartbeat, and collapse. Ingestion of one ounce has caused severe illness but not death. Active irritant on the skin. Not recommended for use in toilet preparations and should never be used on broken skin.

AROMATIC • In the context of cosmetics, a chemical that has an aroma.

AROMATIC BITTERS • Usually made from the maceration of bitter herbs and used to intensify the aroma of perfume. The herbs selected for aromatic bitters must have a persistent fragrant aroma. Ginger and cinnamon are examples.

ARROWROOT • An ingredient in dusting powders and hair dyes made from the root starch of plants. Arrowroot was used by the American Indians to heal wounds from poisoned arrows and is still employed today in plants and animals both free and combined with proteins. It is used as a culture medium and as a medicine. In cosmetics, it is used to help moisturizers penetrate the skin. No known toxicity.

ARSENIC COMPOUNDS • Arsenic is an element that occurs throughout the universe and is highly toxic in most forms. Its compounds are used in hair tonics and hair dyes and have been employed to treat spirochetal infections, blood disorders, and skin diseases. Ingestion causes nausea, vomiting, and death. Chronic poisoning can result in pigmentation of skin and kidney and liver damage. In hair tonic and dyes it may cause contact dermatitis. The limit of arsenic in colors is 0.0002 percent. Arsenic can also cause the skin to be sensitive to light and break out in a rash or to swell.

ARTIFICIAL • In the context of cosmetics, a substance not duplicated in nature. A scent, for instance, may have all natural ingredients, but it must be called artificial if it has no counterpart in nature.

ARTIFICIAL NAILS • Plastics designed to be pasted or self-adhered to one's natural nails to give the appearance of long, lovely, undamaged fingernails. After application, the artificial nails are cut or filed to desired length and shape. Artificial nails were developed from materials used by dentists to fill teeth. The basic ingredients include a vinyl compound (methyl methacrylate is one of the most commonly used vinyls), a catalyst, and a plasticizer. Allergy and irritation to the skin may develop from ingredients in the fake nails or in the adhesive.

ARYLALCANOIC • Rubifacient (*see*) used in Europe.

ASAFOETIDA EXTRACT • **Asafetida. Devil's Dung.** A gum or resin obtained from the roots or rhizome of *Ferula assafoetida*, any of several plants grown in Iran, Turkestan, and Afghanistan. The soft lumps, or "tears," have a garlicky odor and are used as a natural flavoring. The gums have also been used medicinally as an expectorant and to break up intestinal gas. No known toxicity.

ASCORBIC ACID • **Vitamin C.** A preservative and antioxidant used in cosmetic creams, particularly bleach and lemon creams. Vitamin C is necessary for normal teeth bones and blood vessels. The white or slightly yellow powder darkens upon exposure to air. Reasonably stable when it remains dry in air, but deteriorates rapidly when exposed to air while in solution. Nontoxic.

ASCORBYL PALMITATE • A salt of ascorbic acid (*see*), it is used as a preservative and antioxidant in cosmetic creams and lotions to prevent rancidity. Nontoxic.

ASCORBYL STEARATE • See Ascorbyl Palmitate.

ASPARAGINE • A nonessential amino acid (*see*). It is widely found in plants and animals both free and combined with proteins. It is used as a culture medium and as a medicine. In cosmetics, it is used to help moisturizers penetrate the skin. No known toxicity.

ASPARTIC ACID • **DL & L Forms. Aminosuccinate Acid.** A nonessential amino acid (*see*) occurring in animals and plants, sugar cane, sugar beets, and molasses. It is usually synthesized for commercial purposes. No known toxicity.

ASTRINGENT • Usually promoted for oily skin. A clear liquid containing mostly alcohol, but with small amounts of other ingredients such as boric acid, alum, menthol, and/or camphor. A typical astringent formula: ethanol, 50 percent; sorbitol, 2.5 percent (*see both*); perfume oil, 0.1 percent; menthol, 0.1 percent; boric acid, 2.0 percent (*see both*); water, 44.9 percent. In addition to making the skin feel refreshed, it usually gives a tightened feeling from the evaporation of the ingredients. According to the American Medical Association, there is no evidence that astringents tighten or shrink the pores.

Usually toxic when ingested because of denatured alcohol content.

ATTAPULGITE • See Fuller's Earth.

ASPIRIN • **Acetylsalicylic Acid.** It is the most commonly taken drug in the United States. It is widely used as an analgesic, antifever, and anti-inflammatory medicine. It produces allergic reactions in an estimated 2 persons per 100. Of the people with severe asthma, about 5 to 10 percent are aspirin sensitive. Allergy to aspirin occurs most frequently in people between the ages of 40 and 60 years who have a long history of sinusitis, nasal polyps, and high levels of eosinophils (a type of white blood cell). Allergy to aspirin can cause the aforementioned symptoms. It can also cause symptoms that range from rashes, hives, and swelling to asthmatic attacks that may be life threatening. The onset of severe symptoms may come within 15 minutes after ingesting aspirin, or it may not occur for hours. The exact mechanism of the aspirin reaction remains uncertain, because no antibodies to aspirin have been found. However, those allergic to aspirin may also be sensitive to other salicylates (*see*) such as tartrazine used in yellow and orange dyes.

ATOPIC DERMATITIS • A chronic, itching, inflammation of the skin also called eczema (*see*).

AVOIDANCE • Measures taken to avoid contact with allergy-producing substances. Since there are no cures for allergies as of yet, avoiding allergens is the best way to combat them.

AZO DYES • Used in nonpermanent hair rinses and tints. Azo dyes belong to a large category of colorings that are characterized by the way they combine with nitrogen. These are a very large class of dyes made from diazonium compounds and phenol. The dyes usually contain a mild acid, such as citric or tartaric acid. It can cause allergic reactions. People who become sensitized to permanent hair dyes containing paraphenylene diamine (*see*) also develop a cross sensitivity to azo dyes. That is, a person who is allergic to permanent *p*-phenylenediamine dyes will also be allergic to azo dyes. There are reports that azo dyes are absorbed through the skin.

B

BABY CREAM • Aimed at protecting against irritation and soothing baby skin, such formulas usually contain mineral oil, paraffin, lanolin, white beeswax, and ceresin. They may also contain many other ingredients including petrolatum, mineral wax, glyceryl monostearate, methyl and propyl parabens, extract of lanolin, sterols, hydrogenated fatty oils, and spermaceti (*see all*). Lanolin, lanolin derivatives, beeswax, and the parabens are common allergens and if your baby develops a rash, consult your physician.

BABY LOTION • Aimed at protecting, soothing, and cleansing the delicate skins of babies. Usually contains antimicrobials, emulsifiers, humectants to retain moisture, thickeners, and often some perfume. The product may also contain lanolin, mineral oil, cetyl alcohol, preservatives, and antioxidants (*see all*). Few problems are reported by consumers except for an occasional rash. However, a number of the ingredients used can cause allergic responses, particularly the perfumes and the antimicrobials so if your baby develops a rash, read the label and check the product against ingredients listed in this book. Take the information to a physician who can make the definitive diagnosis.

BABY OIL • Aimed at protecting and soothing baby skin. Usually contains mineral oil, palmitate, lanolin, vegetable oils, and lanolin derivatives (*see all*). Mineral oil or vegetable oil right from the pantry will do the same and lessen the chances of allergic contact dermatitis. Check the ingredients on the label, if you suspect the product is causing a rash, and see if they may be allergens for your child. Take the information to your physician who can make the definitive diagnosis.

BABY POWDER • Soothes, dries, and protects baby skin from irritation. Usually contains talc, kaolin, zinc oxide, starch, magnesium carbonate (*see all*), perfume oil, and—although there have been repeated warnings against it—boric acid (*see*). Cornstarch from your pantry shelf does not carry the problems of talc (*see*), will work as well, and is less expensive.

BABY SOAP • Usually a mild sodium soap of coconut and/or palm oil. Some are made of polyunsaturated vegetable oils. Baby soaps may contain colloidal oatmeal, a mild soap-free sudsing agent, lanolin derivatives, and a germ killer such as chlorobutanol. If your baby is known to be allergic to any of the above, check with the company about the soap's ingredients and then check them in the book.

BAK • See Benzalkonium Chloride.

BALM • A variation of the word "balsam." Usually means a soothing ointment, especially a fragrant one, or a soothing application.

BALM MINT • **Balm of Gilead.** The secretion of any of several small evergreen African or Asian trees with leaves that yield a strong aromatic odor when bruised. Known in ancient Palestine as a soothing medication for the skin. Used in cosmetics as an unguent which soothes and heals the skin. It is also used for its fragrance in perfumes. No known toxicity.

BALM OIL • A natural fruit and liquor flavoring agent for beverages, ice cream, candy, and baked goods. The balm leaves may also be used for flavorings in beverages and cosmetics. May cause allergic reactions.

BALSAM MECCA • **Balsam of Gilead.** Obtained from a twig. Insoluble in water, soluble in alcohol. Used to scent perfume. See Balsam for toxicity.

BALSAM PERU • A dark brown viscous liquid with a pleasant lingering odor and a warm bitter taste for use in face masks, perfumes, cream hair rinses, and astringents. Obtained from Peruvian balsam in Central America near the Pacific Coast. Mildly antiseptic and irritating to the skin and may cause contact dermatitis and a stuffy nose. It is one of the most common sensitizers and may crossreact with benzoin, rosin, benzoic acid, benzyl alcohol, cinnamic acid, essential oils, orange peel, eugenol, cinnamon, clove, Tolu balsam, storax, benzyl benzoate, and wood tars.

BALSAM TOLU • An ingredient used in perfumery and soap. Extracted from a tree grown on elevated plains and mountains in South America. Yellowish brown or brown thick fluid with a strong odor and taste. Its vapor has been used as an expectorant. See Balsam Peru for toxicity.

BANANA • The common fruit, high in potassium (*see*), used for dry skin by organic cosmetic enthusiasts. A banana face mask formula: mash one ripe banana and mix thoroughly with 1 tablespoon of almond meal (*see*) plus 2 tablespoons of yogurt. Spread mixture on face and neck. Leave on for 5 to 10 minutes. Remove with lukewarm water. Nontoxic.

BARIUM HYDROXIDE • See Barium Sulfate.

BARIUM SULFATE • **Blanc Fixe.** The salt of the alkaline earth metal, it is a fine, white, odorless, tasteless powder used as a white coloring and as a base for depilatories and other cosmetics. Barium hydroxide is also used in a similar manner. The barium products are poisonous when ingested and frequently cause skin reactions when applied.

BARIUM SULFIDE • Used in depilatories as a base, it is a grayish white to pale yellow powder. A skin irritant, it causes rashes and chemical burns. Should never be applied on broken or inflamed skin.

BARLEY FLOUR • A cereal grass cultivated since prehistoric times. Used in the manufacture of malt beverages, as a breakfast food, and as a demulcent (*see*) in cosmetics. No known toxicity.

BARRIER AGENT • A protective for hand creams and lotions, which acts as a barrier against irritating chemicals. The water-repellent types deposit a film that acts as a barrier to water and water-soluble agents that irritate the skin; oil-repellent types act as barriers against oil and oil-soluble irritants. Silicones (*see*) are widely used as barrier agents. Other skin protective ingredients in barrier agents include petrolatum, paraffin, ozokerite vegetables, beeswax, casein, various celluloses, alginic acid, zein, gum tragacanth, pectin, quince seed, bentonite, zinc oxide, zinc stearate, sodium silicate, talc, stearic acid, and titanium dioxide (*see all*). Covering one's hands with Vaseline or zinc oxide ointment will protect them well and inexpensively.

BASE COAT • Similar to a nail polish (*see*) in form and formulation but does not contain pigment and has an increased amount of resin (*see*). Applied on the nail under nail polish to help prevent chipping and to allow smoother application of the nail enamel. See Nail Enamel for toxicity.

BASIC BLUE 6 • **Medola's Blue.** The zinc chloride salt of benzo(*a*)-phenoxazin-7-ium, 9-(Dimethylamino)-, Chloride. See Basic Dye.

BASIC BLUE 9 • **Methylene Blue.** Prepared from dimethylaniline and thiosulfuric acid. Dark green, odorless crystals used as a stain in bacteriology, as a reagent for several chemicals, as a veterinary antiseptic, and as an antidote to cyanide poisoning.

BASIC BLUE 41 • **Methylbenzothiazolium Chloride.** See Basic Dyes.

BASIC BLUE 99 • **Arianor Steel Blue R.** See Basic Dyes.

BASIC BROWN 1 • **Bismarck Brown Y.** Made from nitrous acid, it is a blackish brown powder that turns yellow and orange in solution. See Aniline Dyes for toxicity.

BASIC BROWN 4 • **Basic Brown R. Bismarck Brown 53.** Prepared from toluene-2-4-diamine (*see*) with nitrous acid, it is a dark, solid brown, which turns reddish brown or violet in solution. Used in hair dyes. See Aniline Dyes for toxicity.

BASIC BROWN 16 • **Arianor Mahogany R.** An azo dye (*see*).

BASIC BROWN 17 • **Arianor Sienna Brown R.** An azo dye (*see*).

BASIC DYE • A group of dyes made from soluble salts, minerals acids, and certain organic acids that form insoluble compounds with acidic fibers. They produce very bright colors but lack good fastness. See Aniline Dyes for toxicity.

BASIC RED 22 • A triazolium dye. See Azo Dyes.

BASIC RED 76 • See Azo Dyes.

BASIC VIOLET 1 • **Methyl Violet.** A bright violet artificial coloring agent. See Aniline Dyes for toxicity.

BASIC VIOLET 3 • **Crystal Violet. Methyl Violet. Gentian Violet.** A triarylmethane color. Dark green powder or greenish pieces with a metallic luster, it is used as an antiseptic and against worms as well as a coloring.

BASIC VIOLET 10 • A xanthene color (*see*). The salt of stearic acid is solvent red 49. The name can be used only when applied to batches of uncertified color. The CTFA adopted name for certified (*see*) batches is D & C Red No. 19, also called rhodamine B. A basic red dye, it is very soluble in water and alcohol and forms a bluish-red fluorescent solution. Used as a dye for paper, wool, silk, and as a biological stain as well as in cosmetics.

BASIC YELLOW 11 • A triazolium dye. See Azo Dyes.

BASIC YELLOW 57 • **Arianor Straw Yellow.** See Basic Dyes.

"BASICOL"™ • A series of essential oils intended for replacement of oils of lavender, geranium, lemon, pine, ylang-ylang, neroli, and orrisroot (*see all*).

BASIL EXTRACT • The extract of the leaves and flowers of *Ocimum basilicum*, an herb having spikes of small white flowers and aromatic leaves used as a seasoning. A natural flavoring distilled from the flowering tops of the plant has a slightly yellowish color and a spicy odor. No known toxicity. GRAS.

BATH LOTION • For after a bath. Usually a cologne with some emollient oil. May also contain isopropyl myristate and fatty acids. The emollient oil also acts as a carrier for the perfume. May cause allergic reactions depending upon your sensitivity and the ingredients used.

BATH OIL • Softens and protects the skin in a foaming or nonfoaming oil. The concentration of perfume in bath oil is usually quite high and may be a source of allergic reactions. The oil is usually a mineral or vegetable oil and includes a surfactant to cause the oil to spread on the surface of the water. A common ingredient of the foaming-type of oil is TEA-lauryl sulfate, and sometimes foam stabilizers, such as saponin or methyl cellulose, are used to give the bubbles longevity. Also the usual chemicals that are added are castor oil, isopropyl myristate, alcohol, lanolin, and certified colors. A number of the ingredients may cause allergic contact dermatitis, so if you develop a rash, check the label.

BATH SALTS • Used to color, perfume, and chemically soften bath water, and to perfume the skin. Usually made from rock salt or sodium thiosulfate, which has been sprayed with alcohol, dye, or perfume. Rock salt is common table salt and has been used for treating inflammation of the skin. Sodium thiosulfate (''hypo'') has been used to treat certain skin rashes and has a low toxicity. The effervescent-type bath salts are due to the added sodium bicarbonate and tartaric acid. The noneffervescent type may add trisodium phosphate and sodium chloride. Among other chemicals that may be in bath salt are borax, sodium hexametaphosphate, starch, sodium carbonate, and sodium sesquicarbonate (*see all*). Phosphate and borax may cause caustic irritation of the skin and mucous membranes; boric acid may cause poisoning when ingested or absorbed through the skin.

BATYL ALCOHOL • Derived from glycerin (*see*), it is isolated from shark oil, bone, and bone marrow. It is soluble in fat solvents. No known toxicity.

BATYL ISOSTEARATE • An ester (*see*) of batyl alcohol and isostearic acid. See Glycerin.

BAY OIL • **Oil of Myrcia.** Astringent and antiseptic oil used in hair lotions and dressings, after-shave lotions, Bay Rum, and perfumes. Distilled from the leaves of the bayberry, it contains 40 to 55 percent eugenol (*see*). May cause allergic reactions and skin irritations.

BAY RUM • The alcoholic, aromatic oil distilled from the leaves of the bayberry and mixed with rum or made by mixing oil from the leaves with alcohol, water, and other oils. Widely used as an after-shave preparation and skin freshener. Also used in hair tonics. The basic formula for Bay Rum: bay oil, 0.20 percent; pimenta oil, 0.05 percent; ethyl alcohol, 50 percent; Jamaica rum, 10 percent; water, 39.75 percent; and caramel coloring. Can cause allergic reactions. See Eugenol for toxicity.

BAYBERRY WAX • Acrid and astringent resin from the dried root bark of the shrub that grows from Maryland to Florida and from Texas to Arkansas. It is used as an astringent in soaps and hair tonics. Formerly used to treat skin ulcers. May be irritating to the skin and cause an allergic reaction.

BEAUTY MASKS • See Face Masks and Packs.

BEER • Used to rinse hair on the theory that it gives a feeling of increased body and manageability. The sugar and protein in the beer are probably responsible for the stiffening effect but, according to the American Medical Association, champagne would have the same effect. Beer leaves an odor on the hair that, unlike champagne, may, after a while, become quite unpleasant. Nontoxic.

BEESWAX • From virgin bees and primarily used as an emulsifier. Practically insoluble in water. Yellow beeswax from the honeycomb is yellowish, soft to brittle, and has a honeylike odor. White beeswax is yellowish white and slightly different in taste but otherwise has the same properties as yellow beeswax. Used in many cosmetics including baby creams, brilliantine hair dressings, cold cream, emollient creams, wax depilatories, eye creams, eye shadow, foundation creams and makeup, lipstick, mascara, nail whiteners, protective creams, and paste rouge. Can cause contact dermatitis (*see*).

BEETROOT JUICE POWDER • The powdered stem base of the beet used for its reddish color in powders and rouges. No known toxicity.

BEHENALKONIUM CHLORIDE • See Quaternary Ammonium Salts.

BEHENAMIDOPROPYL DIMETHYLAMINE • See Quaternary Ammonium Compounds.

BEHENETH-5, -10, -20, -30 • The polyethylene glycol ethers of behenyl alcohol. See Polyethylene Glycol and Behenyl Alcohol.

BEHENIC ACID • **Docosanoic Acid.** Colorless water, soluble, constituent of seed fats, animal fats, and marine animal oils. It is a fatty acid (*see*) used to opacify shampoos. No known toxicity.

BEHENTRIMONIUM CHLORIDE • See Quaternary Ammonium Compounds.

BEHENYL ALCOHOL • **Docosanol.** A mixture of fatty alcohols derived from Behenic Acid, a minor component of vegetable oils and animal fats. Used in synthetic fabrics, lubricants to prevent evaporation of water, and as an insecticide and antihistamine. Low toxicity. See Benhyl Alcohol.

BEHENYL ERUCATE • Used in lipstick. See Behenic Acid and Erucic Acid.

BEHENYL HYDROXYETHYL IMIDAZOLINE • See Imidazoline.

BENTONITE • A white clay found in the midwestern United States and in Canada. Used to thicken lotions, to suspend makeup pigments, emulsify oils, and in makeup lotions, liquid makeup, and facial masks to absorb oil on the face and reduce shine. Also used as a coloring. Inert and generally nontoxic but if injected in rats, it can be fatal.

BENZALDEHYDE • **Artificial Almond Oil.** A colorless liquid that occurs in the kernels of bitter almonds. Lime is used in its synthetic manufacture. As the artificial essential oil of almonds, it is used in cosmetic creams and lotions, perfumes, soaps, and dyes. May cause allergic reactions. Highly toxic.

BENZALKONIUM CHLORIDE (BAK) • A widely used ammonium detergent (*see* Ammonium) in hair tonics, eye lotions, mouthwashes, and after-shave lotions. It is a germicide with an aromatic odor and a very bitter taste. Soluble in water and alcohol but incompatible with most detergents and soaps. Used medicinally as a topical antiseptic and detergent. Allergic conjunctivitis has been reported when used in eye lotions. Lethal to frogs in concentrated oral doses. Highly toxic.

BENZENE • A solvent obtained from coal and used in nail polish remover. Also used in varnishes, airplane dopes, lacquers, and as a solvent for waxes, resins, and oils. Highly flammable. Poisonous when ingested and irritating to the mucous membranes. Harmful amounts may be absorbed through the skin. Also can cause sensitivity to light in which the skin may break out in a rash or swell. Inhalation of the fumes may be toxic. The Consumer Product Safety Commission voted unanimously in February 1978 to ban the use of benzene in the manufacture of many household products. The commission took the action in response to a petition filed by The Consumer Health Research Group, an organization affiliated with consumer advocate Ralph Nader. Earlier in the year, OSHA and the EPA both cited benzene as a threat to public health. For more than a century, scientists have known that benzene is a powerful bone-marrow poison, causing such conditions as aplastic anemia. In the past several decades evidence has been mounting that it also causes leukemia. Derived from toluene or gasoline, it is used in the manufacture of detergents, nylon, artificial leather, airplane fuel, dope, varnish, lacquer, as an antiknock in gasoline, and a solvent for waxes, resins, and oils. It has a chronic effect on bone marrow, destroying the marrow's ability to produce blood cells. Safety standards for cosmetic manufacturing workers and other workers have been set at 10 parts per million during an eight-hour day, but OSHA wants it reduced to 1 part per million.

BENZETHONIUM CHLORIDE • See Quaternary Ammonium Compounds.

BENZOCAINE • **Ethyl Aminobenzoate.** A white crystalline powder slightly soluble in water and a local anesthetic. Used in eyebrow-plucking creams and after-shave lotions. As an anesthetic, it is reported low in toxicity. However, there are reports of babies suffering from methemoglobinemia (lack of oxygen in the blood), due to absorption of benzocaine through the skin. But it is believed that the absorption was enhanced by inflamed skin or rectal fissures. Systemic central nervous system excitation has been reported in adults. However, scientists feel that concentrations in most products have no toxic significance, though there are people who are allergic to benzocaine.

BENZOIC ACID • A preservative that occurs in nature in cherry bark, raspberries, tea, anise, and cassia bark. First described in 1608 when it was found in gum benzoin. Used in chocolate, lemon, orange, cherry, fruit, nut, and tobacco flavorings for beverages, ice cream, ices, candy, baked goods, icings, and chewing gum. Also used in margarine and as an antifungal agent. A mild irritant to the skin, it can cause allergic reactions.

BENZOIN • See Gum Benzoin.

BENZOPHENONES (1 THROUGH 12) • At least a dozen different benzophenones exist. They are used as fixatives (*see*) for heavy perfumes (geranium, for example) and soaps (the smell of "new mown hay"). Obtained as a white flaky solid with a delicate persistent roselike odor, and soluble in most fixed oils and in mineral oil. Also used in the manufacture of hairsprays, and in sunscreens. They help prevent deterioration of ingredients which might be affected by the ultraviolet rays found in ordinary daylight. May produce hives and contact sensitivity. In sunscreens they may cause immediate hives as well as other photoallergic reactions. Toxic when injected.

BENZOXYQUINE • **Benzoxiquine. 8-Hydroxyquinoline Benzoate.** A water-soluble salt of benzoic acid (*see*). Used as an antiseptic. Also used medicinally in the treatment of dysentery. Toxic when ingested. No known skin toxicity.

BENZOYL BENZENE • A fixative for heavy perfumes such as geranium, especially when used in soaps. See Benzophenones.

BENZOYL PEROXIDE • A bleaching agent for flours, blue cheese, gorgonzola, and milk. A catalyst for hardening certain fiberglass resins. A drying agent in cosmetics. Toxic by inhalation. A skin allergen and irritant.

BENZYL ACETATE • A colorless liquid with a pear or flowerlike odor obtained from a number of plants, especially jasmine, for use in perfumery and soap. Can be irritating to the skin, eyes, and respiratory tract. Ingestion causes intestinal upset, including vomiting and diarrhea.

BENZYL ALCOHOL • A solvent in perfumes and a preservative in hair dyes, and a topical antiseptic. It is derived as a pure alcohol and is a constituent of jasmine, hyacinth, and other plants. It has a faint sweet odor. Irritating and corrosive to the skin and mucous membranes. Ingestion of large doses causes intestinal upsets. It may crossreact with Balsam Peru (*see*) in the sensitive.

BENZYL BENZOATE • Plasticizer in nail polishes, solvent and fixative for perfumes. Occurs naturally in balsams Tolu and Peru and in various flower oils. Colorless, oily liquid or white crystals with a light floral scent and sharp burning taste. No known toxicity.

BENZYL CINNAMATE • **Sweet Odor of Balsam.** Colorless prisms, used to give artificial fruit scents to perfumes. See Balsam Peru for toxicity.

BENZYL ETHYL ETHER • Colorless, oily liquid with an aromatic odor, insoluble in water, and miscible in alcohol. Used in flavoring. Narcotic in high concentrations and may be a skin irritant.

BENZYL FORMATE • A synthetic flavoring agent used for its pleasant fruit odor in perfumery. Practically insoluble in water. There is no specific data for toxicity, but it is believed to be narcotic in high concentrations.

BENZYL SALICYLATE • **Salicylic Acid.** A fixative in perfumes and a solvent in sunscreen lotions. It is a thick liquid with a light pleasant odor, and is mixed with alcohol or ether. May cause skin to break out with a rash and swell when exposed to sunlight. See Salicylates.

3-BENZYLIDENE CAMPHOR • **Bicyclo [2,2.1] Heptan-2-one.** See Benzaldehyde and Camphor.

BENZYLPARABEN • See Propylparaben.

BENZYLTRIMONIUM HYDROLYZED ANIMAL PROTEIN • The benzyl trimethyl ammonium salt of hydrolyzed animal protein. See Quaternary Ammonium Compounds and Surfactants.

BERBERINE HYDROCHLORIDE • Mild antiseptic and decongestant in eye lotions. Derived as yellow crystals from various plants. Relatively inactive physiologically, but ingestion of large quantities may cause fatal poisoning. Used as a dressing for skin ulcers.

BERBERIS • **Holly-leaved Barberry. Oregon Grape root. Mountain Grape.** The dried roots of shrubs grown in the United States and British Columbia. Used medicinally to soothe skin ulcers and to break up intestinal gas. Used in creams as a mild antiseptic and decongestant. See Berberine Hydrochloride for toxicity.

BERGAMOT, RED • **Oswego Tea.** A pear-shaped orange whose rind yields a greenish brown oil much used in perfumery and brilliantine hairdressings. It can cause brown skin stains (berloque) when exposed to sunlight and is considered a prime photosensitizer (sensitivity to light). See Berloque Dermatitis.

BERLOQUE DERMATITIS • Some perfumes, which contain oil of bergamot (*see*) and other photosensitizers, may produce increased pigmentation (brown spots) in the area where the perfume has been applied, especially when it is immediately exposed to sunlight. There is no effective treatment and the pigmentation generally persists for some time.

BETA-CAROTENE • **Provitamin A. Beta Carotene.** Found in all plants and in many animal tissues. It is the chief yellow coloring matter of carrots, butter, and egg yolk. Extracted as red crystals or crystalline powder. It is used as a coloring in cosmetics. Also used in the manufacture of Vitamin A. Too much carotene in the blood can lead to carotenemia, a pale yellow-red pigmentation of the skin that may be mistaken for jaundice. It is a benign condition, and withdrawal of carotene from the diet cures it. Nontoxic on the skin.

BETAINE • Occurs in common beets and in many vegetables as well as animal substances. Used in resins. Has been employed to treat muscle weakness medically. No known toxicity.

BETA-NAPHTHOL • Used in hair dyes, skin-peeling preparations, and hair tonics. Prepared from naphthalene, which comes from coal tar. Also used in perfumes. Oral ingestion may cause kidney damage, eye injury, vomiting, diarrhea, convulsions, anemia, and death. Fatal poisoning from external applications has been reported. Local application may produce peeling of the skin, which may be followed by pigmentation, also contact dermatitis. See Naphthas.

BETULA • Obtained from the European white birch and a source of asphalt and tar. Used in hair tonics, it reddens the scalp and creates a warm feeling due to an increased flow of blood to the area. Also used in moisturizing creams and astringents. Betula leaves were formerly used to treat rheumatism. See Salicylates.

BHA • See Butylated Hydroxyanisole.

BHT • See Butylated Hydroxytoluene.

BICHLORIDE OF MERCURY • See Mercury Compounds.

BILBERRY EXTRACT • The extract of *Vaccinium myrtillus*, a plant found in North America and the Alps that differs from the typical blueberry in having single flowers or very small buds.

BINDER • A substance such as gum arabic, gum tragacanth, glycerin, and sorbitol (*see all*), which dispense, swell, or absorb water, increase consistency, and hold ingredients together. For example, binders are used to make powders in compacts to retain their shape; binders in toothpaste provide for the smooth dispensing of the paste.

BIOFLAVONOIDS • **Vitamin P Complex.** Citrus-flavored compounds needed to maintain healthy blood vessel walls. Widely distributed among plants, especially citrus fruits and rose hips. Usually taken from orange and lemon rinds and used as a reducing (*see*) agent. No known toxicity.

BIOTIN • **Vitamin H. Vitamin B Factor.** A whitish crystalline powder used as a texturizer in cosmetic creams. Present in minute amounts in every living cell and in larger amounts in yeast and milk. Vital to growth. It acts as a coenzyme in the formation of certain essential fatlike substances, and plays a part in reactions involving carbon dioxide. It is needed by humans for healthy circulation and red blood cells. Nontoxic.

BIRCH FAMILY • **Betulaceae.** Used as an astringent in creams and shampoos, it is an ancient remedy. The medicinal properties of the plant tend to vary, depending upon which part of the tree is used. It has been used as a laxative, as an aid for gout, to treat rheumatism and dropsy, and to dissolve kidney stones. It is supposedly good for bathing skin eruptions. The oil is used in food flavorings. See Betula.

BISABOL • **Opopanax.** A myrrh-type gum resin obtained from African trees. No known toxicity.

BISMUTH COMPOUNDS • Subgallate, Subnitrate, Oxychloride. Bismuth is a gray-white powder with a bright metallic luster. It occurs in the earth's crust and for many years was used to treat syphilis. Bismuth subgallate, a dark gray, odorless, tasteless form, is used as an antiseptic and in dusting powder. Bismuth subnitrate is odorless and tasteless and is used in bleaching, freckle creams, and hair dyes. Bismuth oxychloride is sometimes called "synthetic pearl" and is used as a skin protective. Most bismuth compounds used in cosmetics have a low toxicity when ingested but may cause allergic reactions when applied to the skin.

BISMUTH CITRATE • Coloring restricted to hair dye only. See Bismuth Compounds.

BISMUTH OXYCHLORIDE • Permanently listed as a coloring in 1977. See Bismuth Compounds.

BISMUTH TRIOXIDE • See Bismuth Compounds.

BISTORT EXTRACT • The extract of the roots of *Polygonum bistorta*, an herb found in Europe and North America. The roots are used as an astringent. No known toxicity.

BISULFITES • Bisulfite straighteners or curl relaxers are used instead of the thioglycolates (*see*). They produce changes in the chemical bonds in the hair. The effectiveness of the bisulfite relaxers is similar to that from hot combing, but it is more permanent. The result is the equivalent to the caustic alkali straighteners and superior to the thioglycolate method. Less irritating to the scalp and less damaging to the hair than other methods but should not be used if the scalp or skin is sensitive, scaly, scratched, sore, or tender. Harmful effects frequently result from not following directions. See also Sodium Bisulfite.

BITTER ALMOND OIL • Almond Oil. Sweet Almond Oil. Expressed Almond Oil. A colorless to pale yellow, bland, nearly odorless, essential, and expressed oil from the ripe seed of the small sweet almond grown in Italy, Spain, and France. It has a strong almond odor and a mild taste. Used in the manufacture of perfumes and as an oil in hair creams, nail whiteners, nail polish remover, eye creams, emollients, soaps, and perfumes. Many people are allergic to cosmetics with almond oil. It causes stuffy nose and skin rashes.

BITTER ORANGE OIL • The pale yellow volatile oil expressed from the fresh peel of a species of citrus and used in perfumes and flavorings. May cause skin irritation and allergic reactions.

BLACK • Inorganic carbon black and iron oxide used to color face powders. Carbon black from carbon or charcoal. Not subject to certification (*see*). Used in coloring candy. See Colors.

BLACK COHOSH • Cimicifuga. Snakeroot. Bugbane. Used in

astringents, it is a perennial herb with a flower that is supposedly distasteful to insects. Grown from Canada to North Carolina and Kansas. It has a reputation for curing snake bites. It is used in ginger ale flavoring. A tonic and antispasmotic. No known toxicity.

BLACK CURRANT EXTRACT • The extract of the fruit of *Ribes nigrum*, a European plant that produces hanging yellow flowers and black aromatic fruit.

BLACK WALNUT EXTRACT • Extract of the leaves or bark of the Black Walnut Tree, *Juglans nigra,* found in eastern North America. It produces nuts with a thick oil and is used as a black coloring.

BLACKBERRY LEAVES • The boiled and strained leaves of the blackberry plant used by organic cosmetic enthusiasts to add to the bath to refresh and soothe the skin. No known toxicity.

BLADDER WRACK EXTRACT • **Fucus. Sea Wrack.** A common black rockweed used in cosmetics such as tanning lotions. No known toxicity.

BLANC FIXE • See Barium Sulfate.

BLEACH • See Hair Bleach; Skin Bleach.

BLEMISH COVER • Pimple and undereye covers may be in stick or cream form. Based on oil, wax, and alcohol. Usually contains titanium dioxide (*see*) and pigments. Applied before makeup for covering marks, dark circles under the eyes, or other minor blemishes.

BLUE COHOSH • **Squawroot. Blueberry Root. Papooseroot.** A tall herb of eastern North America and Asia, it has three pointed leaves and a small greenish-yellow or purple flower. It produces large blueberrylike fruits. The roots were formerly used as an antiseptic. No known toxicity.

BLUE NO. 1 • See FD & C Blue No. 1.

BLUE VIOLET • **Ultramarine Blue. Ultramarine Violet.** Used in ivory face powders. Originally made from lapis lazuli. See Ultramarine Blue.

BLUSHER • Used to put color on cheeks and on other parts of the face. Powder blushers are similar to pressed powder in composition but include lake colors (*see*). Stick blushers are similar in composition to lipsticks (*see*).

BODY-NOTE • The main and characteristic overall odor of the perfume. It has a much longer life than the Top-Note (*see*) and usually contributes to the Dry-Out (*see*).

BOIS DE ROSE OIL • A fragrance from the chipped wood of the tropical rosewood tree obtained through steam distillation. The volatile oil is colorless, pale yellow, with a light camphor odor. It is also used as a food flavoring. No known toxicity.

BORAGE EXTRACT • The extract of the herb, *Borago officinalis*. Contains potassium and calcium and has emollient properties and is used in a "tea" for sore eyes.

BORATES • Widely used as antiseptic agents and preservatives in cosmetics in spite of repeated warnings of medical scientists. Acute poisonings have followed ingestion, injection, enemas, lavage of body cavities, and application of powders and ointments to burned and abraded skin. Affects the central nervous system, the gastrointestinal tract, kidneys, liver, and skin.

BORAX • **Sodium Borate.** A mild alkali found in the Far West, particularly in Death Valley, California. Used in cold creams, foundation creams, hair color rinses, permanent waves, and shaving creams. It is used as a water softener, preservative, and texturizer in cream products. Also used to prevent irritation of the skin by the antiperspirant aluminum chloride (*see*). See Boric Acid for toxicity.

BORIC ACID • An antiseptic with bactericidal and fungicidal properties used in baby powders, bath powders, eye creams, liquid powders, mouthwashes, protective creams, after-shave lotions, soaps, and skin fresheners. It is still widely used despite repeated warnings from the American Medical Association of possible toxicity. Severe poisonings have followed both ingestion and topical application to abraded skin.

BORNEOL • Used in perfumery, it has a peppery odor and a burning taste. Occurs naturally in coriander, ginger oil, oil of lime, rosemary, strawberries, thyme, citronella, and nutmeg. Toxicity is similar to camphor (*see*).

BORNYL ACETATE • Colorless liquid derived from borneol (*see*) in perfumery, flavoring, and as a solvent.

BORNYL FORMATE • Used in perfumes, soaps, and as a disinfectant. See Borneol.

BRAIN EXTRACT • The extract of bovine brains.

BRAZILWOOD • **Redwood. Pernambuco Wood.** Grown in Brazil and used in the manufacture of red lake pigment, which produces warm brown shades in hair colorings. See Colors.

BREATH FRESHENERS • Most breath fresheners contain flavoring, artificial sweeteners, water, and alcohol. They are used in glass or plastic bottles that measure out small amounts, or sprayed from aerosols. However, the propellants in the aerosols may be toxic when used in excess. The spray is really propelled mouthwash.

BRILLIANTINES • Hairdressings that impart a shine to the hair. Cream brilliantines are usually made of mineral oil (25 percent), beeswax, triethanolamine stearate, and water (65 percent). Liquid brilliantine is composed of mineral oil (75 percent) and isopropyl myristate. Solid brilliantines are made of mineral oil, petrolatum, and paraffin. So-called two-layer dressings contain mineral oil, alcohol, and water. They also may contain antiseptics such as hexachlorophene (banned by the FDA), cetyl alcohol, cholesterol, gums such as tragacanth, lanolin, oil of bergamot, and other essential oils, olive oil, synthetic oils, synthetic thickeners, and tars. Toxicity depends upon individual ingredients.

BROMATES • A salt of bromic acid, used in permanent wave neutralizers. Bromates are used as maturing agents and conditioners in bread. Severe poisoning has followed ingestion and topical application to abraded skin.

BROMO ACID • See D & C Red No. 21.

5-BROMO-5-NITRO-1, 3-DIOXANE • **Bronidox L®.** Preservative. May release formaldehyde (*see*).

2-BROMO-2-NITROPROPANE-1, 3-DIOL • **Bronopol®.** Solvent used for nail polishes, fats, oils, and dyes. Also used as an intermediate (*see*) in the manufacture of cosmetics and as a propellant. It inhibits the growth of bacteria, fungi, and yeasts. It is used as a preservative for a wide variety of cosmetics, especially shampoos, creams, lotions, rinses, and eye makeup. It can form nitrosamine or nitrosamide when acting with amines or amides such as triethanolamine or its salts. Of 191 samples tested, 77 contained the powerful cancer causing agent, *N*-nitrosodiethanolamine (NDELA). The preservative also breaks down at neutral and alkaline pHs to produce formaldehyde and one or two or more bromo compounds. Formaldehyde is a suspected carcinogen; therefore, if you see it listed as an ingredient with another compound ending in "amine" or "amide," don't purchase it. It is fifth on the list of preservatives that cause contact dermatitis, according to the American College of Dermatology Test Trays.

BRONZE POWDER • Any metal such as a copper alloy or aluminum in fine flakes, and used as a pigment to give the appearance of a metallic surface. Used in hair coloring to give a shine and as a "frost," or "pearl," in other cosmetics. No known toxicity. Permanently listed as a cosmetic coloring in 1977.

BRUCINE SULFATE • Salt of the poison taken from the seeds of the strychnos shrub. It has a very bitter taste and is used primarily for denaturing alcohols and oils used in cosmetics, and has been patented. As poisonous as strychnine when ingested. Toxicity is unknown on the skin.

BRUSHLESS LATHER • See Brushless Shaving Cream.

BRUSHLESS SHAVING CREAM • Not a soap like lather shaving cream, but a vanishing or cold cream with additional lubricants added.

Because lather creams soften the beard and brushless creams do not, one has to towel the face to effect some softening. Brushless creams usually contain 10 to 20 percent stearic acid (*see*), 3 to 13 percent mineral oil, 0.5 to 2 percent base, up to 5 percent lanolin, up to 0.5 percent gums and thickeners, 6 to 75 percent water, and 0.2 percent preservative. Nontoxic.

BUBBLE BATH • Foams, perfumes, and softens bath water and generally makes bathing something of a special event. Liquid bubble bath may contain TEA-dodecylbenzene sulfonate, fatty acid alkanolamides, perfume, water, and methylparaben. Powdered bubble bath may contain sodium lauryl sulfate, sodium chloride, and perfume. The products may also contain any of the following: alcohol, alkyl benzene sulfonate, various colorings, dioctyl sodium sulfosuccinate, propylene glycol, sodium hexametaphosphate, sodium sulfate, and sodium tripolyphosphate. (See all ingredients above under separate listings.) Ingestion of bubble baths may cause gastrointestinal disturbances, and skin irritations have been reported, especially in children. Reports to the FDA concern skin irritation, urinary and bladder infections, toxic damage to the brain, stomach distress, irritation and bleeding of the genital area, inflammation of the genitals, and eye injury. In 1977, the FDA required manufacturers to keep alkylarylsulfonate below 10 percent, preferably between 2 and 5 percent. Children should not take prolonged and/or unsupervised bubble baths. Adults may aggravate dryness or inflammation of the skin by taking bubble baths.

BUCKTHORN • **Frangula.** A shrub or tree grown on the Mediterranean Coast of Africa, it has thorny branches and often contains a purgative in the bark or sap. Its fruits are used as a source of yellow and green dyes. No known toxicity.

BUFFER • Usually a solution with a relatively constant acidity/alkalinity ratio, which is unaffected by the addition of comparatively large amounts of acid or alkali. A typical buffer solution would be hydrochloric acid and sodium hydroxide (*see*).

BUGLE WEED • **Sweet Bugle.** Extract of the various parts of *Lycopus virginicus* grown in North America. Contains a volatile oil, resin, and tannin. Used in perfumery.

BUGLOSS EXTRACT • Extract of the various parts including the roots, stems, leaves, and fruit of *Lycopsis arvensis*. Cultivated for its beautiful flowers. See Alkanet.

BUMETRIZOLE • An absorbent. See Phenol.

BURDOCK ROOT EXTRACT • **Cocklebur.** An extract of the roots of *Arctium minus*. A volatile bitter oil containing tannin (*see*) and used as a demulcent. No known toxicity.

BUROW'S SOLUTION • See Aluminum Acetate.

BUTADIENE/ACRYLONITRILE COPOLYMER • See Acrylates.

BUTANE • A flammable, easily liquefiable gas derived from petroleum. Used as a propellant or aerosol in cosmetics. The principal hazard is that of fire and explosion, but it may be narcotic in high doses and cause asphyxiation.

BUTCHER'S-BROOM • A shrub native to Europe, with stiff prickle-tipped, flattened stems resembling true leaves, for use in cosmetics. Formerly used as a broom by butchers. No known toxicity.

BUTOXYDIGLYCOL • An ether alcohol. See Diethylene Glycol.

BUTOXYETHANOL • **Butyl Cellosolve®.** A solvent for nitrocellulose (*see*), resins, grease, oil, and albumin. See Polyethylene Glycol for toxicity.

BUTRYIC ACID • A clear, colorless liquid present in butter at 4 to 5 percent. It has a strong, rancid butter odor, and is used in butterscotch, caramel, and fruit flavorings. It is used in chewing gums and margarines, as well as cosmetics. It is found naturally in apples, geraniums, rose oil, grapes, strawberries, and wormseed oil. It has a low toxicity but can be a mild irritant. It caused tumors when applied to the skin of mice in 108 milligram doses per kilogram of body weight and cancer when injected into the abdomen of mice in 18 milligram doses per kilogram of body weight. A NIOSH review has determined it is a positive animal carcinogen.

BUTTER • In cosmetology, substances that are solid at room temperature but that melt at body temperature are called "butters." Cocoa butter is one of the most frequently used in both foods and cosmetics. Newer butters are made from natural fats by hydrogenation (*see*), which increases the butter's melting point or alters its plasticity. Butters may be used in stick or molded cosmetics such as lipsticks or to give the proper texture to a variety of finished products. Nontoxic.

BUTTERMILK • The fluid remaining after butter has been formed from churned creams. It can also be made from sweet milk by the addition of certain organic cultures. Used as an astringent right from the bottle. Apply liberally and let dry about 10 minutes. Rinse off with cool water. Also used as a freckle bleach. Apply one tablespoon of cooking oil or your favorite moisturizer. Mix 7 tablespoons of buttermilk with one tablespoon of grated fresh horseradish (keep it away from your eyes). Combine the ingredients and apply to your face. Leave on for 15 minutes and rinse off with cool water. Then reapply your moisturizer or oil.

BUTYL ACETATE • **Acetic Acid. Butyl Ester.** A colorless liquid with a fruity odor used in perfumery, nail polish, and nail polish remover. Also used in the manufacture of lacquer, artificial leather, plastics, and safety glass. It is an irritant and may cause eye irritation (conjunctivitis). It is a narcotic in high concentrations, and toxic to humans when inhaled at 200 ppm.

BUTYL ACETYL RICINOLEATE • See Ricinoleate.

BUTYL ALCOHOL • A colorless liquid with an unpleasant odor, used as a clarifying agent (*see*) in shampoos; also a solvent for waxes, fats, resins, and shellac. It may cause irritation of the mucous membranes, headache, dizziness, and drowsiness when ingested. Inhalation of as little as 25 ppm causes pulmonary problems in humans. It can also cause contact dermatitis when applied to the skin.

t-BUTYL ALCOHOL • See Butyl Alcohol.

BUTYL/BENZOIC ACID/PHTHALIC/ANHYDRIDE/TRIMETHYLOETHANE COPOLYMER • A polymer (*see*) formed when the phthalic acid has the water removed and is combined with trimethyloethane monomers.

BUTYL BENZYL PHTHALATE • The aromatic ester that is used as a sanitizer.

BUTYL ESTER OF ETHYLENE/MALEIC ANHYDRIDE COPOLYMER • A resin (*see*) made from ethylene and maleic anhydride (*see*). Used in hair sprays, setting lotions, and as a thickener in cosmetics. No known toxicity.

BUTYL ESTER OF PVM/MA COPOLYMER • **Butyl Ester of Poly (Methyl Vinyl Ether, Maleic Acid). Spirit Gum.** Plastic material. Formed from vinyl methyl ether and maleic anhydride. Used in hair sprays, setting lotions, and as a thickener. No known toxicity.

BUTYL GLYCOLATE • A plasticizer in nail lacquers. See Butyl Acetate.

1-BUTYL HYDROQUINONE • See Hydroquinone.

BUTYL MYRISTATE • A fatty alcohol used in nail polishes and nail polish removers, lipsticks, and face and protective creams. It is derived from myristic acid (*see*) and butyl alcohol (*see*). More irritating than ethanol (*see*), but less so than some other alcohols.

BUTYL OLEATE • The ester of butyl alcohol and oleic acid (*see both*). It is a plasticizer, particularly for polyvinyl chloride (*see*) and is used in waterproofing, as a solvent, lubricant, and in polishes. No known toxicity.

BUTYL PABA • The ester of butyl alcohol and aminobenzoic acid (*see both*).

BUTYL PALMITATE • Used in shampoos to leave a gloss on the hair. See Palmitic Acid.

BUTYL PARABEN • Widely used in cosmetics as an antifungal preservative, it is the ester of butyl alcohol and *p*-hydroxybenzoic acid. No known toxicity.

BUTYL PHTHALY BUTYL GLYCOLATE • See Butyl Glycolate.

BUTYLAMINOETHYL METHYLACRYLATE • Used in hair sprays. See Acrylates.

BUTYLATED HYDROXYANISOLE (BHA) • A preservative and antioxidant in cosmetics, foods, and beverages. White to slightly yellow waxy solid with a faint characteristic odor. Can cause allergic reactions.

BUTYLATED HYDROXYTOLUENE (BHT) • A preservative and antioxidant in cosmetics, foods, and beverages. A white crystalline solid with a faint characteristic odor. Prohibited as a food additive in England. Chemically similar to BHA, it can cause allergic reactions.

1, 3 BUTYLENE GLYCOL • It is a humectant most resistant to high humidity and thus valuable in hair sprays and setting lotions. It retains scents and preserves against spoilage.

BUTYROLACTONE • **Butanolide.** Liquid lactone used chiefly as a solvent for resins. It is also an intermediate (*see*) in the manufacture of polyvinylpyrrolidone (*see*) and as a solvent for nail polish. Human toxicity is unknown.

C

C18-36 ACID • A synthetic mixture of waxy, saturated fatty acids containing 18 to 36 carbons in the alkyl (*see*) chain. See Fatty Acids.

C29-70 ACID • **C29-70 Carboxylic Acids.** A mixture of synthetic aliphatic acids with 29 to 70 carbon atoms in the alkyl (*see*) chain. See Fatty Acids.

C18-36 ACID GLYCOL ESTER • Ester of ethylene glycol (*see*) and C18-36 acid. See Fatty Acids.

C18-36 ACID TRIGLYCERIDE • The triester of glycerin (*see*) and C18-36 acid. See Fatty Acids.

C9-11 ALCOHOLS • A mixture of synthetic fatty alcohols with 9 to 11 carbons in the alkyl (*see*) chain. See Fatty Acids.

C12-16 ALCOHOLS • A mixture of synthetic fatty alcohols with 12 to 16 carbons in the alkyl (*see*) chain.

C14-15 ALCOHOLS • A mixture of synthetic fatty alcohols with 14 to 15 carbons in the alkyl (*see*) chain. See Fatty Acids.

C12-15 ALCOHOLS BENZOATE • Ester of benzoic acid (*see*) and C12-15 alcohols. See Fatty Acids.

C12-15 ALCOHOLS LACTATE • The ester of lactic acid and C12-15 alcohols. See Fatty Acids.

C21 DICARBOXYLIC ACID • See Acrylinoleic Acid.
C15-18 GLYCOL • The long chain diol that has 13 to 16 carbons in the alkyl (*see*) chain. See Fatty Acids.
C18-20 GLYCOL ISOSTEARATE • The ester of isostearate with 16 to 18 carbons on the alkyl chain. See Fatty Acids.
C18-20 GLYCOL PALMITATE • The ester that has 12 to 14 carbons on the alkyl (*see*) chain. See Fatty Acids.
C8-9, C9-11, C9-13, C9-14, C10-11, C10-13, C11-12, C11-13, C12-14, C13-14, C13-16, and C20-40 ISOPARAFFINS • Mixtures of aliphatic hydrocarbons with the number of carbons in the alkyl (*see*) chain given by the numbers. See Fatty Acids.
C11-15 PARETH -3, -5, -7, -9, -12, -20, -30, -40 • Mixture of polyethylene glycols, the higher the number the thicker the mixture. See Polyethylene Glycols.
C11-15 PARETH -7 CARBOXYLIC ACID • The polyethylene mixture of Carboxylic Acid (*see*).
C11-15 PARETH-12 STEARATE • The ester of Pareth-15-12 and stearic acid (*see*).
C11-15 PARETH-40 • The polyethylene glycol ether (*see*) of a mixture of synthetic fatty alcohols. See Polyethylene Glycol and Fatty Alcohols.
C12-13 PARETH-3, -7 • Polyethylene glycol ether of a mixture of synthetic fatty alcohols and ethylene glycol (*see all*).
C12-15 PARETH-2, -3, -4, -5, -7, -9, -12 • The polyethylene glycol ethers of fatty alcohols with ethylene oxide. See polyethylene glycol, ethers, and fatty alcohols.
C12-15 PARETH-2 PHOSPHATE • A mixture of the esters of phosphoric acid (*see*) and polyethylene glycol ethers (*see*).
C14-15 PARETH -7, -11, -13 • The polyethylene glycol ether of a mixture of synthetic fatty alcohols with ethylene oxide (*see all*).
C30-46 PISCINE OIL • A marine oil derived from fish. It is used as a thickener. No known toxicity.
C10-18 TRIGLYCERIDES • A mixture of fatty acids and glycerin. Used as a thickener. No known toxicity.
CADMIUM CHLORIDE • A white powder, soluble in water, used in photography and in dye, particularly hair dye. Inhalation of the dust is highly toxic and ingestion can cause death. Caused tumors when injected under the skin in rats and when given intravenously. It also caused cancer in mice when injected under the skin. NIOSH review determined that it was a positive animal carcinogen.
CAFFEINE • **Guaranine. Methyltheobromine. Thein.** An odorless white powder with a bitter taste that occurs naturally in coffee, cola,

guarana paste, tea, and kola nuts. Obtained as a by-product of caffeine-free coffee. Its current use in cosmetics has not been identified, but it is used as a flavoring in beverages and other foods. It is a stimulant for the central nervous system, heart, and respiratory system. Can alter blood sugar release and cross the placental barrier.

CAKE MAKEUP • See Foundation Makeup.

CAKE MASCARA • Mascara (*see*) based on fats or soap molded forms. It is applied with a brush dipped in water. A more liquid product is used in a cylinder into which a brush is inserted and pulled out, coated with mascara. A typical cake mascara formula: triethanolamine stearate, 54.0 percent; carnauba wax, 25.0 percent; paraffin, 12.5 percent; lanolin, 4.5 percent; carbon black, 3.8 percent; propylparaben, 0.2 percent; other, 1.0 percent. (See ingredients above under separate listings.) See Mascara for toxicity.

CALAMINE • Zinc oxide with about 5 percent ferric oxide that occurs as a pink powder. Used in protective creams, astringents, lotions, ointments, washes, and powders in the treatment of skin diseases; also to impart a flesh color. Some calamine formulations contain significant amounts of phenol (*see*), and ingestion or repeated applications over large areas of skin may cause phenol poisoning.

CALCIUM ACETATE • **Brown Acetate of Lime.** A white amorphous powder that has been used medicinally as a source of calcium. Used cosmetically for solidifying fragrances and as an emulsifier and firming agent. Also used in the manufacture of acetic acid and acetone (*see both*) and in dyeing, tanning, and curing skins as well as a corrosion inhibitor in metal containers. Low oral toxicity.

CALCIUM ALGINATE • See Alginates.

CALCIUM BENZOATE • See Benzoic Acid.

CALCIUM CARBONATE • **Chalk.** Absorbent that removes shine from talc. A tasteless, odorless powder that occurs naturally in limestone, marble, and coral. Used as a white coloring in cosmetics and food, an alkali to reduce acidity, a neutralizer and firming agent, and a carrier for bleaches. Also used in dentifrices as a tooth polisher, in deodorants as a filler, in depilatories as a filler, and in face powder as a buffer. A gastric antacid and antidiarrhea medicine, it may cause constipation. No known toxicity.

CALCIUM CARRAGEENAN • See Carrageenan.

CALCIUM CHLORIDE • The chloride salt of calcium. Used in its anhydrous (*see*) form as a drying agent for organic liquids and gases. An emulsifier and texturizer in cosmetics and an antiseptic in eye lotions. Also used in fire extinguishers, to preserve wood, and to melt ice and snow. Employed medicinally as a diuretic and a urinary acidifier. Ingestion can cause stomach and heart disturbances. No known toxicity as a cosmetic.

CALCIUM DISODIUM EDTA • **Edetate Calcium Disodium. Calcium Disodium Ethylenediamine Tetraacetic Acid.** A preservative and sequestrant, white, odorless powder with a faint salty taste. Used as a food additive to prevent crystal formation and to retard color loss. Nontoxic.

CALCIUM HYDROXIDE • **Limewater. Lye.** Used in cream depilatories; also in mortar, plaster, cement, pesticides, fireproofing, as an egg preservative, and as a depilatory. Employed as a topical astringent and alkali in solutions or lotions. Accidental ingestion can cause burns of the throat and esophagus; also death from shock and asphyxia due to swelling of the voice box and infection. Calcium hydroxide also can cause burns of the skin and eyes.

CALCIUM LIGNOSULFONATE • See Lignoceric Acid.

CALCIUM OXIDE • **Lime. Quicklime.** White or gray crystals or powder commercially obtained from limestone. Used as an alkali in cosmetics, as an insecticide and fungicide, and for dehairing hides. A strong caustic that may cause severe irritation of the skin and mucous membranes and can cause both thermal and chemical burns.

CALCIUM PANTOTHENATE • **Pantothenic Acid Calcium Salt. Vitamin B_5.** The calcium salt of pantothenic acid, found in liver, rice, bran and molasses, and essential for metabolism of carbohydrates, fats, and other important substances. Sweetish in taste with a slightly bitter aftertaste, soluble in water, it is a member of the B-complex family of vitamins. It is also found in large amounts in the jelly of the Queen Bee, the so-called royal jelly of cosmetic advertising fame. It is used as an emollient and to enrich creams and lotions. No known toxicity.

CALCIUM PHOSPHATE • White odorless powder used as an anticaking agent in cosmetics and foods. Employed in toothpaste and tooth powder as an abrasive. Practically insoluble in water. No known toxicity.

CALCIUM PROPIONATE • **Propanoic Acid. Calcium Salt.** White crystals or crystalline solid with the faint odor of propionic acid. A mold and rope (slimy strands) inhibitor in breads and rolls, it is used in processed cheese and artificially sweetened fruit jelly. It is used as a preservative in cosmetics and as an antifungal medication for the skin. The FDA has asked for further study for safety.

CALCIUM PYROPHOSPHATE • A fine white, odorless, tasteless powder used as a nutrient, an abrasive in dentifrices, a buffer, and as a neutralizing agent in foodstuffs. No known toxicity.

CALCIUM SACCHARIN • See Saccharin.
CALCIUM SILICATE • **Okenite.** An anticaking agent, white or slightly cream-colored, free-flowing powder used in face powders because it has extremely fine particles and good water absorption. Also used as a coloring agent. Used in baking powder, in road construction and in lime glass. Practically nontoxic orally, but inhalation may cause irritation of the respiratory tract.
CALCIUM STEARATE • Prepared from limewater (*see*), it is an emulsifier used in hair-grooming products. Also used as a coloring agent, in waterproofing, and in paints and printing ink. Nontoxic.
CALCIUM STEAROYL LACTYLATE • It is the calcium salt of the stearic acid ester of lactyl lactate. A free-flowing powder used as a texturizer. Also used to improve the flow of powder. No known toxicity.
CALCIUM SULFATE • **Plaster of Paris.** A fine, white to slightly yellow, odorless, tasteless powder used in toothpaste and tooth powders as an abrasive and firming agent. Also used as a coloring agent in cosmetics. Used in creamed cottage cheese as an alkali and employed industrially in cement, wall plaster, and insecticides. Because it absorbs moisture and hardens quickly, its ingestion may result in intestinal obstruction. Mixed with flour, it has been used to kill rodents. No known toxicity on the skin.
CALCIUM SULPHIDE • A yellow powder formed by heating gypsum with charcoal at 1,000° F degrees. Employed in depilatories. Used in acne preparations.Also used as a food preservative and in luminous paints. It can cause allergic reactions.
CALCIUM THIOGLYCOLATE • Used in cream depilatories and permanent wave lotions. Odorless or with a faint odor. Also used to tan leather. Chronic application has led to thyroid problems in experimental animals. Some people develop skin problems on the hands or scalp with hemorrhaging under the skin.
CALENDULA • Dried flowers of pot marigolds grown in gardens everywhere. Formerly used to soothe inflammation of skin and mucous membranes, now used in "natural" creams, oils, and powders for babies. No known toxicity.
CALFSKIN EXTRACT • An oil extracted from bovine skin.
CALOMEL • **Mercurous Chloride.** A white, odorless, tasteless, heavy powder used in bleach and freckle creams. It slowly decays in sunlight into mercuric chloride and metallic mercury. Banned in July 1973, when the FDA ordered all mercury cosmetics (except for mercury preservatives in eye products) off the market.
CALOPHYLLUM OIL • **Santa Maria Tree.** Extract from a tropical

tree having thick, shiny feather-veined leaves, clustered white flowers, aromatic resinous juice, and oily seeds. Used in moisturizing creams. No known toxicity.

CAMELLIA OIL • A tropical Asiatic evergreen shrub or small tree with reddish or white flowers. Used to scent perfumes. No known toxicity.

CAMOMILE • See Chamomile.

CAMPHOR OIL • Used in emollient creams, hair tonics, eye lotions, preshave lotions, after-shave lotions, and skin fresheners as a preservative and to give a cool feeling to the skin. It is used as a spice flavoring for beverages, baked goods, and condiments. It is also used in horn-rimmed glasses, as a drug preservative, in embalming fluid, the manufacture of explosives, and lacquers, as a moth repellent, and topically in liniments, cold medications, and anesthetics. It is distilled from trees at least 50 years old grown in China, Japan, Taiwan, Brazil, and Sumatra. It can cause contact dermatitis. In 1980 the FDA banned camphorated oil as a liniment for colds and sore muscles because of reports of poisonings through skin absorption and because of accidental ingestion. A New Jersey pharmacist had collected case reports and testified in 1980 before the FDA's Advisory Review Panel on Over the Counter Drugs.

CANANGA OIL • A natural flavor extract obtained by distillation from the flowers of the tree. Light to deep yellow liquid with a harsh, floral odor. Used in cola, fruit, spice, and ginger ale flavoring for beverages, ice cream, ices, candy, and baked goods. May cause allergic reactions.

CANDELILLA WAX • Obtained from candelilla plants for use in lipsticks, solid fragrances, and liquid powders to give them body. Brownish to yellow-brown, hard, brittle, easily pulverized, practically insoluble in water, slightly soluble in alcohol. Used in emollients to protect the skin against moisture loss. Also used in the manufacture of rubber, phonograph records, in waterproofing and writing inks, and hardens other waxes. No known toxicity.

CANTHARIDES TINCTURE • **Spanish Fly.** Obtained from blister beetles that thrive in southern and central Europe and powdered for use in hair tonics to stimulate the scalp. A powerful irritant to the skin and causes blistering. If ingested, it can cause severe intestinal upset, kidney damage, and death. Long reputed to have aphrodisiac effects.

CANTHARIDIN • Skin vesicant, rubefacient in hair tonic. Can cause allergic reaction. See Cantharides.

CANTHAXANTHIN • A color additive. See Carotene.

CAPRACYL BROWN 2R • See Colors; D & C Brown No. 1.

CAPRAMIDE DEA • See Capric Acid.
CAPRIC ACID • Obtained from a large group of American plants. Solid crystalline mass with a rancid odor used in the manufacture of artificial fruit flavors in lipsticks, and to scent perfumes. No known toxicity.
CAPROAMPHOACETATE • See Surfactants.
CAPROAMPHODIACETATE • See Surfactants.
CAPROAMPHODIPROPIONATE • See Surfactants.
CAPROAMPHOHYDROXYPROPYLSULFONATE • See Surfactants.
CAPROIC ACID • **Hexanoic Acid.** A synthetic flavoring that occurs naturally in apples, butter acids, cocoa, grapes, oil of lavender, oil of lavandin, raspberries, strawberries, and tea. Used in butter, butterscotch, fruit, rum, and cheese flavorings. Used also in the manufacture of "hexyl" derivatives such as 4-hexylresorcinol (*see*). No known toxicity.
CAPRYL BETAINE • See Caprylic Acid and Betaine.
CAPRYLAMINE OXIDE • See Caprylic Acid and Capric Acid.
CAPRYLIC/CAPRIC/LAURIC TRIGLYCERIDE • A mixture of triester of glycerin with caprylic, capric, and lauric acids (*see all*). An oily mixture derived from coconut oil, it is used extensively in cosmetics as a vehicle for pigment dispersions in bath oils, hair sprays, and lipsticks. Also used as an emollient to prevent water loss from the skin. Low toxicity.
CAPRYLIC/CAPRIC/STEARIC TRIGLYCERIDE • A mixture of the triester of glycerin with caprylic, capric, and stearic acid (*see all*).
CAPRYLIC ACID • An oil liquid made by the oxidation of octanol (*see*) for use in perfumery. Occurs naturally as a fatty acid in sweat, fusel oil, in the milk of cows and goats, and in palm and coconut oil. No known toxicity.
CAPRYLIC ALCOHOL • See 1-Octanol.
CAPRYLOAMPHOACETATE • See Surfactants.
CAPRYLOAMPHODIACETATE • See Surfactants.
CAPRYLOAMPHODIPROPIONATE • See Surfactants.
CAPRYLOAMPHOHYDROXYPROPYLSULFONATE • See Surfactants.
CAPSICUM • The dried ripe fruit of the capsicum or African chili plant used in hair tonics to stimulate the scalp. Medicinally used to soothe irritated skin and as an internal gastric stimulant. May cause skin irritation and allergic reaction.
CAPTAN • A preservative used in cosmetics. It is a fungicide of low toxicity, but in large doses can cause diarrhea and weight loss. No human poisonings are known.
CARAMEL • Used as a coloring in cosmetics and a soothing agent in

skin lotions. Burnt sugar with a pleasant, slightly bitter taste. Made by heating sugar or glucose and adding small quantities or alkali or a trace mineral acid during heating. Used in food as a flavoring and coloring. The FDA permanently listed caramel in 1981.

CARAWAY SEED AND OIL • The dried ripe seeds of a plant common to Europe and Asia and cultivated in England, the Soviet Union, and the U.S. Volatile, colorless to pale yellow liquid, caraway seed is used in liquor flavorings for beverages, ice cream, baked goods, condiments, and as a spice in baking. The oil is used in grape, licorice, anisette, kummel, liver, sausage, mint, caraway, and rye flavorings for beverages, ice cream, ices, candy, baked goods, chewing gum, meats, condiments, and liquors. The oil is used to perfume soap. Can cause contact dermatitis.

CARBAMIDE • See Urea.

CARBITOL® • **Carbide. Carbon.** A solvent for nail lacquers and enamels. Absorbs water from the air and is mixable with acetone, benzene, alcohol, water, and ether. More toxic than polyethylene glycol (*see*).

CARBOMER -934, -940, -941 • **Carbopol. Carboxypolymethylene.** A white powder, slightly acidic, that reacts with fat particles to form thick stable emulsions of oils in water. Used as a thickening, suspending, dispersing, and emulsifying agent in the cosmetic field. No known toxicity.

CARBON DIOXIDE • Colorless, odorless, noncombustible gas with a faint acid taste. Used as a pressure-dispensing agent in gassed creams. Also used in the carbonation of beverages and as dry ice for refrigeration in the frozen food industry. Used on stage to produce harmless smoke or fumes. May cause shortness of breath, vomiting, high blood pressure, and disorientation if inhaled in sufficient amounts.

CARBOPOL • See Carbomer.

CARBOWAX® • Solid polyethylene glycols used in cosmetics and pharmaceuticals. May cause an allergic reaction. See Polyethylene Glycol.

CARBOXYMETHYL CELLULOSE • **Sodium.** A synthetic gum used in bath preparations, beauty masks, dentifrices, hair-grooming aids, hand creams, rouge, shampoos, and shaving creams. As an emulsifier, stabilizer, and foaming agent, it is a barrier agent (*see*) made from cotton by-products, and occurs as a white powder or in granules. Employed as a stabilizer in ice cream, beverages, and other foods, and medicinally as a laxative or antacid. It has been shown to cause cancer in animals when ingested. Its toxicity on the skin is unknown.

s-CARBOXY METHYL CYSTEINE • Used in astringents and lotions. See Cysteine.

CARBOXYPOLYMETHYLENE • See Carbomer.

CARDAMON OIL • **Grains of Paradise.** A natural flavoring and aromatic agent from the dried ripe seeds of trees common to India, Ceylon, and Guatemala. Used in perfumes and soaps, in butter, chocolate, and other food flavorings. As a medicine, it breaks up intestinal gas. No known toxicity.

CARMINE • **Cochineal.** A crimson pigment derived from a Mexican and Central American species of a scaly female insect that feeds on various cacti. The dye is used in cosmetic colors, red apple sauce, and other food. No known toxicity. The FDA permanently listed carmine for use in food in 1977.

CARMINIC ACID • **Natural Red No. 4.** Used in mascaras, liquid rouge, paste rouge, and red eye shadows. It is the glucosidal coloring matter from a scaly insect (*see* Carmine). Color is deep red in water and violet to yellow in acids. May cause allergic reactions. See Colors. Banned by the FDA.

CARNATION • The essential oil of the double-flowered variety of clove pink. Pale green solid that does not have the characteristic odor of carnations until diluted. Used in fragrances. No known toxicity.

CARNAUBA WAX • The exudate from the leaves of the Brazilian wax palm tree used as a texturizer in foundation makeups, mascara, cream rouge, lipsticks, liquid powders, depilatories, and deodorant sticks. It comes in a hard greenish to brownish solid and rarely causes allergic reactions.

CAROTENE • See Beta-Carotone.

CARRAGEENAN • **Irish Moss.** A stabilizer and emulsifier, seaweed-like in odor, derived from Irish Moss, used in oils in cosmetics and foods. It is completely soluble in hot water and not coagulated by acids. Used medicinally to soothe the skin. Nontoxic. The use of Irish Moss in food and medicine has been known in India for hundreds of years. Its use in the United States began in 1935 but really became common during World War II as a replacement for agar-agar. Sodium carrageenan is on the FDA list for further study. Carrageenan stimulated the formation of fibrous tissue when subcutaneously injected into the guinea pig. When a single dose of it dissolved in saline was injected under the skin of the rat, it caused sarcomas after approximately two years. Its cancer-causing ability may be that of a foreign body irritant, because upon administration to rats and mice at high levels in their diet, it did not appear to induce tumors, although survival of the animals for this period was not good. Its use as a food additive is being studied.

CARROT JUICE POWDER • See Carrot Oil.

CARROT OIL • Either of two oils from the seeds of carrots. A light yellow essential oil which has a spicy odor and is used in liqueurs, flavorings, and perfumes. Rich in Vitamin A, it is also used as a coloring. No known toxicity.

CARROT SEED EXTRACT • Extract of the seeds of *Daucus Carota sativa*.

CARVONE • **(D or L). Oil of Caraway.** A colorless liquid with a characteristic caraway smell used in perfumery and soaps. Found naturally in caraway seed and dill seed oils. Used medicinally to break up intestinal gas and as a stimulant. No known toxicity.

CASCARA • A natural flavoring derived from the dried bark of a plant grown from northern Idaho to northern California. Cathartic. Used in butter, caramel, and vanilla flavoring. Formerly used to treat skin diseases. Used to soothe skin in lotions and creams. No known toxicity.

CASEIN • The principal protein of cow's milk used in protective cream and as the "protein" in hair preparations to make the hair thicker and more manageable. It is a white water-absorbing powder without noticeable odor and is used to make depilatories less irritating and as a film-former in beauty masks. It is also used as an emulsifier in many cosmetics and in special diet preparations. Nontoxic.

CASSIA OIL • **Cloves. Chinese Oil of Cinnamon.** Darker, less agreeable and heavier than true cinnamon. Obtained from a tropical Asian tree and used in perfumes, poultices, and as a laxative. It can cause irritation and allergy such as a stuffy nose.

CASTILE SOAP • A fine, hard, bland soap, usually white or cream-colored, but sometimes green, named for the region of Spain where it was originally made. Made from olive oil and sodium hydroxide (*see*). No known toxicity.

CASTOR • **Castoreum.** Used in perfumes as a fixative (*see*). A creamy orange-brown substance with strong penetrating odor and bitter taste that consists of the dried perineal glands of the beaver and their secretion. The glands and secretions are taken from the area between the vulva and anus in the female beaver and from the scrotum and anus in the male beaver. Professional trappers use castor to scent bait.

CASTOR OIL • **Palm Christi Oil.** The seed of the castor-oil plant. After the oil is expressed from the beans, a residual castor pomace remains, which contains a potent allergen. This may be incorporated in fertilizer which is the main source of exposure, but people who live near a castor bean processing factory may also be sensitized. Used in bath oils, nail polish removers, solid perfumes, face masks, shaving creams, lipsticks and many men's hair dressings. It is also used as a plasticizer in nail polish. It forms a tough shiny film when dried. More than 50 percent of the lipsticks in the United States use a substantial amount of castor oil. Ingestion of large amounts may cause pelvic congestion. Soothing to the skin.

CATALYST • A substance that causes or speeds up a chemical reaction but does not itself change.

CATECHOL • **Catechin.** A modifier in hair colorings used as a drabber. It is a phenol alcohol found in catechu black (*see*).

CATECHU BLACK • A preparation from the heartwood of the acacia catechu used in toilet preparations and for brown and black colorings. Used as an astringent. May cause allergic reactions.

CATIONIC • A group of synthetic compounds employed as emulsifiers, wetting agents, and antiseptics in special hand creams. Their positively charged ions (cations) repel water. Any class of synthetic detergents usually consisting almost entirely of quaternary ammonium compounds (*see*) with carbon and nitrogen. Used also as wetting and emulsifying agents in acid to neutralize solutions or as a germicide or fungicide. Toxicity depends upon ingredients used.

CAUSTIC SODA • See Sodium Hydroxide.

CD • The abbreviation for Completely Denatured alcohol, meaning a poison was added so that it would not be drinkable.

CD ALCOHOL 19 • A denatured alcohol used as a solvent. See Denatured.

CEDAR • **Cedarwood Oil.** The oil from white, red, or various cedars obtained by distillation from fresh leaves and branches. It is often used in perfumes, soaps, and sachets for its warm woodsy scent. Used frequently as a substitute for oil of lavender. There is usually a strong camphor odor that repels insects. Cedar oil can be a photosensitizer, causing skin reactions when the skin is exposed to light.

CEDARWOOD OIL • See Cedar.

CEDRO OIL • See Lemon Oil.

CELLULOID® • A nail finish composed essentially of cellulose nitrate and camphor (*see both*) or other plasticizers. Also used for brushes and combs as well as for photographic film and various household products. No known toxicity.

CELLULOSE • Chief constituent of the fiber of plants. Cotton contains about 90 percent. It is the basic material for cellulose gums (*see*). Used as an emulsifier in cosmetic creams. No known toxicity.

CELLULOSE GUMS • Any of several fibrous substances consisting of the chief part of the cell walls of plants. Ethylcellulose is a film-former in lipstick. Methylcellulose (Methocel®) and hydroxyethylcellulose (Cellosize®) are used as emulsifiers in hand creams and lotions. They are resistant to bacterial decomposition and give uniform viscosity to products. No known toxicity.

CERESIN • **Ceresine®. Earth Wax.** Used in protective creams. It is a white or yellow hard, brittle wax made by purifying ozokerite (*see*) found in the Ukraine, Utah, and Texas. It is used as a substitute for beeswax and paraffin (*see both*); also used to wax paper and cloth, as a polish, and in dentistry for taking wax impressions. May cause allergic reactions.

CERTIFIED • Each batch of coal tar or petrochemical colors, with the exception of those used in hair dyes, must be certified by the FDA as "harmless and suitable for use." The manufacturer must submit samples of every batch for testing and the lot test number accompanies the colors through all subsequent packaging. It costs 25 cents per pound, with a minimum of $160 for each batch tested.

CETALKONIUM CHLORIDE • Derived from ammonium, it is an antibacterial agent used in cosmetics. Soluble in water, alcohol, acetone, and ethyl acetate. See Quaternary Ammonium Compounds.

CETEARALKONIUM BROMIDE • The quaternary ammonium salt that is a blend of cetyl and stearyl radicals.

CETEARETH-3 • **Cetyl/Stearyl Ether.** An oily liquid distilled from a combination of cetyl alcohol made from spermaceti (*see*) and stearyl alcohol made from sperm whale oil. The compound is used as an emollient, an emulsifier, an antifoam agent, and a lubricant in cosmetics. Nontoxic.

CETEARETH-4, -6, -8, -10, -12, -15, -17, -20, -27, -30 • See Ceteareth-3.

CETEARETH-5 • Emollient and emulsifier from cetyl alcohol and ethylene oxide. See Cetyl Alcohol and Ceteareth-3.

CETEARYL ALCOHOL • **Cetostearyl Alcohol.** Emulsifying wax. A mixture chiefly of the fatty alcohols—cetyl and stearyl (*see both*)—and used primarily in ointments as an emulsifier. No known toxicity.

CETEARYL OCTONATE • See Caprylic Acid.

CETETH-1 • See Ceteth-2.

CETETH-2 • **Polyethylene (2) Cetyl Ether.** A compound of derivatives of cetyl, lauryl, stearyl, and oleyl alcohols (*see*) mixed with ethylene oxide, a gas used as a fungicide and a starting material for detergents. Oily liquids or waxy solids. Used as surface-active agents (*see*) and as an emulsifier to allow oil and water to mix and form a smooth cosmetic lotion or cream. See individual alcohols for toxicity.

CETETH-4, -6, -10, -2, -30 • See Ceteth-2.

CETETHYL MORPHOLINIUM ETHOSULFATE • See Quaternary Ammonium Compounds.

CETRIMONIUM BROMIDE • A cationic (*see*) detergent and antiseptic, disinfectant, and cleansing agent in skin-cleaning products and shampoos. It masks or decreases perspiration odors. Can be fatal if swallowed. Can be irritating to the skin and eyes.

CETRIMONIUM CHLORIDE • See Quaternary Ammonium Compounds.

CETRIMONIUM TOSYLATE • A quaternary ammonium compound (*see*).

CETYL- • Means derived from cetyl alcohol (*see*).

CETYL ALCOHOL • An emollient and emulsion stabilizer used in many cosmetics preparations including baby lotion, brilliantine hairdressings, deodorants and antiperspirants, cream depilatories, eyelash creams and oils, foundation creams, hair lacquers, hair straighteners, hand lotions, lipsticks, liquid powders, mascaras, nail polish removers, nail whiteners, cream rouges, and shampoos. Cetyl alcohol is waxy, crystalline, and solid, and found in spermaceti (*see*). It has a low toxicity for both skin and ingestion and is sometimes used as a laxative. Can cause hives.

CETYL AMMONIUM • An ammonium compound, germicide, and fungicide used in cuticle softeners, deodorants, and baby creams. Medicinally an antibacterial agent. See Quaternary Ammonium Compounds for toxicity.

CETYL ARACHIDATE • An ester produced by the reaction of cetyl alcohol and arachidic acid. The acid is found in fish oils and vegetables, particularly peanut oil. A fatty compound used as an emulsifier and emollient in cosmetic creams. Nontoxic.

CETYL BETAINE • Occurs in the common beet and many vegetable and animal substances. Colorless deliquescent crystals with a sweet taste. See Quaternary Ammonium Compounds.

CETYL ESTERS • Synthetic spermaceti (*see*).

CETYL LACTATE • An emollient to improve the feel and texture of cosmetic and pharmaceutical preparations. Produced by the reaction of cetyl alcohol and lactic acid (*see both*). No known toxicity.

CETYL MYRISTATE • Produced by the reaction of cetyl alcohol and myristic acid (*see both*).

CETYL OCTANOATE • The ester of cetyl alcohol and 2-ethylhexanoic acid. See Cetyl Alcohol and Caproic Acid.

CETYL PALMITATE • Produced by the reaction of cetyl alcohol and palmitic acid. Used in the manufacture of soaps and lubricants. Nontoxic.

CETYL PHOSPHATE • A mixture of esters of phospheric acid and cetyl alcohol (*see both*).

CETYL RICINOLEATE • Salt derivative of castor oil used in tanning preparations. See Ricinoleic Acid.

CETYL STEARATE • See Ceteareth-2.

CETYL STEARYL GLYCOL • A mixture of cetyl glycol and stearyl glycol, fatty alcohols that are used as emulsifiers and emollients in cosmetic creams. Nontoxic.

CETYLARACHIDOL • A suds and foam stabilizer that is used in hair and body shampoos and in various types of household detergents. It also has mild conditioning properties, and in some instances it may be used as an emulsifier. See Quaternary Ammonium Compounds for toxicity.

CETYLPYRIDINIUM CHLORIDE • A white powder soluble in water and alcohol. The quaternary salt of pyridine and cetyl chloride (*see both*). A white powder used as an antiseptic and disinfectant in mouthwashes and topical antiseptics and as a deodorant. See Quaternary Ammonium Compounds for toxicity.

CETYLTRYMETHYLAMMONIUM BROMIDE • An antimicrobial preservative that helps destroy and prevent growth of germs. See Quaternary Ammonium Compounds.

CHALK • Purified calcium carbonate (*see*) used in nail whiteners, powders, and liquid makeup to assist in spreading and to give characteristic smooth feeling. A grayish white amorphous powder usually molded into cones for the cosmetic industry. Used medicinally as a mild astringent and antacid. Nontoxic.

CHAMOMILE • **English, Roman, and Hungarian Chamomile.** The daisylike white and yellow heads of these flowers provide a coloring agent known as apigenin. The essential oil distilled from the flower heads is pale blue and added to shampoos to impart the odor of chamomile. Powdered flowers are used to bring out a bright yellow color in the hair. Also used in rinses and skin fresheners. Roman chamomile is used in berry, fruit, vermouth, maple, spice, and vanilla flavorings, and English chamomile is used as a flavoring in chocolate, fruit, and liquor flavorings for beverages, ice cream, ices, candy, and baked goods. Hungarian chamomile oil is used in chocolate, fruit, and liquor flavorings for beverages, ice cream, ices, candy, baked goods, chewing gum, and liquors. Chamomile contains sesquiterpene lactones which may cause allergic contact dermatitis and stomach upsets. See also Matricaria Oil.

CHAPPAREL EXTRACT • The extract of the desert plant chapparel, *Larrea mexicana*.

CHARCOAL BLACK • A black pigment consisting of a charred substance such as wood charcoal or bone black for use in eye shadow. Nontoxic. See Carbon Black.

CHAULMOOGRA OIL • An oil expressed from the seeds of *Taraktogenos kurzii*. Yellow or brownish oil once used in the treatment of leprosy. No known toxicity.

CHEILITIS • Dermatitis of the lips attributed to lipsticks. The symptoms are dryness, chapping, cracked and peeling lips. Sometimes this is accompanied by swelling and blistering. About 95 percent of the symptoms have been found to be caused by the indelible dyes used in most lipsticks. The lips are especially susceptible to irritation and allergic problems due to the absence of the horny or dead layer of skin that protects the rest of the body. Even minute amounts of lipstick can cause gastrointestinal problems such as gastritis, enteritis, and colitis in susceptible women. Many allergic women are able to solve the problem of cheilitis merely by changing brands of lipsticks. Others may be able to use hypoallergenic brands that do not contain the most common sensitizers—lanolin and perfumes or the staining dye, dibromofluorescein (*see*).

CHELATING AGENT • Any compound, usually, that binds and precipitates metals, such as ethylenediamine tetraacetic acid (EDTA), which removes trace metals. See Sequestering Agent.

CHERRY PIT OIL • A natural lipstick flavoring and fragrance extracted from the pits of sweet and sour cherries. Also a cherry flavoring for beverages, ice cream, and condiments. No known toxicity.

CHINA CLAY • See Kaolin.

CHITIN • A white powder similar in structure to cellulose (*see*), it is the principal constituent of the shells of crabs, lobsters, and beetles. It is also found in some fungi, algae, and yeasts. It is used in wound-healing emulsions and in tanning products.

CHLORACETAMIDE • See Quaternary Ammonium Compounds.

CHLORAL HYDRATE • **Knockout Drops.** Transparent, colorless crystals with a slightly acrid odor and bitter taste, it is used in hypnotic drugs, in the manufacture of liniments and in hair tonic. It may cause contact dermatitis, gastric disturbances, and when ingested it is narcotic. The lethal human dose is ten grams.

CHLORAMINE-T • **Sodium p-Toluene Sulfonchloramide.** A preservative and antiseptic used in nail bleaches, dental preparations, and mouthwashes. White crystals fairly soluble in water, which lose moisture at 100° F. It is a powerful antiseptic and is used for washing wounds. May be irritating to the skin and cause allergic reactions.

CHLORHEXIDINE • A white crystalline powder used as a topical antiseptic and skin sterilizing agent in liquid cosmetics and in

European feminine hygiene sprays. May cause contact dermatitis. Strongly alkaline.

CHLORHEXIDINE DIACETATE • The salt of chlorhexidine and acetic acid. Derived from methanol and acetic acid (*see*), which are derived from fruits. It is used as an antiseptic.

CHLORHEXIDINE DIGLUCONATE • See Chlorhexidine.

CHLORHEXIDINE DIHYDROCHLORIDE • Salt of chlorhexidine and hydrochloric acid. Derived from Methanol. Used as a solvent.

CHLOROACETIC ACID • Made by the chlorination of acetic acid (*see*) in the presence of sulfur or iodine. Used in the manufacture of soaps and creams. It is irritating to the skin and mucous membranes and can be toxic and corrosive when swallowed.

CHLOROBUTANOL • A white crystalline alcohol used as a preservative in eye lotions and as an antioxidant in baby oils. It has a camphor odor and taste. Formerly used medicinally as a hypnotic and sedative; today it is employed as an anesthetic and antiseptic. A central nervous system depressant, it is used as a hypnotic drug. No known skin toxicity.

p-CHLORO-m-CRESOL • See Cresol.

CHLOROFORM • Used in products to clean wool or synthetic fabrics, and as a solvent for fats, oils, waxes, resins, and as a cleaning agent. It has many serious side-effects and is considered a carcinogen. Exposure to it may also cause respiratory and skin allergies. Complaints received by the FDA about blisters and inflammation of the gums caused by toothpaste were found to be due to the amount of chloroform in the product. The manufacturer was asked to reduce the amount of the substance. Large doses may cause low blood pressure, heart stoppage, and death. In April 1976, the FDA determined that chloroform may cause cancer and asked drug and cosmetic manufacturers who have not already done so to discontinue using it immediately, even before it was officially banned. The National Cancer Institute made public, in June 1976, the finding that chloroform was found to cause liver and kidney cancers in test animals.

CHLOROMETHOXYPROPYLMERCURIC ACETATE • Preservative. See Mercury Compounds.

2-CHLORO-p-PHENYLENEDIAMINE • See *p*-Phenylenediamine.

2-CHLORO-p-PHENYLENEDIAMINE SULFATE • See *p*-Phenylenediamine.

CHLOROPHYLL • The green coloring matter of plants, which plays an essential part in the plant's photosynthetic process. Used in antiperspirants, dentifrices, deodorants, and mouthwashes as a deodorizing agent. It imparts a greenish color to certain fats and oils, notably olive oil and soybean. Can cause a sensitivity to light.

CHLOROPHYLLIN • **Copper Derivative.** Used as a deodorant agent in mouthwashes, breath fresheners, and body deodorants. Derived from chlorophyll, the green coloring matter of plants. Banned by the FDA. See Chlorophyll.

CHLOROPHYLLIN COPPER COMPLEX • Banned by the FDA as a coloring. See Chlorophyllin.

4-CHLORORESORCINOL • See Resorcinol.

CHLOROTHYMOL • A chloro derivative of thymol (*see*) and a powerful germicide used in mouthwashes, hair tonics, and baby oils. It kills staph germs and is used topically as an antibacterial. Can be irritating to the mucous membranes and can possibly be absorbed through the skin.

CHLOROXYLENOL • See *p*-Chloro-*m*-Xylenol.

p-CHLORO-m-XYLENOL • A white crystalline solid used as an antiseptic, germicide, and fungicide in hair tonics, shampoos, contraceptive douches, deodorants, bath salts, vaginal deodorants, and brushless shaving creams. Penetrates the skin but has no apparent irritating effects when diluted at 5 percent. May cause greenish discoloration of the hair when exposed to chlorinated water.

CHOLESTEROL • A fat-soluble, crystalline, steroid alcohol (*see*) occurring in all animal fats and oils, nervous tissue, egg yolk, and blood. Used as an emulsifier and lubricant in brilliantine hairdressing, eye creams, shampoos, and other cosmetic products. It is important in metabolism but has been implicated as contributing to hardening of the arteries and, subsequently, heart attacks. Nontoxic to the skin.

CHONDRUS • See Carrageenan.

CHROMIUM COMPOUNDS • **Oxides.** Chromium occurs in the earth's crust. Chromic oxide is used for green eye shadow and chromium oxide for greenish mascara. Inhalation of chromium dust can cause irritation and ulceration. Ingestion results in violent gastrointestinal irritation. Application to the skin may result in allergic reaction. The most serious effect of chromium is lung cancer, which may develop 20 to 30 years after exposure. One study showed that the death rate from lung cancer among exposed chromium workers is twenty-nine times that of the normal population.

CHROMIUM HYDROXIDE GREEN • Coloring. Permanently listed for use as a cosmetic coloring in 1977. See Chromium Compounds.

CHROMIUM OXIDE GREEN • Coloring. See Chromium Compounds.

CHROMIUM SULFATE • **Chromic Sulfate.** Violet or red powder used in the textile industries, green paints and varnishes, green ice, ceramics, tanning, and green eye shadows. Can cause contact dermatitis.

CHYPRE • A nonalcoholic type of perfume containing oils and resins.

CINCHONA EXTRACT • The extract of the bark of various species of *Cinchona* cultivated in Java, India, and South America. Quinine is derived from it.

CINNAMAL • **Cinnamaldehyde. Cinnamic Aldehyde.** A synthetic yellowish oily liquid with a strong odor of cinnamon isolated from a wood rotting fungus. Occurs naturally in cassia bark extract, cinnamon bark, and root oils. Used for its aroma in perfume and its flavoring in mouthwash and toothpaste. Also used to scent powder and hair tonic. It is irritating to the skin and mucous membranes, especially if undiluted. One of the most common allergens.

CINNAMIC ACID • Used in suntan lotions and perfumes. Occurs in storax, Balsam Peru, cinnamon leaves, and coca leaves. Usually isolated from wood-rotting fungus. It may cause allergic skin rashes.

CINNAMIC ALCOHOL • Fragrance ingredient. One of the most common allergens in fragrances and flavorings. Used in mouthwashes, toilet soaps, toothpastes, and sanitary napkins. See Cinnamal.

CINNAMIC ALDEHYDE • Found in cinnamon oil, cassia oil, cinnamon powder, patchouli oil, flavoring agents, toilet soaps, and perfumes. It crossreacts with Balsam Peru and benzoin. May cause depigmentation and hives.

CINNAMON • Used to flavor toothpaste and mouthwash and to scent hair tonic and powder. Obtained from the dried bark of cultivated trees. See Cinnamal for toxicity. Extracts have been used to break up intestinal gas and to treat diarrhea, but can be irritating to the gastrointestinal system.

CINNAMON BARK • **Extract and Oil.** From the dried bark of cultivated trees, the extract is used in cola, eggnog, root beer, cinnamon, and ginger ale for beverages, ice cream, baked goods, condiments, and meats. The oil is used in berry, cola, cherry, rum, root beer, cinnamon, and ginger ale flavorings for beverages, condiments, and meats. Can be a skin sensitizer in humans and cause mild sensitivity to light.

CINNAMON OIL • **Oil of Cassia. Chinese Cinnamon.** Yellowish to brown volatile oil from the leaves and twigs of cultivated trees. About 80 to 90 percent cinnamal. It has the characteristic odor and taste of cassia cinnamon and darkens and thickens upon aging or exposure to air. Cinnamon oil is used to scent perfumes and as a flavoring in dentifrices. Can cause contact dermatitis.

CINNAMYL ALCOHOL • Occurs in storax, Balsam Peru, cinnamon leaves, and hyacinth oil. A crystalline alcohol with a strong hyacinth odor used in synthetic perfumes and in deodorants for flavoring and scent. Can cause allergic reactions.

CINNYAMYL ANTHRANILATE • A synthetic flavoring agent and fragrance ingredient used since the 1940s as an imitation grape or cherry flavor. It is used as a fragrance in soaps, detergents, creams, lotions, and perfumes. United States sales equaled more than 2,000 pounds in 1976. The National Cancer Institute reported on December 20, 1980 that it caused liver cancer in male and female mice and caused both kidney and pancreatic cancers in male rats in feeding studies. Earlier studies showed it increased lung tumors in mice. The FDA banned the use of it in food in 1982. Most companies voluntarily stopped using it in cosmetics after publication of the NCI information.

CINOXATE • See Cinnamic Acid.

CITRAL • A flavoring used in foods and beverages. Used in perfumes, soaps, and colognes for its lemon and verbena scents. Found also in detergents and furniture polish. Occurs naturally in grapefruit, orange, peach, ginger, grapefruit oil, oil of lemon, and oil of lime. A light oily liquid isolated from citral oils or made synthetically. The compound has been reported to inhibit wound healing and tumor rejection in animals. Vitamin A counteracts its toxicity, but in commercial products to which pure citral has been added, Vitamin A may not be present.

CITRIC ACID • One of the most widely used acids in the cosmetic industry, it is derived from citrus fruit by fermentation of crude sugars. Employed as a preservative, sequestering agent (*see*), to adjust acid-alkali balance; as a foam inhibitor and plasticizer. It is also used as an astringent alone or in astringent compounds. Among the cosmetic products in which it is frequently found are freckle and nail bleaches, bath preparations, skin fresheners, cleansing creams, depilatories, eye lotions, hair colorings, hair rinses, and hair-waving preparations. The clear, crystalline, water-absorbing chemicals are also used to prevent scurvy, a deficiency disease, and as a refreshing drink with water and sugar added. No known toxicity.

CITRONELLA OIL • A natural food flavoring extract from fresh grass grown in Asia. Used in perfumes, toilet waters, and perfumed cosmetics; also an insect repellant. May cause allergic reactions such as stuffy nose, hay fever, asthma, and skin rash when used in cosmetics.

CITRONELLOL • Used in perfumes. It has a roselike odor. Occurs naturally in citronella oil, lemon oil, lemon grass oil, tea, rose oil, and geranium oil. A mild irritant.

CITRUS OILS • **Eugenol. Eucalyptol.** Anethole, irone, orris, and menthol (*see all*).

CIVET • A fixative in perfumery. It is the civet cat's unctuous secretion from between the anus and genitalia of both male and female. Semisolid, yellowish to brown mass, with an unpleasant odor. No known toxicity.

CLARIFYING AGENT • A substance that removes from liquids small amounts of suspended matter. Butyl alcohol, for instance, is a clarifying agent for clear shampoos.

CLARY • **Clary Sage.** A fixative (*see*) for perfumes. A natural extract of an aromatic herb grown in southern Europe and cultivated widely in England. A well-known spice in food and beverages. No known toxicity.

CLAY PACK • See Face Masks and Packs.

CLAYS • **Bentonite. Veegum®. China Clay.** Used for color in cosmetics as a clarifying agent (*see*) in liquids, as an emollient, and as a poultice. Nontoxic.

CLEANSING CREAMS AND LOTIONS • Used to dissolve sebum, loosen particles of grime, and to facilitate the removal of dirt. They usually contain mineral oil, triethanolamine stearate, and water. Among other ingredients commonly used are alcohol, alkanolamines, allantoins, antibacterials, and preservatives, methyl and propyl parabens, fatty alcohols, lanolin, perfumes, glycerol, propylene glycol, fatty oils, thickeners, and waxes. A typical hypoallergenic cold cream contains water, mineral oil, waxes, borax, and depollenized beeswax. The American Medical Association and dermatologists say that soap and water will serve the same purpose as cleansing creams and lotions, is less expensive, and offers less risk of allergy. (However, soap can be more drying to the skin.) Antibacterials, preservatives, parabens, lanolin, thickeners, and perfumes are all common causes of allergic contact dermatitis (*see all*).

CLEMATIS EXTRACT • **Old Man's Beard Extract.** The extract obtained from the leaves of *Clematis vitalba*. A red or violet herb or woody vine.

CLOFLUCARBAN • See Urea.

CLOVE OIL • Used as an antiseptic and flavoring in tooth powders, a toothache treatment, a scent in hair tonics, a condiment, and flavoring in chewing gum and postage stamp glue. It is 82 to 87 percent eugenol (*see*) and has the characteristic clove oil odor and taste. It is strongly irritating to the skin and can cause allergic skin rashes. Its use in perfumes and cosmetics is frowned upon, although in very diluted forms it is innocuous.

CLOVER • An herb and natural flavoring extract from a plant characterized by three leaves, and flowers in dense heads. Used in fruit flavorings for beverages, ice cream, ices, candy, and baked goods. May cause sensitivity to light.
CLOVER BLOSSOM EXTRACT • **Trifolium Extract.** The extract of the flowers of *Trifolium pratense*. Used in fruit flavorings. May cause sensitivity to light.
CLOVERLEAF OIL • **Eugenia Caryophyllus Leaf Oil.** The volatile oil obtained by steam distillation of the leaves of *Eugenia caryophyllus*. It consists mostly of eugenol (*see*).
COAL TAR • Used in adhesives, creosotes, insecticides, phenols, woodworking, preservation of food, and dyes to make colors used in cosmetics, including hair dyes. Thick liquid or semisolid tar obtained from bituminous coal, it contains many constituents including benzene, xylenes, naphthalene, pyridine, quinoline, phenol, and cresol. The main concern about coal tar derivatives is that they not only cause cancer in animals but are frequent sources of allergic reactions, particularly skin rashes and hives.
COBALT CHLORIDE • A metal used in hair dye. Occurs in the earth's crust; gray, hard, and magnetic. Excess administration can produce an overproduction of red blood cells and gastrointestinal upset. See Metallic Hair Dyes.
COBALT NAPHTHENATE • See Cobalt Chloride.
COCAMIDE (DEA, MEA) • See Coconut Oil.
COCAMIDE MIPA • See Coconut Oil.
COCAMIDE BETAINE • See Coconut Oil.
COCAMIDOPROPYL BETAINE • See Coconut Oil.
COCAMIDOPROPYL DIMETHYLAMINE • See Coconut Oil.
COCAMIDOPROPYL OXIDE • See Coconut Oil.
COCAMIDOPROPYL SULTAMINE • See Coconut Oil.
COCAMIDOPROPYLAMINE OXIDE • See Coconut Oil.
COCAMINE OXIDE • See Coconut Oil.
COCAMINOBUTYRIC ACID • See Coconut Oil and Butyric acid.
COCAMINOPROPIONIC ACID • See Coconut Oil.
COCETH-6 • See Coconut Oil.
COCHINEAL • Banned by the FDA. See Carmine.
COCO SULTAINE • See Coconut Oil.
COCOA • A powder prepared from the roasted and cured kernels of ripe seeds of *theobroma* cacao and other species of *theobroma*. A brownish powder with a chocolate odor, it is used as a flavoring. May cause wheezing, rash, and other symptoms of allergy, particularly in children.

COCOA BUTTER • Theobroma Oil. Softens and lubricates the skin. A solid fat expressed from the roasted seeds of the cocoa plant that is used in eyelash creams, lipsticks, nail whiteners, rouge, pastes, soaps, and emollient creams as a lubricant and skin softener. Frequently used in massage creams and in suppositories because it softens and melts at body temperature. May cause allergic skin reactions.

COCOA EXTRACT • Extract of *theobroma cacao*. See Cocoa Butter.

COCOAMPHOACETATE • See Coconut Oil.

COCOAMPHOCARBOXYMETHYLHYDROXYPROPYLSULFONATE • See Coconut Oil.

COCOAMPHOCARBOXYPROPIONIC ACID • See Coconut Oil.

COCOAMPHODIACETATE • Widely used in cosmetics in the manufacture of toilet soaps, creams, lubricants, chocolate, and suppositories. See Coconut Oil.

COCOAMPHODIPROPIONATE • See Coconut Oil.

COCOAMPHODIPROPIONIC ACID • See Coconut Oil.

COCOAMPHOHYDROXYPROPYLSULFONATE • See Coconut Oil.

COCO-BETAINE • See Coconut Oil.

COCOMORPHOLINE OXIDE • See Coconut Oil.

COCONUT ACIDS • See Coconut Oil.

COCONUT ALCOHOLS • See Coconut Oil.

COCONUT OIL • The white, semisolid, highly saturated fat expressed from the kernels of the coconut. Used in the manufacture of baby soaps, shampoos, shaving lathers, cuticle removers, preshaving lotions, hairdressings, soaps, ointment bases, and massage creams. Stable when exposed to air. Lathers readily and is a fine skin cleanser. Usually blended with other fats. May cause allergic skin rashes.

COCOTRIMONIUM CHLORIDE • Coconut Trimethylammonium Chloride. See Quaternary Ammonium Compounds.

COCOYL HYDROXYETHYL IMIDAZOLINE • See Imidazoline.

COCOYL IMIDAZOLINE • Heterocyclic compound used as a detergent emulsifier. See Cocoa Butter and Ethylenediamine.

COCOYL SARCOSINE • Formed from caffeine by decomposition with barium hydroxide. Used to make antienzyme agents for toothpastes that help to prevent decay. No known toxicity.

COCOYL SARCOSINAMIDE DEA • Diethanolamine Cocyl Sarcosinamide. Used as a detergent emulsifier. See Cocoa Butter.

COD-LIVER OIL • The fixed oil expressed from fresh livers used in skin ointments and special skin creams to promote healing. Pale yellow, with a bland, slightly fishy odor. Contains Vitamins A and D, which promote healing of wounds and abscesses. No known toxicity.

COLD CREAM • Originally developed by the Greek physician,

Galen, the original formula consisted of a mixture of olive oil, beeswax, water, and rose petals. The product was called cold cream because after it was applied to the skin, the water evaporated and gave a feeling of coolness. Cold cream is still used, although the olive oil has been replaced with mineral or other oils that do not become rancid so easily. Beeswax (*see*) can cause allergic contact dermatitis, as can rose petals, perfume, or other additives added to the original formula. See also Cleansing Creams.

COLETH-24 • Emulsifier and emollient derived from cholesterol and ethylene oxide. No known toxicity.

COLLAGEN • Protein substance found in connective tissue. In cosmetics, it is usually derived from animal tissue. The collagen fibers in connective tissues of the skin undergo changes through aging and overexposure to the sun that contribute to the appearance of wrinkles and other outward signs of age. Cosmetics manufacturers have heralded it as a new wonder ingredient but according to medical experts, it cannot affect the skin's own collagen when applied topically. However, it is being used to fill out acne scars and other depressions, including wrinkles, by injection. Allergic reactions are not infrequent. Test spots should be done first to see whether an allergic response is provoked.

COLLODION • A mixture of nitrocellulose, alcohol, and ether in a syrupy, colorless or slightly yellow liquid. It is used as a skin protectant, in clear nail polish, as a corn remover, in the manufacture of lacquers, artificial pearls, and cement. May cause allergic skin reactions.

COLLOIDAL SULFUR • A pale yellow mixture of sulfur and acacia (*see*). Used as an emulsifier. See Sulfur.

COLLYRIUM • A commercial preparation for local application to the eye, usually a wash or lotion. No known toxicity.

COLOCYNTH • **Bitter Apple.** A denaturant used in alcohols for cosmetics. Derived from the dried pulp of a fruit grown in the Mediterranean and Near East regions. It is a supercathartic if ingested and has caused deaths. Has also caused allergic problems in cosmeticians.

COLOGNE • Named originally after a town in Germany, it is usually limited to citrus and floral bases. It has a higher alcohol content than perfume, is usually applied more generously, and leaves a cooling, refreshing feeling on the skin. It is also made as a paste or semisolid stick. May cause allergic reactions depending on ingredients. Those allergic to citrus and floral bases should avoid colognes and try perfumes made of wood or animal scents. No known toxicity to the skin.

COLOGNE, SOLID • Solid colognes are used in sticks or small containers. Such products consist of 80 percent alcohol, about 10 percent sodium stearate, some sorbitol, cologne essence, and water. Gel colognes consist of 60 to 70 percent alcohol, perfume oils, and emulsifiers; and about 30 percent water.

COLORS • Food colors of both natural and synthetic origin are extensively used in cosmetics. When the letters *FD & C* precede a color it means the color can be used in a food, drug or cosmetic. When *D & C* precedes the color, it signifies that it can only be used in drugs or cosmetics, but not in food. *Ext. D & C* before a color means that it is certified for external use only in drugs and cosmetics and may not be used on the lips or mucous membranes. No coal tar colors are permitted for use around the eyes. In fact, the FDA does not allow any color additive to be applied around the area of the eye unless specifically approved for that purpose. There is still a great deal of controversy about the use of coal tar colors because almost all have been shown to cause cancer when injected into the skins of mice. Furthermore, many people are allergic to coal tar products. The bulk of the colors are derived from coal tar. Aniline, a coal tar derivative, is poisonous in its pure state. A provisional listing is a category that is supposed to be abolished. It consists of colors whose safety has not been proven or even studied; in some cases this dates back to when the list was enacted in 1960. Permanent listing means the FDA is convinced that the dye is safe to use as it is now employed in cosmetics. Batch-by-batch certification is used to determine how well the concoction matches the FDA standards—the chemical formula approved. The color additives for which certification is not required are mostly dyes or pigments of vegetable, animal, or mineral origin, and generally require less processing. Many of the colors are vegetable compounds—beet powder, caramel, beta carotene, and grapeskin extract. A few are of animal origin—cochineal extract, taken from the dried bodies of certain insects. Among the natural colors used are alkanet, annatto, carotene, chlorophyll, saffron, and turmeric. The big problem with coal tar colors, of course, is their potential as carcinogens, but they are also potential sensitizers. Each batch of a coal tar color has to be certified as "safe." F & C Red No. 40 is one of the most widely used coal tar colorings. See also Yellow No. 5, Tartrazine, Coal Tar, Catechu Black, and Carmine. The word "pigment," however, usually means a colored or white chemical compound that is insoluble in a particular solvent. The word "dye" generally refers to a chemical compound, most often of coal tar origin, which is soluble. Cosmetic manufacturers have unique problems with coloring their products. They must choose a color substance that is not only safe and stable in a product, but one that will psychologically entice the customer into buying the product. For instance, most hand lotions are either white, pink, cream, or blue. Research sponsored by cosmetic companies has shown that women over twenty-five years of age want pink shades while teenagers prefer blue hand lotions. Many natural colors derived from plants and animals have been in use since humans first started trying to make themselves look better with makeup. Examples of such naturally derived colors are annatto, saffron, chlorophyll, and carotene (*see all*). Inorganic colors used in cosmetics include iron oxides, bronze powder, ultramarines, chromium oxide greens, and a number of white products such as titanium dioxide, barium sulfate, and zinc oxide (*see all*). However, widely used and under FDA scrutiny are the coal tar colors.

In 1900 there were more than 80 dyes in use in cosmetics, foods, and drugs. There were no regulations, and the same dye used to color clothes could also be used to color candy or cosmetics. In 1906 the first comprehensive legislation for food colors was passed. There were only seven colors that, when tested, were shown to be composed of ingredients known to demonstrate no harmful effects. A voluntary system of certification for batches of color dyes was set up. In 1938 new legislation was passed, superseding the 1906 act. The colors were given numbers instead of chemical names, and every batch had to be certified. The manufacturers must submit to the government samples from every batch of coal tar color. Each sample is analyzed today for purity. The lot test number must then accompany the colors through all subsequent packaging. The manufacturer must pay 25¢ a pound and not less than $160 for each batch tested. What is considered a safe color? According to the FDA: "Safety for external color additives will normally be determined by tests for acute oral toxicity, primary irritation, sensitization, subacute skin toxicity on intact or abraded skin and carcinogenicity (cancer causing) by skin application." The FDA commissioner may waive any of such tests if data before him establishes otherwise that such a test is not required to determine safety. Here are the certified colors classified into the following categories according to their chemical ancestry:

1. Nitro Dyes. Containing one atom of nitrogen and two of oxygen, there are only a few certified because they can be absorbed through the skin and are toxic. Ext. D & C Yellow is one. See Nitro.

2. Azo (monoazo). This includes the largest number. They are all characterized by the presence of the azo bond. See Azo Dyes.

3. Triphenylmethane. FD & C Blue No. 1 is the most popular dye of this group and is widely used. See Triphenylmethane Group.

4. Xanthene. This group contains very brilliant, widely used lipstick colors. D & C Orange is one. See Xanthene Group.

5. Quinoline. There are only two certified in this category, D & C Yellow Nos. 10 and 11. They are bright greenish yellows. See Quinoline.

6. Anthraquinone. Widely used in cosmetics because it is not affected by light. Ext. D & C Violet No. 2 is one. See Anthraquinone.

7. Indigo. These dyes have been in use a long time. D & C Blue No. 6 is an example. See Indigo.

There are a few other miscellaneous dyes.

In 1950, children were made ill by certain colorings used in candy and popcorn. These incidents led to the delisting of FD & C Orange Nos. 1 and 2 and FD & C Red No. 32. Since that time, because of experimental evidence of possible harm, Red No. 1, Yellow Nos. 1, 2, 3, and 4 have also been delisted. Violet No. 1 was removed in 1973. In 1976, one of the most widely used of all colors, FD & C Red No. 2, was removed because it was found to cause tumors in rats. In 1976, Red No. 4 was banned for coloring maraschino cherries (its last use), and carbon black was also banned at the same time because they contained cancer-causing agents.

Earlier, in 1960, scientific investigations were required by law to determine the suitability of all colors in use for permanent listing. Citrus Red No. 2 (limited to 2 ppm) for coloring orange skins is permanently listed; Blue No. 1, Red No. 3, Yellow No. 5, and Red No. 40 are permanently listed without restrictions. In 1959, the Food and Drug Administration approved the use of "lakes," in which the dyes have been mixed with alumina hydrate to make them insoluble. See Lakes.

The other food, drug and cosmetic coloring additives remained on the "temporary list." The provisional list permitted colors then in use to continue on a provisional, or interim, basis until completion of studies, when it will be determined whether the colors should be permanently approved or terminated. FD & C Red No. 3 (Erythrosine) is permanently listed for use in food and ingested drugs and provisionally listed for cosmetics and externally applied drugs. It is used in foods such as gelatins, cake mixes, ice cream, fruit cocktail cherries, bakery goods, and sausage casings.

On May 2, 1988 the FDA postponed the closing date for three

provisionally listed color additives—FD & C Red No. 3, D & C Red No. 33 and D & C Red No. 36—to allow additional time to study "complex scientific and legal questions about the colors before deciding to approve or terminate their use in food, drugs, and cosmetics." The Agency asked for 60 days to consider the impact of the October 1987 U.S. Court of Appeals ruling that there is no exception to the Delaney Clause (*see*) which says that cancer-causing agents may not be added to food. On July 13, 1988, the Public Citizens Health Research Group announced that the FDA agreed to revoke by July 15, 1988, the permanent listing of four color additives used in drugs and cosmetics—D & C Red No. 8, D & C Red No. 9, D & C Red No. 19, and D & C Orange No. 17. In a unanimous decision in October 1987, the U.S. Court of Appeals for the District of Columbia said the FDA lacked legal authority to approve two of the colors, D & C Orange No. 17 and D & C Red No. 19, since they had been found to induce cancer in laboratory animals. The Supreme Court ruled against an appeal on April 18, 1988. Meanwhile, Public Citizen also brought a similar suit, challenging the use of D & C Red No. 8 and D & C Red No. 9 before the U.S. Circuit Court of Appeals in Philadelphia. Under an agreement between the FDA and Public Citizen, the case was sent back to the FDA, and the agency delisted these colors as well as D & C Orange No. 17 and D & C Red No. 19. Other countries and the World Health Organization maintain there are inconsistencies in safety data and in the banning of some colors which, in turn, affect international commerce. As of this writing, there is still a great deal of confusion concerning the FDA, which maintains that the cancer risk is minimal—as low as one in a billion—for the colors, and other groups such as Nader's Public Citizen, which maintains that *any* cancer risk for a food additive is unacceptable.

COLTSFOOT • **Wild Ginger.** Used for its soothing properties in shampoos and astringents. From an herb used historically to fight colds and asthma, it reputedly opens pores and allows sweating. It has been used a soothing ointment. No known toxicity.

COMFREY EXTRACT • The extract of the roots and rhizomes of *Symphytum officinale*. Used for centuries by monks as a healer of bruises, a mouthwash and gargle, and as a compress for eye injuries. No known toxicity.

CONCRETES • Wax-like substances prepared from natural raw materials, almost exclusively vegetable in origin, such as bark, flower, herb, leaf, and root and used in perfumes and stick deodorants. No known toxicity.

CONDITIONERS • See Hair Conditioners.

CONDITIONING CREAMS • See Emollients.

CONJUGATED GLYCOPROTEINS • A composition made up of carbohydrates and simple proteins. Used in tanning creams and moisturizers. No known toxicity.

CONTACT DERMATITIS • See Allergic Contact Dermatitis.

CONTACT DERMATITIS OF THE EYELIDS • See Eyelids.

COPAL • A resin obtained as a fossil or as an exudate from various species of tropical plants. Must be heated in alcohol or other solvents. Used in nail enamels. May cause allergic reactions, particularly skin rashes.

COPOLYMER • Result of polymerization (*see* polymer), which includes at least two different molecules, each of which is capable of polymerizing alone. Together they form a new distinct molecule. They are used in the manufacture of nail enamels and face masks.

COPPER, METALLIC POWDER, AND VERSENATE • Used as a coloring agent in cosmetics. One of the earliest known metals. An essential nutrient for all mammals. Naturally occurring or experimentally produced copper deficiency in animals leads to a variety of abnormalities including anemia, skeletal defects, and muscle degeneration. Copper itself is nontoxic, but soluble copper salts, notably copper sulfate, are highly irritating to the skin and mucous membranes, and when ingested, cause serious vomiting. Copper metallic powder was permanently listed as a cosmetic coloring in 1977.

CORIANDER OIL • The volatile oil from the dried ripe fruit of a plant grown in Asia and Europe. Used as a flavoring agent in dentifrices. Colorless or pale yellow liquid with a taste and odor characteristic of coriander, which is also used as a condiment. Can cause allergic reactions, particularly of the skin.

CORN • **Corn Sugar. Dextrose.** Used in maple, nut, and root beer flavorings for beverages, ice cream, ices, candy, and baked goods. The oil is used in emollient creams and toothpastes. The syrup is used as a texturizer and carrying agent in cosmetics. It is also used for envelopes, stamps, sticker tapes, ale, aspirin, bacon, baking mixes, powders, beers, bourbon, breads, cheeses, cereals, chop suey, chow mein, confectioners' sugar, cream puffs, fish products, ginger ale, hams, jellies, processed meats, peanut butters, canned peas, plastic food wrappers, sherbets, whiskeys, and American wines. It may also be found in capsules, lozenges, ointments, suppositories, vitamins, fritters, Fritos, frostings, canned or frozen fruit, graham crackers, gravies, grits, gum, monosodium glutamate, Nescafe, oleomargarine, pablum, paper, peanut butter, tortillas, vinegar, yeasts, bologna, baking powders, bath powders, frying fats, fruit juices, and laxatives. May cause allergic reactions including skin rashes and asthma.

CORN ACID • See Corn Oil.

CORN COB MEAL • The milled powder prepared from the cobs of *Zea mays* (*Indian corn*). See Corn.

CORN FLOUR • A finely ground powder from the seeds of *Zea mays*. Used in face and bath powder. See Corn Oil.

CORN GERM EXTRACT • The extract of the germ of *Zea mays*. See Corn.

CORN OIL • Used in emollient creams, soaps, hair dressings, and toothpastes. Obtained as a by-product by wet milling the grain for use in the manufacture of corn starch, dextrins, and yellow oil. It has a faint characteristic odor and taste and thickens upon exposure to air. No known toxicity, but can cause skin reactions in the allergic.

CORN POPPY EXTRACT • The extract obtained from the petals of the *Papaver rhoeas*.

CORN SILK EXTRACT • Extract of the stigma of *Zea mays*. Used in makeup bases. See Corn Oil.

CORN STARCH • Many containers are powdered with cornstarch to prevent sticking. It is also used in dusting powder and as a demulcent for irritated colons. May cause allergic reactions, including skin rashes and asthma.

CORN SYRUP • **Corn Sugar. Dextrose.** A sweet syrup prepared from cornstarch. Used as a texturizer and carrying agent in cosmetics. Also used for envelopes, stamps and sticking tapes, aspirin, and many food products. May cause allergic reactions.

CORNFLOWER • The dried flowers of *Centaurea cyanus*.

CORNFLOWER EXTRACT • The extract obtained from the flowers of *Centaurea cyanus*. Used as a blue dye.

COSMETICS • One of the most common causes, if not the most common cause, of Allergic Contact Dermatitis and frequently the cause of nasal and lung symptoms, particularly scented products. Until fairly recently, it was believed that cosmetics could not be absorbed through the skin. It is now known that many things can be absorbed through the skin, some chemicals to a greater degree than others depending upon composition and the part of the anatomy to which they are applied. Many cosmetics manufacturers promote their products as "hypoallergenic." A non-allergenic product is impossible because there is always someone who will be allergic to something. There are sixty known ingredients in past or present cosmetics known to cause allergic reactions in many people. Included in this list are such common substances as acacia, benzaldehyde, corn starch, gum arabic, oil of spearmint, and wheat starch (*see all*). By leaving the sixty offenders out of cosmetics or by reducing the number of ingredients altogether, particularly perfumes, manufacturers then claim their products are "hypoallergenic." The FDA has wrestled for years with the claim and asked manufacturers to prove their products unlikely to cause an allergic reaction. As the mandate stands now, it is up to the manufacturer to decide the testing method used to determine the hypoallergenicity of the product. Throughout this book there are ingredients found in cosmetics that often cause allergic reactions. If you read the labels and check the book, you will be able, in most instances, to avoid these products that may be causing you a problem.

COSTUS • A fixative in perfumes. The volatile oil is obtained by steam distillation from dried roots of an herb. Light yellow to brown viscous liquid, with a persistent violetlike odor. Used also as a food flavoring. No known toxicity.

COTTON • A soft white cellulosic substance composed of the fibers surrounding the seeds of various plants of the *mallow* family.

COTTONSEED • The water-soluble, protein material in cottonseed contains one of the most powerful allergens for humans. Occasionally, it contaminates inexpensive cotton stuffing in upholstery, mattresses, and cushions. More often, exposures to the allergens arise from the use of cottonseed meal, which may be a component in fertilizers and feed for cattle, hogs, poultry and dogs. Symptoms usually result from inhalation, but allergic reactions also can occur from ingesting cottonseed meal used in pan-greasing compounds and foods such as some fried cakes, fig bars, and cookies.

COTTONSEED ACID • See Cottonseed Oil.

COTTONSEED FLOUR • Cooked, partly defatted, and toasted flour used for pale yellow color and to make gin. Can cause allergic skin reactions and asthma.

COTTONSEED OIL • The fixed oil from the seeds of the cultivated varieties of the plant. Pale yellow, oily, odorless liquid used in the manufacture of soaps, creams, baby creams, nail polish removers, and lubricants. The oil is used in most salad oils, oleomargarines, most mayonnaises, and salad dressings. Lard compounds and lard substitutes are made with cottonseed oil. Sardines may be packed in it. Most commercial fried products such as potato chips and doughnuts are fried in cottonseed oil, and restaurants use it for cooking. Candies, particularly chocolates, often contain this oil, and it is used to polish fruits at stands. It is also used in cotton wadding or batting in cushions, comforters, mattresses and upholstery, varnishes, fertilizers, and animal feeds. Known to cause many allergic reactions but because of its wide use in cosmetics, foods, and other products, it is hard to avoid.

COUMARIN • Coumarin is present in several plants and essential oils such as Balsam Peru, tonka bean, and sweet clover. It has the odor of new-mown hay. Used in over 300 products in the United States, including acne preparations, antiseptics, deodorants, "skin fresheners," hair dyes, shampoos, soaps, detergents, perfumes, and sunscreens. May produce allergic contact dermatitis (*see*) and photosensitivity (*see*). It was once used as a flavoring, but was banned in food by the FDA because it caused liver injury in experimental animals. No known toxicity on the skin.

COUNTERIRRITANT • An agent applied locally to produce superficial inflammation with the object of reducing existing inflammation in deeper adjacent structures. Iodine (*see*) is an example of a counterirritant.

CRANE'S BILL EXTRACT • The extract of wild geranium, *Geranium maculatum*, or other native geranium species. See Geranium Oil.

CRATAEGUS • The extract of the berries, flowers, and/or leaves of the English hawthorn, *Crataegus oxyacantha*. Used in dyes and skin tonics. Can cause dilation of blood vessels.

CREAM RINSE • **Creme Rinse.** Conditioners (*see*) that are poured on the hair after shampooing and then rinsed with water. A typical formula for a cream rinse: lanolin, 10 percent; mineral oil and lanolin esters, 5 percent; cholesterol, 0.25 percent; sorbitan stearate, 3 percent; preservative, 0.15 percent; distilled water, 78.60 percent; and perfume.

CREAMS • See Emollients; Hand Creams and Lotions; Cold Creams; and Hormone Creams and Lotions.

CREOSOTE • Obtained from wood tar, either almost colorless or yellowish. Used locally as an antiseptic, internally as an expectorant. It has a smoky odor and a caustic, burning taste. Large doses internally may cause stomach irritation, heart problems, and death. It is also used as a mild insect repellent.

CRESOLS • Cresols are obtained from coal tar and wood, used in hair-grooming preparations and eye lotions. They are an antiseptic and disinfectant. Chronic poisoning may occur from oral ingestion or absorption through the skin. They also may produce digestive disturbances and nervous disorders, with fainting, dizziness, mental changes, skin eruptions, jaundice, uremia, and lack of urine. They caused cancer when given orally to rats in doses of 1,000 parts per million. See also Coal Tar.

o-CRESOTIC ACID • White to slightly reddish odorless crystals used in the manufacture of dyes. Slightly soluble in cold water, completely soluble in alcohol. See Salicylic Acid for toxicity.

CROSS-REACTIVITY • When the body mistakes one compound for another of similar chemical composition.

CROTONIC ACID • **Beta-Methacrylic Acid.** Found in clay, soil, and wood, it is used in making resins, polymers, and temporary permanent wave lotions. It is also used in the manufacture of Vitamin A. It is a strong irritant to tissues in its undiluted state.

CTFA • Cosmetic, Toiletries and Fragrance Association, the trade organization of the cosmetics industry.

CUCUMBER JUICE • From the succulent fruit of the vine and used as an astringent by many "natural" cosmetic fans. It has a pleasant aroma and imparts a cool feeling to the skin. Nontoxic.

CUMINALDEHYDE • Used to make perfumes. Colorless to yellowish, oily, with a strong lasting odor. It is a constituent of eucalyptus, myrrh, cassia, cumin, and other essential oils, but often is made synthetically for fragrances. No known toxicity.

CUPRIC ACETATE • The copper salt of acetic acid and copper (*see both*).

CUPRIC CHLORIDE • **Copper Chloride.** A copper salt used in hair dye. A yellow to brown water-absorbing powder that is soluble in diluted acids. It is also used in pigments for glass and ceramics and as a feed additive, disinfectant, and wood preservative. Irritating to the skin and mucous membranes. Irritating when ingested, causing vomiting.

CUPRIC SULFATE • Copper sulfate occurs in nature as hydrocyanite. Grayish white to greenish white crystals. Used as agricultural fungicide, herbicide, and in the preparation of azo dyes (*see*). Used in hair dyes as coloring. Very irritating if ingested. No known toxicity on the skin, and is used medicinally as a skin fungicide.

CURRY RED • A color classed as a monoazo, the name can be used only when applied to uncertified batches of color. The CTFA-adopted name for certified (*see*) batches is FD & C Red No. 40 (*see*).

CUTICLE REMOVERS • Cuticle is the dead skin that covers the base of the nail. Chemicals are used to either plasticize or dissolve the cuticle. Alkalies, such as lye, are used as cuticle softeners and removers. A typical cuticle remover contains coconut oil, potassium phosphate, potassium hydroxide, triethanolamine, and water. Contact dermatitis may occur. Potassium phosphate, potassium hydroxide, and triethanolamine can be irritants. Coconut oil (*see*) can cause allergic reactions.

CYCLAMATE • Artificial sweetening agent about 30 times as sweet as refined sugar, removed from the food market on September 1, 1969, because it was found to cause bladder cancer in rats.

CYCLAMIC ACID • Fairly strong acid with a sweet taste. It is the acid from which cyclamates were derived (*see*).

CYCLOMETHICONE-4, -5 • See Silicones.

O-Cymen-3-OL • See *p*-Cymene.

***p*-CYMENE** • Used as a solvent. A synthetic flavoring, a volatile hydrocarbon solvent that occurs naturally in star anise, coriander, cumin, mace oil, oil of mandarin, and origanum oil. Used in fragrances; also in citrus and spice flavorings for beverages, ice cream, candies, and baked goods. Its ingestion pure may cause a burning sensation in the mouth, and nausea, salivation, headache, giddiness, vertigo, confusion, and coma. Contact with the pure liquid may cause blisters of the skin and inflammation of mucous membranes.

CYPRESS EXTRACT • An extract derived from the leaves and twigs of the cypress tree, *Cupressus sempervirens*.

CYSTEINE, L-FORM • An essential amino acid (*see*), it is derived from hair and used in hair products and creams. Soluble in water, it is used in bakery products as a nutrient. It has been used to promote wound healing. On the list of FDA additives to be studied.

CYSTINE • A nonessential amino acid (*see*) found in urine and in horsehair. Colorless, practically odorless, white crystals, it is used as a nutritional supplement and in emollients. On the FDA list for further study.

D

D & C BLUE NO. 1 ALUMINUM LAKE • **Brilliant Blue Lake.** Insoluble pigment prepared from FD & C Blue No. 1 (*see*). A coal tar derivative, this brilliant blue is used as a coloring in hair dyes and powders, among other cosmetics. Also used in soft drinks, gelatin desserts, and candy. May cause allergic reactions. It will produce malignant tumors at the site of injection in rats. On the FDA permanent list of color additives. Rated 1A for toxicology by the World Health Organization, meaning it is completely acceptable for use in foods and cosmetics. See Colors.

D & C BLUE NO. 2 ALUMINUM LAKE • **Acid Blue 74. Indigetine 1A, Indigo Carmine.** An indigo dye (*see*).

D & C BLUE NO. 4 • **Acid Blue 9 (Ammonium Salt).** Bright greenish-blue. A coal tar, triphenylmethane color used in hair rinses primarily. Permanently listed by the FDA, January 3, 1977. See Colors.

D & C BLUE NO. 6 • **Indigo.** An indigoid, it is used in lipstick, rouges, soaps, hair-waving fluids, and bath salts. See Colors.

D & C BROWN 1 • **Resorcin Brown. Capracyl Brown®. Acid Orange 24.** Light orange-brown. A diazo color (see Colors) permitted for use only in preformed hair colors. But the cosmetic industry has petitioned the FDA to allow wider use. Resorcin is irritating to the skin and mucous membranes. Absorption can cause depletion of oxygen in the body and death. Also used as an antiseptic and fungicide. Permanently listed for external use only in 1976.

D & C GREEN NO. 3 • **Aluminum Lake. Food Green 3.** The aluminum salt of FD & C Green No. 3. A brilliant but not fast dye. See Aniline Dyes for toxicity.

D & C GREEN NO. 5 • **Acid Green 25.** Dullish blue-green. Classed chemically as an anthraquinone color (see Colors). Used in suntan oils, bath salts, shampoos, hair rinses, toothpastes, soaps, and hair-waving fluids. Low skin toxicity but may cause skin irritation and sensitivity. Permanently listed by the FDA in 1982.

D & C GREEN NO. 6 • **Solvent Green 3.** Dull blue-green. Classified chemically as an anthraquinone color. Used in hair oils and pomades. Permanently listed by the FDA in 1982. See Colors.

D & C GREEN NO. 8 • **Solvent Green 7.** Yellowish-green. Classed chemically as a pyrene color. Permanently listed by the FDA in 1976. See Colors.

D & C ORANGE NO. 4 • **Acid Orange 7.** Bright orange. Transparent orange used in lipstick and face powders. Classed chemically as a monoazo color. Permanently listed in 1977. See Colors.

D & C ORANGE NO. 4 ALUMINUM LAKE • **Persian Orange.** Insoluble pigment prepared from D & C Orange No. 4 (*see*). See Colors and Lakes.

D & C ORANGE NO. 5 • **Acid Orange 11. Solvent Red 72. Dibromofluorescein** (*see*). Reddish-orange. An orange stain used in lipsticks, face powders, and talcums. Permanently listed for use in lipsticks, mouthwashes, and dentifrices in 1982. Permanently listed for externally applied drugs and cosmetics in 1984.

D & C ORANGE NO. 5. ALUMINUM LAKE • **Dawn Orange. Manchu Orange.** Insoluble pigment prepared from D & C Orange No. 5 (*see*). See Colors and Lakes.

D & C ORANGE NO. 5 ZIRCONIUM LAKE • **Petite Orange. Dawn Orange. Acid Red 26. Ponceau R.** See Lakes and Zirconium. A monoazo dye. See Azo Dyes.

D & C ORANGE NO. 10 • **Solvent 73. Diiodofluorescein.** Reddish-orange. Classed chemically as a fluoran color. Orange-red powder used in lipsticks and other cosmetics. See Colors.

D & C ORANGE NO. 10 ALUMINUM LAKE • **Solvent Red 73. Erythrosine G.** A xanthene color (*see*).

D & C ORANGE NO. 11 • Clear red. Classed chemically as a

xanthene color. It is the conversion product of D & C Orange No. 10 (*see*) to the sodium or potassium salt. See Colors.

D & C ORANGE NO. 17 • **Permanent Orange. Pigment Orange 5.** Bright orange. Classed chemically as a monoazo color. The FDA permanently listed Orange No. 17, but its ruling was reversed by the United States Court of Appeals in 1987 for the District of Columbia which said the FDA lacked legal authority to approve it since it was found to induce cancer. The court's ruling was in response to a lawsuit by Public Citizen Health Research Group, a consumer advocacy group. See Colors.

D & C ORANGE NO. 17 LAKE • **Permanent Orange. Solvent Red 23. Sudan III.** A diazo dye (*see*) and an approved substrate. See Colors.

D & C RED NO. 2 ALUMINUM LAKE • Insoluble pigment prepared from FD & C Red No. 2 (*see*) and an approved substrate. See Colors.

D & C RED NO. 3 ALUMINUM LAKE • Insoluble pigment prepared from FD & C Red No. 2 (*see*) and aluminum. See Colors.

D & C RED NO. 4 ALUMINUM LAKE • **Food Red 1.** A monoazo color. See Azo Dyes.

D & C RED NO. 6 • **Lithol Rubin B.** Medium red. Classed chemically as a monoazo color. It is the calcium salt of D & C Red No. 7 (*see*). Lithol is a topical antiseptic. Permanently listed in 1983. Nontoxic. See Colors.

D & C RED NO. 6 ALUMINUM LAKE • **Pigment Red 57. Lithol Rubine.** A monoazo color. See Azo Dyes.

D & C RED NO. 6 BARIUM LAKE • **Rubine Lake. Pigment Red 57. Lithol Rubine B.** A monoazo dye. An insoluble pigment prepared from D & C Red No. 6 (*see*) and barium. See Colors and Azo Dyes.

D & C RED NO. 6 POTASSIUM LAKE • An insoluble pigment composed of the potassium salt of D & C Red No. 6. See D & C Red No. 6.

D & C RED NO. 7 • **Lithol Rubin B Ca.** Bluish-red. Classed chemically as a monoazo color. Used in nail lacquers and lipsticks. Lithol is a topical antiseptic. Permanently listed in 1987 for ingested drug and cosmetic lip products, amount not to exceed 5 mg per daily dose of drug. For general cosmetic use according to good manufacturing practices. See Colors.

D & C RED NO. 7 ALUMINUM LAKE • **Pigment Red 57.** See Azo Dyes.

D & C RED NO. 7 BARIUM LAKE • Insoluble pigment prepared from D & C Red No. 7 (*see*). See Colors and Lakes.

D & C RED NO. 7 CALCIUM LAKE • **Pigment Red 57. Lithol**

Rubine B. A monoazo dye. An insoluble pigment prepared from D & C Red No. 7 (*see*) and calcium. See Colors and Azo Dyes.

D & C RED NO. 7 ZIRCONIUM LAKE • Pigment Red 57. Lithol Rubine B. A monoazo color. Carcinogenic in animals. Ruling postponed. See Colors.

D & C RED NO. 8 • Lake Red C. Pigment Red 53. Orange. Classed chemically as a monoazo color. Carcinogenic in animals. Permanently listed in 1987 for ingested drug and cosmetic lip products, amount not to exceed 0.1 percent by weight of finished product, and it is not to be used in mouthwashes. The FDA permanent listing of D & C Red No. 8 has been challenged by a lawsuit by Public Citizen Health Research Group, a consumer advocacy group. See Red No. 19 and Colors.

D & C RED NO. 8 BARIUM LAKE • Acid Red 88. Fast Red A. A monoazo color. See Azo Dyes.

D & C RED NO. 8 SODIUM LAKE • Insoluble pigment prepared from D & C Red No. 8 (*see*). See Colors and Lakes.

D & C RED NO. 9 • Lake Red C Ba. Scarlet coloring. It is the barium salt of D & C Red No. 8 (*see*). Used in face powders. Permanently listed in 1987 for ingested drug and cosmetic lip products, amount not to exceed 0.1 percent of finished product. It is not permitted in mouthwashes. The permanent listing of this color, which has been shown to be carcinogenic in animals, was challenged in 1988 by the Public Citizens Group, a consumer advocacy organization. See Red No. 19 and Colors.

D & C RED NO. 9 BARIUM LAKE • The insoluble pigment prepared from D & C Red No. 9 and barium (*see both*). See also Colors and Lakes.

D & C RED NO. 9 ZIRCONIUM STRONTIUM LAKE • Similar to D & C Red No. 8 (*see*).

D & C RED NO. 10 • Litho Red. Yellowish-red.

D & C RED NO. 17 • Toney Red. Classed chemically as a diazo color. It is used in soaps, suntan oils, hair oils, and pomades. Carcinogenic in animals. No longer used much in lipsticks because of reports of ill-effects. The FDA permanently listed Red No. 17 in 1988, but the ruling was reversed by the United States Court of Appeals for the District of Columbia, which said the FDA lacked legal authority to approve it since Red No. 17 had been found to induce cancer. The court's ruling was in response to a lawsuit by Public Citizen Health Research Group, a consumer advocacy group. See Colors.

D & C RED NO. 19 • Rhodamine B. Magenta. Classed chemically as a xanthene color. Its greenish crystals or yellow powder turns violet in solution. Used in lipsticks, rouges, soaps, bath salts, nail enamels, toothpastes, hair-waving fluids, and face powders. The FDA permanently listed Red No. 19 in 1988, but the ruling was reversed by the United States Court of Appeals for the District of Columbia, which said the FDA lacked legal authority to approve Red No. 19 since it had been found to induce cancer. The court's ruling was in response to a lawsuit by Public Citizen Health Research Group, a consumer advocacy group. See Colors.

D & C RED NO. 19 BARIUM LAKE • Rhodamine B. Magenta. Violet in solution. A xanthene dye (*see*).

D & C RED NO. 19 ZIRCONIUM LAKE • Vat Red 1. Thioindigo Pink R. A thioindigoid dye (*see*). See Vat Dyes and Indigo.

D & C RED NO. 21 • Solvent Red 43. Tetrabromofluorescein (*see*). Classed chemically as a fluoran color. A bluish pink stain used in lipstick, rouges, and nail enamels. Insoluble in water but used to color oils, resins, and lacquers. Permanently listed, 1982. See Colors.

D & C RED NO. 21 ALUMINUM LAKE • Insoluble pigment prepared from D & C Red No. 21 (*see*) and aluminum. See Colors and Lakes.

D & C RED NO. 21 ZIRCONIUM LAKE • Solvent Red 43. Merry Pink. A xanthene dye (*see*).

D & C RED NO. 22 • Eosine YS. Yellowish-pink. Classed chemically as a xanthene color. It is used in soaps, hair rinses, lipsticks and nail polishes. Red crystals with bluish tinge or brownish red powder. Freely soluble in water. Lethal dose in animals is quite small. Permanently listed in 1982. See Colors.

D & C RED NO. 27 • Solvent Red 48. Philoxine B. Veri Pink. A xanthene dye (*see*). Classed chemically as a fluoran color. A deep bluish-red stain used in lipsticks and rouges. Permanently listed, 1982. See Colors.

D & C RED NO. 27 ALUMINUM LAKE • Terabromo Terachloro Fluorescein Lake. Insoluble pigment prepared from D & C Red No. 27 (*see*) and aluminum. See Colors and Lakes.

D & C RED NO. 27 BARIUM LAKE • Solvent Red 48. Petite Pink. A xanthene dye (*see*).

D & C RED NO. 27 ZIRCONIUM LAKE • Solvent Red 48. A xanthene dye (*see*), deep bluish red. Used in lipsticks and rouges.

D & C RED NO. 28 • Phloxine B. Acid Red 92. Classed chemically as a xanthene color. It is the conversion product of D & C Red No. 27 (*see*) to the sodium salt. Permanently listed, 1982. See Colors.

D & C RED NO. 30 • Helindone Pink CN. Vat Red 1. Bluish-pink.

Classed chemically as an indigoid color. It is used in face powders, talcums, lipsticks, rouges, and soaps. See Colors.

D & C RED NO. 30 ALUMINUM LAKE • Vat Red 1. Thioindigoid Pink R. A thioindigoid color. A red vat dye made from indigo and sulfur. See Vat Dyes and Indigo.

D & C RED NO. 30 CALCIUM LAKE • Permanent Pink. Vat Red 1. Thioindigo Pink R. A thioindigo dye. See Vat Dyes and Indigo.

D & C RED NO. 30 LAKE • Insoluble pigment prepared from D & C Red No. 30 (*see*) with an approved metal. See Colors and Lakes.

D & C RED NO. 31 • Brilliant Lake Red R. Classed chemically as a monoazo color. It is used in lipsticks and nail enamels. See Colors.

D & C RED NO. 31 CALCIUM LAKE • Brilliant Lake Red R. Monoazo color used in lipsticks and nail enamels. See Azo Dyes.

D & C RED NO. 33 • Acid Red 33. Dull bluish-red. Classed chemically as a monoazo color. It is used in lipsticks, rouges, soaps, bath salts, and hair rinses. Was to be permanently listed in 1988 but the ruling has been postponed to allow the FDA "additional time to study complex scientific and legal questions about it." See Azo Dyes and Colors.

D & C RED NO. 34 • Fanchon Maroon. Deep Maroon. Classed chemically as a monoazo color. It is used in face powders, talcums, nail lacquers, lipsticks, rouges, toothpastes, and soaps. See Colors.

D & C RED NO. 34 CALCIUM LAKE • Insoluble pigment prepared from D & C Red No. 34 (*see*). See Colors and Lakes.

D & C RED NO. 36 • Pigment Red 4. Tiger Orange. A monoazo dye. It is a bright orange used in lipsticks, rouges, face powders, and talcums. Was to be permanently listed in 1988 but the ruling has been postponed to allow the FDA "additional time to study complex scientific and legal questions about it." See Colors and Azo Dyes.

D & C RED NO. 36 BARIUM LAKE • Pigment Red 4. Permanent Red 12. Orange hue. A monoazo color. See Azo Dyes.

D & C RED NO. 36 LAKE • Chlorinated Para Lake. Tang Orange. Insoluble pigment prepared from D & C Red No. 36 (*see*). See Colors and Lakes.

D & C RED NO. 36 ZIRCONIUM LAKE • Pigment Red 4. See D & C Red No. 36 Barium Lake.

D & C RED NO. 37 • Rhodamine B-Stearate. Banned in 1988. See Solvent Red 49:1.

D & C RED NO. 37 CALCIUM LAKE • Rhodamine B. Stearate Solvent. See D & C Red No. 37.

D & C RED NO. 39 • An azo dye containing benzoic acid (*see*). Used for coloring quaternary ammonium compounds (*see*) germicidal solutions for external applications only. Must not exceed 0.1 percent by weight of the finished product. Must be certified (*see*).

D & C RED NO. 40 • Bluish-pink. Classed chemically as a xanthene color (*see*). Used in soaps.

D & C VIOLET NO. 2 • **Alizurol Purple SS. Solvent Violet 13.** Classed chemically as an anthraquinone color. It is a dull bluish violet used in suntan oils, pomades, and hair colors.

D & C YELLOW NO. 5 ALUMINUM LAKE • Greenish-yellow. Insoluble pigment prepared from FD & C Yellow No. 5 (*see*) and aluminum. See Colors and Lakes.

D & C YELLOW NO. 5 ZIRCONIUM LAKE • An insoluble pigment prepared from FD & C Yellow No. 5 (*see*) and zirconium. See Colors and Lakes.

D & C YELLOW NO. 6 ALUMINUM LAKE • Insoluble pigment prepared from FD & C Yellow No. 6 (*see*) and aluminum. See Colors and Lakes.

D & C YELLOW NO. 7 • **Acid Yellow 73. Fluorescein.** Classed chemically as a fluoran color. It is a water-absorbing, yellowish-red powder freely soluble in water. The fluorescence disappears when the solution is made acid and reappears when it is made neutral. No toxic action on fish, and believed to be nontoxic to humans. See Colors.

D & C YELLOW NO. 8 • **Uranine. Sodium Fluorescein. Naphthol Yellow S.** Classed chemically as a xanthene color. It is the sodium salt of D & C Yellow No. 7 (*see*). Light yellow or orange-yellow powder soluble in water. See Colors.

D & C YELLOW NO. 10 • **Acid Yellow 3. Quinoline Yellow.** Classed chemically as a quinoline color. It is a bright greenish-yellow used in hair-waving fluids, toothpastes, bath salts, soaps, and shampoos. It is a potential allergen. It is present in yellow Irish Spring®, Pink Dove® and Caress Bath Soap®. It may crossreact with other quinoline colors used in drugs.

D & C YELLOW NO. 10 ALUMINUM LAKE • Insoluble pigment prepared from D & C Yellow No. 10 (*see*) and aluminum. See Colors and Lakes.

D & C YELLOW NO. 11 • **Solvent Yellow 33.** Classed chemically as a quinoline color. It is a bright greenish-yellow used in soaps, shampoos, suntan oils, hair oils, and pomades. See Colors.

DAISY EXTRACT • **Extract of Daisy.** Extract of the flowers of the English Daisy, *Bellis perennis*. Certain plants of the daisy family may cause blister-like eruptions when crushed on the skin. Used in sachets. Also included in love potions by ancient herbalists.

DAMAR • Resin used to produce a gloss and adhesion in nail lacquer. It is a yellowish white semitransparent exudate from a plant grown in the East Indies and the Philippines. Comes in varying degrees of hardness. It has a bitter taste. Also used for preserving animal and vegetable specimens for science laboratories. May cause allergic contact dermatitis.

DANDELION LEAF AND ROOT • **Lion's Tooth.** Used as a skin refreshing bath additive. Obtained from *Taraxacum* plants that grow abundantly in the United States. The common dandelion weed eaten as a salad green was used by the Indians for heartburn. Rich in Vitamins A and C, it is also used as a flavoring. No known toxicity.

DANDRUFF, HUMAN • The allergen in human skin flakes has been recognized for a long time and has been used as a test to determine a general tendency towards allergy. In one study, more than 90 percent of asthma patients had a positive skin test reaction in contrast to "normals" who showed no reaction to the test. The reaction rate is even higher in those with allergic contact dermatitis or eczema. The subject of human allergen is a matter of controversy among allergists. Some point out that it is a "chemically modified-self antigen"; others say it is part of the allergenic house dust antigen, and still others say it is not a true allergen.

DANDRUFF SHAMPOOS • Usually shampoos that combine detergents with dry skin dissolvers. They contain sulfur, salicylic acid, resorcinol, and hexachlorophene. There are also after-shampoo dandruff rinses that contain quaternary ammonium compounds. And there are scalp lotions with antiseptics and stimulants such as resorcinol and/or chloral hydrate or tincture of capsicum. Hair dressings with zinc and cetalkonium chloride are also used to treat dandruff. Among other ingredients in dandruff products are allantoin for its healing properties and salicylanilide. A typical antidandruff formulation contains zinc pyrithione and a detergent. Another contains salicylic acid, sulfur, lanolin, cholesterol, and petrolatum. Certain ingredients are common allergens such as sulfur, tar, lanolin, and salicylic acid and may cause allergic contact dermatitis.

DEA • The abbreviation for diethanolamine (*see*).

DEA-ACRYLINOLEATE • The diethanolamine (*see*) salt of acrylinoleic acid.

DEA-COCOAMPHODIPROPIONATE • See Coconut Oil and Quaternary Ammonium Compounds.

DEA-DODECYLBENZENESULFONATE • See Quaternary Ammonium Compounds.

DEA-ISOSTEARATE • See Diethanolamine and Isosteric Acid.

DEA-LAURAMINOPROPIONATE • The diethanolamine salt of propionic acid (*see both*).

DEA-LAURETH SULFATE • See Quaternary Ammonium Compounds.

DEA-LAURYL SULFATE • See Quaternary Ammonium Compounds.

DEA-LINOLEATE • See Linoleic Acid.

DEA-METHOXYCINNAMATE • The diethanolamine salt of methoxycinnamic acid. See Diethanolamine and Cinnamic Acid.

DEA-METHYL MYRISTATE SULFONATE • **Biterge.** See Quaternary Ammonium Compounds.

DEA-MYRETH SULFATE • The diethanolamine salt of ethyoxylated myristyl sulfate. See Quaternary Ammonium Compounds.

DEA-MYRISTATE • The diethanolamine salt of myristic acid. Also called diethanolamine myristate. See Quaternary Ammonium Compounds.

DEA-OLETH-3 • See Oleth-20.

DEA-OLETH-10 PHOSPHATE • The diethanolamine salt of a mixture of esters of phosphoric acid and oleth-10. See Quaternary Ammonium Compounds.

DEA-STYRENE/ACRYLATES/DIVINYLBENZENE COPOLYMER • The diethanolamine salt of a polymer of styrene, divinylbenzene, and two or more monomers consisting of acrylic acid, methacrylic acid or their esters. Used as an opacifier. See Acrylates, Styrene, Vinyl, and Benzene.

DECANOIC ACID • A synthetic flavoring agent that occurs naturally in anise, butter acids, oil of lemon, and oil of lime, and is used in cosmetic fragrances. Also used to flavor butter, coconut, fruit, liquor, and cheese. No known toxicity.

DECETH-7-CARBOXYLIC ACID • See Myristic Acid.

DECYL ALCOHOL • An intermediate (*see*) for surface-active agents, an antifoam agent, and a fixative in perfumes. Occurs naturally in sweet orange and ambrette seed. Derived commercially from liquid paraffin (*see*). Colorless to light yellow liquid. Used also for synthetic lubricants and as a synthetic fruit flavoring. Low toxicity in animals. No known toxicity for the skin.

DECYL BETAINE • See Betaine.

DECYL ISOSTEARATE • See Decyl Alcohol and Isostearic Acid.

DECYL MERCAPTOMETHYLIMIDAZOLE • See Imidazole.

DECYL OLEATE • See Decyl Alcohol.

DECYL SUCCINATE • **Decyl Hydrogen Succinate.** Produced by the reaction of decyl alcohol (*see*) and succinic acid (*see*). Used in the manufacture of perfumes and in cosmetic creams as a buffer and neutralizing agent. No known toxicity.

DECYL TETRADECANOL • See Decanoic Acid.

DECYLAMINE OXIDE • **Capric Dimethylamine Oxide.** See Capric Acid.

DEDM HYDANTOIN • See Hydantoin.

DEDM HYDANTOIN DILAURATE • See Hydantoin and Lauric Acid.

DEHYDRATED • With the water removed.

DEHYDROACETIC ACID • **DHA. Sodium Dehydroacetate.** A weak acid that forms a white odorless powder with an acrid taste. Used as an antienzyme agent in toothpastes to prevent tooth decay and as a preservative for shampoos. Also used as a fungi and bacteria-destroying agent in cosmetics. The presence of organic matter decreases its effectiveness. Not irritating or allergy-causing, but it is a kidney-blocking agent and can cause impaired kidney function. Large doses can cause vomiting, imbalance, and convulsions.

DELAYED HYPERSENSITIVITY • Manifested primarily as contact dermatitis due to drugs such as neomycin or to parabens (*see both*), a common preservative in topical medications. Certain multiple allergic reactions to drugs such as penicillin, nitrofurantoin, and hydantoins may also fall into this category.

DELTA CADINENE • A sequiterpenes occurring in essential oils from Juniper species and cedars (oil of cade). Used in perfumery. See Sequiterpenes.

DEMULCENT • A soothing, usually thick, oily, or creamy substance used to relieve pain in inflamed or irritated mucous surfaces. The gum acacia, for instance, is used as a demulcent.

DENATONIUM BENZOATE • A denaturant for alcohol that is to be used in cosmetics. It is intended to make alcohol unpalatable for drinking purposes and, therefore, is unpleasant to smell and taste. No known toxicity. See Denatured Alcohol.

DENATURANT • A poisonous or unpleasant substance added to alcoholic cosmetics to make them undrinkable. It is also considered a substance that changes another substance's natural qualities or characteristics.

DENATURED ALCOHOL • Ethyl alcohol must be made unfit for drinking before it can be used in cosmetics. Various substances such as denatonium benzoate (*see*) are added to alcohol to make it malodorous and obnoxious in order to completely prevent its use or recovery for drinking purposes.

DENTIFRICES • Their primary purpose is to clean accessible surfaces of the teeth with a toothbrush. Such cleansing is important to the appearance of teeth and gum health and prevents mouth odor. Dentifrices usually come in the form of a paste or powder. Despite the brand claims, most dentifrices contain similar ingredients: binders, abrasives, sudsers, humectants, flavorings, unique additives, and liquids. Binders include karaya gum, bentonite, sodium alginate, methylcellulose, carrageenan, and magnesium aluminum silicate. Among the abrasives are calcium carbonate, dibasic calcium phosphate, calcium sulfate, tricalcium phosphate, and sodium metaphosphate hydrated alumina. Sudsers include hard soap and the detergents sodium lauryl sulfate, sodium lauryl sulfoacetate, dioctyl sodium sulfosuccinate, sulfocolaurate, and sodium lauryol sarcosinate. Humectants include glycerin, proylene glycol, and sorbitol. The most popular flavors are spearmint, peppermint, wintergreen, and cinnamon, but there are also such odd ones as bourbon, rye, anise, clove, caraway, coriander, eucalyptus, nutmeg, and thyme. Fluorides are added to reduce decay; also added are antienzyme ingredients (sodium dehydroacetate) and tooth whiteners (sodium perborate). Still other ingredients in dentifrices are sodium benzoate, ammonium antiseptics, sodium coconut monoglyceride sulfonate, sodium copper chlorophyllin, chloroform, starch, sodium chloride, calcium sulfate, strontium chloride, *p*-hydroxybenzoate as a preservative, and sodium dehydroacetate. Toothpastes promoted for sensitive teeth are questionable according to the American Dental Association. The most popular toothpaste contains sodium fluoride, calcium pyrophosphate, glycerin, sorbitol, and a blend of anionic surfactants (*see* Anionic Detergents); its competitor contains sodium *n*-lauryol sarcosinate, and sodium monofluorophosphate. Complaints to the FDA about dentifrices include sore mouth and gums, tooth enamel worn away, sore tongue, and sloughing of mucous membranes. Some toothpastes contained too much chloroform, which was reduced by the manufacturer upon the FDA's request. Plaque control became the "buzz word" in the 1980s and most toothpastes promoted it.

DEODORANTS • Includes antiperspirants. It is not the normal secretions of the skin that produce an objectionable odor but the action of bacteria and chemicals on sweat that creates the unpleasant smell. The difference between deodorants and antiperspirants is in sequence. Deodorants control perspiration odors, but antiperspirants retard the flow of perspiration. Deodorants inhibit the growth of microorganisms, which produce the malodors; antiperspirants, which contain a hydrolyzing metal salt, develop a low pH (increased acidity) and inhibit moisture. The inhibiting action may be enhanced by antiseptics that deodorize. Aluminum salts are the most widely used for inhibiting perspiration; urea (*see*) may be added to neutralize the fabric-damaging acidity of the metal. Organic compounds such as hexachlorophene (*see*) inhibit the growth of skin microorganisms. Such antiseptics may be incorporated into deodorant soaps. Deodorants, formerly called "unscented toilet waters" and "sanitary liquid preparations," once contained formaldehyde or benzoic acid, which have been replaced with quaternary ammonium compounds (*see*). Deodorant-action liquid antiperspirants today usually contain aluminum chloride, urea, propylene glycol, and about 75 percent water. Deodorant-action cream antiperspirants contain aluminum chlorhydroxide, sorbitan monostearate, poloxamers, stearic acid, boric acid, petrolatum, perfume, propylene glycol, and water. Spray deodorants have the same ingredients as liquid ones but are mixed with a propellant. The aluminum, alcohol, and zinc salts in deodorants and antiperspirants can cause skin and gastrointestinal irritations. Deaths from intentional inhalation of deodorant sprays have been reported. Vision has been affected from spray in the eyes. With all deodorants there can be stinging and burning, itching, sebaceous cysts, enlarged sweat glands, pimples under the arms, and lung and throat irritation. Seven causes of lung tumors attributed to underarm deodorant sprays were reported at the 1971 American Thoracic Society meeting in Los Angeles. See Vaginal Deodorants.

DEODORIZED KEROSENE • **Deo-Base.** Derived from petroleum, it is a mobile, water-white transparent liquid that has been deodorized and decolorized by washing kerosene with fuming sulfuric acid. It is a solvent used in brilliantines, emulsified lotions and creams, and as a constituent of hand lotions. It is a skin irritant, and dermatitis often occurs. Because of its solvent action on fats, it can cause a defatting and drying of the skin. In cosmetics, however, when it is used with fatty substances, its fat-solvent action is minimized and it is considered innocuous.

DEPILATORIES • The most effective chemical hair removers yet discovered are the sulfides (*see*), particularly hydrogen sulfide, but they have an unpleasant odor that is hard to mask. Most sulfides have been replaced with salts of thioglycolic acid (*see*), which take more time to act but smell better and are not as irritating as sulfides. However, persons who have difficulty with detergent hands, ammonia, or strong soaps often have difficulty with thioglycolic depilatories. Also ingestion of thioglycolic depilatories may cause severe gastrointestinal irritation. Cream depilatories that act by dissolving the hair usually contain calcium thioglycolate, calcium carbonate, calcium hydroxide, cetyl alcohol, sodium lauryl sulfate (a detergent), water, and a strong perfume (so as to remain stable in an alkali medium). Another type of depilatory made of wax acts by hardening around the hair and pulling it out. Such products usually contain rosin, beeswax, paraffin, and petrolatum. (See above ingredients under separate listings.) Among injuries recently reported to the FDA concerning depilatories were skin irritation, headaches, scars on legs, skin burns, and rash. They can cause allergic reactions. See Flaxseed.

DEQUALINIUM CHLORIDE • See Quaternary Ammonium Compounds.

DERMATITIS • Inflammation of the skin.

DESAMIDO ANIMAL COLLAGEN • Animal collagen that has been modified to change the amide group into carboxylic acid groups to change its texture and odor for use in "youth creams."

DESAMIDOCOLLAGEN • See Desamido Animal Collagen.

DETERGENT • Any of a group of synthetic, organic, liquid, or water-soluble cleansing agents that, unlike soap, are not prepared from fats and oils and are not inactivated by hard water. Most of them are made from petroleum derivatives but vary widely in composition. The major advantage of detergents is that they do not leave a hard water scum. They also have wetting-agent and emulsifying-agent properties. Quaternary ammonium compounds (*see*), for instance, through surface action, exert cleansing and antibacterial effects. PHisoDerm is an example of a liquid detergent and Dove is an example of a solid detergent. Toxicity of detergents depends upon alkalinity. Dishwasher detergents, for instance, can be dangerously alkaline while detergents used in cosmetic products have an acidity-alkalinity ratio near normal skin, 5 to 6.5 pH.

DEXTRAN • A term applied to polysaccharides produced by bacteria growing on sugar. Used as a thickening agent in cuticle removers, it is also employed as a foam stabilizer in beer. Injection into the skin has caused cancer in rats.

DEXTRIN • **British Gum. Starch Gum.** White or yellow powder produced from starch. Used as a diluting agent for dry extracts and emulsions and as a thickener in cream and liquid cosmetics. May cause an allergic reaction.

DIACETIN • A mixture of the diesters (*see*) of glycerin (*see*) and acetic acid (*see*), used as a plasticizer, softening agent or as a solvent for cellulose derivatives, resins, and shellacs. No known toxicity.

DIACETONE ALCOHOL • Used as a solvent for nail enamels, fats, oils, waxes, and resins. Also used as a preservative. Prepared by the action of an alkali such as calcium hydroxide on acetone (*see*).

Highly flammable with a pleasant odor, it mixes easily with other solvents. May be narcotic in high concentration and has caused kidney and liver damage, as well as anemia in experimental animals when given orally.

DIACETYL • A catalyst (*see*) in the manufacture of fake nails. It occurs naturally in cheese, cocoa, pears, coffee, raspberries, strawberries, and cooked chicken, but is usually prepared by a special fermentation of glucose. It is a yellowish green liquid. Also used as a carrier of aroma of butter, vinegar, coffee, and to flavor oleomargarine. Diacetyl compounds have been associated with cancer when ingested by experimental animals.

DIAMINONAPTHALINE • A black dye. See Coal Tar.

DIAMINOPHENOL • A brown dye. See Phenol.

DIAMINOPHENOL HYDROCHLORIDE • A black-brown dye. See Phenol.

2, 4-DIAMINOPHENOL • Manufactured from aniline (*see*) and used in hair dye. For toxicity see *p*-Phenylenediamine.

2, 4-DIAMINOPHENOXYETHANOL HCL • An aromatic amine salt used as a fixative, bactericide, and insect repellent. See Quaternary Ammonium Compounds.

2, 6-DIAMINOPYRIDINE • See Pyridine.

DIAMMONIUM CITRATE • **Ammonium Salt of Citric Acid, Dibasic.** See Citric Acid.

DIAMMONIUM DITHIODIGLYCOLATE • Acetic Acid, 2,2′-dithiobis-diammonium salt used in hair removal and hair waving. See Thioglycolic Acid Compounds.

DIAMMONIUM LAURYL SULFOSUCCINATE • The ammonium salt of lauryl alcohol. See Quaternary Ammonium Compounds.

DIAMMONIUM OLEAMIDO-PEG-2-SULFOSUCCINATE • An ammonium soap used as an emulsifying agent. See Quaternary Ammonium Compounds.

DIAMMONIUM SODIUM SULFOSUCCINATE • The sodium salt of the diester of amyl alcohol and sulfosuccinic acid. A wetting agent and emulsifier. See Surfactants.

DIAMYLHYDROQUINONE • **Santovar A®.** An antioxidant for resins and oils and a polymerization inhibitor. See Hydroquinone.

DIATOMACEOUS EARTH • **Kieselguhr.** A porous and relatively pure form of silica formed from fossil remains of diatoms—one-celled algae with shells. Inert when ingested. Used in pomades, dentifrices, nail polishes, face powders, as a clarifying agent, and as an absorbent for liquids, because it can absorb about four times its weight in water. The dust can cause lung damage after long exposure to high concentrations. Not recommended for use on teeth or skin because of its abrasiveness.

DIAZO- • A compound containing two nitrogen atoms such as diazolidinyl urea (*see*), one of the newer preservatives or diazepam, a popular muscle relaxant.

DIAZO DYES • Coloring agents that contain two linked nitrogen atoms united to an aromatic group and to an acid radical. See Heliotropin.

DIAZOLIDINYL UREA • **Germall II®.** One of the newer cosmetic preservatives, not much has been reported about it except that it may be a sensitizer. See Urea.

DIBA • The abbreviation for dihydroxyisobutylamine.

DIBEHENYL/DIARACHIDYL DIMONIUM CHLORIDE • See Quaternary Ammonium Compounds.

DIBEHENYL METHYLAMINE • **Methyl Dibenehenylamine.** See Behenic Acid.

DIBEHENYLDIMONIUM CHLORIDE • See Quaternary Ammonium Compounds.

DIBENZOTHIOPHENE • **Thioxanthene. Diphenylene Sulfide.** Prepared from thioxanthrone, it gives a green fluorescence. Used in dandruff treatment shampoos and products. Colorless crystals made from alcohol, chloroform, and sulfur. Used as a psychopharmaceutical to treat mental disorders. When ingested can affect the central nervous system, the blood, and blood pressure. However, no known toxicity when applied to the skin.

DIBENZYLIDENE SORBITOL • See Sorbitol.

DIBROMOFLUORESCEIN • Used in indelible lipsticks, it is made by heating resorcinol and phthalic anhydride (*see both*) to produce fluorescent orange red crystals. Ingestion can cause gastrointestinal symptoms. Skin application can cause skin sensitivity to light, inflamed eyes, skin rash, and even respiratory symptoms. See Colors.

DIBROMOPROPAMIDINE DIISETHIONATE • The salt of isethionic acid mixed with propane. Almost insoluble in alcohol and water and fixed oils, it is used as an antiseptic and antimicrobial. May be irritating to the skin.

DIBROMOSALAN • **4, 5-Dibromosalicylanilide.** An antibacterial agent used as an antiseptic and fungicide in detergents, toilet soaps, creams, lotions, and powders. No oral toxicity reported in humans but has caused skin sensitivity to light, causing rash and swelling.

DIBUCAINE • **Nupercaine.** Bitter, water-absorbing crystals. Used as a local anesthetic for the skin, particularly in wax depilatories to prevent pain. Similar to cocaine when applied to the skin. Highly toxic when injected into the abdomens of rats; only one part per kilogram of body weight is lethal. No known toxicity is reported in humans.

DIBUTYL ADIPATE • The diester of Butyl Alcohol and Adipic Acid (*see both*). A thickener in cosmetic products.

DIBUTYL PHTHALATE • The ester of the salt of phthalic acid (*see*), which is isolated from a fungus. The colorless liquid is used as a plasticizer in nail polish, as a perfume solvent, fixative, and antifoam agent. It is also an insect repellent. Has a low toxicity but if ingested can cause gastrointestinal upset. The vapor is irritating to the eyes and mucous membranes.

DIBUTYL SEBACATE • **Sebacic Acid.** A synthetic fruit flavoring usually obtained from castor oil and used for beverages, ice cream, and baked goods. Used in fruit-fragrance cosmetics. No known toxicity.

DIBUTYLENE TETRAFURFURAL • Derived from bran, rice hulls, or corn cobs, it is used in the manufacture of medicinals and as a solvent and flavoring in cosmetics and food. Toxic when absorbed by the skin. Irritating to the eyes.

DI-t-BUTYLHYDROQUINONE • A yellow powder used as an oxidizing agent. See Hydroquinone.

DICALCIUM PHOSPHATE • Tooth polisher for dentifrices. See Calcium Phosphate.

DICAPRYL/DICAPRYLOYL DIMONIUM CHLORIDE • See Quaternary Ammonium Compounds.

DICAPRYL ADIPATE • The diester of capryl alcohol and adipic acid (*see both*).

DICAPRYLOYL CYSTINE • See Caprylic Acid and Cystine.

DICAPRYLSODIUM SULFOSUCCINATE • The sodium salt of the diester of capryl alcohol and sulfosuccinic acid. See Quaternary Ammonium Compounds.

DICETYL ADIPATE • The diester of cetyl alcohol and adipic acid (*see both*).

DICETYL THIODIPROPIONATE • The diester of cetyl alcohol and thiodipropionic acid (*see both*).

DICETYLDIMONIUM CHLORIDE • See Quaternary Ammonium Compounds.

DICHLOROBENZYL ALCOHOL • An insecticide. See Benzyl Alcohol.

DICHLOROPHENE • A fungicide and bactericide used in dentifrices, shampoos, antiperspirants, deodorant creams, powder, and toilet waters. It is a potent allergen and is closely related to hexachlorophene (*see*).

DICHLORO-m-XLENOL • A phenol used as a bactericide in soaps and as a mold inhibitor and preservative. See Phenol.

DICOCAMINE • See Coconut Acid.

DICOCODIMETHYLAMINE DILINOLEATE • The diamine salt of dimer acid and dimethyl cocamine (*see both*) used as a plasticizer. See Coconut Acid.

DICOCODIMETHYLAMINE DIMERATE • See Dicocodimethylamine Dilinoleate.

DICOCODIMONIUM CHLORIDE • See Quaternary Ammonium Compounds.

DICYCLOHEXYL SODIUM SULFOSUCCINATE • See Quaternary Ammonium Compounds.

DIDECYLDIMONIUM CHLORIDE • See Quaternary Ammonium Compounds.

DIESTER- • A compound containing two ester groupings. An ester is formed from an alcohol and an acid by eliminating water. Usually employed in fragrant liquids for artificial fruit perfumes and flavors.

DIETHANOLAMIDOOLEAMIDE DEA • See Quaternary Ammonium Compounds.

DIETHANOLAMINE • Colorless liquid or crystalline alcohol. It is used as a solvent, emulsifying agent, and detergent. Also employed in emollients for its softening properties and as a dispersing agent and humectant in other cosmetic products. It may be irritating to the skin and mucous membranes. See Ethanolamines.

DIETHANOLAMINE BISULFATE • See Ethanolamines.

DIETHOXYETHYL SUCCINATE • See Succinic Acid.

N, N-DIETHYL-m-AMINOPHENOL • See Phenol.

N, N-DIETHYL-m-AMINOPHENOL SULFATE • See Phenol.

DIETHYL ASPARATE • The diester of ethyl alcohol and aspartic acid (*see both*).

DIETHYL GLUTAMATE • See Glutamate.

DIETHYL PALMITOYL ASPARTATE • See Aspartic Acid.

DIETHYL PHTHALATE • Made from ethanol and phthalic acid (*see both*). Used as a solvent, a fixative for perfume, and a denaturant (*see*) for alcohol. It has a bitter and unpleasant taste. Irritating to mucous membranes. Produces central nervous system depression when absorbed through the skin.

DIETHYL SEBACATE • See Sebacic Acid.

DIETHYL TOLUAMIDE • Made from *m*-toluoyl chloride and diethylamine in benzene or ether. A liquid soluble in water, it is used as an insect repellent. Irritating to the eyes and mucous membranes but not to the skin. Ingestion can cause central nervous system disturbances.

DIETHYLAMINE • Used in detergent soaps. Prepared from menthol (*see*) and ammonia (*see*), very soluble in water, and forms a strong alkali. Has a fishy odor. Irritating to the skin and mucous membranes.

DIETHYLAMINO METHYL COUMARIN • See Coumarin.

DIETHYLAMINOETHYL PEG-5-LAURATE • See Polyethylene Glycol and Lauric Acid.

DIETHYLAMINOETHYL STEARAMIDE • See Diethylamine.

DIETHYLAMINOETHYL STEARATE • See Stearic Acid and Amines.

DIETHYLENE GLYCOL • Made by heating ethylene oxide and glycol. A clear, water-absorbing, almost colorless liquid; it is mixable with water, alcohol, and acetone. Used as a solvent, humectant, and plasticizer in cosmetic creams and hair sprays. A wetting agent (*see*) that enhances skin absorption. Can be fatal if swallowed. Not usually irritating to the skin, but can be absorbed through the skin, and the use of glycols on extensive areas of the body is considered hazardous.

DIETHYLENE GLYCOL DIOCTANOATE/DIISONOATE • Used in hair sprays. See Diethene Glycol.

DIETHYLENE GLYCOLAMINE/EPICHLOROHYDRIN/PIPERAZINE COPOLYMER • A polymer formed by the reaction of a mixture of diethylene glycolamine and piperazine with epichlorohydrin, used as a solvent. See Epichlorohydrin.

DIETHYLENE TRICASEINAMIDE • See Casein.

DIFFUSIVE • A term used to describe a perfume compound odor which spreads quickly and widely. This quality is good in perfumes but may be disliked in other products such as hair sprays and deodorants.

DIGALLOYL TRIOLEATE • From digallic acid and oleic acid. An oily sunscreen ingredient devoid of anesthetic properties and stable under long periods of ultraviolet radiation. It may cause the skin to break out and redden when exposed to light.

DIGLYCERYL STEARATE MALATE • The mixed ester of stearic acid and malic acid and glycerin polymer (*see all*).

DIHEPTYL SODIUM SULFOSUCCINATE • Available as a waxlike solid. Used as a wetting agent in bath oil preparation. No known toxicity to the skin.

DIHEPTYLUNDECYL ADIPATE • See Adipic Acid.

DIHEXYL ADIPATE • A low-temperature plasticizer. See Adipic Acid.

DIHEXYL SODIUM SULFOSUCCINATE • See Quaternary Ammonium Compounds.

DIHYDROABIETYL ALCOHOL • See Abietyl Alcohol; Abietic Acid.

DIHYDROABIETYL METHACRYLATE • See Abietyl Alcohol.

DIHYDROACETIC ACID • Used in tanning creams. See Acetic Acid.

DIHYDROCHOLESTEROL • See Cholesterol.

DIHYDROCHOLESTERYL OCTYLDECANOATE • See Cholesterol and Octyldecanoic Acid.

DIHYDROCHOLETH-15 • The polyethylene glycol (*see*) ether of dihydrocholesterol. See Cholesterol.

DIHYDROCHOLETH-30 • The polyethylene glycol (*see*) ether of dihydrocholesterol. See Cholesterol.

DIHYDROGENATED TALLOW BENZYLMONIUMCHLORIDE • See Quaternary Ammonium Compounds.

DIHYDROGENATED TALLOW METHYLAMINE • See Tallow and Hydrogenated.

DIHYDROGENATED TALLOW PHTHALATE • See Tallow.

DIHYDROPHYTOSTERYL OCTYLDECANOATE • See Octyldecanoic Acid.

DIHYDROXYACETEONE • The Food and Drug Administration declared in 1973 that this color additive is safe and suitable for use in cosmetics or drugs that are applied to color the skin. A white powder that turns colorless in liquid form, it colors the skin an orange-brown shade, giving it a suntanned appearance. It is an ingredient in some suntan lotions for use indoors without sunlight. Obtained by the action of certain bacteria on glycerol, it has a sweet taste and characteristic odor. It is a strong reducing agent (*see*). It is converted by alkali to the fruit sugar fructose. Lethal when injected in large doses into rats. No known skin toxicity and the FDA has exempted it from color additive certification, which means there is no need to test each batch as a means of protecting consumers as there is with coal tar colors. However, it can cause allergic contact dermatitis (*see*).

DIHYDROXYACETONE • Coloring for externally applied cosmetics intended to impart a color to the human body (fake suntan). Permanently listed in 1973. Also used as an emulsifier, humectant, and fungicide. No known toxicity.

DIHYDROXYETHYL C9-11 ALKOXYPROPYLAMINE OXIDE • See Quaternary Ammonium Compounds.

DIHYDROXYETHYL C12-15 ALKOXYPROPYLAMINE OXIDE • See Thioglycolic Compounds.

DIHYDROXYETHYL COCAMINE OXIDE • See Coconut Oil.

DIHYDROXYETHYL SOYA GLYCINATE • See Quaternary Ammonium Compounds.

DIHYDROXYETHYL SOYAMINE DIOLEATE • The diester of oleic acid and dihydroxyethyl soyamine. See Thioglycolic Compounds.

DIHYDROXYETHYL STEARAMINE OXIDE • See Stearic Acid.
DIHYDROXYETHYL STEARYL GLYCINATE • See Quaternary Ammonium Compounds.
DIHYDROXYETHYL TALLOW AMINE OXIDE • See Tallow.
DIHYDROXYETHYLOLEYL GLYCINATE • See Glycine.
DIISOBUTYL SODIUM SULFOSUCCINATE • The sodium salt of the diester of isobutyl alcohol and sulfosuccinic acid, used as an alkalizer. See Succinic Acid.
DIISOCETYL ADIPATE • The diester of hexadecyl alcohol and adipic acid. See Adipic Acid.
DIISOPROPANOLAMINE • See Isopropylamine.
DIISOPROPYL ADIPATE • An emollient that helps prevent dryness and protects the skin by softening and lubricating it to minimize moisture loss. See Adipic Acid.
DIISOPROPYL DILINOLEATE • See Dilinoleate.
DIISOPROPYL DIMERATE • See Dilinoleate.
DIISOPROPYL SEBACATE • See Isopropyl Alcohol and Sebacic Acid.
DILAURYL CITRATE • See Lauryl Alcohol and Citric Acid.
DILAURYL THIODIPROPIONATE • An antioxidant. White crystalline flakes with a sweet odor. No known toxicity.
DILAURYLDIMONIUM CHLORIDE • See Quaternary Ammonium Compounds.
DILINOLEATE • **Dimer Acid.** Widely used as an emulsifier, it is derived from Linoleic Acid (*see*).
DILINOLEIC ACID • See Linoleic Acid.
DILUENT • Any component of a color additive mixture that is not of itself a color additive, and has been intentionally mixed therein to facilitate the uses of the mixture in coloring cosmetics or in coloring the human body, food, and drugs. The diluent may serve another functional purpose in cosmetics, as, for example, emulsifying or stabilizing. Ethylcellulose is an example.
DIMER ACID • See Dilinoleate.
DIMETHICONE • **Dimethicone Copolyol.** A silicone (*see*) oil, white, viscous, used as an ointment base ingredient, as a topical drug vehicle, and as a skin protectant. Very low toxicity.
DIMETHICONE COPOLYOL • See Dimethicone.
DIMETHICONOL • See Dimethicone.
DIMETHYL BEHENAMINE • See Behenic Acid.
DIMETHYL BRASSYLATE • Used in polyethylene films and water-resistant products.
DIMETHYL COCAMINE • See Coconut Oil.

DIMETHYL HYDROGENATED TALLOWAMINE • See Hydrogenated Tallowamine.

N, N-DIMETHYL-N-HYDROXYETHYL-3-NITRO-p-PHENYLENE DIAMINE • See *p*-Phenylenediamine.

DIMETHYL ISOSORBIDE • See Sorbitol.

DIMETHYL LAURAMINE • See Lauric Acid.

DIMETHYL LAURAMINE OLEATE • See Lauric Acid and Oleic Acid.

DIMETHYL MYRISTAMINE • See Myristic Acid.

DIMETHYL OCTYNEDIOL • See Citronellol.

DIMETHYL PALMITAMINE • See Palmitic Acid.

N, N-DIMETHYL-p-PHENYLENE DIAMINE SULFATE • See *p*-Phenylenediamine.

DIMETHYL PHOSPHATE • See Phosphoric Acid.

DIMETHYL PHTHALATE • **Phthalic Esters.** A colorless, aromatic oil insoluble in water. A solvent, especially for musk (*see*). Used to compound calamine lotion and as an insect repellent. See Phthalic Acid for toxicity.

DIMETHYL SOYAMINE • See Soya Acid.

DIMETHYL STEARAMINE • See Stearic Acid.

DIMETHYL SULFATE • **Sulfuric Acid. Dimethyl Ester.** Colorless, oily liquid used as a methylating agent (to add methyl) in the manufacture of cosmetic dyes, perfumes, and flavorings. Methyl salicylate is an example (*see*). Extremely hazardous, dimethyl sulfate has delayed lethal qualities. Liquid produces severe blistering, necrosis of the skin. Sufficient skin absorption can result in serious poisoning. Vapors hurt the eyes. Ingestion can cause paralysis, prostration, kidney damage, coma, and death.

DIMETHYL SULFONE • An organic compound that is used as an emulsifier. See Sulfonated Oils.

DIMETHYL TALLOWAMINE • See Tallow.

DIMETHYL-o-TOLUIDINE • Coal tar derivative. Lightly yellow liquid becoming reddish brown when exposed to air. Used in the manufacture of hair dyes. See Aniline Dyes for toxicity.

DIMETHYLAMINE • Prepared from methanol (*see*) and ammonia (*see*), it is very soluble in water and in alcohol. Used in the manufacture of soaps and detergents. It also promotes hardening of plastic nails. Irritating to the skin and mucous membranes.

DIEMTHYLAMINOETHYL METHYLCRYLATE • See Acrylates.

DIEMTHYLAMINOPROPYL OLEAMIDE • See Oleic Acid.

DIEMTHYLAMINOPROPYL STEARAMIDE • See Stearic Acid.

3-DIEMTHYLAMINOPROPYLAMINE • See Ethanolamines.

DIMETHYLOL UREA • A preservative. May release Formaldehyde (*see*).

DIMYRISTYL THIODIPROPIONATE • The diester of myristyl alcohol and thiodipropionic acid (*see both*).

2, 5-DINITROPHENOL • Yellow crystals made from dinitrobenzene. Used in the manufacture of hair dyes. See *p*-Phenylenediamine for toxicity.

DINKUM OIL • See Eucalyptus Oil.

DINONOXYNOL-9-CITRATE • The diester of citric acid and nonoxynol-9. See Citric Acid and Nonoxynol-2.

DINONYL PHENOL • See Phenols.

DIOCTYL- • Containing two octyl groups. Octyl is obtained from octane, a liquid paraffin found in petroleum.

DIOCTYL ADIPATE • See Adipic Acid.

DIOCTYL DILINOLEATE • See Dilinoleic Acid.

DIOCTYL MALEATE • See Malic Acid.

DIOCTYL PHTHALATE • An oily ester (*see*) used chiefly as a plasticizer, solvent, and fixative in perfumes and nail enamels. Because of its bitter taste, also used as a denaturant for alcohol (*see*). Irritating to mucous membranes, and a central nervous system depressant if absorbed through the skin.

DIOCTYL SODIUM SULFOSUCCINATE • **Docustae Sodium.** A waxlike solid that is very soluble in water. It is used as a dispersing and solubilizing agent in foods and cosmetics. No known skin toxicity.

DIOCTYL SUCCINATE • A white wax, soluble in water, it is a wetting agent used in compounding calamine lotion. No known skin toxicity.

DIOCTYLAMINE • **Di-2-Ethylhexyl-Amine.** See Amines.

DIOLETH-8-PHOSPHATE • The mixture of diesters of phosphoric acid and oleth-8 (*see both*).

DIPA • The abbreviation for diisopropanolamine.

DIPALMETHYL HYDROXYETHYLMONIUM METHOSULFATE • See Quaternary Ammonium Compounds.

DIPENTENE • See Limonene.

DIPERODON HYDROCHLORIDE • Obtained by condensing a piperidine and glycerol chlorohydrin with an alkali. Bitter taste. Soluble in alcohol. Used as an anesthetic in solution. No known toxicity.

DIPHENHYDRAMINE HCL • The amine salt that is used as an antihistamine and central nervous system depressant. Toxic.

DIPHENOLIC ACID • Prepared by condensing phenol (*see*) with another acid. Soluble in hot water. It is an intermediate for lubricating oil additives. Used in cosmetics as a surfactant and plasticizer. See Phenol for toxicity.

DIPHENYL METHANE • **Benzyl Benzene.** Used chiefly as a perfume in soaps. Prepared from methylene chloride and benzene with aluminum chloride as a catalyst. Smells like oranges and geraniums. A petroleum distillate and like all such substances, when imposed, can produce local skin irritation and, more rarely, a skin reaction to sunlight, which includes prickling, swelling, and sometimes pigmentation.

DIPHENYLENE SULFIDE • See Dibenzothiophene.

DIPOTASSIUM AZELATE • The salt of azelic acid. Used as a plasticizer. No known toxicity.

DIPOTASSIUM EDTA • See Ethylenediamine Tetraacetic Acid.

DIPOTASSIUM GLYCYRRHIZATE • The dipotassium salt of glycyrrhizic acid (*see*).

DIPOTASSIUM PHOSPHATE • A sequestrant. A white grain, very soluble in water. Used as a buffering agent to control the degree of acidity in solutions. It is used medicinally as a saline cathartic. No known toxicity.

DIPROPYLENE GLYCOL • See Propylene Glycol.

DIPROPYLENE GLYCOL DIBENZOATE • Light-colored liquid that is used as a plasticizer. See Propylene Glycol and Benzoic Acid.

DIPROPYLENE GLYCOL SALICYLATE • Insoluble in water, it is used as a plasticizer and in sunscreen lotions. See Propylene Glycol and Salicylates.

DIRECT BLACK 51 • Classed as a diazo color (*see*).

DIRECT BROWN 1 • **Benzochrome. Brown G. Benzamine Brown.** See Azo Dyes and Direct Dyes.

DIRECT DYES • These compounds need salts to be effective. When combined with aniline, they improve in fastness. They are used in hair dyes and in some pigments. See Aniline Dyes for toxicity.

DIRECT RED 23 • **Fast Scarlet 4BSA.** Classed chemically as a diazo color. See Colors.

DIRECT RED 80 • Classed chemically as a diazo color, it is a brilliant red. See Coal Tar.

DIRECT RED 81 • **Benzo Fast. Red 8 BL.** A diazo dye. See Azo Dyes and Direct Dyes.

DIRECT VIOLET 48 • A diazo dye. See Azo Dyes and Direct Dyes.

DIRECT YELLOW 12 • **Chrysophenine G.** A diazo dye. See Azo Dyes and Direct Dyes.

DISELENIUM SULFIDE • An antidandruff agent used in prescription items and over-the-counter brands. See Selenium Sulfide.

DISODIUM ADENOSINE TRIPHOSPHATE • A preservative derived from adenylic acid. See Adenosine Triphosphate.

DISODIUM C12-15 PARETH SULFOSUCCINATE • See Surfactants.

DISODIUM CETEARYL SULFOSUCCINATE • The disodium salt of cetearyl alcohol and sulfosuccinic acid (*see both*).

DISODIUM COCAMIDO MIPA-SULFOSUCCINATE • See Coconut Oil and Surfactants.

DISODIUM DECETH-6 SULFOSUCCINATE • See Sulfonated Oils.

DISODIUM EDTA • Permanently listed as a coloring for shampoos in 1974. See Ethylenediamine Tetraacetic Acid (EDTA).

DISODIUM EDTA-COPPER • **Cooper Versenate.** Used as a sequestering agent. See Ethylene Tetraacetic Acid for toxicity.

DISODIUM HYDROGENATED COTTONSEED GLYCERIDE SULFOSUCCINATE • See Sulfonated Oils.

DISODIUM HYDROGENATED TALLOW GLUTAMATE • See Hydrogenated Tallow.

DISODIUM ISODECYL SULFOSUCCINATE • See Sulfonated Oils.

DISODIUM ISOSTEARAMINO MEA-SULFOSUCCINATE • See Surfactants.

DISODIUM LANETH-5-SULFOSUCCINATE • See Sulfonated Oils.

DISODIUM LAURAMIDE PEG-2 SULFOSUCCINATE • See Surfactants.

DISODIUM LAURAMIDO MEA-SULFOSUCCINATE • See Surfactants.

DISODIUM LAURETHSULFOSUCCINATE • See Surfactants.

DISODIUM LAURIMINODIPROPIONATE • See Surfactants.

DISODIUM LAURYL SULFOSUCCINATE • See Surfactants.

DISODIUM MONOCOCAMIDOSULFOSUCCINATE • See Dioctyl Sodium Sulfosuccinate.

DISODIUM MONOLAURETHSULFOSUCCINATE • See Dioctyl Sodium Sulfosuccinate.

DISODIUM MONOLAURYLAMIDOSULFOSUCCINATE • See Dioctyl Sodium Sulfosuccinate.

DISODIUM MONOLAURYLSULFOSUCCINATE • See Dioctyl Sodium Sulfosuccinate.

DISODIUM MONOMYRISTAMIDOSULFOSUCCINATE • See Dioctyl Sodium Sulfosuccinate.

DISODIUM MONOOLEAMIDOSULFOSUCCINATE • See Dioctyl Sodium Sulfosuccinate.

DISODIUM MONORICINOLEAMIDO MEA-SULFOSUCCINATE • See Sulfonated Oils.

DISODIUM MYRISTAMIDO MEA-SULFOSUCCINATE • See Dioctyl Sodium Sulfosuccinate.

DISODIUM NONOXYNOL-10 SULFOSUCCINATE • See Surfactants.

DISODIUM OLEAMIDO MIPA-SULFOSUCCINATE • See Surfactants.

DISODIUM OLEAMIDO PEG-2 SULFOSUCCINATE • See Surfactants.

DISODIUM OLEYL SULFOSUCCINATE • See Surfactants.

DISODIUM PARETH-25 SULFOSUCCINATE • See Surfactants.

DISODIUM PEG-4 COCAMIDO MIPA-SULFOSUCCINATE • See Surfactants.

DISODIUM PYROPHOSPHATE • **Sodium Pyrophosphate.** An emulsifier and texturizer used to decrease the loss of fluid from a compound. It is GRAS for use in foods as a sequestrant. See Sodium Pyrophosphate.

DISODIUM RICINOLEAMIDO MEA-SULFOSUCCINATE • Widely used as a surfactant, it is the disodium salt of ethanolamide and sulfosuccinic acid (*see both*).

DISODIUM STEARMIDO MEA-SULFOSUCCINATE • See Surfactants.

DISODIUM STEARMINODIPROPIONATE • See Steareth-2.

DISODIUM STEARYL SULFOSUCCINATE • See Sulfonated Oils.

DISODIUM SUCCINATE • See Succinic Acid.

DISODIUM TALLAMIDO MEA-SULFOSUCCINATE • See Surfactants.

DISODIUM TALLOWAMINODIPROPIONATE • See Surfactants.

DISODIUM WHEAT GERMAMIDO MEA-SULFOSUCCINATE • See Surfactants.

DISODIUM WHEAT GERMAMIDO PEG-2 SULFOSUCCINATE • See Wheat Germ Oil and Surfactants.

DISOYADIMONIUM CHLORIDE • See Quaternary Ammonium Compounds.

DISOYAMINE • See Soybean Oil.

DISPERSANT • A dispersing agent, such as polyphosphate, for promoting the formation and stabilization of a dispersion of one substance in another. An emulsion, for instance, would consist of a dispersed substance and the medium in which it is dispersed.

DISPERSE BLACK 9 • **Nacelan Diazine Black JS.** Classed chemically as an azo color (*see*).

DISPERSE BLUE 1 • **1, 4, 5, 8-Tetraaminoanthraquinone.** Classed chemically as an anthraquinone (*see*) color.

DISPERSE BLUE 3 • **Disperse Fast Blue.** An anthraquinone (*see*) dye. See also Disperse Dyes.

DISPERSE BLUE 3:1 • **Nacelan Brilliant Blue NR.** Classed chemically as an anthraquinone (*see*) color.

DISPERSE DYES • These compounds are only slightly soluble in water but are readily dispersed with the aid of sulfated oils. Used on nylon knit goods, sheepskins, and furs, they are in human hair dyes as well as resins, oils, fats, and waxes. Not permanently listed as safe.

DISPERSE VIOLET 1 • Classed as an anthraquinone color (*see*).

DISPERSE VIOLET 4 • **Solvent Violet 12.** Classed chemically as an anthraquinone color. See Colors.

DISPERSE VIOLET 11 • **Nacelan Violet 5RL.** Classed chemically as an anthraquinone color. See Colors.

DISPERSE YELLOW 1 • **Disperse Fast Yellow PR.** See Disperse Dyes.

DISPERSE YELLOW 3 • **Disperse Fast Yellow. Yellow G.** A monoazo dye. See Azo Dyes and Disperse Dyes.

DISTARCH PHOSPHATE • A combination of starch and sodium metaphosphate. It is a water softener, sequestering agent, and texturizer. It is used in dandruff shampoos. No known toxicity.

DISTEARETH-6 DIMONIUM CHLORIDE • See Quaternary Ammonium Compounds.

DISTEARYL THIODIPROPIONATE • The diester of stearyl alcohol and thiodipropionic acid used as a stabilizer (*see all*).

DISTEARYLDIMONIUM CHLORIDE • See Quaternary Ammonium Compounds.

DISTEARYLDIMETHYLAMINE DILINOLEATE • See Dimer Acid.

DISTEARYLDIMETHYLAMINE DIMERATE • See Dimer Acid.

DISTILLED • The result of evaporation and subsequent condensation of a liquid, as when water is boiled and steam is condensed.

DITALLOWDIMONIUM CHLORIDE • See Quaternary Ammonium Compounds and Tallow.

DI-TEA-PALMITOYL ASPARTATE • See Aspartic Acid.

DITHIODIGLYCOLIC ACID • See Thioglycolic Compounds.

DITRIDECYL ADIPATE • The diester of tridecyl alcohol and adipic acid (*see both*).

DITRIDECYL DILINOLEATE • The diester of tridecyl alcohol and dilinoleic acid. See Dilinoleate.

DITRIDECYL SODIUM SULFOSUCCINATE • See Sulfonated Oils.

DITRIDECYL THIODIPROPIONATE • The diester of tridecyl alcohol and thiodipropionic acid (*see both*).

DM HYDANTOIN • See Hydantoin.

DMDM • The abbreviation for diemethylol dimethyl.

DMDM HYDANTOIN • A preservative. May release formaldehyde (*see*). See also Hydantoin.

DMHF • The abbreviation for the resin formed by heating hydantoin and formaldehyde (*see both*).

DODECANEDIONIC ACID/CETEARYL ALCOHOL/GLYCOL COPOLYMER • The polymer of dodecanedioic acid, cetearyl alcohol, and ethylene glycol monomers, used to form a wax (*see all*).

DOCECYL GALLATE • The ester of gallic acid derived from tannin and used in ink.

DODECYLBENZENE SULFONIC ACID • A sulfonic acid anionic (*see*) detergent. Made from petroleum. May cause skin irritation. If swallowed will cause vomiting.

DODECYLBENZYLTRIMONIUM CHLORIDE • See Quaternary Ammonium Compounds.

DODECYLTETRADECANOL • See Myristic Acid.

DODECYLXYLDITRIMONIUM CHLORIDE • See Quaternary Ammonium Compounds.

DODOXYNOL-5, -6, -7, -9, -12 • See Phenols.

DOLOMITE • A common mineral, colorless to white or yellowish gray, containing calcium, phosphorus, and magnesium. It is one of the most important raw materials for magnesium and its salts. It is used in toothpaste as a whitener. No known toxicity.

DOMIPHEN BROMIDE • Clear, colorless, odorless crystalline powder with a slightly bitter taste. Soluble in water, but incompatible with soap, it is used as an antiseptic and detergent in cosmetics. No known toxicity.

DRIED BUTTERMILK • The dehydration of the liquid recovered from churning cow's milk. Used as an emollient.

DRIED EGG YOLK • The dehydration of the yolk of chicken eggs used in shampoos.

DROMETRIOZOLE • A derivative of benzene used as a solvent in nail polish. See Benzene.

DROSERA • **Common Sundew**. A dried flowering plant that grows in Europe, Asia, and in North America as far south as Florida. Formerly used to treat chest disorders. Used as a mild astringent in skin lotions and perfumes. No known toxicity.

DRY SHAMPOOS • Usually consist of a water-absorbent powder such as talc (*see*) and a mild alkali. The product is placed in the hair and then brushed out, carrying with it any oil or dirt. Many women use baby powder or bath powder to "dry" wash their hair. See Shampoos.

DRYING AGENTS • See Rosin.

DRY-OUT • Just as the Top-Note (*see*) is the first impression of a perfume, this is the last impression. It may begin to become apparent after an hour or several hours or even the next day. The Dry-Out notes show the fixative (*see*) effects of the components and will reveal the Body-Note (*see*). The Dry-Out depicts the tenacity of the composition, and the fixative's ability to hold the scent. The better the perfume, usually, the better the Dry-Out.

DULCAMARA EXTRACT • **Bitter Sweet Nightshade.** Extract of the dried stems of *Solanum dulcamara*. Belonging to the family of the nightshades, it is used as a preservative. The ripe berries are used for pies and jams. The unripened berries are deadly. It is made into an ointment by herbalists to treat skin cancers and burns. It induces sweating. See also Horse Nettle.

DUSTING POWDER • See Powder.

E

EAR ALLERGY • The condition, *Serous otitis*, which is fullness in the ears associated with the formation of thick mucous behind the eardrum is sometimes an allergic phenomenon. The first sympton may be hearing loss, and allergies of the nose contribute to the problem. Allergic contact dermatitis in and around the ear is not uncommon. Nickel in earrings, eye glasses, hair dye, cologne or perfume, ear drops, and ointments applied to the ear are among the most common offenders.

EAR LOBE • Frequently a site of allergic contact dermatitis from earrings containing nickel. May also be affected by hair products.

EARTH WAX • General name for ozocerite, ceresin, and montan waxes. See Waxes.

EGG • Particularly associated with eczema in children. May also cause reactions ranging from hives to anaphylaxis. Eggs may also be found in root beer, soups, sausage, coffee, and in cosmetics.

EGG OIL • A mixture of the fat-soluble emollients and emulsifiers extracted from the whole egg. Provides protection against dehydration and has lubricating and antifriction properties when rubbed on the skin.

EGG POWDER • Used in many cosmetics including shampoos, ointments, creams, face masks, and bath preparations. Dehydrated egg powder is often incorporated into shampoos on the theory that protein is beneficial to damaged hair. There is little scientific evidence to substantiate this, but the egg coating does make the hair more cohesive and more manageable. The oil of egg yolk, which mixes easily with other oils, is used in ointment bases and cosmetic creams. Egg albumin is used in facial masks to give the characteristic tight feeling. For a homemade egg treatment four beaten eggs are required, with a jigger of rum mixed in. Then the solution is massaged into the scalp, followed by a rinse with cold (never hot) water; the hot water would make the egg sticky. For persons not allergic to egg products, the ingredient is harmless.

EGG YOLK • The yellow matter of chicken eggs.

EGG YOLK EXTRACT • The exact of egg yolk. See Egg Oil.

ELASTIN • A protein in connective tissue.

ELASTOMERS • Used for face masks. Rubberlike substances that can be stretched from twice to many times their length. Upon their release they rapidly return to almost their original length. Synthetic elastomers have similar properties and are actually superior to the natural ones. They have been in use since 1930. Thiokol was the first commercial synthetic elastomer. It is a condensation polymer (*see*), for example, neoprene, and silicone rubber.

ELDER FLOWERS • **Sambucus.** Extracted from the honey-scented flowers of the elder tree. Used in skin and eye lotions and bath preparations. Mildly astringent, it supposedly keeps the skin soft and clean. Old-time herb doctors used it. Elder flowers increase perspiration and therefore reduce body water. Used to scent perfumes and lotions. No known toxicity.

ELDERBERRY JUICE POWDER • Dried powder from the juice of the edible berry of a North American elder tree. Used for red coloring. Nontoxic.

ELEMI • A soft, yellowish, fragrant, plastic resin from several Asiatic and Philippine trees. Slightly soluble in water but readily soluble in alcohol. Used for gloss and adhesion in nail lacquer and to scent soaps and colognes. No known toxicity.

EMBRYO EXTRACT • An oil extracted from fetal calves, often promoted in "youth-restoring" creams and lotions.

EMOLLIENTS • **Creams, Lotions, Skin Softeners, and Moisturizers.** An emollient by whatever designation—night cream, hand cream, eye cream, skin softener, moisturizer, and so on—remains an emollient. The selection of a cream, spray, or lotion is really a matter of taste and the influence of advertising and packaging. The AMA's Committee on Cutaneous Health finds little difference between liquid, cream, lotion, drop, or dew emollients since they all perform the same function. These preparations do help to make the skin feel softer and smoother, to reduce the roughness, cracking, and irritation of the skin, and they may possibly help retard the fine wrinkles of aging. However, in any application of oil to the skin, what happens is that the roughened, scaly surface is coated with a smooth film, cementing down the dry flakes. And although the oil retards the evaporation of water, as far as the oil penetrating the skin, dermatologists say this has been overemphasized. Any dryness would be in the layer known as the stratum corneum, and it is due to insufficient water in the skin. Exposure to low humidities in artificially heated or cooled rooms, aging, and heredity may all contribute to dry skin. The ancient Greek physician, Galen, is credited with making the first emollient of beeswax, spermaceti, almond oil, borax, and rosewater (*see all*). Most emollients today are still a mixture of oils. If the oils have a low melting point, the emollient will feel greasy; with a high melting point, it disappears from the skin. Because emollients are usually colorless, and seem to be absorbed rapidly, they are called vanishing creams. But, according to the AMA, it is the water in such creams, and not the oil that benefits dry skin. Experiments with a specimen of calloused skin placed in oils for three years could not make it flexible again. However, when a brittle piece of callus is placed in water, it soon becomes flexible. Most emollients are intended to remain on the skin for a significant period of time, including overnight. Petrolatum (Vaseline) is one of the least expensive and one of the most efficient emollients. It tends to keep the loss of natural moisture from the skin at a minimum. Next in efficiency and also inexpensive is zinc oxide (*see*). Mineral oil, vegetable oil, and shortening also work well. All may be found on your supermarket shelf. Vitamin A and hormone creams (*see both*) are added to keep the skin moist and supple. However effective they are in doing so is a matter of medical controversy. Glycerin (*see*) is widely used in emollients and has been found to work best in humid air because it draws moisture from the air. (When the humidity is high, most people do not need emollients.) A simple condition or emollient cream may contain lanolin, petrolatum, and oil of sweet almond. A moisturizing cream may contain mineral oil, stearic acid, lanolin, beeswax, sorbitol, and polysorbates (*see all*). Among other ingredients in emollients and lotions are natural fatty oils such as olive, coconut, corn, peach kernel, peanut, and sesame oils in hydrogenated form; natural fats such as cocoa butter and lard; synthetic fatty oils such as paraffin; alcohols such as cetyl, stearyl, and oleyl; emulsifiers, preservatives, and antioxidants, including Vitamin E and paraben; and antibacterials and perfumes, especially methol and camphor (*see all*). Among the problems with creams and lotions reported to the FDA were body and hand rashes, swelling of the eyes and face, blood vessels on the surface of the nose, red and painful eyes, burning of the face, and skin eruptions and irritations.

EMULSIFIERS • Agents used to assist in the production of an emulsion. Among common emulsifiers in cosmetics are stearic acid soaps such as potassium and sodium stearates, sulfated alcohols such as sodium lauryl sulfate, polysorbates, poloxamers, and pegs, and sterols such as cholesterol. (See all under separate listings.)
EMULSIFYING OIL • **Soluble Oil.** An oil, which when mixed with water, produces a milky emulsion. Sodium sulfonate is an example.
EMULSIFYING WAX • Waxes that are treated so that they mix more easily.
EMULSION • What is formed when two or more non-mixable liquids are shaken so thoroughly together that the mixture continues to appear to be homogenized. Most oils form emulsions with water.
ENCAPSULATION • Scents can be encapsulated in gelatin and are released when a fragrance product is placed in hot water. Some microencapsulated products contain coated perfume granules that are so small they give the impression of free-flowing powder.
ENFLEURAGE • The technique of making perfumes from flowers, such as roses and orange blossoms that cannot be subjected to steam distillation. It includes the use of glass trays that are lined with lard, on which flowers picked early in the morning are scattered. The trays are stacked on one another. The next day the flowers are removed from the fat and replaced with fresh ones. The cycle is repeated for several weeks. The lard is then scraped from the trays and mixed with alcohol. The alcohol in turn is removed by distillation, leaving behind the flower-scented essential oil, or "absolute." The process usually takes 36 days and is therefore expensive and done only for fine perfumes.
ENGLISH OAK EXTRACT • Extract of the bark of the *Quercus robur*. The wood is used for cabinet-making. The extract is used in chestnut brown dye.
ENZYME • Any of a unique class of proteins which catalyze a broad spectrum of biochemical reactions. Enzymes are formed in living cells. One enzyme can cause a chemical process that no other enzyme can do. Among the enzymes used in cosmetics are amylase and Papain (*see both*).
EOSIN • Red crystalline powder soluble in alcohol and acetic acid. It is used as a coloring in cosmetic products. See Fluorescein.
EOSINE YELLOW • See Tetrabromofluorescein.
EPICHLOROHYDRIN • A colorless liquid with an odor resembling chloroform. It is soluble in water but mixes readily with alcohol and ether. Used as a solvent for cosmetic resins and nitrocellulose (*see*) and in the manufacture of varnishes, lacquers, and cements for celluloid articles; also a modifier for food starch. A strong skin irritant and

sensitizer. Daily administration of 1 milligram per kilogram of body weight to skin killed all of a group of rats in four days, indicating a cumulative potential. Chronic exposure is known to cause kidney damage. A 30-minute exposure to air concentrations of 8,300 parts per million was lethal to mice. Poisoned animals showed cyanosis, muscular relaxation or paralysis, convulsions, and death.

EPILATORIES • Waxlike products that are softened by heat and applied when cool and then "yanked" off, taking embedded hair with them. (Some epilatories do not have to be heated.) They may be formulated from roses, paraffin, beeswax, ceresin, carnauba wax, mineral and linseed oils, and petrolatum. (See ingredients under separate listings.) Sometimes benzocaine is added in low concentrations for its local anesthetic effect. Nontoxic. See Depilatories.

ERGOCALCIFEROL • Vitamin D_2.

ERUCAMIDE • **Erucylamide.** An aliphatic amide slightly soluble in alcohol and acetone. Used as a foam stabilizer, solvent for waxes, resins, and emulsions, and as an antiblock agent for polyethylene.

ERUCYL ARACHIDATE • The ester of erucyl alcohol and arachidic acid. See Arachidic Acid.

ERYCYL ERUCATE • The ester of erucyl alcohol and erucic acid. A fatty alcohol derived from erucic acid used as a lubricant, surfactant, and in plastics and textiles.

ERYTHORBIC ACID • **Isoascorbic Acid.** Antioxidant. White, slightly yellow crystals, which darken on exposure to light. Isoascorbic acid contains $\frac{1}{20}$th the vitamin capacity of ascorbic acid (*see*). Nontoxic.

ERYTHROSINE • Sodium or potassium salt of tetraiodofluorescein, a coal tar derivative. A brown powder that becomes red in solution. FD & C Red No. 3 is an example. It is used in rouge. See Coal Tar for toxicity.

ESCIN • A saponin occurring in the seeds of the horse chestnut tree, *Aesculus hippocastanum*. Practically insoluble in water, it is used as a sunburn protective.

ESCULIN • Occurs in the bark and leaves of the horse chestnut tree. It has been used as a skin protectant in ointments and creams. No known toxicity.

ESSENCE • An extract of a substance that retains its fundamental or most desirable properties in concentrated form, such as a fragrance or flavoring.

ESSENCE OF MIRBANE • **Nitrobenzene.** Used to scent cheap soap. A colorless to pale yellow, oily, poisonous liquid (nitric acid and benzene). It is rapidly absorbed through the skin. Workers are warned not to get it in their eyes or on their skin. Workers are also warned not to breath the vapor. Exposure to essence of mirbane may cause headaches, drowsiness, nausea, vomiting, lack of oxygen in the blood (methemoglobinemia), and cyanosis.

ESSENTIAL OIL • The oily liquid obtained from plants through a variety of processes. The essential oil usually has the taste and smell of the original plant. Essential oils are called volatile because most of them are easily vaporized. The only theories for calling such oils essential are (1) the oils were believed essential to life and (2) they were the "essence" of the plant. The use of essential oils as preservatives is ancient. A large number of oils have antiseptic, germicidal, and preservative action; however, they are primarily used for fragrances and flavorings. No known toxicity when used on the skin. A teaspoon may cause illness in an adult and less than an ounce may kill.

ESTER • A compound formed from an alcohol and an acid by elimination of water, as ethyl acetate (*see*). Usually, they are fragrant liquids used for artificial fruit perfumes and flavors. Esterification of rosin, for example, reduces rosin's allergy causing properties. Toxicity depends on the ester.

ESTRADIOL • Most potent of the natural estrogenic female hormones. See Hormone Creams and Lotions. Also used in perfumes.

ESTRADIOL BENZOATE • See Estradiol.

ESTROGEN • A female hormone. See Hormone Creams and Lotions.

ESTRONE • A follicular hormone that occurs in the urine of pregnant women and mares, in human plancenta, and in palm-kernel oil (*see*). Used in creams and lotions as a "hormone" to improve the skin. Usually, there is not enough in the creams to have an effect. It can have harmful systemic effects if used by children.

ETHANOL • **Ethyl Alcohol. Rubbing Alcohol. Ordinary Alcohol.** An antibacterial used in mouthwashes, nail enamel, astringents, liquid lip rouge, and many other cosmetic products. Clear, colorless, and very flammable, it is made by the fermentation of starch, sugar, and other carbohydrates. Used medicinally as a topical antiseptic, sedative, and blood vessel dilator. Ingestion of large amounts may cause nausea, vomiting, impaired perception, stupor, coma, and death. When it is deliberately denatured (*see*), it is poisonous.

ETHANOLAMIDE OF LAURIC ACID • Used in soapless shampoos, it is derived from coconut oil. It is a mild irritant but does not cause allergic reactions. See Lauric Acid.

ETHANOLAMINE DITHIODIGLYCOATE • See Ethanolamines.

ETHANOLAMINE THIOGLYCOLATE • See Ethanolamines.

ETHANOLAMINES • Three compounds—monoethanolamine, diethanolamine, and triethanolamine—with low melting points, colorless and solid, which readily absorb water and form viscous liquids and are soluble both in water and alcohol. They have an ammonia smell and are strong bases. Used in cold permanent wave lotions as a preservative. Also form soaps with fatty acids (*see*) and are widely used as detergents and emulsifying agents. Very large quantities are required for a lethal oral dose in mice (2,140 milligrams per kilogram of body weight). They have been used medicinally as sclerosal agents for varicose veins. Can be irritating to skin if very alkaline.

ETHER • An organic compound. Acetic ether (*see* ethyl acetate) is used in nail polishes as a solvent. Water insoluble, fat insoluble liquid with a characteristic odor. It is obtained chiefly by the distillation of alcohol with sulfuric acid and is used chiefly as a solvent. A mild skin irritant. Inhalation or ingestion causes central nervous system depression.

ETHIODIZED OIL • The ethyl ester of the fatty acids derived from poppy seeds with iodine. It is used as an antiseptic. See Iodine.

ETHOXYDIGLYCOL • A liquid solvent prepared from ethylene oxide, a petroleum product. It is used as a solvent and thinner in nail enamels. Absorbs water. More toxic orally in animals than polyethylene glycol (*see*). No specific human data is available. It is nonirritating and nonpenetrating when applied to human skin.

ETHOXYDIGLYCOL ACETATE • **Carbitol Acetate.** Used as a solvent and plasticizer for nail enamels, resins, and gums. Less toxic than ethoxydiglycol alone by ingestion but is more toxic when applied to the skin.

ETHOXYETHANOL • **Cellosolve. Ethylene Glycol Monoethyl Ether.** A solvent for nail enamels and a stabilizer in cosmetic emulsions. Obtained by heating ethylene chloride with alcohol and sodium acetate. Colorless and practically odorless. Acute toxicity is several times greater than polyethylene glycol (*see*) in animals. Produces central nervous system depression and kidney damage. Can penetrate the intact skin.

ETHOXYETHANOL ACETATE • **Cellosolve Acetate.** Used to give high gloss to nail polish and to retard evaporation. A colorless liquid with a pleasant odor. Somewhat less toxic than ethoxyethanol alone, it is a central nervous system depressant but does not cause as much kidney damage. It can be readily absorbed through the skin.

4-ETHOXY-m-PHENYLENEDIAMINE SULFATE • See Phenylenediamine.

2-ETHOXYETHYL-p-METHOXYCINNAMATE • Slightly yellow, viscous liquid, practically odorless, almost insoluble in water. UV absorber in suntan preparation.

ETHYL ACETATE • A colorless liquid with a pleasant fruity odor that occurs naturally in apples, bananas, grape juice, pineapple, raspberries, and strawberries. A very useful solvent in nail enamels and nail polish remover. Also an artificial fruit essence for perfumes. It is a mild local irritant and central nervous system depressant. The vapors are irritating and prolonged inhalation may cause kidney and liver damage. Irritating to the skin. Its fat solvent action produces drying and cracking and sets the stage for secondary infections.

ETHYL ALCOHOL • See Ethanol.

ETHYL ANTHRANILATE • Colorless liquid, fruit odor, soluble in alcohol and propylene glycol. Used in perfumery and flavors. See Aminobenzoate.

ETHYL ARACHIDONATE • The ester of ethyl alcohol and arachidonic acid (*see both*).

ETHYL ASPARATE • The ester of ethyl alcohol and aspartic acid (*see both*).

ETHYL BENZOATE • **Essence de Niobe.** An artificial fruit essence used in perfumes. Almost insoluble in water. Also used in strawberry and raspberry flavorings. No known toxicity.

ETHYL BUTYRATE • **Pineapple Oil.** An ingredient in perfumes, colorless, with a pineapple odor. It occurs naturally in apples and strawberries. Also used in synthetic flavorings such as blueberry and raspberry. No known toxicity.

ETHYL CAPROATE • Colorless to yellowish liquid, pleasant odor, soluble in alcohol and ether. Used in artificial fruit essences.

ETHYL CARBONATE • **Carbonic Acid Diethyl Ester.** Pleasant odor. Practically insoluble in water. Solvent for nail enamels. No known toxicity.

ETHYL CELLULOSE • **Cellulose Ether.** Binding, dispersing, and emulsifying agent used in cosmetics, particularly nail polishes and liquid lip rouge. Prepared from wood pulp or chemical cotton by treatment with an alkali. Also used as a diluent (*see*). Not susceptible to bacterial or fungal decomposition. No known toxicity.

ETHYL CINNAMATE • An almost colorless oily liquid with a faint cinnamon odor. Used as a fixative for perfumes; also to scent heavy oriental and floral perfumes in soaps, toilet waters, face powders, and perfumes. Insoluble in water. Also used as a synthetic food flavoring. No known toxicity for the skin.

ETHYL DIHYDROXYPROPYL PABA • The ester of ethyl alcohol and *p*-dihydroxypropyl aminobenzoic acid. See Ethyl Alcohol and PABA.

ETHYL DIISOPROPYLCINNAMATE • See Cinnamic Acid.

ETHYL ESTER OF HYDROLYZED ANIMAL PROTEIN • The ester of ethyl alcohol and the hydrolysate of collagen (*see*).

ETHYL ESTER OF PVM/MA COPOLYMER • Used for its setting properties, it yields a nontacky film and is water-resistant. It is used in hair setting and bodying preparations. See Vinyl Polymers.

ETHYL GLUTAMATE • The ester of ethyl alcohol and glutamic acid. See Glutamate.

ETHYL HEXANEDIOL • See Sorbic Acid.

ETHYL HEXYL-*p*-METHOXYCINNAMATE • Used as a sunscreen in hypoallergenic cosmetics. See Methoxycinnamate.

ETHYL HYDROXYMETHYL OLEYL OXAZOLINE • A synthetic wax. No known toxicity.

ETHYL ISOVALERATE • Colorless, oily liquid with a fruity odor derived from ethanol and valerate. Used in essential oils, perfumery, artificial fruit essences, and flavoring. See Valeric Acid.

ETHYL LACTATE • Colorless liquid with a mild odor. Derived from lactic acid with ethanol. Used as a solvent for nitrocellulose, lacquers, resins, enamels, and flavorings. See Lactic Acid.

ETHYL LAURATE • The ester of ethyl alcohol and lauric acid used as a synthetic flavoring. It is a colorless oil with a light, fruity odor. It is also used as a solvent. No known toxicity.

ETHYL LEVULINATE • Colorless liquid soluble in water. Used as a solvent for cellulose acetate and starch and flavorings. See Levulic Acid.

ETHYL LINOLEATE • See Linoleic acid.

ETHYL LINOLENATE • The ester of ethyl alcohol and linoleic acid (*see*). Vitamin F. See Fatty Acids.

ETHYL MALONATE • Colorless liquid, sweet ester odor. Insoluble in water. Used in certain pigments and flavoring. No known toxicity.

ETHYL METHACRYLATE • The ester of ethyl alcohol and methacrylic acid. See Acrylates.

ETHYL METHYLPHENYLGLYCIDATE • **Strawberry Aldehyde.** Colorless to yellowish liquid having a strong odor suggestive of strawberry. Used in perfumery and flavors.

ETHYL MORRHUATE • **Lipinate.** Salt of morrhuic acid, a fatty acid obtained from cod liver oil. Used in creams and lotions. No known toxicity.

ETHYL MYRISTATE • The ester of ethyl alcohol and myristic acid (*see both*).

ETHYL OLEATE • An ingredient in nail polish remover; yellowish, oily, insoluble in water. It is made from carbon, hydrogen, oxygen, and oleic acid (*see*) and used as a synthetic butter and fruit flavoring. No known toxicity.

ETHYL PALMITATE • The ester of ethyl alcohol and palmitic acid (*see both*).

ETHYL PEG-15 COCAMINE SULFATE • See Coconut Oil.

ETHYL PELARGONATE • The ester of ethyl alcohol and pelargonic acid (*see both*) used in the manufacture of lacquers and plastics, derived from rice bran. Pelargonic acid is a strong irritant.

ETHYL PERSATE • **Persic Oil Acid, Ethyl Ester.** The ethyl ester of the fatty acids derived from either apricot kernel oil or peach kernel oil. See Apricot and Peach Kernel Oil.

ETHYL PHENYLACETATE • A fixative for perfumes, colorless, or nearly colorless liquid, with a sweet honey rose odor. Also a synthetic flavoring agent in various foods. No known toxicity.

ETHYL PHTHALYL ETHYL GLYCOLATE • **Aromatic ester.** A solvent, a fixative for perfumes, and a denaturant. See Polyethylene and Phthalic Acid for toxicity.

ETHYL SALICYLATE • Used in the manufacture of artificial perfumes. Occurs naturally in strawberries and has a pleasant odor. Also used as a synthetic flavoring agent in fruit drinks, baked goods, and so on. At one time it was used to treat rheumatics. It may cause allergic reactions, especially in those who are allergic to other salicylates including those used in sunscreen lotions.

ETHYL SERINATE • The ester of ethyl alcohol and serine (*see both*).

ETHYL STEARATE • The ester of ethyl alcohol and stearic acid (*see both*).

ETHYL TOLUENESULFONAMIDE • Plasticizer for cellulose acetate, and for ethylating. See Toluene.

ETHYL UROCANATE • The ester of ethyl alcohol and urocanic acid. See Imidazoline.

ETHYL VANILLIN • An ingredient in perfumes. Colorless flakes, with an odor and flavor stronger than vanilla. Also a synthetic food flavoring. No known toxicity.

ETHYLENE/ARCYLATE COPOLYMER • See Acrylates and Copolymers.

ETHYLENE/MALEIC ANHYDRIDE COPOLYMER • Plastic material made from ethylene and maleic anhydride. Maleic anhydride is a powerful irritant causing burns. Contact with skin should be avoided. Ethylene is used in the manufacture of plastics and alcohols. High concentrations can cause unconsciousness.

ETHYLENE/VA COPOLYMER • Provides a continuous film for nail enamels or controls film in hair sprays.

ETHYLENE DICHLORIDE • The halogenated aliphatic hydrocarbon derived from the action of chlorine on ethylene. It is used in the manufacture of vinyl chloride (*see*); as a solvent for fats, waxes, and resins; as a lead scavenger in antiknock gasolines; in paint, varnish, and finish removers; as a wetting agent; as a penetrating agent; in organic synthesis; and in the making of polyvinyl chloride (PVP) (*see*). EDC is also used as an ingredient in cosmetics and as a food additive. It is one of the highest volume chemicals produced. It can be highly toxic whether taken into the body by ingestion, inhalation, or skin absorption. It is irritating to the mucous membranes. In cancer testing, the National Cancer Institute found this compound caused stomach cancer, vascularized cancers of multiple organs, and cancers beneath the skin in male rats. Female rats exposed to EDC developed mammary cancers—in some high-dose animals as early as the twentieth week of the study. The chemical also caused breast cancers as well as uterine cancers in female mice and respiratory tract cancers in both sexes.

ETHYLENE DEHYDROGENATED TALLOWAMIDE • See Tallow.

ETHYLENE DIOLEAMIDE • See Fatty Acids.

ETHYLENE DISTEARAMIDE • See Fatty Acids.

ETHYLENE GLYCOL • A slightly viscous liquid with a sweet taste. Absorbs twice its weight in water. Used as an antifreeze and humectant (*see*); also as a solvent. Toxic when ingested, causing central nervous system depression, vomiting, drowsiness, coma, respiratory failure, kidney damage, and possibly death.

ETHYLENE UREA • See Urea.

ETHYLENEDIAMINE • Colorless, clear, thick, and strongly alkaline, it is a component of a bacteria-killing component in processing sugar cane. Also used as a solvent for casein, albumin, and shellac. Has been used as a urinary acidifier. It can cause sensitization leading to asthma and allergic skin rashes.

ETHYLENEDIAMINE TETRAACETIC ACID (EDTA) • An important compound in cosmetics used primarily as a sequestering agent (*see*), particularly in shampoos. It may be irritating to the skin and mucous membranes and cause allergies such as asthma and skin rashes. Also used as a sequesterant in carbonated beverages. When ingested, it may cause errors in a number of laboratory tests, including those for calcium, carbon dioxide, nitrogen, and muscular activity. It is on the FDA list of food additives to be studied for toxicity. It can cause kidney damage. The trisodium salt of EDTA was fed to rats and mice for nearly two years. According to a summary of the report: "Although a variety of tumors occurred among test and control animals of both species, the test did not indicate that any of the tumors observed in the test animals were attributed to EDTA. The tests were part of the National Cancer Institute's Carcinogenesis Bioassay Program."

2-ETHYLHEXOIC ACID • A mild-scented liquid, slightly soluble in water, it is used in paint and varnish driers and to convert some mineral oils to greases. Its esters (*see*) are used as plasticizers. No known toxicity.

ETHYLHEXYL PALMITATE • An emollient used in cosmetic creams. See Palmitic Acid.

ETHYLHEXYL PELARGONATE • Used in makeup. See Ethyl Pelargonate.

ETHYLPARABEN • See Propylparaben.

ETIDRONIC ACID • See Benzyl Alcohol.

ETOCRYLENE • The organic ester derived from acrylic acid widely used in nail polish. See Acrylates.

EUCALYPTOL • A chief constituent of eucalyptus and cajeput oils. Occurs naturally in allspice, star anise, bay, calamus, and peppermint oil. An antiseptic, antispasmodic, and expectorant. Used to flavor toothpaste and mouthwash and to cover up malodors in depilatories. It is not used in hypoallergenic cosmetics. Fatalities followed ingestion of doses as small as 3 to 5 milliliters (about a teaspoon), and recovery has occurred after doses as large as 20 to 30 milliliters (about 4 to 5 teaspoons).

EUCALYPTUS EXTRACT • See Eucalyptus Oil.

EUCALYPTUS OIL • **Dinkum Oil.** Used in skin fresheners. The colorless to pale yellow volatile liquid from the fresh leaves of the eucalyptus tree. It is 70 to 80 percent eucalyptol and has a spicy cool taste and a characteristic aromatic, somewhat camphorlike odor. Used as a local antiseptic. It can cause allergic reactions, and fatalities have followed ingestion of doses as small as 3 to 5 milliliters (about equal to a teaspoon), and about one milliliter has caused coma.

EUGENOL • An ingredient in perfumes and dentifrices obtained from clove oil. Occurs naturally in allspice, basil, bay leaves, calamus, pimiento, and laurel leaves. It has a spicy, pungent taste. Used as a fixative in perfumes and flavorings. Eugenol also acts as a local antiseptic. When ingested, may cause vomiting and gastric irritation. Because of its potential as an allergen, it is left out of hypoallergenic cosmetics.

EURPHRASIA • **Eyebright Herbs.** A derivative from any of several herbs and regarded as a remedy for eye ailments. It is used to soothe the eye in a rinse. No known toxicity.

EVERLASTING EXTRACT • An extract derived from the flowering plant *Helichrysum italicum* and related species.

EXALTING FIXATIVES • A material that acts as an odor carrier, improving and fortifying transportation of the vapors of other perfume materials. Musk and civet are examples. See Fixatives.

EXCIPIENT • A more or less inert substance added to a prescription as a diluent or vehicle, or to give form or consistency when the medication is in pill form. Not infrequently, excipients may be "hidden" allergens.

EXT. D & C VIOLET NO. 2 • Classed chemically as an anthraquinone color. Bluish scarlet. Permitted only for use in preformed hair colors but textbooks list use in bath salts, soaps, and hair-waving fluids as well. The cosmetics industry has petitioned the FDA to allow wider use. Permanently listed for external use, 1982. See Colors.

EXT. D & C YELLOW NO. 7 • Formerly FD & C Yellow No. 1. Greenish yellow. A coal tar color. Classed chemically as a nitro color. It is the disodium salt of 2, 4-Dinitro-1-Naphthol-7-Sulfonic Acid. Used in hair rinses and shampoos. See Colors.

EXT. D & C YELLOW NO. 7 ALUMINUM LAKE • **Naphthol Yellow Lake.** A coal tar color. Light yellow or orange-yellow powder. An insoluble pigment prepared from Ext. D & C Yellow No. 7 (*see*). See Colors.

EXTENDER • A substance added to a product, especially a diluent or modifier (*see both*). Petroleum jelly would be an example.

EXTRACT • The solution that results from passing alcohol or an alcohol-water mixture through a substance. Examples of extracts would be the alcohol-water mixture of vanillin, orange, or lemon extracts found among the spices and flavorings on the supermarket shelf. Extracts are not as strong as essential oils (*see*).

EYE ALLERGY • There are many forms of allergy of the eye. The mucous membranes of the eye may be involved in allergic rhinitis. Such allergic conjunctivitis may also occur by itself without irritation of the nose. Another form, spring "pinkeye" is probably due to allergens in the air. Dust, mold spores, foods, and eye medications may all cause conjunctivitis. There is also a less severe, chronic form of allergic conjunctivitis. Symptoms include prolonged photophobia, itching, burning, and a feeling of dryness. There may be a watery discharge, and finding the source of the allergy is often difficult.

EYE CREAMS • **Eye Wrinkle Creams.** So-called eye creams are slightly modified emollient creams (*see*), usually with the perfume omitted. There is less subcutaneous fat in the skin around the eyes, and it is likely for this reason that wrinkles first begin to develop there. According to the American Medical Association, eye creams will not prevent wrinkles but may make them less noticeable. Most eye creams contain essentially the same ingredients: lecithin, cholesterol, beeswax, lanolin, sodium benzoate, boric acid, mineral oil, ascorbyl palmitate, and almond oil (*see all*).

EYE MAKEUP REMOVER • Pads saturated with ingredients to remove eye makeup. They may contain a solvent such as acetone (*see*), an oil and/or lanolin (*see*), and perfume. Hypoallergenic (*see*) cosmetic manufacturers use cotton pads saturated with pure mineral oil. Eye irritations from eye makeup removers have been reported to the FDA within the past several years.

EYE MASCARA • Mascara is used to color and thicken eyelashes. Early mascara was composed of a pigment and soap. Today it still contains a salt of stearic acid (*see*) with pigments and/or lanolin, paraffin, and carnauba wax (*see all*). Within the past two years there have been a number of complaints of itching, burning, and swelling of eyes and eye irritation due to mascara.

EYE SHADOW • Shades of blue, green, brown, red, yellow, and white are used to color the lid and area under the eyebrow to highlight the eyes. The waterless type of eye shadows uses colors mixed with a lightening agent such as titanium dioxide (*see*) and are then mixed with petrolatum (*see*) on a roller mill. Eye shadows may also contain lanolin, beeswax, ceresin, calcium carbonate, mineral oil, sorbitan oleate, and talc (*see all*). The iridescent effect is achieved by adding very pure aluminum. There have been reports in recent years of eye irritation from eye shadow, one complaint of a package shattering in the eye and another of a sharp foreign article in the product applicator.

EYEBRIGHT HERBS • See Eurphrasia.

EYEBROW DYES • No permanent dyes are approved for use around the eyes.

EYEBROW PENCILS • Usually contain lampblack, petrolatum, and paraffin (*see all*) and sometimes aluminum silicate and stearic acid (*see both*). See also Eyeliners.

EYEBROW PLUCKING CREAM • Used to soften the skin, allowing the hair to be pulled more easily and to alleviate the discomfort. Most eyebrow plucking creams contain benzocaine a pain killer, and cold cream (*see both*). Nontoxic if uncontaminated.

EYEDROPS, LOTIONS, AND WASHES • Soothe and clear eyes of redness. Work by constricting the blood vessels in the eyes, by anesthetizing and soothing the eyes with anesthetics and emollients. Mild astringents such as boric acid or sodium chloride are used. Mild anesthetics used are antipyrine hydrastine hydrochloride and berberine hydrochloride. To contract the blood vessels tetrahydrozoline hydrochloride is used. Included for their pleasant smell are camphor, peppermint, or witch hazel. Among the preservatives used are phenols, cresol, and formaldehyde. A wetting agent such as benzalkonium is also usually included. Reports of eye irritations are infrequent from eye treatment products, but the largest danger is from contamination because eye solutions are good mediums for the growth of bacteria and molds; therefore they must be kept sterile.

EYELASH CREAMS • Used to make the lashes soft and shiny. Such creams usually contain lanolin, cocoa butter, paraffin, cetyl alcohol, and peach-kernel oil (*see all*). Nontoxic if uncontaminated. However, may cause reactions in persons who are allergic to specific ingredients.

EYELASH DYES • **Includes Eyebrow Dyes.** Brown, black, and blue certified oil-soluble dyes are used. Because of possible damage to the eyes only certain ingredients and colors may be used in these preparations (see Colors). The U.S. Food and Drug Administration forbids the use of coal tar dyes (*see*) in the area of the eye. Highly purified inorganic pigments must be used; among them carbon black, charcoal black, black iron oxide, and ultramarine blue for black and blue shades. Iron oxides are used also for yellow and brown shades, carmine for red, chromic oxides for green, and titanium dioxide or zinc oxide for white (*see all*). See Colors for toxicity.

EYELASH OILS • Used to make the lashes soft and shiny. Such oils usually contain lanolin, cocoa butter, cetyl alcohol, alcohol (ethanol), water, and olive oil. Nontoxic if uncontaminated. However, reactions may occur in persons allergic to specific ingredients.

EYELIDS • The skin of the eyelids is a common site of allergic contact dermatitis. The lesions, at first, may be swollen, red, and scaly, but as the victim tries to control the condition, the situation may become chronic and the skin of the lids thicken and roughen. Nail polish and perfume are among the most common allergens, but artificial eyelashes are also a source of trouble. Common allergens affect the eyelids, and the eyes are therapeutic agents. A number of the ophthalmic medications are sensitizers, including local anesthetics and antibiotics.

EYELINERS • Used to outline and accentuate the eyes, eyeliners may be in pencil or liquid form or in the newer pencil-brush container. Eyeliners usually contain an alkanolamine, a fatty alcohol, polyvinyl pyrrolidone, cellulose ether, methylparaben, antioxidants, perfumes, and titanium dioxide (*see all*). Waterproof eyeliners resist tears, moisture in the air, and perspiration. Some also resist ordinary soap and water. Most of the waterproof eyeliners are made of a pigment suspended in a gum or resin solution or a pigmented waxy base dissolved in a volatile solvent. Waterproof eyeliners must be removed with a solvent such as mineral oil or similar oils. Most facial cleansing lotions and creams contain such solvents. The U.S. Food and Drug Administration has found a persistent problem of bacterial contamination in some liquid eyeliners. Since bacterial infections around the eyes can lead to serious problems, it is probably better to purchase nonliquid eyeliners. There are also a significant number of persons allergic to eyeliners and other such products. The American Medical Association recommends that women stop using an eyeliner or eye makeup product if their skin becomes red, itchy, or swollen whenever an eye cosmetic is applied. The AMA also points out that because the eyelids are easily irritated, eye makeup, particularly eyeliner, should be removed with care and the repeated application of eye makeup at one session should be avoided. There have been a number of reports of swollen eyelids and eye irritation from well-known products.

The use of eyeliner pencils applied to the upper and lower border of the eyelids inside the lashes rather than to the eyelid behind the lashes is not recommended by physicians. According to a report by an eye specialist quoted by the American Medical Association, this may lead to various problems, including permanent pigmentation of the mucous membrane lining of the inside of the eye, moderate redness and itching, tearing and blurring of vision.

EYEWASHES • See Eyedrops, Lotions and Washes.

F

FABA BEAN EXTRACT • **Fava Bean. Common Bean**. The extract of the seeds of *Vicia faba*. Inhalation or ingestion of the pollen of its flower can cause fever and headache in certain sensitized individuals. Little is known about the toxicity of the seed extract.

FACE MASKS AND PACKS • Claims are made for face masks and for the thicker face packs that they shrink pores, remove wrinkles, and relieve tension. Only the last may be true. According to the American Medical Association, there is no evidence that any cosmetic can safely shrink pores and only surgery removes wrinkles. However, the apparent cooling or tight feeling derived from their use may induce a clean feeling. Clay face masks usually contain purified siliceous earth, kaolin, glycerin, and water. Face packs usually contain zinc stearate, zinc oxide, tragacanth, alcohol, glycerin, and limewater. Both masks and packs may also contain acacia, Balsam Peru, glyceryl monostearate, hexachlorophene, magnesium carbonate, wax, salicylic acid, spermaceti, Turkey-red oil, talc, titanium oxide and/or zinc sulfate.

(See ingredients above under separate listings.) Complaints to the FDA about face masks and packs include burning sensation, swelling, blisters and lumps, eye ailments, skin irritation, and corneal ulcers.

FAKE NAILS • See Artificial Nails.

FALSE EYELASHES • False eyelashes are made of real or synthetic hair on a thin stringlike base that is pasted over the natural eyelashes on the eyelid. There have been cases of eye irritation and one cause of blindness reported to the FDA. Whether the problems were the result of the adhesive used, the dye on the eyelashes, or other materials, is not clear.

FARNESOL • Used in perfumery to emphasize the odor of sweet floral perfumes such as lilac. Occurs naturally in ambrette seed, star anise, cassia, linden flowers, oils of musk seed, citronella, rose, and balsam. Also a food flavoring. No known toxicity.

FAST GREEN FCF • A name applied to uncertified FD & C Green No. 3 (*see*).

FATIGUE • Everyone's nose becomes "fatigued" when smelling a certain odor. No matter how much you like a fragrance, you can only smell it for a short interval. It is nature's way of protecting humans from overstimulation of the olfactory sense.

FATTY ACID ESTERS • See Ester. The fatty acid esters of low molecular weight alcohols are widely used in hand products because they are oily but nongreasy when applied to the skin. They are emollients and emulsifiers. No known toxicity.

FATTY ACIDS • Fatty acids are used in bubble baths and lipsticks, but chiefly for making soap and detergents. One or any mixture of liquid and solid acids, capric, caprylic, lauric, myristic, oleic, palmitic, and stearic. In combination with glycerin, they form fat. Necessary for normal growth and healthy skin. In foods they are used as emulsifiers, binders, and lubricants. See Stearic Acid. No known toxicity.

FATTY ALCOHOLS • **Cetyl. Stearyl. Lauryl. Myristyl.** Solid alcohols made from acids and widely used in hand creams and lotions. Cetyl and stearyl alcohols form an occlusive film to keep skin moisture from evaporating and they import a velvety feel to the skin. Lauryl and myristyl are used in detergents and creams. Very low toxicity.

FD & C BLUE NO. 1 • **Brilliant Blue FCF.** A coal tar derivative, triphenylmethane, used for hair colorings, face powders, and other cosmetics. Also used as a coloring in bottled soft drinks, gelatin, desserts, cereals, and other foods. May cause allergic reactions. On the FDA permanent list of color additives. Rated 1A, that is, completely acceptable for nonfood use, by the World Health Organization.

However, it produced malignant tumors at the site of injection and by ingestion in rats. See Colors.

FD & C BLUE NO. 2 • Moderate bright green. A coal tar derivative, triphenylmethane, used in hair rinses and in mint-flavored jelly, frozen desserts, candy, confections, and cereals. It is a sensitizer in the allergic. Permanently listed for surgical sutures in 1971 and for food and ingested drug use in 1987. Produced malignant tumors at the site of injection when introduced under the skin of rats. See Colors.

FD & C BRILLIANT BLUE NO. 1 ALUMINUM LAKE • Aluminum salt of certified Brilliant Blue No. 1 (*see*). See Colors and Lakes.

FD & C GREEN NO. 3 • Permanently listed by the FDA for use in food, drugs and cosmetics in 1982, except in the area of the eye.

FD & C RED NO. 2 • **Amaranth.** Formerly one of the most widely used cosmetic and food colorings. A dark, reddish-brown powder that turns bright red when mixed with fluid. A monoazo color, it was used in lipsticks, rouges, and other cosmetics as well as in cereals, maraschino cherries, and desserts. The safety of this dye was questioned by American scientists for more than twenty years. Two Russian scientists found that FD & C Red No. 2 prevented some pregnancies and caused some stillbirths in rats. The FDA ordered manufacturers using the color to submit data on all food, drug, and cosmetic products containing it. Controversial tests at the FDA's National Center for Toxicological Research in Arkansas showed that in high doses Red No. 2 caused a statistically significant increase in a variety of cancers in female rats. The dye was banned by the FDA in January 1976.

FD & C RED NO. 3 • **Erythrosine. Bluish Pink.** A coal tar derivative, a xanthene color, used in toothpaste and in canned fruit cocktail, fruit salad, and cherry pie mixes as well as maraschino cherries. Has been determined a carcinogen. The FDA postponed the closing date for FD & C to allow the agency additional time to study complex scientific and legal questions about the color before deciding to approve or terminate its use. FD & C Red No. 3 is permanently listed for use in food and ingested drugs but only provisionally listed for cosmetics and externally applied drugs.

FD & C RED NO. 3 ALUMINUM LAKE • The aluminum salt of certified FD & C Red No. 3 (*see*). See Colors and Lakes.

FD & C RED NO. 4 • A monoazo color and coal tar dye. Used in mouthwashes, bath salts, and hair rinses. It was banned in food by the FDA in 1964 when it was shown to damage the adrenal glands and bladders of dogs. The agency relented and gave it provisional license for use in maraschino cherries. It was banned in all foods in 1976 because it was shown to cause urinary bladder polyps and atrophy of the adrenal glands in animals. It was also banned in orally taken drugs but is still permitted in cosmetics for external use only. See also Colors.

FD & C RED NO. 20 • Permanently listed by the FDA in 1983 for general use in drugs and cosmetics (except in areas around the eyes).

FD & C RED NO. 22 • Permanently listed by the FDA in 1983 for general use in drugs and cosmetics (except in areas around the eyes).

FD & C RED NO. 40 • **Allura Red AC**. Newest color. Used widely in the cosmetics industry. Approved in 1971, Allied Chemical has an exclusive patent on it. It is substituted for FD & C Red No. 4 in many cosmetics, food, and drug products. Permanently listed in 1971 because, unlike the producers of "temporary" colors, this producer supplied reproductive data. However, many American scientists feel that the safety of Red No. 40 is far from established particularly because all the tests were conducted by the manufacturer. Therefore, the dye should not have received a permanent safety rating. The National Cancer Institute reported that *p*-credine, a chemical used in the preparation of Red No. 40, was carcinogenic in animals. See also Azo Dyes.

FD & C YELLOW NO. 5 • **Tartrazine.** A coal tar derivative, it is used as a coloring in hair rinses, hair-waving fluids, and in bath salts. A pyrazole color, it is also found in prepared breakfast cereals, imitation strawberry, jelly, bottled soft drinks, gelatin desserts, ice cream, sherbets, dry drink powders, candy, confections, bakery products, spaghetti, and puddings. Causes allergic reactions in persons sensitive to aspirin. The certified color industry petitioned for permanent listing of this color in February 1966, with no limitations other than good manufacturing practice. However, in February 1966, the FDA proposed the listing of this color with a maximum rate of use of 300 parts per million in food. The color industry objected to the limitations. Yellow No. 5 was thereafter permanently listed as a color additive without restrictions. Rated 1A by the World Health Organization—acceptable in food. It is estimated that half the aspirin-sensitive people plus 47,000 to 94,000 others in the nation are sensitive to this dye. It is used in about 60 percent of both over-the-counter and prescription drugs. Efforts were made to ban this color in over-the-counter pain relievers, antihistamines, oral decongestants, and prescription anti-inflammatory drugs. Aspirin-sensitive patients have been reported to develop life-threatening asthmatic symptoms with ingestion of this yellow. Since 1981, it is supposed to be listed on the label if it is used.

FD & C YELLOW NO. 5. ALUMINUM LAKE • See FD & C Yellow No. 5, Colors and Lakes.

FD & C YELLOW NO. 6 • **Sunset Yellow FCF.** A coal tar, monoazo color, used in hair rinses as well as other cosmetics, carbonated beverages, gelatin, desserts, and dry drink powders. It is not used in products that contain fats and oils. May cause allergic reactions. Permanently listed for food, drugs, and cosmetics in 1986. Labeling requirements began in 1989 because of its potential for causing allergic reactions. See Colors.

FD & C YELLOW NO. 6 ALUMINUM LAKE • See FD & C Yellow No. 6, Colors, and Aluminum Lakes.

FEMININE HYGIENE SPRAYS • See Vaginal Deodorants.

FENNEL • One of the earliest known herbs from the tall beautiful shrub. Used in astringents and perfumes. The fennel flowers appear in June and are bright yellow. Compresses of fennel tea are used by organic cosmeticians to soothe the inflamed eyelids and watery eyes. May cause allergic reactions.

FENUGREEK SEED • **Greek Hay.** An annual herb grown in southern Europe, North Africa, and India, and used in hair tonic supposedly to prevent baldness; also added to powders, poultices, and ointments. The seeds are used in making curry.

FERRIC AMMONIUM FERROCYANIDE • **Iron Blue.** An inorganic salt used as a dark blue coloring for cosmetics. Permanently listed in 1977. See Iron Salts.

FERRIC CHLORIDE • Brownish yellow or orange iron compound. Absorbs water readily. Used as a styptic and astringent. Irritating to the skin and not suitable for wide use.

FERRIC FERROCYANIDE • **Prussian Blue.** A coloring for externally applied cosmetics including the eye area. Permanently listed in 1978. See Colors.

FERROUS SULFATE • **Green or Iron Vitriol.** Pale bluish-green, odorless crystals, efflorescent in dry air. An astringent deodorant. Used in hair dyes. A source of iron used medicinally. No known toxicity.

FIELD POPPY EXTRACT • Extract of the petals of *Papaver rhoeas* used in coloring and as an odorant.

FINGERNAIL POLISH • See Nail Polish.

FINGERNAIL POLISH REMOVER • See Nail Polish Remover.

FINISHING RINSE • A product that coats only the surface fibers of the hair and that is used to add sheen and remove tangles.

FIR NEEDLE OIL • **Fir Oil.** An essential oil obtained by the steam distillation of needles and twigs of several varieties of pine trees native to both Canada and Siberia. Used as a scent in perfumes and as a flavoring agent.

FISH GLYCERIDES • See Fish Oil and Glycerin.

FISH OIL • A fatty oil in soap manufacturing derived from fish or marine animals.

FIXATIVE • A chemical that reduces the tendency of an odor or flavor to vaporize, by making the odor or flavor last longer. An example is musk (*see*), which is used in perfume.

FLAXSEED • The seed of the flax plant may be "hidden" in cereals and the milk of cows fed flaxseed. It is also in flaxseed tea and the laxative, flaxolyn. It is a frequent allergen when ingested, inhaled, or in direct contact. Flaxseeds are the source of linseed oil. Among other hidden sources are: dog food, wave-setting preparations, shampoos, hair tonics, depilatories, patent leather, insulating materials, rugs and some cloths, Roman meal, cough remedies, and muffins.

FLORAL BOUQUET • One of the basic perfume types, it is a blending of flower notes with no particular standouts. For balance and body, it may contain a medley of basic notes such as amber, musk, vetiver, as well as a touch of the aromatic, but there is definitely the scent of bouquet of flowers.

FLUORESCEIN • A yellow granular or red crystalline dye giving a brilliant yellow green fluorescence in an alkaline solution. Very visible. See Tetrabromofluorescein for toxicity.

FLUORESCENT BRIGHTENERS • **(46, 47, 52).** Colorless, water- or solvent-soluble aromatic compounds with an affinity for fibers. They are usually violet, blue, or blue green colors, and are capable of increasing both the blueness and the brightness of a substrate with a resulting marked whitening effect. They improve the brightness of tints and are included in detergents of all kinds to enhance cleansing action.

FLUORIDE • An acid salt used in toothpaste to prevent tooth decay. See Stannous Fluoride.

FLUOROSALAN • A salicylide used as an antiseptic agent. See Salicylides.

FOAM STABILIZERS • Used in soft drinks and brewing. See Vegetable Gums.

FOLIC ACID • A yellowish orange compound and member of the Vitamin B-Complex, used as a nutrient. Used in cosmetic emollients. Occurs naturally in liver, kidney, mushrooms, and green leaves. Aids in cell formation, especially red blood cells. No known toxicity.

FOOD RED 6 • **Formerly Ext. D & C Red No. 15, FD & C Red No. 1, and Ponceau 3 R.** One of the first approved certified coal tar colors. Food Red 6 was delisted as a food additive, as possibly harmful. Dark red powder, it changes to cherry red in solution. See Colors.

FOREST BLENDS • One of the basic perfume types, these blends are woody, mossy-leafy, or resinous. They either stand out alone with the aromatic notes of an individual nature, such as sandalwood, rosewood, the balsams, or cedarwood, or they have a combination of these notes. Quite often, the more pungent notes of geranium, lavender, fern, and herbs are used to give an earthy quality.

FORMALDEHYDE • A colorless gas obtained by the oxidation of methyl alcohol and generally used in watery solution. Vapors are intensely irritating to mucous membranes. It has been estimated that 4 to 8 percent of the general population may be sensitized to it. It is used in nail hardeners, nail polish, soap, and hair growing products. It is widely used in cosmetics as a disinfectant, germicide, fungicide, defoamer, and preservative. Ingestion can cause severe abdominal pain, internal bleeding, loss of ability to urinate, vertigo, coma, and death. Skin reactions after exposure to it are very common because the chemical can be both irritating and allergy producing. Physicians have reported severe reactions to nail hardeners containing formaldehyde. Its use in cosmetics is banned in Japan and Sweden. Some surfactants, such as the widely used lauryl sulfate, may contain formaldehyde as a perservative, and other surfactants may have it without listing it on the label. Formaldehyde is an inexpensive and effective preservative, but there are serious questions about its safety. It is a highly reactive chemical that is damaging to the hereditary substances in the cells of several animal species. It causes lung cancer in rats and has a number of other harmful biological consequences. Researchers from the Division of Cancer Cause and Prevention of the National Cancer Institute recommended in April 1983 that, since formaldehyde is involved in DNA damage and inhibits its repair, and potentiates the toxicity of X-rays in human lung cells, and, since it may act in concert with other chemical agents to produce mutagenic and carcinogenic effects, it should be "further investigated." Some shampoos contain formaldehyde. Among them at this writing, Breck Shampoo and L'Oréal Ultra Rich Gentle Shampoo.

FORMIC ACID • Used as a rubefacient (*see*) in hair tonics; also a synthetic food flavoring. Colorless, pungent, highly corrosive, it occurs naturally in apples and other fruits. Also used as a decalcifier and for dehairing hides. Chronic absorption is known to cause albuminuria—protein in the urine. It caused cancer when administered orally in rats, mice, and hamsters in doses from 31 to 49 milligrams per kilogram of body weight.

FOUNDATION MAKEUP • Aimed at covering blemishes, protecting the skin from drying out, and giving a glowing, healthy look. There is a cream-type foundation that vanishes from the skin but leaves a smooth, protective base for the application of pigmented makeup. Such creams are usually about 75 percent water, 15 percent stearic acid, and the remainder either sorbitan stearate or sorbitol. The pigmented foundation creams, which are designed to tint and cover the skin, usually contain about 50 percent water, and mineral oil, stearic acid, lanolin, cetyl alcohol, propylene glycol, triethanolamine, borax, and insoluble pigments. They may also contain emulsifiers and detergents; humectants to absorb and retain water such as propylene glycol, glycerin, and sorbitol; lanolin derivatives; perfume; preservatives such as paraben; special barrier agents such as zinc stearate; cellulose derivatives and silicone; synthetic esters; thickeners such as sodium alginate, gum tragacanth, quince seed, and mucilage; and such waxes as beeswax and spermaceti. Stick-type makeup is made from isopropyl myristate, beeswax, carnauba wax, mineral oil, perfume, and dry pigment. Cake makeup, which is used by applying a wet sponge to the material and then applying the sponge to the face, is usually made of finely ground pigment, talc, kaolin, zinc, titanium oxide, precipitated calcium carbonate, and such inorganic pigments as iron oxides. To these may be added sorbitol, propylene glycol, lanolin, mineral oil, and perfume. If you check the entries for the above ingredients, you will see many—such as lanolin, perfume, beeswax, and parabens—are quite common allergens. However, by the very nature of the allergic response, you may not be allergic to a common allergen but to an uncommon one. The more ingredients to which you are exposed, of course, the greater the chances of developing an allergic response.

FRESHENER • See Skin Freshener.

FRUCTOSE • A sugar occurring naturally in large numbers of fruits and honey. It is the sweetest of the foodstuffs. It is also used as a medicine and preservative. It caused tumors in mice when injected under the skin in 5,000 milligram doses per kilogram of body weight.

FRUITY BLENDS • One of the basic perfume types, fruit blends have other notes present but are desired for their clean, fresh citrus notes, or a smooth, mellow, peachlike warmth.

FULLER'S EARTH • Used in dry shampoos, hair colorings, beauty masks, and as a dusting powder; also used for lubricants and soaps. A white or brown, naturally occurring, earthy substance. A nonplastic variety of kaolin (*see*) containing an aluminum magnesium silicate. Used as an absorbent and to decolorize fats and oils. No longer permitted in cosmetics.

FUMITORY EXTRACT • The extract of the leaves, twigs, and flowers of *Fumaria officinalis*. Used as an odorant. No known toxicity.

FURFURAL • **Artificial Ant Oil.** Used as a solvent, insecticide, fungicide, to decolor resins, and as a synthetic flavoring in food. A colorless liquid with a peculiar odor. Occurs naturally in angelica root, apples, coffee, peaches, and skim milk. Darkens when exposed to air. It irritates mucous membranes and acts on the central nervous system. Causes tearing and inflammation of the eyes and throat. Ingestion or absorption of 0.06 grams produces persistent headache. Used continually, it leads to nervous disturbances and eye disorders.

G

GALACTURONIC ACID • Obtained from plant pectins by hydrolysis, it is used in combination with allantoin (*see*) in creams and lotions.

GARDENIA • The white or yellow flowers used in fragrances. Obtained from a large genus of Old World tropical trees and shrubs. No known toxicity.

GARLIC EXTRACT • An extract from *Allium sativum*, a yellowish liquid with a strong odor used in fruit and garlic flavorings. Is being tested as an antibiotic and has been used to counteract intestinal worms.

GEL • A semisolid, apparently homogenous substance that may be elastic and jellylike (gelatin) or more or less rigid (silica gel) formed in various ways such as coagulation or evaporation.

GELATIN • Used in protein shampoos because it sticks to the hair and gives it "more body," peelable face masks, and as a fingernail strengthener. Gelatin is a protein obtained by boiling skin, tendons, ligaments, or bones with water. It is colorless or slightly yellow, tasteless, and absorbs 5 to 10 times its weight of cold water. Also used as a food thickener, stabilizer, and base for fruit gelatins and puddings. Employed medicinally to treat malnutrition and brittle fingernails. No know toxicity.

GERANIOL • Used in perfumery to compound artificial attar of roses and artificial orange blossom oil. Also used in depilatories to mask odors. Oily sweet, with a rose odor, it occurs naturally in apples, bay leaves, cherries, grapefruit, ginger, lavender, and a number of other essential oils. Geraniol is omitted from hypoallergenic cosmetics. Can cause allergic reactions.

GERANIUM OIL • Used in perfumery, dusting powder, tooth powder, and ointments. It is the light yellow to deep yellow oil of plants of the genus *Pelargonium* or of rose geranium leaves, with the characteristic odor of rose and geraniol. A teaspoon may cause illness in an adult and less than an ounce may kill. May affect those allergic to geraniums.

GERANYL ACETATE • **Geraniol Acetate.** Clear, colorless liquid with the odor of lavender, it is a constituent of several essential oils. Used in perfumery and flavoring. See Geraniol.

GERANYL BUTYRATE • **Geraniol Butyrate.** Colorless liquid which occurs in several essential oils, it is used in perfumes, soaps, flavorings, and as a synthetic attar of rose. See Geraniol.

GERANYL FORMATE • **Geraniol Formate.** Colorless liquid with a roselike odor, insoluble in alcohol, it occurs in several essential oils. Used in perfumes, and soaps and flavorings as a synthetic neroli oil (*see*). See Geraniol.

GERANYL PROPIONATE • **Geraniol Propionate.** Colorless liquid with a roselike odor, it is soluble in most oils and is used in perfumery and flavoring. See Geraniol.

GERIANAL • See Citral.

GERIANALDEHYDE • See Citral.

GHATTI GUM • **Indian Gum.** The gummy exudate from the stems of a plant abundant in India and Ceylon. Used as an emulsifier and in butter, butterscotch, and fruit flavorings for beverages. Has caused an occasional allergy but when ingested in large amounts it has not caused obvious distress.

GINGER OIL • Obtained from the dried rhizomes of *Zingiber officinale*, it is used in flavorings. Also used in perfumes. Employed medicinally to break up intestinal gas. No known toxicity.

GINKGO EXTRACT • **Maidenhair.** An extract of *Ginkgo biloba*. A sacred tree of the Chinese, the fruit has an offensive odor but is resistant to smoke, disease, and insects. Used in perfumes and as an insecticide. No known toxicity.

GINSENG • Root of the ginseng plant grown in China, Korea, and the United States. It produces a resin, a sugar starch, glue, and volatile oil. Widely used in Oriental medicine as an aromatic bitter. It is used in American cosmetics as a demulcent (*see*). No known toxicity.

GLAUBER'S SALT • Crystalline sodium sulfate (*see*) used as an opacifier in shampoos and as a detergent in bath salts. Named for a German chemist, Johann R. Glauber, who died in 1668. Also used as a laxative medicinally. Skin irritations may occur.

GLOSS WHITE • No longer permitted as a coloring in cosmetics.

GLUCAMINE • An organic compound that is prepared from glucose (*see*).

GLUCOSE • Used as a flavoring, to soothe the skin, and as a filler in cosmetics. Occurs naturally in blood, grape, and corn sugars. A source of energy for plants and animals. Sweeter than sucrose (*see*). No known toxicity in cosmetics but confectioners frequently suffer erosions and fissures around their nails, and the nails loosen and sometimes fall off.

GLUCOSE GLUTAMATE • Used as a humectant in hand creams and lotions, it occurs naturally in animal blood, grape, and corn sugars, and is a source of energy for plants and animals. It is sweeter than sucrose. Glucose syrup is used to flavor sausage, hamburger, and other processed meats. Also used as an extender in maple syrup and medicinally as a nutrient. Glutamate is the salt of glutamic acid and is used to enhance natural food flavors. The FDA has asked for further studies as to its potential mutagenic, teratogenic, subacute, and reproductive effects. No known skin toxicity.

GLUCURONIC ACID • A carbohydrate that is widely distributed in the animal kingdom.

GLUTAMATE • Ammonium and monopotassium salt of glutamic acid (*see*). Used to enhance natural flavors and to improve the taste of tobacco. It is used as an antioxidant in cosmetics to prevent spoilage. It is being studied by the FDA for mutagenic, teratogenic, subacute, and reproductive effects.

GLUTAMIC ACID • A white, practically odorless, free-flowing crystalline powder, a nonessential amino acid (*see*) usually manufactured from vegetable protein. A salt substitute, it has been used to treat epilepsy and to correct stomach acids. It is used to enhance food flavors, as an antioxidant in cosmetics, and a softener in permanent wave solutions to help protect against hair damage. It is being studied by the FDA for its mutagenic, teratogenic, subacute, and reproductive effects.

GLUTAMINE • A nonessential amino acid (*see*) used as a medicine and culture medium. Nontoxic.

GLUTARAL • **Glutaraldehyde.** An amino acid (*see*) that occurs in green sugar beets. Used in creams and emollients. It has a faint agreeable odor. See Glutaric Acid.

GLUTARIC ACID • **Pentanedioic Acid.** A crystalline fatty acid that is soluble in oil. Widely used in Oriental medicine as an aromatic bitter. It is used in American cosmetics as a demulcent (*see*). No known toxicity.

GLUTEN • A mixture of proteins from wheat flour.

GLY- • The abbreviation for glycine (*see*).

GLYCEL • A compound said to be developed by Christiaan Barnard, the pioneer heart surgeon, in Switzerland, to counteract wrinkles. The project says it "contains many natural plant extracts . . . enhancing its capacity for elasticity and the amount of energy-producing oxygen available thereby accelerating cell renewal." If that were proven, it would have to be a drug, not a cosmetic.

GLYCERETH-26 • **Liponic EG-1**. See Glycerin.

GLYCERIDES • Any of a large class of compounds that are esters (*see*) of the sweet alcohol, glycerin. They are also made synthetically. They are used in cosmetic creams as texturizers and emollients. No known toxicity.

GLYCERIN • **Glycerol.** Any by-product of soap manufacture, it is a sweet, warm tasting, oily fluid obtained by adding alkalies (*see*) to fats and fixed oils. A solvent, humectant, and emollient in many cosmetics, it absorbs moisture from the air and, therefore, helps keep moisture in creams and other products, even if the consumer leaves the cap off the container. Also helps the products to spread better. A humectant in foods and a solvent for food colors and flavors. Among the many products containing glycerin are cream rouge, face packs and masks, freckle lotions, hand creams and lotions, hair lacquer, liquid face powder, mouthwashes, protective creams, skin fresheners, and toothpastes. In concentrated solutions it is irritating to the mucous membranes, but as used, nontoxic, nonirritating, nonallergenic.

GLYCERYL-p-AMINOBENZOATE • A semisolid waxy mass or syrup with a faint aromatic odor, liquefying and congealing very slowly, used in cosmetic sunscreen preparations. See Benzoic Acid.

GLYCERYL CAPRATE • The monoester of glycerin and caprylic acid (*see both*).

GLYCERYL CAPRYLATE • See Glycerin and Caprylic Acid.

GLYCERYL CAPRYLATE/CAPRATE • A mixture of caprylic acid and capric acid (*see both*).

GLYCERYL COCONATE • See Glycerin and Coconut Oil.

GLYCERYL DILAURATE • See Glycerin and Lauric Acid.

GLYCERYL DIOLEATE • The diester of glycerin and oleic acid (*see both*).

GLYCERYL DISTEARATE • The diester of glycerin and stearic acid (*see both*).

GLYCERYL ERUCATE • See Glycerin and Euric Acid.

GLYCERYL HYDROSTEARATE • See Glyceryl Monostearate.

GLYCERYL HYDROXYSTEARATE • The monoester of glycerin and hydroxystearic acid (*see both*).

GLYCERYL ISOSTEARATE • See Glyceryl Monostearate.

GLYCERYL LANOLATE • The monoester of glycerin and lanolin (*see both*).

GLYCERYL LINOLEATE • The monoester of glycerin and linoleic acid (*see both*).

GLYCERYL MONOSTEARATE • An emulsifying and dispersing agent used in baby creams, face masks, foundation cake makeup, liquid powders, hair conditioners, hand lotions, mascara, and nail whiteners. It is a mixture of two glyceryls, a white waxlike solid, or beads, and is soluble in hot organic solvents such as alcohol. Lethal when injected in large doses into mice. No known toxicity.

GLYCERYL MYRISTATE • See Glycerin and Myristic Acid.

GLYCERYL OLEATE • See Glycerin and Oleic Acid.

GLYCERYL PABA • The ester of glycerin and *p*-aminobenzoic acid (*see both*).

GLYCERYL PALMITATE LACTATE • The lactic acid ester (*see*) of glyceryl palmitate.

GLYCERYL RICINOLEATE • See Glycerin.

GLYCERYL SESQUIOLEATE • See Glycerin.

GLYCERYL STARCH • See Starch and Glycerin.

GLYCERYL STEARATE • An emulsifier. See Glycerin.

GLYCERYL STEARATE SE • See Glycerin Monostearate.

GLYCERYL TRIMYRISTATE • See Glycerin and Myristic Acid.

GLYCERYL TRIOCTANOATE • The triester of glycerin and 2-ethylhexoic acid (*see both*).

GLYCERYL TRIUMDECANOATE • The triester of glycerin and undecanoic acid (*see both*).

GLYCINE • Used as a texturizer in cosmetics. An amino acid (*see*) classified as nonessential. Made up of sweet-tasting crystals, it is used as a dietary supplement and as a gastric antacid. No known toxicity.

GLYCOFUROL • The ethoxylated ether of tetrahydrofurfuryl alcohol. See Furfural.

GLYCOGEN • Distributed throughout cell protoplasm, it is an animal starch found especially in liver and muscle. Used as a violet dye and in biochemical research. No known toxicity.

GLYCOL DISTEARATE • Alcohol from glycol. See Glycols.

GLYCOL STEARATE SE • An emulsifier. See Glycols and Stearic Acid.

GLYCOLIC ACID • Contained in sugarcane juice, it is an odorless, slightly water-absorbing acid used to control the acid/alkali balance in cosmetics and whenever a cheap organic acid is needed. It is also used in copper brightening, decontamination procedures, and in dyeing. It is a mild irritant to the skin and mucous membranes.

GLYCOLS • **Propylene Glycol. Glycerine. Ethylene Glycol. Carbitol. Diethylene Glycol.** Literally it means "glycerin" plus "alcohol." A group of syrupy alcohols derived from hydrocarbons (*see*) and widely used in cosmetics as humectants. The FDA cautions manufacturers that glycols may cause adverse reactions in users. Propylene glycol and glycerin (*see both*) are considered safe. Other glycols in low concentrations may be harmless for external application, but ethylene glycol, carbitol, and diethylene glycol are hazardous in concentrations exceeding 5 percent even in preparations for use on small areas of the body. Therefore, in sunscreen lotions and protective creams where the area of application is extensive, they should not be used at all. Wetting agents (*see*) increase the absorption of glycols and therefore their toxicity.

GLYCOSAMINOGLYCANS • An ingredient in wrinkle creams. See Chitin and Mucopolysaccharides.

GLYCRETH-26 • **Liponic.** See Glycerin.

GLYCYRRHETINIC ACID • Used as a flavoring, to soothe skin, and as a carrier. Prepared from licorice root, it is soluble in chloroform, alcohol, and acetic acid (*see*). It has been used medicinally to treat a disease of the adrenal gland. No known toxicity when used in cosmetics.

GLYCYRRHETINYL STEARATE • The stearic acid ester of glycyrrhetinic acid (*see*).

GLYCYRRHIZIC ACID • Used as a flavoring, coloring, and to soothe the skin in cosmetics. Extracted from licorice, the crystalline material is soluble in hot water and alcohol. See Glycyrrhetinic Acid.

GLYOXYLIC ACID • Used as a coloring. Syrup or crystals that occur in unripe fruit, young leaves, and baby sugar beets. Malodorous and strong corrosive. Forms a thick syrup, very soluble in water, sparingly soluble in alcohol. It absorbs water from the air and condenses with urea to form allantoin (*see*) and gives a nice blue color with sulfuric acid. It is a skin irritant and corrosive.

GOLD • Used as a coloring and to give shine to cosmetics. The soft yellow metal occurring in the earth's crust and used in jewelry, gold plating, and medicine to treat arthritis. The pure metal is nontoxic but the gold salts can cause allergic skin reactions.

GOLDENROD • Any of a group of American plants belonging to the *Solidago*, found in North America. Used as a natural rubber. No known toxicity.

GOURD EXTRACT • The extract of various species of *Cucurbitaceae.*

GRAPE EXTRACT • The extract of the pulp of *Vitis vinifera* used as a coloring.

GRAPE JUICE • The liquid expressed from fresh grapes used as a coloring.

GRAPE LEAF EXTRACT • The extract obtained from the leaves of *Vitis vinifera.*

GRAPEFRUIT EXTRACT • The extract of the seeds of the grapefruit, *Citrus paradisi.*

GRAPEFRUIT OIL • An ingredient in fragrances obtained by expression from the fresh peel of the grapefruit. The yellow, sometimes reddish liquid is also used in fruit flavorings. No known toxicity.

GRAPE-SEED OIL • Expressed from grape seeds and used widely in hypoallergenic lubricating creams because it does not cause problems with the allergic. Also used as a lubricant for fine watches. Nontoxic.

GRAPHITE • **Black Lead.** Obtained by mining, especially in Canada and Ceylon. Usually soft, black, lustrous scales. A pigment for cosmetics. Also used in lead pencils, stone polish, and as an explosive. The dust is mildly irritating to the lungs. No longer permitted in cosmetics.

GRAS • The Generally Recognized As Safe list was established in 1958 by Congress. Those substances that were being added to food over a long time, which under conditions of their intended use were generally recognized as safe by qualified scientists, would be exempt from pre-market clearance. Congress had acted on a very marginal response—on the basis of returns from those scientists who sent questionnaires. Approximately 355 out of 900 responded, and only about 100 of those responses had substantive comments. Three items were removed from the originally published list. Since then, developments in the scientific fields and in consumer awareness have brought to light the inadequacies of the testing of food additives and, ironically, the complete lack of testing of the Generally Recognized As Safe list. President Nixon directed the FDA to reevaluate items on the GRAS list. The reevaluation was completed and a number of items were removed from the list. A number were put on a priority list for further studies but as of this writing, nothing new has been reported.

GRAY HAIR RINSES • To cover yellowish tinge that often appears in gray hair. Usually compounded with acids such as adipic or citric (*see both*) and color rinses such as Acid Violet 99 and Acid Black 2 (*see both*).

GREEN • Chrome oxide green used in face powders. See Colors.

GREEN BEAN EXTRACT • The extract of the unripe beans of domesticated species of *Phaseolus*.

GREEN SOAP • A liquid soap made with potassium hydroxide and any vegetable oil except coconut or palm kernel oil.

GRINDELIA • A coarse, bumpy, or resinous herb grown in western America. It has flower heads with spreading tips. The dried leaves and stumps of these various gum weeds are used internally as a remedy in bronchitis and topically to soothe poison ivy rashes. Grindelia contains resin and an oil used in cosmetics. No known toxicity.

GROUNDSEL EXTRACT • Extract of *Senecio vulgaris*, a North American maritime shrub or tree.

GUAIACOL • Obtained from hardwood tar or made synthetically. White or yellow crystalline mass with a characteristic odor. Darkens when exposed to light. Used as an antiseptic both externally and internally. Ingestion causes irritation of the intestinal tract and heart failure. Penetrates the skin. Produces pain and burning and then loss of sensitivity when applied to mucous membranes. Causes the nose to run and the mouth to salivate. Deep irritant on the skin. Also used as a flavoring.

GUAIACWOOD OIL • Yellow to amber semisolid mass with a floral odor. Soluble in alcohol. Derived from steam distillation of guaiacwood (*see*). Used as a perfume fixative and modifier, soap odorant, and in frangrances.

GUAIAZULENE • A color additive also called azulene. Permanently listed as a cosmetic for external use only in 1978. See Azulene.

GUANIDINE CARBONATE • Used to adjust pH (*see*) and to keep cosmetics moist. Colorless crystals, soluble in water, found in turnip juice, mushrooms, corn germ, rice hulls, mussels, and earthworms. Occurs as water-absorbing crystals, which are very alkaline. Used in organic synthesis and as a rubber accelerator. It is a muscle poison if ingested. No known toxicity to the skin.

GUANINE • **Pearl Essence.** Obtained from scales of certain fish, such as alewives and herring, by scraping. It is mixed with water and used in nail polish. However, it has been greatly replaced with either synthetic pearl (bismuth oxychloride; see Bismuth Compounds) or aluminum and bronze particles. Lethal when injected into the abdomen of mice but no known toxicity in humans. Permanently listed as a cosmetic coloring in 1977.

GUANOSINE • An organic compound that is found in the pancreas, clover, coffee plant, and pine pollen. Usually prepared from yeast. It is used in biochemical research. No known toxicity.

GUAR GUM • Used in emulsions, toothpastes, lotions, and creams.

From ground nutritive seed tissue of plants cultivated in India, it has 5 to 8 times the thickening power of starch. Employed also as a bulk laxative, appetitie suppressant, and to treat peptic ulcers. A stabilizer in foods and beverages. No known toxicity.

GUAR HYDROXYPROPYLTRIMONIUM CHLORIDE • See Quaternary Ammonium Compounds.

GUM ARABIC • **Acacia Gum.** The exudate from acacia trees grown in the Sudan used in face masks, hair sprays, setting lotions, rouge, and powders for compacts. Serves as an emulsifier, stabilizer, and gelling agent. It may cause allergic reactions such as hay fever, dermatitis, gastrointestinal distress, and asthma.

GUM BENZOIN • Used as a preservative in creams and ointments and as a skin protective. It is the balsamic resin from benzoin grown in Thailand, Cambodia, Sumatra, and Cochin China. Also used to glaze and polish confections. May cause allergic reactions.

GUM DAMMAR • See Dammar.

GUM GUAIAC • Resin from the wood of the guaiacum used widely as an antioxidant in cosmetic creams and lotions. Brown or greenish-brown. Formerly used in treatment of rheumatism. No known toxicity.

GUM KARAYA • **Sterculia Gum.** Used in hair sprays, beauty masks, setting lotions, depilatories, rouge, powder for compacts, shaving creams, denture adhesive powder, hand lotions, and toothpastes. It is the dried exudate of a tree native to India. Karaya came into wide use during World War I as a cheaper substitute for gum tragacanth (*see*). Karaya swells in water and alcohol, but does not dissolve. It is used in finger wave lotions, which dry quickly and are not sticky. Because of its high viscosity at low concentrations, its ability to produce highly stable emulsions, and its resistance to acids, it is widely used in frozen food products. In 1971, however, the FDA put this additive on the list of chemicals to be studied for teratogenic, mutagenic, subacute, and reproductive effects. It can cause allergic reactions such as hay fever, dermatitis, gastrointestinal diseases, and asthma. It is omitted from hypoallergenic cosmetics.

GUM ROSIN • See Rosins.

GUM SUMATRA • See Gum Benzoin.

GUM TRAGACANTH • An emulsifier used in brilliantines, shaving creams, toothpastes, face packs, foundation creams, hair sprays, mascara, depilatories, compact powder, rouge, dentifrices, setting lotions, eye makeup, and hand lotions. It is the gummy exudate from a plant grown in Iran and Asia Minor. Its acid forms a gel. It may cause allergic reactions such as hay fever, dermatitis, gastrointestinal distress, and asthma.

GUMS • The true plant gums are the dried exudates from various plants obtained when the bark is cut or otherwise injured. They are soluble in hot or cold water, and sticky. Today, the term "gum" usually refers to water-soluble thickeners, either natural or synthetic; thickeners that are insoluble in water are called "resins." Gums are used in perfumes, dentifrices, emollient creams, facepowders, hair-grooming aids, hair straighteners, hand creams, rouges, shampoos, skin bleach creams, and wave sets. No known toxicity other than individual allergic reactions to specific gum.

GUTTA-PERCHA • **Gummi Plasticum.** The purified, coagulated, milky exudate of various trees grown in the Malay Archipelago. Related to rubber; on exposure to air and sunlight, it becomes brittle. Used in dental cement, in fracture splints for broken bones, and to cover golf balls. No known toxicity.

H

HAIR BLEACH • Among the most ancient of cosmetic preparations the Roman maidens used were various native minerals such as quicklime mixed with old lime, to produce reddish-gold tresses. The most widely used bleach today is simply hydrogen peroxide. It has been employed to bleach hair since 1867. Reports of problems with hair bleach include nausea, burned scalp, severe life-threatening allergic reactions, and swelling of the face.

HAIR COLOR RINSES • This is a temporary hair color that covers the cuticle layer of the hair only and does not affect natural color pigment inside the hair shaft. Used after shampooing it is usually washed out with the next shampooing. There are color shampoos formulated with a synthetic detergent and color, and there are powders, crayons, wave sets, and lacquers that are also used for temporary coloring. The most common color rinses today combine azo dyes (*see*). Acids used in hair color rinses are usually citric and tartaric. The rinses may also contain fatty acids, alcohols or amides, borax, glycols, thickening agents, and isopropyl alcohol. Recent complaints to the FDA about hair rinses include ear numbness, headaches, and hair turning the wrong color. One of the problems with hair rinses is that when customers are allergic to permanent dyes, they become allergic to rinses, although the chemicals are not the same.

HAIR COLORING • Permanent hair-coloring products change the color of the hair. They cannot be shampooed away but remain until the hair grows out or is cut off. The root hair must be "retouched" as it grows in. There are basically three types: natural organics, synthetics, and metallics. Natural organics such as henna and chamomile have been used for centuries to color hair. Such dyes are placed on the hair and removed when the desired shade has been obtained. They are more difficult to apply, less reliable than manufactured dyes, and less predictable as far as color is concerned. They can cause allergic reactions to specific ingredients but are harmless otherwise. Synthetic dyes such as para- or amino derivatives work by oxidation, that is, they are applied cold and depend on the development of the shade by the action of the compound such as hydrogen peroxide to liberate oxygen. They frequently cause skin rashes and allergic skin reactions, and the laws in most states require that patch-testing be done before use. This means applying the dye to the skin 24 hours in advance to see if any irritation or reaction occurs. This precaution is rarely observed. Furthermore, there is evidence that *p*-phenylenediamine products may cause skin cancer. Semi-permanent dyes, which also carry a warning to patch-test, require no mixing before use; there is a notice that they will last only for four or five shampoos. Metallic hair dyes offer no shade selection, and directions indicate the shades develop gradually with each use. Recent reports to the FDA of injuries from hair coloring include scalp irritation, hair breakage and loss, contact dermatitis, swelling of the face, and itching. In 1977, the National Cancer Institute reported that studies on laboratory animals showed that those fed large amounts of hair dye developed thyroid and skin tumors. The agency warned that the studies indicated potential cancer danger to women who might absorb cancer-causing agents through their scalps. In 1978, a New York University Medical Center researcher reported that a study of 129 women with breast cancer and 193 without showed that the breast tumors were more likely to develop among hairdye users who would otherwise be considered "at lower natural risks" for breast cancer. The cancers appeared about 10 years after dyes were in use. The cosmetic manufacturers voluntarily removed 4-MMPD, the dye ingredient known to be a cancer-causing agent. However, others in the phenylalamine group and other coal tar derivatives remain, and women continue to dye their hair. In 1979, the FDA attempted to force cosmetic manufacturers to include a cancer warning on coal tar hair dyes containing 4-methoxy-*o*-phenylenediamine and 2,4-diamino-anisole. Japanese researchers showed that another hair dye intermediate, 2,4-diaminotoluene (2,4-DAT) caused cancer in animals. It was removed from most hair dyes in 1971 but was still a part of seven dyes in late 1977. The National Cancer Institute data shows that two other hair dye components cause cancer in laboratory animals,

2-nitro-*p*-phenylenediamine, contained in at least 354 hair dyes in 1979, and 4-amino-2-nitrophenol, contained in at least 90 hair dyes. Six other hair dye ingredients are positive on the AMES test, which shows that 150 of 169 permanent hair dyes are mutagenic. The AMES test used genetic damage in bacteria as a signal that a chemical is potentially carcinogenic. Available evidence indicates that chemicals related to hair dyes can be absorbed through the skin and distributed throughout the body in small but significant amounts. The scalp is a good route for absorption of hair dyes into the system because it is a large surface with a large number of sebaceous glands.

HAIR CONDITIONERS • Hair conditioners try to undo the damage from other hair preparations, particularly bleaches and dyes, and from the drying effects of the sun as well as the aging process. They include humectants, finishing agents, and emulsions. Hair is softened by water. Consequently, humectants bring moisture into the hair and reduce brittleness. Glycerin, propylene glycol, sorbitol, and urea (*see all*) help retain moisture and keep water from evaporating and consequently keep hair softer. Finishing agents, which include cream rinses, are added to shampoos or applied after shampooing. They leave a film on the hair to make it feel soft and look shiny. Isopropyl myristate and balsam are examples (*see both*). Emulsions, including cream and protein conditioners, are applied before, during, or after shampooing and sometimes between shampoos. They should be nonsticking and if rubbed between the hands, they should disappear. Such products usually contain lanolin, alcohols, sterols, glyceryl monostearate, spermaceti, glycerin, mineral oil, water, and perfume (*see all*). The aerosol type of hair conditioner is made by preparing a "concentrate" from lanolin, isopropyl palmitate (*see*), perfume oil, and some propellant. Protein conditioners contain a protein (*see*) such as beer or egg, aimed at replacing lost protein. However, according to the American Medical Association, there is little, if any evidence, to substantiate their effectiveness. There is no proof that protein from hair conditioners can penetrate the hair shaft and reconstruct healthy hair. If there is any effect, it is merely a coating similar to those of cream rinses (*see*). Except for individual allergies, hair conditioners are nontoxic.

HAIR LACQUERS AND SPRAYS • These products "hold the set" and keep the hair looking as if it were just done at the beauty parlor. Once strictly a woman's product, men now freely spray their hair. Hair lacquers usually come in either a plastic squeeze bottle or an aerosol. The early products contained shellac, and some still do. The shellac type is made by dissolving perfume in alcohol and then adding shellac (the excretion of certain insects), and then adding a mixture of triethanolamine (*see*) and water. PEGs, lanolin alcohols, and castor oil may also be included in the mixture (*see all*). The early shellacs made hair shine but caused it to be brittle to the touch. The addition of lanolin, castor oil, and glycol counteract this effect. The newer hair lacquers contain a product used as a blood extender in medicine—polyvinylpyrrolidone (PVP). Related to plastics and similar to egg albumin in texture, it slightly stiffens the hair to keep it in place. PVP is dissolved in ether and then glycerin and perfume is added. The solution may also include polyethylene glycol, cetyl alcohol, and lanolin alcohols (*see all*). Pressurized hair sprays contain PVP, alcohol, sorbitol, and water. Additional ingredients may be lanolin, perfume, shellac, silicone, sodium alginate, or vegetable gums such as gum karaya, acacia, or gum tragacanth (*see all*). Most sprays can cause eye and lung damage and should be used with caution. The pump sprays are a better choice than aerosols because they are not as fine and thus, not as easily inhaled. Complaints to the FDA about hair sprays include headache, hair loss, rash, change in hair color, throat irritation, suspected lung lesions, and death. In one case the hair ignited after a cigarette was lit. See Aerosols.

HAIR RINSES • Aimed at improving the feel and appearance of hair. Usually made of water-soluble material that can be dissolved and dispersed after application. When water has evaporated, a deposit is left behind, which forms a film. Among ingredients used as gums, certain protein derivatives, and synthetic polymers. A basic cream rinse contains glyceryl monostearate, 3 percent; benzalkonium chloride, 3 percent; water, about 94 percent; perfume, and coloring. The American Medical Association maintains that cream rinses cannot repair damaged hair as claimed in advertisements. See Hair Conditioners.

HAIR SPRAYS • See Hair Lacquers and Sprays.

HAIR STRAIGHTENERS • Half the population wants curly hair and the other wants straight hair: There are three methods, none perfect, for straightening hair; pomades that coat the hair and glue it straight; the much advertised hot combs and irons; and chemical straighteners. Pomades, of course, are the least effective but the least damaging. Heating the hair, when done properly at 300° to 500° F, does straighten the strands when tension is applied. Burns of the scalp are not uncommon, and the hair is dried out and may become very brittle. Chemical straighteners are effective but can cause burns, irritations, and hair damage. They usually contain either thioglycolic acid compounds (*see*) or alkalies such as sodium hydroxide as well as polyethylene glycol, cetyl alcohol, stearyl alcohol, a triethanolamine, propylene glycol (*see all*), perfume, and water. The glycols and alcohols may be caustic. The thioglycolate curl relaxers require the application of a neutralizer to the hair to stop the straightening process. Although there are some hair-straightening kits, there is a fine line between enough straightening and too much. If possible, the procedure should be done by a professional. The alkali curl relaxants, which are more effective for kinky hair, straighten the hair in about 5 to 10 minutes while a comb is run through. The hair is then rinsed with water to stop the chemical action. Again, there is a fine line between enough and too much, and the procedure should be done by a professional. Alkali straighteners contain strong burning ingredients, and first to third degree chemical burns can occur. They can also cause allergic reactions and swelling of the face and scalp. The greatest danger from these products is eye damage. Extreme caution must be used to avoid contact with the eyes. The hair will become fragile with any form of chemical or heat straightening. Bleached hair is particularly susceptible, and straightening of bleached hair is usually not recommended. Recent reports to the FDA of injuries include scalp irritation, loss of hair, and scalp burns.

HAIR THICKENERS • See Hair Tonics, Lotions, and Thickeners.

HAIR TONICS, LOTIONS, AND THICKENERS • Hair tonics and lotions are designed to keep the hair in place and looking healthy. There are three basic types: alcoholic, emulsion, and drug/tonic. Alcoholics may consist of an oil mixed with alcohol, glycerin (*see*), and perfume. Emulsions may be made by heating mineral oil and stearic acid (*see*), mixing it with hot water and triethanolamine (*see*), and adding perfume. The tonic or drug-type hairdressing usually contains antiseptics and may affect the function or structure of the human body or they are designed to treat a diseased condition. They also contain low concentrations of rubefacients (these are products that cause a reddening and thus stimulation of the skin). Antiseptics employed may be creosols, phenols, chlorothymol, or resorcinol (*see all*). There is another type of hairdressing, used mostly by men, which is similar to a wave set common to women. It contains natural gums such as tragacanth, and karaya, or sodium alginate with alcohol, water, perfume, and glycerol. Among other chemicals in hair tonics and lotions are benzalkonium chloride, beta-naphthol, biothiniol, camphor, cantharides tincture, chloral hydrate, hexachlorophene, phosphoric acid, pilocarpine, glycols, quinine, sorbitan derivatives, salicylic acid, and tars (*see all*). Hair thickeners contain oils and proteins that coat the hair with an invisible film, thus giving it body. The thickeners make the hair feel smoother, and it is more manageable. A common hair tonic formula contains resorcinol, 0.8 percent; chloral hydrate, 1.5 percent; ethanol 80 percent; beta-naphthol 0.8 percent. Turkey-red oil, 16.9 percent; perfume; and color (*see all*). Complaints to the FDA about hair conditioners and dressings include loss of hair, eye irritation, pimples, inflamed scalp, hair shrunk into knots, face irritation, dryness, and rash.

HAMAMELIS WATER • See Witch Hazel.

HANDS • See Contact Dermatitis.

HAND CREAMS AND LOTIONS • These are emollients, which apply easily and without stickiness. Most contain stearic acid, lanolin, and water. They may also contain cetyl alcohol, mineral oil, glycerin, potassium hydroxide, perfume, and glyceryl monostearate. The newer formulas may also contain healing agents such as allantoin (*see*) and water repellent silicones (*see*) to protect the hands against further irritation from water, detergents, or wind. Most leading hand creams and lotions are uncolored, though surveys show that pink or blue hand creams are preferred; women over 25 years prefer pink and teenagers, blue. The pH level (*see*) of most hand creams and lotions is between 5 and 8. A typical formula for hand cream contains cetyl alcohol, 2 percent; lanolin, 1 percent; mineral oil, 2 percent; stearic acid, 13 percent; glycerin, 12 percent; methylparaben, 0.15 percent; potassium hydroxide, 1 percent; water, 68 percent; and perfume in sufficient amounts (*see all*). A typical hand lotion contains cetyl alcohol, 0.5 percent; lanolin, 1 percent; stearic acid, 3 percent; glycerin, 2 percent; methylparaben, 0.1 percent; triethanolamine, 0.75 percent; water, 85 percent; and perfume in sufficient amounts (*see all*). Among problems reported to the FDA concerning hand preparations were rash, blisters, and swollen feet. Lanolin derivatives, colors and perfumes, of course, are possible allergens.

HANDKERCHIEF PERFUMES • A woman's perfume in a retail shop. The name was derived from the practice of dabbing scent on a handkerchief to allow the sniffer to distinguish between perfume compounds.

HAWKWEED EXTRACT • An extract of the various species of *Hieracium*.

HAYFLOWER EXTRACT • An extract of hayflowers used in bath salts.

HAZEL NUT OIL • The oil obtained from the various species of the hazel nut tree, genus *Corylus*.

HC • The abbreviation for hair color.

HC BLACK NO. 1 • **Calcozine Black CBF.** Commercial hair coloring. See Colors.

HC BLUE NO. 1 • N^4, N^4-Bis (2-Hydroxyethyl)-N^1-Methyl-2-Nitro-*p*-Phenylenediamine. Commercial hair coloring. See *p*-Phenylenediamine and Colors.

HC BLUE NO. 2 • N^1, N^4, N^4-(2-Hydroxyethyl)-2-Nitro-p-Phenylenediamine. Commercial hair coloring. See *p*-Phenylenediamine and Colors.

HC BLUE NO. 3 • Cibalan Blue FBL. Commercial hair coloring. See Colors.

HC BLUE NO. 4 • A reaction product of diaminoanthraquinone, epichlorohydrin, and monothanolamine. It contains benzendiamine. See *p*-Phenylenediamine.

HC BLUE NO. 5 • A reaction product of 2-nitro-*p*-phenylenediamine (*see*), epichlorohydrin, and diethanolamine. Contains benzenediamine. See *p*-Phenylenediamine.

HC BROWN NO. 1 • Capracyl Brown 2R. Commerical hair coloring. See Colors.

HC ORANGE NO. 1 • 2-Nitro-4-Hydroxydiphenylamine. Commercial hair coloring. See *p*-Phenylenediamine and Colors.

HC RED NO. 1 • 4-Amino-2-Nitrodiphenylamine. Commercial haircoloring. See *p*-Phenylenediamine and Colors.

HC RED NO. 3 • N^1-(2-Hydroxyethyl)-2-Nitro-p-Phenylenediamine. Commerical hair coloring. See *p*-Phenylenediamine and Colors.

HC RED NO. 6 • Formerly FD & C Red No. 1 and Food Red 6. A monoazo dye. See Azo Dyes.

HC YELLOW NO. 2 • N-(2-Hydroxyethyl)-2-Nitroaniline. Commercial hair coloring. See Aniline Dyes and Colors.

HC YELLOW NO. 3 • N^1-Tris (Hydroxymethyl)-Methyl-4-Nitro-o-Phenylenediamine. Commercial hair coloring. See *p*-Phenylenediamine and Colors.

HC YELLOW NO. 5 • N^1-(2-Hydroxyethyl)-4-Nitro-o-Phenylenediamine. Commercial hair coloring. See *p*-Phenylenediamine.

HCL • The abbreviation for hydrochloride.

HEALING AGENTS • Medications added to hand creams and lotions (*see*) to treat chapped and irritated hands. Allantoin (*see*) is probably the most widely used healing agent in hand creams and lotions. Urea (*see*) has also been used.

HEATHER EXTRACT • An extract of *Calluna vulgaris,* also called Ling Extract.

HECTORITE • An emulsifier and extender. A clay consisting of silicate of magnesium and lithium, it is used in the chill-proofing of beer. The dust can be irritating to the lungs. No known toxicity of the skin.

HEDTA • **Hydroxyethyl Ethylenediamine Triacetic Acid.** A liquid with an ammonia odor, it is used in textile finishing compounds, antiquing agents, dyestuffs, cationic surfactants, resins, rubber products, insecticides, and medicines. Low toxicity.

HELIOTROPE • **Desert Heliotrope.** Bluish-purple flowers on a stem that coils in the shape of a fiddle neck. It grows through the southwestern United States and is a frequent cause of allergic contact dermatitis on the legs and ankles of persons walking through the desert.

HELIOTROPIN • **Piperonal**. A purple diazo dye used in perfumery and soaps. Consists of colorless, lustrous crystals that have a heliotrope odor. Usually made from oxidation of piperic acid. Ingestion of large amounts may cause central nervous system depression. Applications to the skin may cause allergic reactions and skin irritations. Not recommended for use in cosmetics or perfumes.

HENNA • **Henna Leaves.** An ancient hair cosmetic obtained from the ground-up, dried leaves and stems of a shrub found in North Africa and the Near East. A paste of henna and water is applied directly to the hair and a reddish color is produced. There is no known toxicity, but allergic skin rashes may occur. However, those who are allergic to other dyes may be able to use henna without problems. Although it is rather messy and unpredictable to use, there is renewed interest in the dye because of the desire to return to "natural" products rather than using man-made cosmetics. The FDA ruled that henna is safe for coloring hair only. It may not be used for coloring eyelashes or eyebrows or in the area of the eyes. Permanently listed in 1965.

HEPTANAL • **Heptaldehyde.** Oily, colorless liquid with a penetrating fruit odor made from castor oil. Used in perfumery, pharmaceuticals and flavoring.

HEPTANE • An aliphatic hydrocarbon. Volatile, colorless liquid derived from petroleum and used as an anesthetic and solvent. Highly flammable. Toxic by inhalation.

HEPTANOIC ACID • **Enanthic Acid.** Found in various fusel oils and in rancid oils, it has the faint odor of tallow. It is made from grapes and is a fatty acid used chiefly in making esters (*see*) for flavoring materials. No known toxicity.

2-HEPTANONE • Used in perfumery as a constituent of artificial carnation oils. Found in oil of cloves and in cinnamon bark oil. It has a peppery fruity odor that is very penetrating. Heptanone is responsible for the peppery odor of Roquefort cheese. Can be irritating to human mucous membranes and is narcotic in high doses.

1-HEPTYL ACETATE • Liquid with fruit odor used in artificial fruit essences. See 2-Heptanone.

n-HEPTYL ALCOHOL • **1-Heptanol.** Colorless, fragrant liquid miscible with alcohol. Used in perfumery. See 2-Heptanone.

n-HEPTYL FORMATE • Used in artificial fruit essences. See 2-Heptanone.

HEPTYL HEPTOATE • Colorless liquid with fruity odor used in artificial fruit essences. See 2-Heptanone.

HEPTYL PELARGONATE • Liquid with pleasant odor used in flavors and perfumes. See 2-Heptanone.

n-HEPTYLIC ACID • See Heptanoic Acid.

HEPTYLUNDECANOL • Synthetic Queen Bee Substance secreted by the jaw glands of queen bees to keep other bees from becoming rivals. See 2-Heptanone.

HERB ROBERT EXTRACT • Extract of the entire plant, *Geranium robertianum.* See Geranium Oil.

HERBAL SHAMPOOS • Many contain saponins, a class of substances found in many plants. They possess the common properties of foaming, or making suds when agitated in water. They also hold resins and fatty substances in suspension in water. These products clean the scalp and reduce scaliness. Here is the typical formula for herbal shampoos: quillaja bark, powdered, 5 percent; ammonium carbonate, 1 percent; borax, 1 percent; bay oil, 1 percent (*see all*); and water, 9.2 percent. Saponins can be irritating when applied to the skin, and when given internally can cause nausea. Toxicity of herbal shampoos depends on ingredients and amounts used. The allergic potential of the shampoos also depends on sensitivity and the herbs used as well as the other ingredients such as quillaja bark and ammonium carbonate.

HEXACHLOROPHENE • An antibacterial used in baby oil, baby powder, brilliantine hairdressings, cold creams, emollients, deodorants, antiperspirants, face masks, hair tonics, shampoos, and medicated cosmetics products. In 1969 scientists reported microscopically visible brain damage in rats from small concentrations of the antibacterial. The company that had the patent on hexachlorophene, the Swiss-based Givaudan Corporation, sold the chemical only to those companies that could demonstrate a safe and effective use for it. Givaudan refused to sell hexachlorophene for use in toothpastes and mouthwashes. However, when the patents expired in the mid-1960s, the FDA allowed hexachlorophene to be used in toothpastes and mouthwashes. In 1971 the chemical was an ingredient of nearly 400 products ranging from fruit washes to baby lotion. Chloasma, a pigmenting of the face, was reported in 1961 in persons who had used hexachlorophene-containing products. Coma was reported in burn patients washed in hexachlorophene products in 1968. On March 29, 1971, August Curly and Robert E. Hawk of the U.S. Environmental Protection Agency presented a paper in Los Angeles at the American Chemical Society meeting stating that hexachlorophene had been found toxic to experimental animals, capable of penetrating the skin, and present in the blood of some human beings. Tests on 13 human volunteers showed hexachlorophene levels of one part in a billion parts of blood to 89 ppb. Curley, chief research chemist at the EPA at the time, said that the agency thought the material was absorbed through the skin. He pointed out: "For over two decades, hexachlorophene has been widely used as a bactericide in the United States. However, realtively little quantitative data is available concerning its dermal absorption in either experimental animals or humans." On May 17, 1971, the American Academy of Pediatrics warned that products containing hexachlorophene that are intended for oral use, such as certain toothpastes or throat lozenges, may be poisonous to children. In December 1971 the FDA curbed the use of hexachlorophene containing detergents and soaps for total body bathing. Winthrop, the makers of pHisohex, which contained 3 percent hexachlorophene, sent out further information to doctors saying that the product should not be used as a lotion, left on the skin after use, used as a wet soak or compress, or transferred to another container that would allow for misuse. It should always be rinsed thoroughly from the skin after any use, should be used in strict accordance with directions, and it should always be kept out of reach of children. The FDA has limited it up to 0.75 percent. Products containing up to 0.75 percent will be able to continue on the market with a warning: "Contains hexachlorophene. For external use only. Rinse thoroughly." According to the summary of the report included in the Federal Register, the cancer testing program showed that hexachlorophene did not cause tumors in rats under test conditions.

HEXADECYL METHICONE • A silicone wax. See Silicones.

HEXADIMETHRINE CHLORIDE • See Polymers.

HEXAMETHYLDISILOXANE • See Silicates.

HEXAMIDINE DIISETHIONATE • An organic salt that is used as a topical antiseptic derived from petroleum distillate (*see*).

HEXANEDIOL DISTEARATE • The diester of hexanediol and stearic acid used as a wax and a plasticizer. It is derived from ethyl alcohol and stearic acid (*see both*).

1, 2, 6-HEXANETRIOL • An alcohol used as a solvent. No known skin toxicity.

HEXANOL • **Hexyl Alcohol.** Used as an antiseptic and preservative in cosmetics, it occurs as the acetate (*see*) in seeds and fruits of *Heracleum sphondylium* and *Umbelliferae*. Colorless liquid, slightly soluble in water, it is miscible with alcohol. No known toxicity.

HEXYL ALCOHOL • Used in antiseptics and in perfumery. See Hexanol.

HEXYL LAURATE • See Lauric Acid.

HEXYL NICOTINATE • The ester of hexyl alcohol and nicotinic acid (*see both*).

HEXYLENE GLYCOL • See Polyethylene Glycol.

4-HEXYLRESORCINOL • Used in mouthwashes and sunburn creams. A pale yellow heavy liquid that becomes solid upon standing at room temperature. It has a pungent odor and a sharp astringent taste and has been used medicinally as an antiworm medicine and antiseptic. It can cause severe gastrointestinal irritation; bowel, liver, and heart damage have been reported. Concentrated solutions can cause burns of the skin and mucous membranes.

HINOKITIOL • The organic compound distilled from the leaves of *Arbor vitae*, it is a pale yellow oil with a camphor smell, and is used in perfumery and flavoring. Low toxicity.

HISTAMINE • A chemical released by mast cells and considered responsible for much of the swelling and itching characteristics of hay fever and other allergies.

HISTIDINE • A basic essential amino acid (*see*) used as a nutrient. It is a building block of protein and is used in cosmetic creams.

HOMOSALATE • **Heliphan.** See Cresol.

HONEY • Used as a coloring, flavoring, and emollient in cosmetics. Formerly used in hair bleaches. The common, sweet, viscous material taken from the nectar of flowers and manufactured in the sacs of various kinds of bees. The flavor and color depend upon the plants from which it was taken.

HONEYDEW MELON JUICE • Liquid expressed from fresh honeydew.

HONEYSUCKLE • The common fragrant tubular flowers, filled with honey, which are used in perfumes. No known toxicity.

HOPS • Used in perfumes and flavorings. Derived from the carefully dried pineconelike fruit of the hop plant grown in Europe, Asia, and North America. Light yellow or greenish, it is an oily liquid with a bitter taste and aromatic odor. Used also in beer brewing and for food flavorings. Hops at one time was used as a sedative. Can cause allergic reactions.

HOPS OIL • See Hops.

HORMONE CREAMS • The cosmetic manufacturers claim that hormone creams containing estrogen or progesterone are cosmetics, and many dermatologists and some staff members of the U.S. Food and Drug Administration maintain they are drugs. Cosmetic manufacturers, ever aware of the human desire to stay young forever, have advertised the hormone creams as wrinkle preventatives and youthful skin restoratives. According to the American Medical Association, there is little scientific evidence that locally applied hormones can thicken the thinning skin of aging and that simple emollient creams may do a better job. In a review of the experimental data on the use of sex steroids in cosmetics, there was some evidence that topically applied steroidal hormones, both active and inactive biologically, do cause a slight thickening of aged skin. However, the effects are negligible, and in the amounts considered safe to use in cosmetics, topically applied hormones have no effect on human oil glands and oil secretion. Estrogen may be added at not more than 10,000 international units per ounce. Progesterone content may not exceed 5 mg per ounce. Enlargement of the breast in boys using estrogen-containing hair lotion, La Cade®, was reported in *The American Journal of the Diseases of Childhood,* July 1982, p. 587 by Deborah Edidin, M.D. and Lynne Levitsky, M.D.

HORSE CHESTNUT • The seeds of *Aesculus hippocastanum.* A tonic, natural astringent for skin, ad fever-reducing substance that contains tannic acid (*see*). No known toxicity.

HORSERADISH EXTRACT • **Scurvy Grass.** A condiment ingredient utilizing the grated root from the tall, coarse, white-flowered herb native to Europe. Often combined with vinegar or other ingredients. Contains ascorbic acid (*see*) and acts as an antiseptic in cosmetics. No known toxicity.

HOT OIL TREATMENT • Used to restore luster to bleach-damaged hair. The hair is completely doused with oil and then heated by a lamp or an electric cap. Oils include mineral and vegetable.

HOUSELEEK EXTRACT • Extract of the common houseleek *Sempervivum tectorum.* Old herbal remedy for soothing the skin.

HUMAN PLACENTAL PROTEIN • Protein derived from the sac that surrounds the fetus. Obtained from normal afterbirth. Used in "anti-aging" creams.

HUMAN UMBILICAL EXTRACT • Used in "anti-aging" creams.

HUMECTANT • A substance used to preserve the moisture content of materials, especially in hand creams and lotions. The humectant of glycerin and rose water, in equal amounts, is the earliest known hand lotion. Glycerin, propylene, glycol, and sorbitol (*see all*) are widely used humectants in hand creams and lotions. Humectants are usually found in antiperspirants, baby preparations, beauty masks, dentifrices, depilatories, hair-grooming aids, and wave sets. See individual substances for toxicity.

HYACINTH • Used in perfumes and soaps. It is the extract of the very common fragrant flower. Also used as a flavoring for chewing gum. Dark green liquid with a penetrating odor, the juice of hyacinth is very irritating to the skin and can cause allergic reactions.

HYALURONIC ACID • A natural protein found in umbilical cords and the fluids around the joints. Used as a cosmetic oil. No known toxicity.

HYBRID SAFFLOWER OIL • The oil derived from the seeds of a genetic strain which contains mostly oleic acid triglyceride as distinct from safflower oil.

HYDANTOIN • Derived from methanol (*see*), it is used as an intermediate in the synthesis of lubricants and resins. It caused cancer when injected into the abdomens of rats in doses of 1,370 mg per kilogram of body weight and when given orally to rats in doses of 1,500 mg per kilogram.

HYDRATED • Combined with water.

HYDRATED ALUMINA • See Aluminum Hydroxide.

HYDRATED SILICA • An anticaking agent to keep loose powders free-flowing. See Silica and Hydrated.

HYDROABIETYL ALCOHOL • Used in eyebrow pencils. See Abietic Acid.

HYDROCARBONS • A large class of organic compounds containing only carbon and hydrogen. Petroleum, natural gas, coal, and bitumens are common hydrocarbon products. Hydrocarbons such as petrolatum, mineral oils, paraffin wax, and ozokerite have been used in sunscreens, hand creams, lotions, and nail polish. They are believed to work by forming a water-repellent film that keeps water from evaporating from the skin.

HYDROCHLORIC ACID • Acid used in hair bleaches to speed up oxidation in rinses and to remove color. Also a solvent. A clear, colorless, or slightly yellowish, corrosive liquid, it is a water solution of hydrogen chloride of varying concentrations. Inhalation of the fumes causes choking and inflammation of the respiratory tract. Ingestion may corrode the mucous membranes, esophagus, and stomach, and cause diarrhea.

HYDROCHLOROFLUOROCARBON, 22, 142b, 152a • Propellants and refrigerants derived from chlorofluorcarbon, any of several compounds comprised of carbon, fluorine, chlorine, and hydrogen. Though safer than many propellant gases, their use has diminished because of suspected effects on stratospheric ozone.

HYDROGEN PEROXIDE • A bleaching and oxidizing agent, a detergent, and antiseptic. Used in skin bleaches, hair bleaches, cold creams, mouthwashes, toothpastes, and in cold permanent waves. An unstable compound readily broken down into water and oxygen. It is made from barium peroxide and diluted phosphoric acid. Generally recognized as safe as a preservative and germ killer in cosmetics as well as in milk and cheese. A three percent solution is used medicinally as an antiseptic and germicide. A strong oxidizer, undiluted it can cause burns of the skin and mucous membranes.

HYDROGENATED ANIMAL GLYCERIDE • The end product of the hydrogenation (*see*) of animal glyceride (*see*).

HYDROGENATED C6-14 OLEFIN POLYMERS • Low molecular weight polymers of olefin monomers. Olefin is a class of unsaturated hydrocarbons obtained by "cracking" naphtha or other petroleum products and used in the manufacture of surfactants (*see*).

HYDROGENATED CASTOR OIL • Used as a wax. See Castor Oil and Hydrogenation.

HYDROGENATED COCO-GLYCERIDES • See Coconut Oil, Triglycerides, and Hydrogenation.

HYDROGENATED COCONUT ACID • See Coconut Oil and Hydrogenation.

HYDROGENATED COCONUT OIL • See Coconut Oil and Hydrogenation.

HYDROGENATED COTTONSEED GLYCERIDE • See Cottonseed Oil and Hydrogenation.

HYDROGENATED COTTONSEED OIL • See Cottonseed Oil and Hydrogenation.

HYDROGENATED DITALLOW AMINE • An amine derived from Hydrogenated Tallow Acid. See Tallow Oil.

HYDROGENATED FATTY OILS • Used in baby creams and lipsticks. See Fatty Acids and Hydrogenation.

HYDROGENATED HONEY • Controlled hydrogenation (*see*) of honey.

HYDROGENATED JOJOBA OIL, WAX • See Jojoba and Hydrogenation.

HYDROGENATED LANETH-5, -20, -25 • See Hydrogenated Lanolin.

HYDROGENATED LANOLIN • A light yellow to white tacky solid which is soluble in ethyl ether but insoluble in water. It retains the emollient and adhering characteristics of lanolin but loses the latter's odor, taste, color, and tackiness. Used in eye makeup preparations; colognes and toilet water; manicuring preparations; waving preparations; skin care preparations such as creams, lotions, powders, and sprays; and suntan and sunscreen preparations.

HYDROGENATED LANOLIN ALCOHOL • See Hydrogenated Lanolin.

HYDROGENATED LARD GLYCERIDE • See Lard and Hydrogenation.

HYDROGENATED PALM GLYCERIDES. • See Palm Oil and Hydrogenation.

HYDROGENATED PALM-KERNEL OIL • See Palm-Kernel Oil and Hydrogenation.

HYDROGENATED PALM-KERNEL OIL PEG-6 COMPLEX • See Palm-Kernel Oil, Hydrogenation, and Polyethylene Glycol.

HYDROGENATED PALM OIL • See Palm Oil and Hydrogenation.

HYDROGENATED PEANUT OIL • See Peanut Oil and Hydrogenation.

HYDROGENATED POLYISOBUTENE • See Isobutyric Acid and Hydrogenation.

HYDROGENATED RICE BRAN WAX • See Rice Bran and Hydrogenation.

HYDROGENATED SHARK-LIVER OIL • See Shark Liver and Hydrogenation.

HYDROGENATED SOY GLYCERIDE • See Soybean Oil and Hydrogenation.

HYDROGENATED SOYBEAN OIL • See Soybean Oil and Hydrogenation.

HYDROGENATED STARCH HYDROSYLATE • The end product of the hydrogenation of corn syrup. See Corn Syrup and Hydrogenation.

HYDROGENATED TALLOW ACID • See Tallow and Hydrogenation.

HYDROGENATED TALLOW BETAINE • See Betaine and Hydrogenation.

HYDROGENATED TALLOW GLYCERIDE • See Tallow and Hydrogenation.

HYDROGENATED TALLOWTRIMONIUM CHLORIDE • See Quaternary Ammonium Compounds.

HYDROGENATED VEGETABLE GLYCERIDE • An emollient to prevent the skin from losing moisture. See Vegetable Oils and Hydrogenation.

HYDROGENATION • The process of adding hydrogen gas under high pressure to liquid oils. It is the most widely used chemical process in the edible fat industry. Used in the manufacture of petrol from coal, and in the manufacture of margarine and shortening. Used primarily in the cosmetics and food industries to convert liquid oils to semisolid fats at room temperature. Reduces the amount of acid in the compound and improves color. Usually, the higher the amount of hydrogenation, the lower the unsaturation in the fat and the less possibility of flavor degradation or spoilage due to oxidation. Hydrogenated oils still contain some unsaturated components that are susceptible to rancidity. Therefore, the addition of antioxidants is still necessary.

HYDROLYZED • Subject to hydrolysis or turned partly into water. *Hydrolisis* is derived from the Greek *hydro*, meaning "water," and *lysis,* meaning "a setting free." It occurs as a chemical process in which the decomposition of a compound is brought about by water, resolving into a simpler compound. Hydrolysis also occurs in the digestion of foods. The proteins in the stomach react with water in an enzyme reaction to form peptones and amino acids (*see*).

HYDROLYZED ANIMAL ELASTIN • The hydrolyzed animal connective tissue used in emollients and creams.

HYDROLYZED ANIMAL KERATIN • See Keratin and Hydrolyzed.

HYDROLYZED ANIMAL PROTEIN • Improves the ability to comb hair. See Proteins and Hydrolyzed.

HYDROLYZED CASEIN • See Casein and Hydrolyzed.

HYDROLYZED ELASTIN • The hydrolysate of animal connective tissue, particularly the ligaments, used in "youth" creams.

HYDROLYZED HUMAN PLACENTAL PROTEIN • See Human Placental Protein and Hydrolyzed.

HYDROLYZED KERATIN • The hydrolysate of keratin derived by acid, enzyme, or other forms of hydrolysis. See Keratin.

HYDROLYZED MUCOPOLYSACCHARIDES • A mixture of polysaccharides derived from the hydrolysis of animal connective tissue.

HYDROLYZED SILK • The hydrolysate (turned partly into water) of silk protein derived by acid, alkaline, or enzymatic hydrolysis.

HYDROLYZED SOY PROTEIN • See Soy Bean and Hydrolyzed.

HYDROLYZED VEGETABLE PROTEIN • The hydrolysate (liquification) of vegetable protein derived by acid, enzyme, or other method of hydrolysis.

HYDROLYZED YEAST • The hydrolysate of yeast (liquification) derived from acid, enzyme, or other method of hydrolysis.

HYDROLYZED YEAST PROTEIN • See Hydrolyzed Yeast.

HYDROQUINOL • An alkaline solution that turns brown in air and is made up of white leaflets that are soluble in water. Used as an antiseptic and reducing agent (*see*) in cosmetics. Has caused skin cancer in mice.

HYDROQUINONE • Used in bleach and freckle creams and in suntan lotions. A white crystalline phenol (*see*) that occurs naturally but is usually manufactured in the laboratory. Hydroquinone combines with oxygen very rapidly and becomes brown when exposed to air. Death has occurred from the ingestion of as little as 5 grams. Ingestion of as little as one gram (1/30th of an ounce) has caused nausea, vomiting, ringing in the ears, delirium, a sense of suffocation, and collapse. Industrial workers exposed to the chemical have suffered clouding of the eye lens. Application to the skin may cause allergic reactions. It can cause depigmentation in a 2 percent solution. When injected into the abdomens of mice in 28-milligram doses per kilogram of body weight, it caused bladder cancers, but other studies in which animals were fed the chemical did not show it to induce cancer. However, it did cause atrophy of the liver and aplastic anemia.

HYDROQUINONE DIBENZYL ETHER • Tan powder insoluble in water. Used as a solvent and in perfumes, soap, plastics, and pharmaceuticals. See Hydroquinone.

HYDROQUINONE DIMETHYLETHER • White flakes with sweet clover odor used as a fixative in perfumes, dyes, cosmetics, and especially in suntan preparations. See Hydroquinone.

p-HYDROXYANISOLE • See Guaiacol.

HYDROXYANTHROQUINONEAMINOPROPYL METHYL MORPHOLIUMIUN METHOSULFATE • A solvent for resins and waxes, an antioxidant, and plasticizer. May be irritating to the skin.

o-HYDROXYBENZOIC ACID • See Salicylic Acid.

p-HYDROXYBENZOIC ACID • Prepared from *p*-bromophenol. Used as a preservative and fungicide. See Benzoic Acid for toxicity.

HYDROXYBENZOMORPHOLINE • **4-Salicylomorpholine.** Used medically to stimulate the liver.

HYDROXYCETETH-60 • See Polyethylene Glycol and Hexadecanoic Acid.

HYDROXYCITRONELLAL • **Laurine®.** Colorless liquid obtained by the addition of water to citronellol (*see*). Used as a fixative (*see*) and a fragrance in perfumery for its sweet lilylike odor. It has been known to cause allergic reactions.

HYDROXYETHYL CARBOXYMETHYL COCAMINOPROPYLATE • See Coconut Oil.

HYDROXYETHYL CELLULOSE • Used as a thickener in cosmetic creams and lotions. See Cellulose.

HYDROXYETHYL CETYLDIMONIUM CHLORIDE • See Quarternary Ammonium Compounds.

HYDROXYETHYL CETYLDIMONIUM PHOSPHATE • See Quaternary Ammonium Compounds.

HYDROXYETHYL PEI-1000, -1500 • See PEI.

HYDROXYETHYLAMINO-5-NITROANISOLE • See Ethanol.

HYDROXYLAMINE HCL • An antioxidant for fatty acids and soaps, sodium nitrite (*see*). May be slightly irritating to skin, eyes, and mucous membranes, and may cause a depletion of oxygen in the blood when ingested. In the body it is reportedly decomposed to sodium nitrite.

HYDROXYLAMINE SULFATE • A hair-waving component in permanent wave solutions, it is a crystalline ammonium sulfate compound. It is also used for dehairing hides, in photography, as a chemical reducing agent, and to purify aldehydes (*see*) and ketones (*see*). No known toxicity to the skin. The lethal dose given in the abdomens of rats is small.

HYDROXYLATE • The product of hydroxylation (*see*).

HYDROXYLATED LANOLIN • It is better than plain lanolin because the hydroxylation (*see*) makes it mix better with water and be more absorbable on the skin. It is widely used in make-up and skin care preparations.

HYDROXYLATED LECITHIN • The product obtained by the hydroxylation (*see*) of lecithin (*see*).

HYDROXYLATION • The process in which an atom of hydrogen and an atom of oxygen are introduced into a compound to make that compound more soluble.

HYDROXYLYCINE • Lycine which has been hydroxylated to make it more soluble and supposedly to increase the protein content of a product. Used in tanning products. See Lycine and Hydroxylation.

HYDROXYMETHYLCELLULOSE • Thickener and bodying agent derived from plants. Used to thicken cosmetics and as a setting aid in hair products. See Carboxymethylcellulose.

HYDROXYOCTACOSANYL HYDROXYSTEARATE • See Stearic Acid and Hydroxylation.

HYDROXYPHENYL GLYCINAMIDE • Derived from the nonessential amino acid glycine (*see*) used as a buffering agent and as a violet scent.

HYDROXYPROLINE • **L-Proline.** The hydroxylated (*see*) amino acid used to add "protein" to cosmetics.

HYDROXYPROPYL CELLULOSE • A thickener. See Hydroxymethylcellulose.
HYDROXYPROPYL GUAR • **Guar Gum, 2-Hydroxypropyl Ether.** See Guar Gum.
HYDROXYPROPYL METHYLCELLULOSE • See Cellulose Gums.
HYDROXYPROPYLAMINE NITRITE • See Isopropanolamine Nitrite.
HYDROXYPROPYLCELLULOSE • See Cellulose Gums.
HYDROXYQUINOLINE • See Oxyquinoline Sulfate.
8-HYDROXYQUINOLINE SULFATE • Pale yellow powder with a slight saffron odor and burning taste. It is used as an antiseptic, antiperspirant, deodorant, and fungicide.
HYDROXYSTEARMIDE MEA • A mixture of ethanolamides of hydroxystearic acid. See Stearic Acid.
HYDROXYSTEARIC ACID • See Stearic Acid.
HYDROXYSTEARYL METHYLGLUCAMINE • An amino sugar. See Glucose.
HYPERICUM • **Hypericin.** Blue-black needles obtained from pyridine (*see*). The solutions are red or green with a red cast. Small amounts seem to be a tranquillizer and have been used as an antidepressant in medicine. It can produce a sensitivity to light.
HYPERSENSITIVITY • The condition in persons previously exposed to an antigen in which tissue damage results from an immune reaction to a further dose of the antigen. Classically, four types of hypersensitivity are recognized, but the term is often used to mean the type of allergy associated with hay fever and asthma.
HYPO- • Prefix from the Greek, meaning "under," or "below," as in "hypoacidity"—acidity in a lesser degree than is usual or normal.
HYPOALLERGENIC • A term for cosmetics supposedly devoid of common allergens that most frequently cause allergic reactions. However, spokesmen for both the FDA and the AMA find insufficient the claims of scientific proof for their efficacy. When first marketed in the 1930s, these cosmetics were called nonallergic, which implied they could not cause an allergic reaction. The term was abandoned because there are always people who will be allergic to almost any substance. The term "hypoallergenic" means "least likely to cause a reaction." Not only the user, but his or her companion may suffer allergic reaction to cosmetics. For instance, a wife to her husband's shaving lotion; a child to its mother's hair spray.
HYSSOP EXTRACT • Extract of *Hyssopus officinalis*. A synthetic flavoring from the aromatic herb. Used in bitters. The extract is a liquor flavoring for beverages, ice cream, and ices. The oil is a liquor and spice flavoring. No known toxicity.

I

ICELAND MOSS EXTRACT • The extract of *Lichen islandicus*. A water-soluble gum which gels on cooling. Used to flavor alcoholic beverages, as a food additive and in comedic gels. No known toxicity.

ICHTHAMMOL • Pale yellow or brownish black, thick viscous liquid, which smells like coal. It mixes with water, glycerol, fats, oils, and waxes, and is used medicinally as a topical antiseptic. It has slight bacteria-killing properties and is used in ointments for the treatment of skin disorders. It is also a feeble skin irritant. Formerly used medicinally as an expectorant. Large doses caused stomach upset and diarrhea.

IMIDAZOLE • **Glyoxaline, 1, 3-Diazole.** Derived from benzene (*see*). Consists of orange-colored needles. It is an antimetabolite and inhibitor of histamine and is used to control pests. It is an inhibitor of growth rather than toxin.

IMIDAZOLIDINYL UREA • The most commonly used cosmetic preservative after the parabens, it is the second most identified cosmetic preservative causing contact dermatitis, according to the American Academy of Dermatology's standards on Vehicle and Preservative Patch Testing Tray results. It is colorless, odorless, and tasteless and is employed in baby shampoos, lotions, oils, powders, and in eye shadow, permanent waves, rinses, fragrances, hair tonics, colognes, creams, bath oils, blushers, rouges, moisturizers, and fragrances. No know toxicity.

IMIDAZOLINE AMPHOTERIC • Surfactant used in "no tears" shampoos. An "anti-irritant" that neutralizes the effects of a cosmetic. See Imidazolidinyl Urea.

IMINO-BIS-PROPYLAMINE • See Propylamine.

IMITATION • With reference to a fragrance, containing all or some portion of nonnatural materials. For instance, unless a strawberry flavoring used in lipstick is made entirely from strawberries, it must be called imitation.

INDIAN CRESS EXTRACT • **Phytelene of Capucine.** The extract obtained from the flowers of *Trapaeolum majus*.

INDIGO • Probably the oldest known dye. Prepared from various *Indigofera* plants native to Bengal, Java, and Guatemala. Dark blue powder with a coppery luster. No known skin irritation but continued use on hair can cause hair to become brittle.

INDOLE • A white, lustrous, flaky substance with an unpleasant odor, occurring naturally in jasmine oil and orange flowers and used in perfumes. Also extracted from coal tar and feces; in highly diluted solutions the odor is pleasant. Large doses have been lethal in dogs. No known toxicity on the skin.

INOSITOL • A dietary supplement of the Vitamin B family used in emollients. Found in plant and animal tissues. Isolated commercially from corn. A fine, white, crystalline powder, it is odorless with sweet taste. Stable in air. No known toxicity.

INSOLUBLE METAPHOSPHATE • See Sodium Metaphosphate.

INTERMEDIATE • A chemical substance found as part of a necessary step between one organic compound and other, as in the production of dyes, pharmaceuticals, or other artificial products that develop properties only upon oxidation. For instance, it is used for hair-dye bases that have dyeing action only when exposed to oxygen.

IODINE • Discovered in 1811 and classed among the rarer earth elements, it is found in the earth's crust as bluish black scales. Nearly 200 products contain this chemical. They are prescription and over-the-counter medications. Iodine compounds are used in expectorants and thinners, particularly in the treatment of asthma and in contrast media for X-rays and fluoroscopy. They can produce a diffuse red pimply rash, hives, asthma, and sometimes, anaphylactic shock. If you are going to have X-rays with contrast, inform your physician of your sensitivity to iodine. Even if you've not had a problem with it before, it might be wise to inform the doctor if you have a number of allergies. Among the drugs that may contain iodine are cough medicines such as Tussi-Organidin™, Anbesol Liquid®, a topical antiseptic and anesthetic, and betadine, an antiseptic. Iodine is also used as an antiseptic and germicide in cosmetics.

IONONE • Used as a scent in perfumery and as a flavoring agent in foods, it occurs naturally in *Boronia*, an Australian shrub. Colorless to pale yellow with an odor reminiscent of cedarwood or violets. It may cause allergic reactions.

IPECAC • Used as a denaturant in alcohol. From the dried rhizome and roots of a creeping South American plant with drooping flowers. Used to induce vomiting in poisonings. Fatal dose in humans is as low as 20 milligrams per kilogram of body weight. Irritating when taken internally but no known toxicity on the skin.

IRISH MOSS • See Carrageenan.

IRON OXIDES • Used to color cosmetics. Any of several natural or synthetic oxides of iron (that is, iron combined with oxygen), varying in color from red to brown, black to orange or yellow, depending on the degree of water added, and the purity. Ocher, sienna, and iron oxide red are among the colors used to tint face powders, liquid powders, and foundation creams. Black iron oxide is used for coloring eye shadow. See Colors for toxicity. Permanently listed in 1977.

IRON SALTS • Iron Sources: Ferric, Choline Citrate; Ferric Orthophosphate; Ferric Phosphate; Ferric Sodium Pyrosphosphate; Ferrous Fumarate; Ferrous Gluconate; Ferrous Lactate; and Ferrous Sulfate. Widely used as enrichment for foods, they are used in cosmetics mainly for coloring and as astringents. Ingestion of large quantities can cause gastrointestinal disturbances but there is no known toxicity in cosmetics.

IRONE • The fragrant principle of violets, usually isolated from the iris, and used in perfumery. A light yellow viscous liquid, it gives off the delicate fragrance of violets when put in alcohol. It is also used to flavor dentifrices. See Orris for toxicity.

ISO • Greek for "equal." In chemistry, it is a prefix added to the name of one compound to denote another composed of the same kinds and numbers of atoms but different in structural arrangement.

ISOAMIDOPROPYL ETHYDIMONIUM ETHOSULFATE • See Quaternary Ammonium Compounds.

ISOAMYL ACETATE • A synthetic flavoring agent that occurs naturally in bananas and pears. Colorless, pearlike odor and taste, it is used in perfumery. Exposure to 950 ppm for one hour has caused headache, fatigue, shoulder pain, and irritation of the mucous membranes.

ISOAMYL LAURATE • The ester of isoamyl alcohol and lauric acid (*see both*) used as a synthetic fruit flavoring.

ISOAMYL p-METHOXYCINNAMATE • See *p*-Methoxycinnamic acid.

ISOBORNYL ACETATE • A synthetic pine odor in bath preparations. Also used as a synthetic fruit flavoring for beverages. No known toxicity.

ISOBUTANE • A constituent of natural gas and illuminating gas, colorless and insoluble in water, and used in refrigeration plants. A propellant used for cosmetic sprays. See Paraffin and Propellants.

ISOBUTOXYPROPANOL • See Isopropyl Alcohol.

ISOBUTYL ACETATE • The ester of isobutyl alcohol and acetic acid. Used as a synthetic flavoring agent. A clear, colorless liquid with a fruity odor, it may be mildly irritating to the mucous membranes and in high concentrations, it is narcotic.

ISOBUTYL MYRISTATE • The ester of isobutyl alcohol and myristic acid (*see both*).

ISOBUTYL PABA • See Propylparaben.

ISOBUTYL PALMITATE • See Palmitate.

ISOBUTYL PARABEN • See Parabens.

ISOBUTYL PELARGONATE • The ester of isobutyl alcohol and pelargonic acid (*see both*).

ISOBUTYL SALICYLATE • See Salicylates.

ISOBUTYL STEARATE • The ester of isobutyl alcohol and stearic acid. See Fatty Alcohols. Used in waterproof coatings, polishes, face creams, rouges, ointments, soaps, dyes, and lubricants. No known toxicity.

ISOBUTYLATED LANOLIN • The partial ester of lanolin oil (*see*).

ISOBUTYLENE/ISOPRENE COPOLYMER • A copolymer of isobutylene and isoprene monomers derived from petroleum and used as resins.

ISOBUTYLENE/MALEIC ANHYDRIDE COPOLYMER • A copolymer of isobutylene and maleic anhydride monomers derived from petroleum and used as a resin. Strong irritant.

ISOBUTYRIC ACID • A pungent liquid that smells like butyric acid (*see*). A mild irritant used chiefly in making fragrance materials.

ISOCETEARETH-8 STEARATE • See Ethylene Oxide and Stearic Acid.

ISOCETETH-10, -20, -30 • The polyethylene glycol ethers of isocetyl alcohol. See Cetyl Alcohol.

ISOCETETH-10 STEARATE • The ester of isoceteth-10 and stearic acid. See Stearic Acid.

ISOCETYL ALCOHOL • See Cetyl Alcohol.

ISOCETYL ISODECANOATE • See Cetyl Alcohol.

ISOCETYL PALMITATE • See Ceytl Alcohol and Palmitate.

ISOCETYL STEARATE • See Cetyl Alcohol and Stearic Acid.

ISOCETYL STEAROYL STEARATE • The ester of isocetyl alcohol, stearic alcohol, and stearic acid. See Fatty Acids.

ISODECETH-4, -5, -6 • See Polyethylene Glycol and Isodecyl Alcohol.

ISODECYL HYDROXYSTEARATE • See Decyl Alcohol and Stearic Acid.

ISODECYL ISONONANOATE • See Decyl Alcohol.

ISODECYL LAURATE • The ester of decyl alcohol and lauric acid (*see both*). Used as a wetting agent (*see*).

ISODECYL MYRISTATE • See Decyl Alcohol and Myristic Acid.

ISODECYL NEOPENTANOATE • See 1-Pentanol.

ISODECYL OLEATE • An emollient. See Decyl Alcohol and Oleic Acid.

ISODECYL PALMITATE • See Decyl Alcohol and Palmitic Acid.

ISODECYLPARABEN • The ester of decyl alcohol and *p*-hydroxybenzoid acid. See Propylparaben.

ISOEUGENOL • An aromatic liquid phenol oil obtained from eugenol (*see*) by mixing with an alkali. Used chiefly in perfumes but also employed in hand creams and in making the flavoring vanillin. Strong irritant. Not recommended for use.

ISOHEXYL LAURATE • See Lauryl Alcohol.

ISOHEXYL PALMITATE • See Palmitic Acid.

ISOLAURETH-3, -6, -10 • See Polyethylene Glycol and Lauric Acid.

ISOLEUCINE • An essential amino acid not synthesized within the human body. Isolated commercially from beet sugar, it is a building block of protein. GRAS.

ISONONYL ISONONANOATE • The ester (*see*) produced by the reaction of nonyl alcohol with nonanoic acid. Used in fruit flavorings for lipsticks and mouthwashes. Occurs in cocoa, oil of lavender. No known toxicity.

ISOPENTANE • Volatile flammable liquid hydrocarbon found in petroleum and used as a solvent in cosmetics. A skin irritant. Narcotic in high doses.

ISOPROPYL ACETATE • The ester of isopropyl alcohol and acetic acid, a colorless liquid with a strong odor, it is used as a solvent for resin, gums, cellulose, for lacquers, and in perfumery. Flammable.

ISOPROPYL ALCOHOL • **Isopropanol.** An antibacterial, solvent, and denaturant (*see*). Used in hair color rinses, body rubs, hand lotions, after-shave lotions, and many other cosmetics. It is prepared from propylene, which is obtained in the cracking of petroleum. Also used in antifreeze compositions and as a solvent for gums, shellac, and essential oils. Ingestion or inhalation of large quantities of the vapor may cause flushing, headache, dizziness, mental depression, nausea, vomiting, narcosis, anesthesia, and coma. The fatal ingested dose is around a fluid ounce. No known toxicity to the skin.

ISOPROPANOLAMINE • An emulsifying agent with a light ammonia odor that is soluble in water. It is used as a plasticizer and in insecticides as well as in cosmetic creams. No known toxicity.

ISOPROPYL CRESOLS • See Cresols.

ISOPROPYL ESTER OF PVM/MA COPOLYMER • A polymer (*see*) used as a resin. See Polyvinyl Alcohol.

ISOPROPYL ISOSTEARATE • See Stearic Acid and Propylene Glycol.

ISOPROPYL LANOLATE • A mixture of isopropyl esters of lanolin acids. After purification, the acids are esterified (see Ester) with isopropanol (*see*). One of the more versatile lanolin derivatives because of its surfactant (*see*) properties and pigment-dispersing ability, it is used in combination with mineral oil and isopropyl palmitate (*see*) for pigments such as Titanium Dioxide, Oxy Red and

Red No. 9. In lipsticks, creams, lotions, and aerosol emulsions, it acts as a lubricant and gives high gloss. It has been used for more than twenty years. May cause skin sensitization and its effects on lung tissue have not been studied, although it is used as an aerosol. See Lanolin.

ISOPROPYL LAURATE • See Lauric Acid.

ISOPROPYL LINOLEATE • See Linoleic Acid.

ISOPROPYL MYRISTATE • A widely used fatty compound derived from isopropyl alcohol and myristic acid. It causes blackheads and is being removed from many of the newer formulations. However, a more serious potential exists in that when nitrate compounds such as *N*-nitrosodiethanolamine, NDELA, an impurity in many cosmetic preparations, was applied in isopropyl myristate, its absorption was increased 230 times. NDELA may be a reaction product of di- or triethanolamine used in many cosmetic formulations. Scientists are concerned that when isopropyl myristate is applied over large areas of the skin for long periods of time—such as in suntanning lotion—there will be a significant absorption of NDELA if the contaminant is present.

ISOPROPYL PALMITATE • An emollient. See Palmitic Acid.

ISOPROPYLPARABEN • See Parabens.

ISOPROPYL RICINOLEATE • See Isopropyl Alcohol and Ricinoleic Acid.

ISOPROPYL STEARATE • An emollient. See Stearic Acid.

ISOPROPYL TALLOWATE • See Fatty Acids.

ISOPROPYLAMINE DODECYLBENZENESULFONATE • See Quaternary Ammonium Compounds.

ISOSTEARAMIDOPROPALKONIUM CHLORIDE • See Surfactants.

ISOSTEARAMIDOPROPYL BETAINE • See Surfactants.

ISOSTEARAMIDOPROPYL DIMETHYLAMINE GLYCOLATE • See Surfactants.

ISOSTEARAMIDOPROPYL DIMETHYLAMINE LACTATE • See Surfactants.

ISOSTEARAMIDOPROPYL ETHYLDIMONIUM ETHOSULFATE • See Quaternary Ammonium Compounds.

ISOSTEARAMIDOPROPYL MORPHOLINE LACTATE • See Surfactants.

ISOSTEARAMIDOPROPYLAMINE OXIDE • See Surfactants.

ISOSTEARETH-2 THROUGH-20 • See Fatty Alcohols.

ISOSTEARIC ACID • A complex mixture of fatty acids similar to stearic acid (*see*).

ISOSTEARIC HYDROLYZED ANIMAL PROTEIN • Used in creams. See Protein and Hydrolyzation.

ISOSTEAROAMPHOGLYCINATE • See Surfactants.
ISOSTEAROAMPHOPROPIONATE • See Surfactants.
ISOSTEAROYL HYDROLYZED ANIMAL PROTEIN • See Surfactants.
ISOSTEARYL ALCOHOL • See Stearyl Alcohol.
ISOSTEARYL BENZYLIMIDONIUM CHLORIDE • See Surfactants.
ISOSTEARYL DIGLYCERYL SUCCINATE • See Surfactants.
ISOSTEARYL ERUCATE • See Surfactants.
ISOSTEARYL ETHYLIMIDONIUM ETHOSULFATE • See Surfactants.
ISOSTEARYL HYDROXYETHYL IMIDAZOLINE • See Surfactants.
ISOSTEARYL IMIDAZOLINE • See Surfactants.
ISOSTEARYL ISOSTEARATE • See Stearyl Alcohol.
ISOSTEARYL LACTATE • See Surfactants.
ISOSTEARYL NEOPENTANOATE • See Surfactants.
ISOSTEARYL PALMITATE • See Surfactants.
ISOSTEARYL STEAROYL STEARATE • See Surfactants.
ISOTRIDECYL ISONONANOATE • See Tridecyl Alcohol.
ISOVALERIC ACID • Occurs in valerian, hops oil, tobacco, and other plants. Colorless liquid with a disagreeable taste and odor but is used in dilution for flavors and perfumes. See Valeric Acid.
IVY EXTRACT • Extract of climbing plant with evergreen leaves native to Europe and Asia. Produces a color that ranges from dark grayish green to yellowish. No known toxicity.

J

JABORANDI • **Pilocarpus.** A tincture from the leaves of the pilocarpus plant grown in South America. It supposedly stimulates the sebaceous glands and scalp and was formerly used to induce sweating. Used in hair tonics. A source of pilocarpine (*see*). Poisonous when ingested. No known toxicity on the skin.
JAGUAR GUM • See Guar Gum.
JALAP RESIN • A resin (*see*) used in cosmetics. The dried purgative tuberous root of a Mexican plant. Was once used as a drastic cathartic. No known toxicity on the skin.
JAPAN WAX • **Vegetable Wax. Japan Tallow.** A fat squeezed from the fruit of a tree grown in Japan and China. Pale yellow flat cakes, disks or squares, with a fatlike rancid odor and taste. Used as a substitute for beeswax in cosmetic ointments; also floor waxes and polishes. It is related to poison ivy and may cause allergic contact dermatitis.
JASMINE • Used in perfumes. The essential oil extracted from the

extremely fragrant white flowers of the tall climbing, semi-evergreen jasmine shrub. May cause allergic reactions.

JASMINE ABSOLUTE • Oil of jasmine obtained by extraction with volatile or nonvolatile solvents. Sometimes called the "natural perfume" because the oil is not subjected to heat and distilled oils. See Absolute. May cause allergic reactions.

JOJOBA BUTTER • Obtained from jojoba oil (*see*).

JOJOBA OIL • Increasingly used in cosmetics, it is the oil extracted from the beanlike seeds of the desert shrub, *Simondsia chinensis.* A liquid wax used as a lubricant and as a substitute for sperm oil, carnauba wax, and beeswax. Mexicans and American Indians have long used the bean's oily wax as a hair conditioner and skin lubricant. United States companies are now promoting the ingredient in shampoos, moisturizers, sunscreens, and conditioners as a treatment for "crow's feet," wrinkles, stretch marks, and dry skin. May cause allergic reactions.

JOJOBA WAX • The semisolid fraction of jojoba oil (*see*).

JONQUIL EXTRACT • Extract of *Narcissus jonquilla.*

JUGLONE • A coloring for hair dyes. Yellow needles, slightly soluble in hot water but soluble in alcohol. It is the active coloring principle in walnuts. When mixed in solution with an alkali, it gives a purplish red color. It has antihemorrhaging activity. The lethal oral dose in mice is only 2.5 milligrams per kilogram of body weight. No known skin toxicity.

JUNIPER TAR • **Oil of Cade.** The volatile oil from the wood of a pine tree. Dark brown, viscous, with a smoky odor and acrid, slightly aromatic taste. Very slightly soluble in water. It is used as a skin peeler and antiitching factor in hair preparations and as a scent in perfumes. Less corrosive than phenol (*see*).

K

KANGAROO PAW FLOWER • An Australian sedgelike spring-flowering herb related to the amaryllis. It has clustered flowers covered with greenish wool. Used in Australian-imported hair sprays. No known toxicity.

KAOLIN • **China Clay.** Aids in the covering ability of face powder and in absorbing oil secreted by the skin. Used in baby powder, bath powder, face masks, foundation cake makeup, liquid powder, face powder, dry rouge, and emollients. Originally obtained from Kaoling Hill in Kiangsi Province in southeast China. Essentially a hydrated aluminum silicate (*see*). It is a white or yellowish white mass or powder, insoluble in water and absorbent. Used medicinally to treat intestinal disorders, but in large doses it may cause obstructions, perforations, or granuloma (tumor) formation. It is also used in the manufacture of porcelain, pottery, bricks, and color lakes (*see*). No known toxicity for the skin.

KARAYA GUM • See Gum Karaya.

KELP • Recovered from the giant Pacific marine plant *Macrocystis pyriferae,* it is used as a fertilizer and in plastics. No known toxicity.

KERATIN • Protein (*see*) obtained from the horns, hoofs, feathers, quills, and hairs of various creatures. Yellowish brown powder. Insoluble in water, alcohol, or ether but soluble in ammonia. Used in permanent wave solutions and hair rinses. Nontoxic.

KERATIN AMINO ACIDS • See Animal Keratin Amino Acids.

KEROSENE • See Deodorized Kerosene.

KETONES • **Acetone, Methyl, or Ethyl.** Aromatic substances obtained by the oxidation of secondary alcohols. Ethereal or aromatic odor, generally insoluble in water, but soluble in alcohol or ether. Solvents used in nail polish and nail polish removers. When injected into the abdomens of rats, intermediate dosages are lethal. See Acetone for skin toxicity.

KIDNEY BEAN EXTRACT • Extract of *Phaseolus vulgaris,* the beans were used as a nutrient and a laxative by the American Indians. No known toxicity.

KRAMERIA EXTRACT • **Bhatany Extract.** A synthetic flavoring derived from the dried root of either of two American shrubs. Used in raspberry, bitters, fruit, and rum flavorings. Used in cosmetics as an astringent. Low oral toxicity. Large doses may produce gastric distress. Can cause tumors and death after injection, but not after ingestion.

L

LABDANUM • **Synthetic Musk.** Used in perfumes, especially as a fixative, it is a volatile oil obtained by steam distillation from gum extracted from various rockrose shrubs. Golden yellow, viscous, with a strong balsamic odor and a bitter taste. Also used as a synthetic flavoring in foods.

LABRADOR TEA EXTRACT • **Hudson's Bay Tea. Marsh Tea.** The extract of the dried flowering plant or young shoots of *Ledum palustre* or *Ledum groelandicum,* a tall, resinous evergreen shrub found in bogs and swamps and moist meadows. Brewed like tea, it has a pleasing antiscorbutic and stimulating quality. It was used by the American Indians and settlers as a tonic supposed to purify blood. It was also employed to treat wounds. The *Ledum palustre* contains, among other things, tannin and valeric acid (*see both*). No known toxicity.

LACQUER • A Japanese lacquer tree contains a lacquer related to poison ivy. See Shellac.

LACTIC ACID • Used in skin fresheners. Odorless, colorless, usually a syrupy product normally present in blood and muscle tissue as a product of the metabolism of glucose and glycogen. Present in sour milk, beer, sauerkraut, pickles, and other food products made by bacterial fermentation. Also an acidulant. It is caustic in concentrated solutions when taken internally or applied to the skin. In cosmetic products, it may cause stinging in sensitive people, particularly in fair-skinned women.

LACTIC YEASTS • Obtained from milk. See Lactic Acid.

LACTOSE • **Milk Sugar.** Used widely as a base in eye lotions. Present in the milk of mammals. Stable in air but readily absorbs odors. Used in preparing food for infants, in tablets, as a general base and diluent in pharmaceutical and cosmetic compounding, and in baked goods. In large doses it is a laxative and diuretic, but generally nontoxic. However, it was found to cause tumors when injected under the skin of mice in 50-milligram doses per kilogram of body weight.

LADY'S MANTLE EXTRACT • From the dried leaves and flowering shoots of *Achemilla vulgaris*. A common European herb covered with spreading hairs, it has been used for centuries by herbalists to concoct love potions.

LAKES, COLOR • A lake is an organic pigment prepared by precipitating a soluble color with a form of aluminum, calcium, barium potassium, strontium, or zirconium, which then makes the colors insoluble. Not all colors are suitable for making lakes.

LAMPBLACK • Used in eye makeup pencils. It is a bluish-black fine soot deposited on a surface by burning liquid hydrocarbons (*see*) such as oil. It is duller and less intense in color than other carbon blacks and has a blue undertone. It is also used in pigments for paints, enamels, and printing inks. See Carbon Black for toxicity.

LANETH-5 THROUGH-40 • Emulsifiers. See Lanolin Alcohols.

LANETH-9 AND -10 ACETATE • Emulsifiers. See Lanolin Alcohols.

LANOLIN • **Wool Fat. Wool Wax.** A product of the oil glands of sheep. Used in lipstick, liquid powder, mascara, nail polish remover, protective oil, rouge, eye shadow, foundation creams, foundation cake makeup, hair conditioners, eyecreams, cold creams, brilliantine hairdressings, ointment bases, and emollients. A water-absorbing base material and a natural emulsifier, it absorbs and holds water to the skin. Chemically a wax instead of a fat. Contains about 25 to 30 percent water. Advertisers have found that the words "contains lanolin" help to sell a product and have promoted it as being able to "penetrate the skin better than other oils," although there is little scientific proof of this. Lanolin has been found to be a common skin sensitizer, causing allergic contact skin rashes. It will not prevent or cure wrinkles, and will not stop hair loss. It is not used in pure form today because of its allergy-causing potential. Products derived from it are less likely to cause allergic reactions.

LANOLIN ACID • See Lanolin.

LANOLIN ALCOHOLS • **Sterols, Triterpene Alcohols. Aliphatic Alcohols.** Derived from lanolin (*see*), lanolin alcohols are available commercially as solid waxy materials that are yellow to amber in color, or as liquids that are pale to golden yellow in color. They are widely used as emulsifiers and emollients in hand creams and lotions, and while less likely to cause an allergic reaction than lanolin, still may do so in the sensitive.

LANOLIN LINOLEATE • See Lanolin.

LANOLIN OIL • Used as the oil in baby oils, it consists of 15 to 17 percent cholesterol with the remainder liquid lanolin. See Lanolin for toxicity.

LANOLIN RICINOLEATE • See Lanolin Alcohols.

LANOLIN WAX • An emollient. See Lanolin.

LANOLINAMIDE DEA • See Lanolin.

LANOSTEROL • A widely used skin softener in hand creams and lotions, it is the fatty alcohol derived from the wool fat of sheep. See Lanolin.

LANTHANUM CHLORIDE • An inorganic salt. A rare earth mineral that occurs in cerite, monazerite, orthite, and certain fluorspars. Used as a reagent (*see*) and catalyst (*see*) in cosmetic preparations. No known toxicity from topical use but a small oral dose is lethal in rats.

LAPIS LAZULI • No longer authorized for use in cosmetics. See Colors.

LAPPA EXTRACT • **Burdock Extract.** The extract of the roots of *Arctium lappa,* it contains tannic acid (*see*) and is used to soothe the skin. No known toxicity.

LAPYRIUM CHLORIDE • See Quaternary Ammonium Compounds.

LARD • Easily absorbed by the skin, it is used as a lubricant, emollient, and base in shaving creams, soaps, and various cosmetic creams. It is the purified internal fat from the abdomen of the hog. It is a soft white unctuous mass, with a slight characteristic odor and a bland taste. Insoluble in water. No known toxicity.

LARD GLYCERIDE • See Lard.

LATEX • **Synthetic Rubber.** The milky, usually white, juice or exudate of plants obtained by tapping. Used in beauty masks (*see* Face Masks and Packs) for its coating ability. Any of various gums, resins, fats, or waxes in an emulsion of water and synthetic rubber of plastic are now considered latex. Ingredients of latex compounds can be poisonous, depending upon which plant products are used. Can cause skin rash.

LATHER • Produced by action of air bubbles in a soap solution. For satisfactory shaving, a lather must be dense. The air bubbles must be fine and stable for the duration of the shave. In bubble baths the air bubbles must be large and light.

LAURALKONIUM BROMIDE • See Quaternary Ammonium Compounds.

LAURALKONIUM CHLORIDE • See Quaternary Ammonium Compounds.

LAURAMIDE DEA • A mixture of ethanolamides of lauric acid, the principal fatty acid of coconut oil, it is widely used in cosmetic soaps and detergents as a softener and foam inhibitor. See Lauric Acid.

LAURAMIDE MEA • See Lauric Acid.

LAURAMIDE MIPA • A mixture of isopropanolamides of lauric acid widely used as a wetting agent in soaps and detergents. See Lauric Acid.

LAURAMIDOPROPYL DIMETHYLAMINE • See Lauric Acid and Dimethylamine.

LAURAMINE OXIDE • See Lauric Acid.

LAURAMINOPROPIONIC ACID • See Propionic Acid.

LAURETH-1, -23 • See Lauryl Alcohol.

LAURIC ACID • **n-Dodecanoic Acid.** A common constituent of vegetable fats, especially coconut oil and laurel oil. Its derivatives are widely used as a base in the manufacture of soaps, detergents, and lauryl alcohol (*see*) because of their foaming properties. Has a slight odor of bay and makes large copious bubbles when in soap. A mild irritant but not a sensitizer.

LAURIC ALDEHYDE • See Lauric Acid.

LAURIC DEA • Creates a good, long-lasting foam in shampoos. See Lauric Sulfate.

LAUROAMPHOACETATE • A preservative. See Imidazolium.

LAUROAMPHODIACETATE • A preservative. See Imidazolium.

LAUROAMPHODIPROPIONATE • See Propionic Acid and Lauric Acid.

LAUROAMPHODIPROPIONIC ACID • A preservative. See Lauric Acid and Propionic Acid.
LAUROAMPHODROXYPROPYLSULFONATE • See Imidazolium.
LAUROAMPHOPROPINOATE • See Lauric Acid and Propionic Acid.
LAUROYL HYDROLYZED ANIMAL PROTEIN • A condensation product of lauric acid chloride and hydrolyzed animal protein (*see*) used in soaps.
LAUROYL SARCOSINE • See Sarcosines.
LAURTRIMONIUM CHLORIDE • See Quaternary Ammonium Compounds.
LAURYL ALCOHOL • **1-Dodecanol.** A colorless, crystalline compound that is produced commercially from coconut oil. Used to make detergents because of its sudsing ability. Has a characteristic fatty odor. It is soluble in most oils but is insoluble in glycerin. Used in perfumery. See Lauric Acid for toxicity.
LAURYL AMINE • See Lauric Acid.
LAURYL AMINOPROPYLGLYCINE • See Lauryl Alcohol and Glyceric Acid.
LAURYL BETAINE • See Lauric Acid.
LAURYL DIETHLENDIAMINEGLYCINE • See Lauryl Alcohol.
LAURYL DIMETHLAMINE ACRYLINOLATE • See Lauric Acid and Dimethylamine.
LAURYL DIMETHYLAMINE ACRYLINOLEATE • See Acrylinic Acid.
LAURYL GLYCOL • See Lauryl Alcohol and Glycol.
LAURYL HYDROXYETHYL IMIDAZOLINE • See Imidazoline.
LAURYL ISOQUINOLINIUM BROMIDE • A quaternary ammonium compound (*see*) active against a microorganism believed to cause a type of dandruff. Used in hair tonics and cuticle softeners. Slightly greater toxicity than benzalkonium chloride in rats. No skin irritation or sensitization in concentrations of 0.1 percent and lower. Used also as an agriculture fungicide.
LAURYL ISOSTEARATE • The ester of lauryl alcohol and isosteric acid (*see both*).
LAURYL LACTATE • See Lauric Acid and Lactic Acid.
LAURYL METHACRYLATE • See Lauric Acid and Acrylates.
LAURYL PALMITATE • The ester (*see*) of lauryl alcohol and palmitic acid (*see both*).
LAURYL PYRIDINIUM CHLORIDE • See Quaternary Ammonium Compounds.
LAURYL STEARATE • The ester of lauryl alcohol and stearic acid (*see both*).
LAURYL SULFATE • Derived from lauryl alcohol (*see*). Its potas-

sium, zinc, magnesium, sodium, calcium, and ammonium salts are used in shampoos because of their foaming properties. See Sodium Lauryl Sulfate.

LAURYL SULTAINE • See Lauryl Alcohol and Betaine.

LAVANDIN OIL • Used in soaps and perfumes. It is the essential oil of a hybrid related to the lavender plant. Fragrant, yellowish, with a camphor lavender scent. No known toxicity.

LAVENDER OIL • Used in skin fresheners, powders, shaving preparations, mouthwashes, dentifrices, and perfumes. The volatile oil from the fresh, flowering tops of lavender. Also used in a variety of food flavorings. It can cause allergic reactions and has been found to cause adverse skin reactions when the skin is exposed to sunlight. Related to the lavender plant. Fragrant, yellowish, with a camphor lavender scent. No known toxicity.

LAWSONE • Derived from the leaves of *Lawsonia inermis,* it is used as a sunscreen agent. No known toxicity.

LEAD ACETATE • **Sugar of Lead.** Colorless white crystals or grains with an acetic odor. Bubbles slowly. It has been used as a topical astringent but is absorbed through the skin, and therefore might lead to lead poisoning. Also used in hair dyeing and printing colors and in the manufacture of chrome yellow (*see* Colors). Still used to treat bruises and skin irritations in animals. Not recommended for use because of the possibility of lead buildup in the body. Permission was given in 1981 by the FDA to use this in progressive hair dyes, although it is a proven carcinogen. Permanently listed as a color component of hair dye in 1969 with a caution that it "should not be used on cut or abraded scalp." See Lead Compounds.

LEAD COMPOUNDS • Used in ointments and hair dye pigments. Lead may cause contact dermatitis. It is poisonous in all forms. It is one of the most hazardous of toxic metals because its poison is cumulative and its toxic effects are many and severe. Among them are leg cramps, muscle weakness, numbness, depression, brain damage, coma, and death. Ingestion and inhalation of lead cause the most severe symptoms.

LECITHIN • From the Greek, meaning "egg yolk." A natural antioxidant and emollient used in eye creams, lipsticks, liquid powders, hand creams and lotions, soaps, and many other cosmetics. Also a natural emulsifier and spreading agent. It is found in all living organisms, and is frequently obtained from common egg yolk and soybeans for commercial purposes. Egg yolk is 8 to 9 percent lecithin. Nontoxic.

LECITHINAMIDE DEA • A reaction product of lecithin and diethanolamine with ammonia. See Quaternary Ammonium Compounds.

LEMON • The common fresh fruit and fruit extract is the most frequently used acid in cosmetics. It is 5 to 8 percent citric acid. Employed in cream rinses, hair color rinses, astringents, fresheners, skin bleaches, and for reducing alkalinity of many other products. Do-it-yourselfers can squeeze two lemons into a strainer, add the juice of 1 cup of water, and use it as a rinse after shampooing to remove scum and to leave a shine on the hair. Lemon can cause allergic reactions.

LEMON BALM • **Sweet Balm. Garden Balm.** Used in perfumes and as a soothing facial treatment. An Old World mint cultivated for its lemon-flavored, fragrant leaves. Often considered a weed, it has been used by herbalists as a medicine and to flavor foods and medicines. It reputedly imparts long life. Also used to treat earache and toothache. Nontoxic.

LEMON EXTRACT • See Lemon Oil.

LEMON JUICE • See Lemon.

LEMON OIL • **Cedro Oil.** Used in perfumes and food flavorings, it is the volatile oil expressed from the fresh peel. A pale yellow to deep yellow, it has a characteristic odor and taste of the outer part of fresh lemon peel. It can cause an allergic reaction and has been suspected of being a co-cancer-causing agent.

LEMON VERBENA EXTRACT • Extract of *Lippia citriodoral.* See Lemongrass Oil.

LEMONGRASS OIL • **Indian Oil of Verbena.** Used in perfumes, especially those added to soap. It is the volatile oil distilled from the leaves of lemon grasses. A yellowish or reddish brown liquid, it has a strong odor of verbena. Also used in insect repellents and in fruit flavorings for foods and beverages. Death was reported when taken internally, and autopsy showed lining of the intestines was severely damaged. Skin toxicity unknown.

LETTUCE EXTRACT • An extract of various species of *Lactuca.* Used in commercial toning lotions and by herbalists to make skin-soothing decoctions.

LEUCINE • An essential amino acid (*see*) for human nutrition not manufactured in the body. It is isolated commercially from gluten, casein, and keratin (*see all*). No known toxicity.

LICORICE • **Liquorice. Glycyrrhizin.** A black substance derived from the plant, *Glycyrrhiza glabra,* "sweet root," belonging to the *Leguminosae* and cultivated from southern Europe to Central Asia. It is used in fruit, licorice, anise, maple, and root beer flavorings for beverages, ice cream, ices, candy, baked goods, gelatin, chewing gum, and syrups. Licorice root is used in licorice and root beer flavorings for beverages, candy, baked goods, chewing gum, tobacco, and medicines. Some people known to have eaten licorice candy regularly and generously had raised blood pressure, headaches, and muscle weakness. It can cause asthma, intestinal upsets, and contact dermatitis. No known skin toxicity.

LIDOCAINE • Needles from benzene or alcohol, insoluble in water. A local anesthetic, it relieves itching, pain, soreness, and discomfort due to skin rashes, including eczema and minor burns, but can cause an allergic reaction.

LIGHT • Sensitivity to light may be caused by drugs, cosmetics, or foods, or light alone may cause an allergic reaction. When some people are exposed to sunlight, their skins erupt with eczema, hemorrhages, hives, and scales. In severe sunlight allergy, the person may break out all over with large hives, feel dizzy, and may fall into shock. The allergy may appear suddenly, last for years, and then disappear, or it may remain for a lifetime. Some people allergic to sunlight are also sensitive to fluorescent light.

LIGNOCERIC ACID • Obtained from beechwood tar or by distillation of rotten oak wood. Occurs in most natural fats. Used in shampoos, soaps, and plastics. No known toxicity.

LIGNOL • See Lignoceric Acid.

LILAC • Used in perfumes. Derived from the plant, especially the European shrub variety. It has fragrant bluish to purple pink flowers. No known toxicity.

LILY OF THE VALLEY • **Convallaria Flowers.** A perfume ingredient extracted from the low perennial herb. It has oblong leaves and fragrant, nodding, bell-shaped white flowers. Has been used as a heart stimulant. No known toxicity for the skin.

LIME • A perfume ingredient from the small greenish yellow fruit of a spicy tropical tree. Its very acid pulp yields a juice used as a flavoring agent and as an antiseptic. A source of Vitamin C. Can cause an adverse reaction when skin is exposed to sunlight.

LIME OIL • A natural flavoring extracted from the fruit of a tropical tree. Colorless to greenish. Used in grapefruit, lemon, lemon-lime, lime, orange, cola, fruit, rum, nut, pineapple, ginger, and ginger-ale flavorings for beverages, ice cream, ices, candy, baked goods, gelatin desserts, chewing gum, syrups, and condiments. May cause a sensitivity to light.

LIME SULFUR • Topical antiseptic. A brown clear liquid prepared by boiling sulfur and lime with water. Can cause skin irritation.

LIME WATER • An alkaline water solution of calcium hydroxide that absorbs carbon doxide from the air, forming a protective film of calcium carbonate (*see*) on the surface of the liquid. Used in medicines, as an antacid, and as an alkali in external washes, face masks, and hair-grooming products. No known toxicity.

LIMONENE • D, L, and DL Forms. A synthetic flavoring agent that occurs naturally in star anise, buchu leaves, caraway, celery, oranges, coriander, cumin, cardamon, sweet fennel, common fennel, mace, marigold, oil of lavandin, oil of lemon, oil of mandarin, peppermint, petitgrain oil, pimento oil, orange leaf, orange peel (sweet oil), origanum oil, black pepper, peels of citrus, macrocarpa bunge, and hops oil. Used in lime, fruit, and spice flavorings for beverages, ice cream, ices, candy, baked goods, gelatin desserts, and chewing gum. A skin irritant and sensitizer.

LINALOE OIL • Bois de Rose Oil. An ingredient in perfumes that is the colorless to yellow volatile essential oil distilled from a Mexican tree. It has a pleasant flowery scent and is soluble in most fixed oils. May cause allergic reactions.

LINALOOL • Linalol. Used in perfumes and soaps instead of bergamot or French lavender. It is a fragrant, colorless liquid that occurs in many essential oils such as linaloe, Ceylon cinnamon, sassafras, orange flower, and bergamot. Also used in food flavorings such as blueberry, chocolate, and lemon. May cause allergic reactions.

LINALYL ACETATE • A colorless, fragrant liquid, slightly soluble in water, it is the most valuable constituent of bergamot and lavender oils, which are used in perfumery. It occurs naturally in basil, jasmine oil, lavandin oil, lavender oil, and lemon oil. It has a strong floral scent. Also used as a synthetic flavoring in food. No known toxicity.

LINDEN EXTRACT • A natural flavoring agent from the flowers of the tree grown in Europe and the United States. Used in fragrances in raspberry and vermouth flavorings. No known toxicity.

LINOLEAMIDE • See Linoleic Acid.

LINOLEAMIDE DEA • Alkyl amides produced by a diethanolamine (*see*) condensation of linoleic acid. Used as a foaming agent in soaps and shampoos. See Linoleic Acid.

LINOLEIC ACID • Used as an emulsifier. An essential fatty acid (*see*) prepared from edible fats and oils. Component of Vitamin F and a major constituent of many vegetable oils, for example, cottonseed and soybean. Used in emulsifiers and vitamins. Large doses can cause nausea and vomiting. No known skin toxicity and, in fact, may have emollient properties.

LINOLENIC ACID • Colorless liquid glyceride found in most oils. Insoluble in water, soluble in organic solvents. Used to make nail polishes dry faster. Slightly irritating to mucous membranes.

LINSEED ACID • See Linseed Oil.

LINSEED OIL • Oil used in shaving creams, emollients, and medicinal soaps. Soothing to the skin. It is the yellowish oil expressed or extracted from flaxseed. Gradually thickens when exposed to air. It has a peculiar odor and a bland taste and is also used in paint, varnish, and linoleum. Can cause allergic reactions.

LIP BRUSH • A brush to trace a sharp outline of the lips with lipstick.

LIP CREAM • A mixture of oils that melts on contact with the skin to soften and soothe the lips. Almost identical to night creams or moisturizers. See Emollients.

LIP GLOSS • Usually comes in jars, sticks, sometimes in tubes. Contains different proportions of the same ingredient as lipstick but usually has less wax and more oil to make the lips shinier. Used alone or with lipstick and applied with the fingertip.

LIP PENCIL • A colored wax mixture in wood or metal casing for the same purpose as a lip brush (*see*).

LIP PRIMER • A stick similar to lipstick but containing less wax, used to soften the lips and to serve as a base for the lipstick. Makes the lips shinier.

LIPSTICK • **Regular, Frosted, Medicated, Sheer.** Primarily a mixture of oil and wax in a stick form with a red-staining certified dye dispersed in oil, red pigments similarly dispersed, flavoring, and perfume. Bromo acid, D & C Red No. 21 and related dyes are most often used. Among other common lipstick dyes are D & C Red No. 27, and insoluble dyes known as lakes such as D & C Red No. 34 Calcium Lake, and D & C Orange No. 17 Lake. Pinks are made by mixing titanium dioxide with various reds. Among the oils and fats used are olive, mineral, sesame, castor, butyl stearate, polyethylene glycol, cocoa butter, lanolin, petrolatum, lecithin, hydrogenated vegetable oils, carnauba and candelilla waxes, beeswax, ozokerite, and paraffin. Colors of lipsticks on the market remain essentially the same, but the names such as "strawberry rose" are frequently changed to induce customers to buy. A typical lipstick formula contains castor oil, about 65 percent; beeswax, 15 percent; carnauba wax, 10 percent; lanolin, 5 percent; certified dyes, soluble; color lakes, insoluble, and perfume. Frosted lipstick includes a pearlizing agent that adds luster to the color. Such an agent may be bismuth compound or guanine. Medicated lipstick is used to treat or prevent chapped or sun-dried lips. It may or may not combine coloring with ingredients but usually contains petrolatum, mineral wax, and oils. It may or may not contain menthol or a sunscreen. Sheer lipsticks include transparent coloring and no indelible dyes so as to give a more natural look to the lips. The main difficulty with lipsticks results from allergy to the dyes or to specific ingredients. See Cheilitis.

LIPSTICK HOLDER • See Nickel.

LIQUEFYING CREAM • Cleansing cream designed to liquefy when rubbed into the skin. It usually contains paraffin, a wax, stearic acid, sodium borate, liquid petrolatum (54 percent) (*see all*), and water (26 percent).

LIQUID MAKEUP • See Foundation Makeup.

LIQUID POWDER • See Foundation Makeup.

LITHIUM CHLORIDE • A crystalline salt of the alkali metal, used as a scavenger in purifying metals, to remove oxygen, and in soap and lubricant bases. The crystals absorb water and then become neutral or slightly alkaline. It is also used in the manufacture of mineral waters, in soldering, and in refrigeration machines. Formerly used as a salt substitute. Prolonged absorption may cause disturbed electrolyte balance in humans and impair kidney function and cause central nervous system problems.

LITHIUM HYDROXIDE • Used in making cosmetic resins and esters (*see both*). A granular, free-flowing powder, acrid, and strongly alkaline. It is the salt of the alkaline metal that absorbs water from the air and is soluble in water. Used in photo developers and in batteries. Very irritating to the skin, and flammable in contact with the air.

LITHIUM STEARATE • White, fatty, solid, and soluble in water and alcohol. A metallic soap used as an emulsifier, lubricant, and plasticizer in various cosmetic creams and lotions. Also a coloring agent. No known toxicity.

LIVER EXTRACT • Extract of bovine livers used in anti-wrinkle creams. No known toxicity.

LOCUST BEAN GUM • **St. John's Bread. Carob Bean Gum.** A thickener and stabilizer in cosmetics and foods. Also used in depilatories. A natural flavor extract from the seed of the carob tree cultivated in the Mediterranean area. The history of the carob tree dates back more than two thousand years when the ancient Egyptians used locust bean gum as an adhesive in mummy binding. It is alleged that the "locust" (through confusion of the locusts with carob) and wild honey, which sustained John the Baptist in the wilderness, was from this plant, thus the name "St. John's Bread." The carob pods are used as feed for stock today because of their high protein content. No known toxicity from cosmetic use. It is on the FDA list for study of side-effects.

LOGWOOD • An active ingredient known as hematoxylin from the very hard brown or brownish red heartwood of a tree common to the

West Indies and Central America. It was widely used as a liquid or as a solid extract obtained by evaporation in black hair colorings and for neutralizing red tones in dyed hair. It is also a mild astringent. May cause allergic reactions in the hypersensitive. No longer authorized for use in cosmetics.

LOVAGE • An ingredient in perfumery from an aromatic herb native to southern Europe and grown in monastery gardens centuries ago for medicine and food flavoring. It has a hot, sharp, biting taste. The yellow brown oil is extracted from the root or other parts of the herb. It has a reputation for improving health and inciting love; Czechoslovakian girls reportedly wear it in a bag around their necks when dating boys. It supposedly has deodorant properties when added to bath water. No known toxicity.

LUBRICATING CREAM • See Emollients.

LUPIN EXTRACT • **Lupine**. Extract of *Lupinus alba*. The seed has been used as a food since earliest times. It produces a light blue dye. No known toxicity.

LYCOPODIUM • **Ground Pine. Ground Fir.** A dusting powder derived from erect or creeping evergreen plants grown in North America, Europe, and Asia. The plant's pores create a fine yellow powder that sticks to the fingers when touched. It is odorless and absorbent. It may cause a form of inflammatory reaction in wounds or exposed tissues and can cause allergic reactions such as a stuffy nose and hay fever.

LYSINE • An essential amino acid (*see*) isolated from casein, fibrin, or blood. It is used to improve the protein quality of a product. No known toxicity.

M

MACADAMIA OIL • **Queensland Nut Oil.** Derived from the nut of a small evergreen tree, it is widely cultivated. Used in emollients.

MACERATION • The extraction of flower-oil by immersion in warm fats.

MAGNESIA • A skin freshener and dusting powder ingredient. Slightly alkaline white powder taken from any one of several ores such as periclase. Named after Magnesia, an ancient city in Asia Minor. An antacid. No known toxicity.

MAGNESIUM • A silver white, light, malleable metal that occurs abundantly in nature and is widely used in combination with various chemicals as a powder. It was reevaluated by the FDA in 1976 and found not harmful at presently used levels. The World Health Organization recommended further studies because of kidney damage found in dogs that ingested it.

MAGNESIUM ALUMINUM SILICATE • A silver white, light, malleable metal that occurs abundantly in nature and is widely used in combination with various chemicals as a powder. It is used primarily as a thickener in cosmetics. It was reevaluated by the FDA in 1976 and found not harmful at presently used levels. The World Health Organization recommended further studies because of kidney damage found in dogs that ingested it.

MAGNESIUM CARBONATE • Perfume carrier, anticaking agent, and coloring agent. Used in baby powder, bath powder, tooth powders, face masks, liquid powders, face powders, dry rouge. It is a silver white, very crystalline salt that occurs in nature as magnetite or dolomite. Can be prepared artificially and is also used in paint, printing ink, table salt, and as an antacid. Nontoxic to the intact skin but may cause irritation when applied to abraded skin.

MAGNESIUM CITRATE • Used in hair sets or hair-bodying agents. The magnesium salt of citric acid. Soluble in water. It leaves a glossy film after drying. No known toxicity.

MAGNESIUM COCOATE • The magnesium salt of coconut acid (*see*).

MAGNESIUM HYDROXIDE • Used as an alkali in dentifrices and skin creams, in canned peas, and as a drying agent and color retention agent for improved gelling in the manufacture of cheese. Slightly alkaline crystalline compound obtained by hydration of magnesia (*see*) or precipitation of seawater by lime. Toxic when inhaled. Harmless to skin and in fact soothes it.

MAGENESIUM LANOLATE • Magnesium salt of lanolin. See Magnesium and Lanolin.

MAGNESIUM LAURETH SULFATE • Widely used as a surfactant because of its low irritation potential in shampoos. See Surfactants and Anionic.

MAGNESIUM LAURYL SULFATE • A detergent. See Sodium Lauryl Sulfate.

MAGNESIUM MYRISTATE • The magnesium salt of myristic acid (*see*).

MAGNESIUM OLEATE • Salt of magnesium used in liquid powders as a texturizer. It is a yellowish powder of mass that is insoluble in water. No known toxicity.

MAGNESIUM SILICATE • An insoluble, effervescent, white powder that is slowly decomposed by acids to form a soluble salt and an insoluble silica, which has strong absorptive properties. Used to opacify shampoos; also medicinally to reduce stomach acidity, with slow neutralizing action. Nontoxic.

MAGNESIUM STEARATE • Coloring agent used in face powder, protective creams, and baby dusting powders. It is a white soapy powder, insoluble in water. Also used for tablet-making. No known toxicity.

MAGNESIUM TALLOWATE • The magnesium salt of tallow acid (*see*).

MAGNESIUM TRISILICATE • Coloring agent. See Magnesium Aluminum Silicate.

MAGNOLIA • **Sweet Bay.** Used in perfumery. A genus of North American and Asian shrubs and trees named after the French botanist, Pierre Magnol. The plants have evergreen or deciduous leaves and usually snowy white, yellow, rose, or purple flowers appearing in early spring. The dried bark is used in folk medicine to induce sweating and as a bitter tonic. No known toxicity.

MAIDENHAIR FERN EXTRACT • **Venus Hair.** Extract of the leaves of the fern, *Adiantum capillus-veneris*. Used in herbal creams to soothe irritated skin.

MAKEUP BASE, FOUNDATION • See Foundation Makeup.

MALIC ACID • A colorless, crystalline compound with a strong acid taste that occurs naturally in a wide variety of fruits, including apples and cherries. An alkali in cosmetics, foods, and wines. Also used as an antioxidant for cosmetics and as an ingredient of hair lacquer. Irritating to the skin and can cause allergic reaction when used in hair lacquers.

MALLOW EXTRACT • From the herb family. A moderate purplish red that is paler than magenta rose. Used in coloring and also as a source of pectin (*see*). No known toxicity.

MALONIC ACID • An antioxidant prepared synthetically. Occurs naturally in many plants. The colorless crystals obtained from the oxidation of malic acid are used in the manufacture of barbituates. It is a strong irritant. Large doses injected into mice are lethal.

MALT EXTRACT • Extracted from barley that has been allowed to germinate, then heated to destroy vitality, and dried. It contains sugars, proteins, and salts from barley. The extract is mixed with water and allowed to solidify. It is used as a nutrient and in cosmetics as a texturizer. No known toxicity.

MALTITOL • Obtained by the hydrogenate from maltose (*see*).

MALTODEXTRIN • The sugar obtained by hydrolysis of starch.

MALTOSE • **Malt Sugar.** Colorless crystals derived from malt extract and used as a nutrient, sweetener, culture medium, and stabilizer. No known toxicity.

MAMMARIAN EXTRACT • The extract of cow's mammary tissue.

MANGANESE SULFATE • Usually prepared by dissolving dolomite (*see*) or magnetite in acid. It is the salt of the element of manganese, a metal ore. Its pale red crystals are used in red hair dye and to make red glazes on porcelain. Also used medicinally as a purgative and as a dressing for cotton goods. No known toxicity to the hair or scalp, but very small doses injected into mice are lethal.

MANGANESE VIOLET • **Burgundy Violet. Permanent Violet. Ammonium Manganese Pyrophosphate.** A moderate purple that is redder and duller than heliotrope and bluer than amethyst. Toxic when inhaled. Permanently listed in 1976 for cosmetic coloring, including around the eyes.

MANNITAN LAURATE • The monoester of lauric acid and mannitol (*see both*).

MANNITOL • A humectant in hand creams and lotions and used in hair-grooming products as an emulsifier and antioxidant. It is widespread in plants but mostly prepared from seaweed. White, crystalline solid, odorless, and sweet tasting. Its use as a food additive is under study by the FDA because it can cause gastrointestinal disturbances. However, there is no known toxicity from its use as a cosmetic.

MARITIME PINE EXTRACT • Extract of the bark and pine buds of *Pinus maritima*. See Pine Tar.

MARJORAM OIL • Used in hair preparations, perfumes and soaps, it is the yellowish essential oil from sweet marjoram. Insoluble in water, soluble in alcohol and chloroform. Can irritate the skin. The redness, itching, and warmth experienced when marjoram is applied to the skin are caused by local dilation of the blood vessels or by contraction of smooth muscles in the skin. May produce allergic reactions. Essential oils, such as marjoram, are believed to penetrate the skin easily and produce systemic effects.

MASCARA • A cosmetic for coloring the eyelashes and eyebrows. Contains insoluble pigments, carnauba wax, triethanolamine stearate, paraffin, and lanolin. Pigments in eye makeup must be inert and are usually carbon black, iron oxides, chromium oxide, ultramarine, or carmine. Coal tar dyes are not permitted. The excipients may contain beeswax, cetyl alcohol, and glyceryl monostearate; gums such as tragacanth, mineral oil, and perfume; preservatives such as *p*-hydroxybenzoic acid, propylene glycol, and spermaceti; synthetics such as isopropyl myristate; and vegetable oils. The newer lash extenders may carry certain tiny fibers of rayon or nylon. Almost any one of the ingredients may cause an allergic reaction in the susceptible.

MATE EXTRACT • **Paraguay Tea Extract. St. Bartholomew's Tea. Jesuit's Tea.** A natural flavoring extract from small gourds grown in South America where mate is a stimulant beverage. Among its constituents are caffeine, purines, and tannins. See Caffeine and Tannic Acid for toxicity. GRAS.

MATRICARIA EXTRACT • **Wild Chamomile Extract.** Extract of the flower heads of *Matricaria chamomilla*. Used internally as a tonic and externally as a soothing medication for contusions and other inflammation. See Tannic Acid.

MATRICARIA OIL • **Chamomile Oil.** The volatile oil distilled from the dried flower head of *Matricaria chamomilla*. See Matricaria Extract.

MATTE FINISH MAKEUP • Designed to be an all-in-one makeup combining foundation and powder. It is a more concentrated version of standard makeup and contains more powder, pigment, and emollient than standard makeup. Effective in covering blemishes. Skin toxicity depends upon ingredients used.

MAYONNAISE • The common salad dressing. Semisolid, made with eggs, vegetable oil, and vinegar or lemon juice. Used by natural cosmeticians as a dry hair conditioner. The hair is rubbed liberally with mayonnaise, a hot towel is wrapped around the hair and is kept on for 15 minutes, and then removed. Two soapings and plenty of rinsing follow. As effective as any of the more expensive commercial products.

MDM • Abbreviation for monomethylol dimethyl.

MDM HYDANTOIN • **Monomethylol Dimethyl Hydantoin.** Used as a preservative in cosmetic preparations, the compound liberates an allergen, steadily at a slow rate in the presence of water. The resin is used in hair lacquers.

MEA • The abbreviation for monoethanolamine.

MEA-BORATE • The ester of ethanolamine borate. See Ethanolamine and Boric Acid.

MEA-HYDROLYZED ANIMAL PROTEIN • The monoethanolamine salt of hydrolyzed animal protein (*see*).

MEA-LAURETH SULFATE • The monoethanolamine salt of ethylated lauryl sulfate. See Quaternary Ammonium Compounds.

MEA-LAURYL SULFATE • The monoethanolamine salt of sulfated lauryl alcohol.

MEDICATED MAKEUP • Cosmetic manufacturers advertise medicated makeup that both "covers" and treats the skin simultaneously.

Such cosmetics contain antibacterials such as tribromsalan. The American Medical Association frowns on such preparations because such antiinfective agents are useful in medical preparations for the treatment of minor cuts and abrasions, but in cosmetics and toilet preparations, they serve merely to limit the bacterial contamination of the product during use. Furthermore, their potential harm often outweighs their benefit, because such agents may cause allergic reactions and sensitivity to sunlight or bright lights; when the skin is exposed, it breaks out or reddens.

MEK • **Methyl Ethyl Ketone.** A flammable, colorless liquid compound resembling acetone and most often made by taking the hydrogen out of butyl alcohol. Used chiefly as a solvent. Similar to, but more irritating than acetone; its vapor is irritating to the mucous membranes and eyes. Central nervous system depression in experimental animals has been reported, but the irritating odor usually discourages further inhalation in humans. No serious poisonings reported in humans, except for skin irritation when nail polish was applied with MEK as a solvent. Large doses inhaled by rats are lethal.

MELAMINE • White, free-flowing, powdered resin. Used in nail enamel. First introduced into industry in 1939, it is now used in a wide variety of products including boil-proof adhesives and scratch-resistant enamel finishes. Combined with urea resins, it forms the heat-resistant amino plastics. It may cause skin rashes, but that is believed to be caused by the formaldehyde component rather than the melamine.

MENADIONE • **Vitamin K_3.** Used as a preservative in emollients. A synthetic with properties of Vitamin K. Bright yellow crystals which are insoluble in water. They are used medically to prevent blood clotting and in food to prevent souring of milk products. Can be irritating to mucous membranes, the respiratory tract, and the skin.

MENHADEN OIL • **Pogy Oil. Mossbunker Oil.** Obtained along the Atlantic coast from menhaden fish, which are a little larger than herrings. The fish glycerides of menhaden are reddish and have a strong fishy odor. Used in soaps and creams. No known toxicity.

MENTHOL • Used in perfumes, emollient creams, hair tonics, mouthwashes, shaving creams, preshave lotions, after-shave lotions, body rubs, liniments, and skin fresheners. It gives that "cool" feeling to the skin after use. It can be obtained naturally from peppermint or other mint oils and can be made synthetically by hydrogenation (*see*) of thymol (*see*). It is a mild local anesthetic. It is nontoxic in low doses, but in concentrations of 1 percent or more it exerts an irritant action that can, if continued long, induce changes in all layers of the mucous membranes.

MENTHYL SALICYLATE • The ester of menthol and salicylic acid used in medicines and sunscreen preparations. See Salicylic Acid.

MERCAPTOPROPIONIC ACID • See Thioglycolic Acid Compounds.

MERCURIC OXIDE • **Red Mercuric Oxide. Yellow Mercuric Oxide.** Derived by heating mercurous nitrate, it is used in perfumery as a topical disinfectant and as a fungicide. Highly toxic.

MERCURY COMPOUNDS • **Quicksilver.** Until July 5, 1973, mercury was widely used in cosmetics, including wax face masks, hair tonics, medicated soaps, and bleach and freckle creams. Mercury compounds are heavy, silver liquids from the metal that occurs in the earth's crust. Mercury is potentially dangerous by all portals of entry, including the skin. It may cause a variety of symptoms ranging from chronic inflammation of the mouth and gums to personality changes, nervousness, fever, rash; and, if ingested in small amounts, may be fatal. The ban on mercury was brought about because it was found that its use in bleaching creams and other products over a long period of time caused mercury buildup in the body. Mercury is still used as a preservative in eye preparations to inhibit growth of germs. This is now the only use permitted. Because the prevention of eye infection warrants the use of mercury, eye makeup contains up to 0.0065 percent.

MEROXAPOL-105, -108, -171, -172, -174, -178, -251, -252, -254, -255, -258, -311, -312, -314 • **Pluronic.** The polyoxypropylene block polymer that is derived from petroleum, it is a liquid nonionic—resists freezing and shrinkage—surfactant used in hand creams. The numbers after identify the liquidity of the compound; the higher, the more solid.

METABROMOSALAN • See Bromates.

METALLIC HAIR DYES • Metals such as copper are used to change the color of hair. They are not used very often because they tend to dull the hair. However, they are used in products that are designed for daily application over a week or so to effect color changes gradually. Combs impregnated with dye or hair lotions may contain metals for this purpose. See Hair Coloring for further information, including toxicity.

METHACRYLOYL ETHYL BETAINE/METHACRYLATES COPOLYMER • See Methacrylic Acid.

METHANOL • **Methyl Alcohol. Wood Alcohol.** A solvent and denaturant obtained by the destructive distillation of wood. Flammable, poisonous liquid with a nauseating odor. Better solvent than ethyl alcohol. See Ethanol for skin toxicity.

METHENAMINE • An odorless, white, crystalline powder made from formaldehyde and ammonia. Used as an antiseptic and bacteria killer in deodorant creams and powders, mouthwashes, and medicines.

It is one of the most frequent causes of skin rashes in the rubber industry and is omitted from hypoallergenic cosmetics. Skin irritations are believed to be caused by formic acid, which occurs by the action of perspiration on the formaldehyde.
METHICONE • See Silicones.
METHIONINE • An essential amino acid (*see*) that occurs in protein. Used as a texturizer in cosmetic creams. Also used as a dietary substance and is attracted to fat. Nontoxic.
4-METHOXY-m-PHENYLENEDIAMINE SULFATE • See Phenylenediamine.
METHOXY PEG-22/DODECYL GLYCOL • See Polymers.
p-METHOXYACETOPHENONE • ***p*-Acetanisole.** Crystalline solid with a pleasant odor. Soluble in alcohol and fixed oils and derived from the interaction of anisole and acetyl chloride with aluminum chloride and carbon disulfide. Used in perfumery as a synthetic floral odor and in flavoring.
METHOXYDIGLYCOL • See Polyethylene Glycol.
METHOXYETHANOL • See Ethanol.
p-METHOXYPHENYL • See Guaiacol.
2- AND 4-METHOXY-m-PHENYLENEDIAMINE • See *p*-Phenylenediamine.
2-METHOXY-p-PHENYLENEDIAMINE SULFATE • See Phenylenediamine.
METHOXYPROPANOL • See Propylene Glycol.
METHOXYSALEN • **8-Methoxypsoralen.** White to cream colored, odorless, crystalline solid; slightly soluble in alcohol and almost insoluble in water. Used as a suntan accelerator and a sunburn protectant.
4-METHOXYTOLUENE-2, 5-DIAMINE HCL • A colorless liquid used in perfumery and flavorings. See Toluene.
METHYL ACETAMIDE • See Methyl Acetate.
METHYL ACETATE • **Acetic Acid.** Colorless liquid that occurs naturally in coffee, with a pleasant apple odor. Used in perfume to emphasize floral notes (*see*), especially that of rose, and in toilet waters having a lavender odor. Also naturally occurs in peppermint oil. Used as a solvent for many resins and oils. May be irritating to the respiratory tract and, in high concentrations, may be narcotic. Since it has an effective fat solvent drying effect on skin, it may cause skin problems such as chafing and cracking.
METHYL ACRYLATE • **2-Propanoic Acid. Methyl Ester.** Derived from ethylene chlorohydrin, it is transparent and elastic. See Acrylates.
METHYL ALCOHOL • See Methanol.
METHYL ANTHRANILATE • Used as an "orange" scent for oint-

ments, in the manufacture of synthetic perfumes, and in suntan lotions. Occurs naturally in neroli, ylang-ylang, bergamot, jasmine, and other essential oils. Colorless to pale yellow liquid with a bluish fluorescence and a grapelike odor. It is made synthetically from coal tar (*see*). Can irritate the skin.

METHYL BENZOATE • **Essence of oil of Niobe.** Made from methanol and benzoic acid (*see both*). Used in perfumes. Colorless, transparent liquid with a pleasant fruity odor. Also used as a flavoring in foods and beverages. No known toxicity.

METHYL CAPROATE • **Methyl Hexanoate.** The ester produced by the reaction of methyl alcohol and caproic acid. Used as a stabilizer and plasticizer for hand and face creams. No known toxicity.

METHYL CAPRYLATE • See Methyl Caproate.

METHYL CINNAMATE • White crystals, strawberrylike odor, and soluble in alcohol. Derived by heating methanol, cinnamic acid, and sulfuric acid. Used in perfumes and flavoring. See Cinnamic Acid.

METHYL COCOATE • **Methyl Alcohol and Fatty Acids.** See Methanol and Coconut Oil.

6-METHYL COUMARIN • A synthetic compound once used in suntan products. A potent photosensitizer. Not recommended for use in fragrance ingredients.

METHYL DEHYDROABIETATE • See Abietic Acid.

METHYL ETHYL KETONE • See MEK.

METHYL EUGENOL • **Eugenol. Methyl Ether.** See Eugenol and Ether.

METHYL GLUCETH-10 OR -20 • The polyethylene glycol ether of methyl glucose. See Glucose Glutamate.

METHYL GLUCETH-20 SESQUISTERATE • **Glucamate.** See Glucose Glutamate.

METHYL GLUCOSE SESQUIOLEATE • A mixture of diesters of methyl glucoside and oleic acid. See Glutamic Acid.

METHYL GLUCOSE SESQUISTEARATE • A mixture of diesters of methyl glucoside and stearic acid. See Glutamic Acid.

METHYL HYDROGENATED ROSINATE • The ester of methyl alcohol and hydrogenated acids derived from rosin (*see*).

2-METHYL-5-HYDROXYETHLAMINOPHENOL • See Phenol.

METHYL HYDROXYMETHYL OLEYL OXAZOLINE • A synthetic wax. See Oxazoline.

2-METHYL-4-HYDROXYPYRROLINE • A plasticizer derived from acetylene and formaldehyde. See latter for toxicity.

METHYL HYDROXYSTEARATE • The ester of methy alcohol and

hydroxystearic acid used in cosmetic creams. See Methanol and Stearic Acid.

METHYL LACTATE • The ester of menthol *(see)* and lactic acid z. See Lactic Acid..

METHYL LAURATE • The ester of methyl alcohol and lauric acid. Derived from coconut oil, it is used in detergents, emulsifiers, wetting agents, stabilizers, resins, lubricants, plasticizers, and flavorings. No known toxicity.

METHYL LINOLEATE • The ester of methyl alcohol and linoleic acid, it is a colorless oil derived from safflower oil and used in detergents, emulsifiers, wetting agents, stabilizers, resins, lubricants, and plasticizers. No known toxicity.

METHYL MYRISTATE • See Myristic Acid.

METHYL NICOTINATE • Derived from nicotinic acid and used as a rubefacient (*see*). No known toxicity.

METHYL OLEATE • See Oleic Acid.

METHYL PALMITATE • The ester of methyl alcohol and palmitic acid. Colorless liquid derived from palm oil. Used in detergents, emulsifiers, wetting agents, stabilizers, resins, lubricants, and plasticizers. Low toxicity.

METHYL PARABEN • One of the most widely used preservatives in cosmetics, it has a broad spectrum of animicrobial activity and is relatively nonirritating, nonsensitizing, and nonpoisonous. It is stable over the acid-alkalinity range of most cosmetics and is sufficiently soluble in water to produce the effective concentration in the water phase. Can cause allergic reactions.

METHYL PELARGONATE • **Nonanoic Acid. Methyl Ester.** The ester of ethyl alcohol and pelargonic acid used in perfume and flavorings. No known toxicity.

METHYL PHENYLACETATE • Colorless liquid with a honeylike odor used in perfumery and as a flavoring. See Phenylacetate.

METHYL PHTHALYL ETHYL GLYCOLATE • See Phthalic Acid and Polyethylene Glycol.

METHYL RICINOLEATE • The ester of methyl alcohol and ricinoleic acid. A colorless liquid used as a plasticizer, lubricant, cutting oil, and wetting agent. See Castor Oil.

METHYL ROSINATE • **Rosin Acid. Methyl Ester.** The ester of acids recovered from Rosin (*see*).

METHYL SALICYLATE • **Oil of Wintergreen.** A counterirritant, local anesthetic, and disinfectant used in perfumes, toothpaste, tooth powder, and mouthwash. The volatile oil obtained by maceration and subsequent steam distillation in a species of leaves, including those of sweet birch, cassie, and wintergreen. A strong irritant to the skin and mucous membranes and may be absorbed readily through the skin. Used as a flavor in foods, beverages, and pharmaceuticals, and used as an odorant, in perfumery, and in sunburn lotions as an ultraviolet absorber. Toxic by ingestion. Use in foods restricted by the FDA. Lethal dose 30 cc in adults, 10 cc in children.

METHYL SILICONE • Prepared by hydrolyzing (*see*) dimethyldichlorosilane or its esters, it is used to help compounds resist oxidation. No known toxicity. See Silicones.

3-METHYLAMINO-4-NITROPHENOXYETHANOL • See *p*-Methylaminophenol Sulfate.

p-METHYLAMINOPHENOL • See *p*-Methylaminophenol Sulfate.

p-METHYLAMINOPHENOL SULFATE • Crystals that discolor in air and are soluble in water. They are used in photographic developers, for dyeing furs, and for hair dyes. May cause skin irritation, allergic reactions, and a shortage of oxygen in the blood. In solution applied to the skin, restlessness, and convulsions have been produced in humans.

METHYLATED SPIRITS • **Toilet Quality.** Alcohol denatured with methanol (*see*). Used in fragrances and other cosmetic products in amounts of over 85 percent ethyl alcohol, 5 percent methyl alcohol, and 5 percent water. See Ethanol for toxicity.

METHYLBENZETHONIUM CHLORIDE • **Diaparine Chloride.** A quaternary ammonium compound used as a germicide in cosmetics and baby products such as baby oils. Also used as topical disinfectant. See Quaternary Ammonium Compounds for toxicity.

METHYLCELLULOSE • **Cellulose Methyl Ether.** A binder, thickener, dispersing, and emulsifying agent used in wave-setting lotions, foam stabilizers, bath oils, and other cosmetic products. It is prepared from wood pulp or chemical cotton by treatment with alcohol. Swells in water. Soluble in cold water and insoluble in hot. See also Carboxymethyl Cellulose. A dose injected into the abdomens of rats causes cancer. Nontoxic on the skin.

METHYLCHLOROISOTHIAZOLINONE • A preservative used in shampoos, taken from industry, to replace formaldehyde. While it has been shown to be a sensitizer in animals, it has not been shown to be a sensitizer in humans.

METHYLENE CHLORIDE • A solvent for nail enamels and for cleansing creams. A colorless gas that compresses into a colorless liquid of pleasant odor and sweet taste. Used as an anesthetic in medicine. High concentrations are narcotic. Damage to the liver, kidney, and central nervous system can occur, and persistent postrecovery symptoms after inhalation include headache, nervousness, insomnia, and tremor. Can be absorbed through the skin and is then converted to carbon monoxide which, in turn, can cause stress in the cardiovascular system. It is also a skin irritant.

METHYLISOTHIAZOLINONE • Used with methylchloroisothiazolinone as a preservative in shampoos to replace formaldehyde. While it is a sensitizer in animals, it has not been shown to be a sensitizer in humans.

METHYLPARABEN • **Methyl p-Hydroxybenzoate.** Used in bubble baths, cold creams, eyeliners, and liquid makeup. It is an antimicrobial and preservative made of small, odorless, colorless crystals that have a burning taste. Nontoxic in small amounts but can cause allergic skin reactions.

METHYLPHENYLPOLYSILOXANE • Cresol (*see*) with a blend of silicone (*see*) oils. An oily, fluid resin, stable over a wide temperature range, used in lubricating creams. No known toxicity.

2-METHYLRESORCINOL • **Orcin.** An aromatic compound with white crystalline prisms derived from lichen and used in medicine as a reagent for sugars and starches. See Resorcinol.

METHYLSTYRENE/VINYLTOLUENE COPOLYMER • The polymer of methylstyrene and vinyltoluene monomers. Used as a wax. See Styrenes.

MIBK • **Methyl Isobutyl Ketone.** Colorless liquid with a pleasant odor that is used as a solvent for paints, varnishes, nitrocellulose lacquers, and as a denaturant for alcohol. Hazardous by either ingestion or inhalation.

MICA • Any of a group of minerals that are found in crystallized, thin elastic sheets that can be separated easily. They vary in color from pale green, brown, or black to colorless. Ground and used as a lubricant and coloring in cosmetics. Irritant by inhalation, may be damaging to the lungs. Nontoxic to the skin. Coloring permanently listed for cosmetic use in 1977 and used according to general manufacturing practices.

MICROCRYSTALLINE CELLULOSE • The colloid crystalline portion of cellulose fibers. See Cellulose Gums.

MICROCRYSTALLINE WAX • Any of various plastic materials that are obtained from petroleum. They are different from paraffin waxes (*see*) in that they have a higher melting point and higher viscosity and have much finer crystals that can be seen only under a microscope. Used in nail polishes and in cake cosmetics. No known toxicity.

MILFOIL • See Yarrow.

MILK • Used in bath preparations and face masks as a soothing skin cleanser. Also used by natural cosmeticians as a face wash; for dry skin, cream is used; for oily skin, they use skimmed milk. It is as effective as many more expensive products. Nontoxic, but if not rinsed thoroughly from the skin with water, rancidity sets in and becomes a focus of bacteria. Consequently, the skin may break out with pimples.

MIMOSA • Reddish yellow solid with a long-lasting, pleasant odor resembling ylang-ylang used in perfumes. Derived from trees, shrubs, and herbs native to tropical and warm regions. Mimosa droops and closes its leaves when touched. Also used in tanning. May produce allergic skin reactions.

MINERAL OIL • **White Oil.** Used in baby creams, baby lotions, bay oil, brilliantine hairdressings, cleansing creams, cold creams, emollients, moisturizing creams, eye creams, foundation creams and makeup, hair conditioners, hand lotions, lipsticks, mascaras, rouge, shaving creams, compact powders, makeup removers, suntan creams, oils, and ointments. Also a cosmetic lubricant, protective agent, and binder. It is a mixture of refined liquid hydrocarbons (*see*) derived from petroleum. Colorless, transparent, odorless, and tasteless. When heated, it smells like petroleum. It stays on top of the skin and leaves a shiny, protective surface. Nontoxic.

MINERAL SPIRITS • **Ligroin.** A refined solvent of naphtha. Contains naphthenes and paraffin (*see*). Used as a solvent in cosmetic oils, fats, and waxes. See Kerosene for toxicity.

MINERAL WAX • See Ceresin.

MINK OIL • Used in emollients, it supposedly softens the skin. It became popular as a cosmetic ingredient when a mink farmer noticed his hands were softer after handling minks. According to the American Medical Association, mink oil is no more effective than other oils in minimizing the evaporation of moisture from the skin and smoothing the surface scales of excessively dry skin. No known toxicity.

MINKAMIDOPROPYL DIETHYLAMINE • Fatty acids derived from mink oil.

MINT • See Spearmint Oil, Peppermint Oil, Wintergreen Oil, and Sassafras Oil.

MIPA • Abbreviation for monoisopropanolamine.

MIPA-DODECYLBENZENESULFONATE • See Quaternary Ammonium Compounds.

MIPA-LAURYL SULFATE • The monoisoproanolamine salt of lauryl sulfate. See Quaternary Ammonium Compounds.

MIXED ISOPROPANOLAMINES MYRISTATE • A mixture of amine salts formed by neutralizing myristic acid with mixed isopropanolamines. See Myristic Acid and Isopropyl Alcohol.

MIXED TERPENES • Terpenes are a class of organic compounds widely distributed in nature. They are components of volatile or essential oils and are found in substantial amounts in cedarwood oil, camphor, thymol, eucalyptol, menthol, turpentine, and pure oil. They are used in cosmetics as wetting agents and surfactants. Can cause local irritation.

MODERN BLENDS • One of the basic perfume types, it has indefinable top-notes (*see*) which cannot be linked to either the floral or the oriental. These blends contain aldehydes (*see*) meaning that whether they are basically floral or woody, they have a sparkle in their more insistent notes, which enhances all the others.

MODIFIED HETEROPOLYSACCHARIDES • Gums that have been made more soluble.

MODIFIED SEA SALT • Salt derived from sea water with a reduced sodium chloride content.

MODIFIER • A term in cosmetics to describe a substance that induces or stabilizes certain shades in hair coloring.

MOISTURIZERS • **Emollients. Skin Softeners. Creams. Lotions.** The selection of a night cream, hand cream, eye cream, skin softener, moisturizer, etc., is really the selection of an emollient. They all perform the same function—to make the skin feel softer and smoother and to reduce the roughness, cracking, and irritation of the skin. Most are a mixture of oils. The most common ingredients are: mineral oil, stearic acid, lanolin, beeswax, sorbitol, and polysorbates. Among the other ingredients added may be natural fatty oils such as olive, coconut, corn, peach, and sesame oils; natural fats such as stearate and diglycol laurate; hydrocarbon solids such as paraffin; alcohols such as cetyl, stearyl, and oleyl; emulsifiers, preservatives, and antioxidants, including Vitamin E and paraben; antibacterials and perfumes, especially menthol and camphor. As you can see from the list above, many of the ingredients are common allergens described in this book.

MONOAZO COLOR • A dye made from diazonium and phenol, both coal tar derivatives (*see* Coal Tar).

MONOBENZONE • **Hydroquinone Monobenzyl Ether.** Prepared synthetically and used as an antioxidant and to retard melanin production. Used also in bleach and freckle creams. It may cause blotchiness and allergic skin reactions.

MONOMER • A molecule that by repetition in a long chain builds up a large structure, or polymer (*see*). Ethylene, the gas, for instance, is the monomer of polyethylene (*see*).

MONOSACCHARIDE LACTATE CONDENSATE • The condensation product of sodium lactate and the sugars, glucose, fructose, ribose, glucosamine, and deoxyribose.

MONTAN WAX • A clay forming the main ingredient of bentonite (*see*) and Fuller's earth (*see*). Used in the petroleum industry as a carrier. Inhalation of the dust can cause respiratory irritation.

MORDANTS • Chemicals that are insoluble compounds that serve to fix a dye, usually a weak dye, to hasten the development of the desired shade or to modify it in hair colorings. Toxicity depends upon specific ingredients.

MORINGA OIL • **Ben Oil.** Oil from the seeds of the tropical tree *Moringa oleafera.*

MORPHOLINE • Used as a surface-active agent (*see*) and an emulsifier in cosmetics. Prepared by taking the water out of diethanolamine (*see*). A mobile, water-absorbing liquid that mixes with water. It has a strong ammonia odor. A cheap solvent for resins, waxes, and dyes. Also used as a corrosion inhibitor, antioxidant, plasticizer, viscosity improver, insecticide, fungicide, local anesthetic, and antiseptic. Irritating to the eyes, skin, and mucous membranes. It may cause kidney and liver injury, and can produce sloughing of the skin.

MORPHOLINE STEARATE • A coating and preservative. See Morpholine.

MOUNTAIN ASH EXTRACT • The extract from the berries of the European tree or shrub, *Sorbus aucuparia.* High in Vitamin C, it has been used by herbalists to cure and prevent scurvy and to treat nausea. Used in cosmetics as an antioxidant. No known toxicity.

MOUTHWASH • Promoted as a method to cleanse the mouth and overcome objectionable odors. Claims for such abilities have not been proven. Among ingredients used in mouthwashes are: sodium bicarbonate, alcohol, mixed flavoring oils, cinnamon, methyl salicylate, menthol, anethole, thyme, certified colors, resorcinol, sorbitol, urea, methyl salicylate, boric acid, benzalkonium chloride, benzoic acid, propylene glycol, cetylpyridium chloride, and chlorophyllin. Several of the above, particularly the colorings and the flavorings, are common allergens. Resorcinol is a resin (*see*) and methylsalicylate is related to aspirin and other salicylates.

MUCILAGE • A solution in water of the sticky principles of vegetable substances. Used as a soothing application to the mucous membranes.

MUCOPOLYSACCHARIDES • A complex of proteins (*see*). Used in moisturizers.

MUCOUS MEMBRANES • The thin layers of tissues that line the respiratory and intestinal tracts, which are kept moist by a sticky substance called "mucous." These membranes line the nose and other parts of the respiratory tract, and are found in other parts of the body that have communication with air.

MUDPACKS • Long in use as a facial treatment. Today, they consist of a paste for the face composed chiefly of Fuller's earth and astringents (*see both*). There is no evidence that mudpacks are effective. No known toxicity.

MUGWORT • The extract of the flowering herb, *Artemisia absinthium.* See Wormwood and Sesquiterpene Lactones.

MUIRA PUAMA EXTRACT • A wood extract used as an aromatic resin and fat. No known toxicity.

MULBERRY EXTRACT • An extract of the dried leaves of various species of *Morus,* which produces a purplish black dye.

MULLEIN EXTRACT • The extract of common mullein, *Verbascum thapsis,* used in henna dyes.

MUSCLE EXTRACT • The oil extracted from cow muscle.

MUSHROOM EXTRACT • The extract of various species of mushrooms, used as an oil and plasticizer.

MUSK • Used in perfumes. It is the dried secretion from preputial follicles of the northern Asian, small, hornless deer, which has musk in its glands. Musk is a brown, unctuous, smelly substance associated with attracting the opposite sex and which is promoted by stores for such purposes. Also used in food flavorings and at one time was a stimulant and nerve sedative in medicine. Can cause allergic reactions.

MUSK AMBRETTE • A synthetic fixative, it is widely used as a fragrance agent in perfumes, soaps, detergents, creams, lotions, and dentifrices in the United States at an estimated 100,000 pounds per year. It reportedly damages the myelin, the covering of nerve fibers. It can cause photosensitivity (*see*) and contact dermatitis. The problem is mostly with after-shave lotions. Musk tetralin, in use for twenty years as a fragrance ingredient, was identified as a neurotoxin and removed from the market in 1978. Musk Ambrette has been generally recognized as safe as a food additive by the FDA.

MUSTARD OIL • **Allyl Isothiocynate.** The greenish yellow, bland, fatty oil expressed from the seeds of the mustard plant. Used in soaps, liniments, and lubricants. It has an intensely pungent odor that can be irritating. It is a strong skin blisterer and is used diluted as a counterirritant (*see*) and rubefacient (*see*). Can cause allergic reactions.

MYRCIA • **Bay Rum.** See Bay Rum.

MYRETH-3 • The polyethylene glycol ether of myristyl alcohol (*see*).

MYRETH-3 CAPRATE • **Myristic Ethoxy Caprate.** See Capric Acid.

MYRETH-3 LAURATE • The ester of lauric acid and myreth-3 (*see both*).

MYRETH-3 MYRISTATE • The ester of myristic acid and myreth-3 (*see both*).

MYRETH-4 • The polyethylene glycol ether of myristyl alcohol (*see*).

MYRISTALKONIUM CHLORIDE • See Quaternary Ammonium Compounds.

MYRISTAMIDE DEA • **Myristic Diethanolamide.** See Myristic Acid and Diethanolamide.

MYRISTAMIDE MIPA • A mixture of isopropanolamides of lauric acid (*see*).

MYRISTAMIDOPROPYL BETAINE • See Surfactants.

MYRISTAMIDOPROPYL DIETHYLAMINE • See Quaternary Ammonium Compounds.

MYRISTAMIDOPROPYLAMINE OXIDE • See Quaternary Ammonium Compounds.

MYRISTAMINE OXIDE • See Myristic Acid.

MYRISTAMINOPROPIONIC ACID • See Propionic Acid and Myristic Acid.

MYRISTATE • The ester of myreth-3 and myristic acid (*see both*).

MYRISTIC ACID • Used in shampoos, shaving soaps, and creams. A solid, organic acid that occurs naturally in butter acids (such as nutmeg butter to the extent of 80 percent), oil of lovage, coconut oil, mace oil, *cire d'abeille* in palm seed fats, and in most animal and vegetable fats. Also used in food flavorings. When combined with potassium, myristic acid soap gives a very good copious lather. No known toxicity.

MYRISTIMIDE MEA • A mixture of ethanolamide of myristic acid (*see*).

MYRISTOAMPHOACETATE • See Surfactants.

MYRISTOYL HYDROLYZED ANIMAL PROTEIN • The condensation product of myristic acid and hydrolyzed animal protein (*see both*). Used as a setting agent and film-former, it allows the incorporation of protein into nonwater-based cosmetics.

MYRISTOYL SARCOSINE • See Sarcosine.

MYRISTYL ALCOHOL • Used as an emollient in hand creams, cold creams, and lotions to give them a smooth velvety feel. It is made up of white crystals prepared from fatty acids (*see*). Practically insoluble in water. Nontoxic.

MYRISTYL BETAINE • See Myristyl Alcohol.

MYRISTYL HYDROXYETHYL IMIDAZOLINE • See Myristyl Alcohol and Imidazoline.

MYRISTYL ISOSTEARATE • See Myristyl Alcohol and Stearic Acid.

MYRISTYL LACTATE • Used in tanning creams. See Myristyl Alcohol and Myristic Acid.
MYRISTYL LIGNOCEREATE • The ester of myristyl alcohol and lignoceric acid. See Myristyl Alcohol.
MYRISTYL MYRISTATE • An emollient ingredient. See Myristyl Alcohol and Myristic Acid.
MYRISTYL NEOPENTANOATE • **Ceraphyl.** An emollient used to improve the texture and feel of cosmetics. See Valeric Acid.
MYRISTYL PROPIONATE • See Myristic Acid and Propionic Acid.
MYRISTYL STEARATE • See Myristic Acid and Stearic Acid.
MYRISTYLEICOSANOL • See Myristyl Alcohol.
MYRISTYLEICOSYL STEARATE • See Myristyl Alcohol.
MYRISTYLOCTADECANOL • See Myristyl Alcohol.
MYRRH • Used in perfumes, dentifrices, and skin topics. One of the gifts of the Magi, it is a yellow to reddish brown, aromatic, bitter gum resin that is obtained from various trees, especially from East Africa and Arabia. Used by the ancients as an ingredient of incense and perfumes and as a remedy for localized skin problems. Also used in food and beverage flavorings. The gum resin has been used tobreak up intestinal gas and as a topical stimulant. No known toxicity.
MYRTLE EXTRACT • The extract of *Myrtus communis*, a European shrub.
MYRTRIMONIUM BROMIDE • See Quaternary Ammonium Compounds.

N

NAIL, ARTIFICIAL • See Artificial Nails.
NAIL BLEACHES • Compounds designed to remove ink, nicotine, vegetable, and other stains from fingernails. They consist mainly of an oxidizing agent and chlorinated compounds. A typical formula includes titanium dioxide, 20 percent; talc, 20 percent; zinc peroxide, 7.5 percent; petrolatum, 26 percent; mineral oil, 26.5 percent; and perfume (*see all*). Toxicity depends upon ingredients used.
NAIL ENAMEL • See Nail Polish.
NAIL FINISHES • **Top Coat.** Usually a colorless nail polish (*see*) or it can be slightly pink. Contains celluloid, amyl acetate, and acetone (*see all*). Protects the nail by strengthening it physically, helps to keep the nail polish from chipping, and produces a shiny surface.
NAIL HARDENERS • Keep the nails from breaking or chipping. Most

nail hardeners formerly contained formaldehyde but now contain polyesters, acrylics, and polyamides. Sensitization rarely occurs.

NAIL MENDING KITS • Tissue paper, high solids, and enamel. May have acrylic adhesives, which are sensitizers. Can be an eye irritant.

NAIL POLISH • Used to paint the nails with colors, usually some shade of red. Polishes contain cellulose nitrate (nitrocellulose), butyl acetate, ethyl acetate, toluene, dibutyl phthalate, alkyl esters (amyl acetate, ethyl acetate), dyes, glycol derivatives, gums, hydrocarbons (aromatic and aliphatic), ketones (acetone, methyl, ethyl), lakes, and phosphoric acid. Common colors used are D & C Red No. 19 or 31 (*see*). Skin rashes of the eyelids and neck are common in those allergic to nail polish. Among recent complaints to the FDA about nail polishes were irritation of the nail area, discolored nails, nails permanently stained black, splitting of nails, and nausea.

NAIL POLISH REMOVER • Usually a liquid, it is used to remove nail polish. It contains acetone, toluene, alcohol, amyl acetate, butyl acetate, benzene, and ethyl acetate. It also contains castor oil, lanolin, cetyl alcohol, olive oil, perfume, spermaceti, and synthetic oil (ethyl oleate, butyl stearate) (*see all*). Many components are very toxic and can cause central nervous system depression, especially the toluene and aliphatic acetates. A report to the FDA described a "tight smothering feeling in the chest" after use of a nail polish remover.

NAIL STRENGTHENERS • See Nail Hardeners.

NAIL WHITENERS • The cream nail whiteners may contain titanium dioxide, beeswax, cetyl alcohol, petrolatum, cocoa butter, sodium borate, tincture of benzoin (*see all*), and water. The liquid nail whites may contain titanium dioxide, glyceryl monostearate, beeswax, almond oil, petrolatum (*see all*), and water. Toxicity is dependent upon ingredients.

NAILS, PRESS ON • Fake nails made of resins and acrylic glues. The acrylic glues may sensitize.

NAPHTHALENE • A coal tar (*see*) derivative, it is used to manufacture dyes, solvents, lubricants, as a moth repellent, and a topical and internal antiseptic. It has been used as a dusting powder to combat insects on animals. Can cause allergic contact dermatitis.

NAPHTHAZOLINE HYDROCHLORIDE • **Privine Hydrochloride.** Prepared from acids, it is composed of bitter-tasting crystals, which are soluble in water. Used as a nasal and eye decongestant. It may cause sedation in infants, and high blood pressure and central nervous system excitement followed by depression in adults.

1, 5-NAPHTHALENEDIOL • See Naphthas.

2, 7-NAPHTHALENEDIOL • See Naphthas.

NAPHTHAS • Obtained from the distillation of petroleum, coal tar, and shale oil. It is a common diluent (*see*) found in nail lacquer. Among the common naphthas that are used as solvents are coal tar/naphtha and petroleum/naphtha. See Kerosene for toxicity.

NAPHTHOL • A coal tar (*see*) derivative, it is used as an antiseptic, in hair dyes, and to treat eczema, ring worm, and psoriasis. May cause allergic contact dermatitis.

1-NAPHTHOL • **a-Naphthol.** Used in hair dyes and the treatment of skin diseases, as an antiseptic, and as an antioxidant for fats and oils. Also used in perfumery. White crystals with phenolic odor and disagreeable burning taste. Slightly soluble in water. Toxic by ingestion and skin absorption.

2-NAPHTHOL • **b-Naphthol.** Used as an antiseptic and modifier in hair preparations, with a tendency to darken gray hair. Sometimes used in treatment of eczema, ringworm, and psoriasis. See 1-Naphthol for toxicity.

B-NAPHTHYL ETHYL ETHER • White crystals with an orange-blossom odor. Used in perfumes, soaps, and flavoring. See Nerolin.

B-NAPHTHYL METHYL ETHER • White crystals with a menthol odor. Used to perfume soaps. See Naphthol.

NASTURTIUM EXTRACT • The extract of the leaves and stems of *Tropaeolum majus*. A member of the mustard family, it has pungent and tasty leaves. It is very rich in Vitamins A and C as well as containing Vitamins B and B_2. It is soothing to the skin and supposedly has blood thinning factors and increases the flow of urine. No known toxicity.

NATURAL COSMETICS • See Organic Cosmetics.

NATURAL RED 26 • **Carthamic Acid.** A red crystalline glucoside coloring constituting the coloring matter of the safflower (*see*). No known toxicity.

NEAT'S-FOOT OIL • Lubricant used in creams and lotions. A pale yellow fatty oil made by boiling the feet and shinbones of cattle. Used chiefly as a leather dressing and waterproofing. Can cause allergic reactions in the hypersensitive.

NENOLONE HEMISUCCINATE • See Succinic Acid.

NEODECANOIC ACID • Colorless liquid used in plasticizers and lubricants. See Decanoic Acid.

NEOMYCIN • Used in underarm deodorants. It is produced from the growth of microorganisms inhabiting the soil. It inhibits the growth of bacteria and, therefore, the odor from sweat. It can cause the skin to swell, redden, or break out when exposed to light. It produces allergic reactions in many people. Highly toxic to the eighth nerve, which involves hearing, and to the kidneys. The FDA does not believe the use of neomycin in deodorants is justified, because it caused resistant strains of staphylococci to develop. Such staph infections are extremely difficult to treat and could be lethal.

NEOPENTYL GLYCOL DICAPRATE • The diester of neopentyl glycol and decanoic acid used as a plasticizer. No known toxicity.

NEROL • A primary alcohol used in perfumes, especially in rose and orange-blossom scents. Occurs naturally in oil of lavender, orange leaf, palmarosa oil, rose, neroli, and oil of petitgrain. It is colorless, with the odor of rose. Also used in food flavorings. Similar to geraniol (*see*) in toxicity.

NEROLI BIGARADE OIL • Used chiefly in cologne and in perfumes. Named for the putative discoverer, Anna Maria de la Tremoïlle, princess of Nerole (1670). A fragrant, pale yellow, essential oil obtained from the flowers of the sour orange tree. It darkens upon standing. Also used in food flavorings. No known toxicity.

NEROLIDOL • A sesquiterpene alcohol. A straw-colored liquid with an odor similar to rose and apple. Occurs naturally in Balsam Peru and oils of orange flower, neroli, sweet orange, and ylang-ylang. Also made synthetically. Used in perfumery and flavoring. See Nerol.

NETTLES • Used in hair tonics and shampoos. It is obtained from the troublesome weed, with stingers. It has a long history and was used in folk medicine. Its flesh is rich in minerals and plant hormones, and it supposedly stimulates hair growth and shines and softens hair. Also used to make tomatoes resistant to spoilage, to encourage the growth of strawberries, and to stimulate the fermentation of humus. No known toxicity.

NGDA • See Nordehydroguaiaretic Acid.

NIACIN • **Nicotinic Acid.** White or yellow crystalline powder, it is an essential nutrient that participates in many energy-yielding reactions. It is a component of the B-Vitamin Complex.

NIACINAMIDE • **Niotinamide. Vitamin B.** Used as a skin stimulant. A white or yellow crystalline, odorless powder used to treat pellagra, a vitamin deficiency disease, and in the assay of enzymes for substrates. No known skin toxicity.

NICKEL • Metal that occurs in the earth.

NICKEL SULFATE • Used in hair dyes and astringents. Occurs in the earth's crust as a salt of nickel. Obtained as green or blue crystals and is used chiefly in nickel plating. It has a sweet astringent taste and acts as an irritant, and causes vomiting when swallowed. Its systemic effects include blood vessel, brain, and kidney damage, and nervous depression. Frequently causes skin rash when used in cosmetics.

NICOTINE REMOVERS • See Nail Bleaches.

NITRIC ACID • Used as an oxidizer in hair dyes and as a stabilizer in cosmetics. A corrosive, colorless, inorganic acid made by the action of ammonia on sulfuric acid and nitrate. Used chiefly as an oxidizing agent in the manufacture of fertilizers, explosives, and nitroparaffin. The fumes in moist air give off a choking odor. Ingestion can cause burning and corrosion of the mouth, esophagus, and stomach, and can result in death. Chronic inhalation of vapors can cause bronchitis. Can be irritating to the skin.

NITRILOTRIACETIC ACID • **NTA.** Cheleting and sequestering agent. Used in detergents. Can be irritating.

NITRO- • A prefix denoting one atom of nitrogen and two of oxygen. Nitro also denotes a class of dyes derived from coal tars. Nitro dyes can be absorbed through the skin. When absorbed or ingested, they can cause a lack of oxygen in the blood. Chronic exposure may cause liver damage. See Colors.

NITROCELLULOSE • Any of several esters (*see*) obtained as white, fibrous, flammable solids by adding nitrate to cellulose, the cell walls of plants. Used in skin protective creams, nail enamels, and lacquers. No known toxicity.

NITROGEN • A gas that is, by volume, 78 percent of the atmosphere, and essential to all living things. Odorless. Used as a preservative for cosmetics, in which it is nontoxic. In high concentrations, it can asphyxiate. Toxic concentration in humans is 90 ppm; in mice, 250 ppm.

3-NITRO-4-AMINOPHENOXYETHANOL • An aromatic ether alcohol used as a fungicide. See *o*-Phenylphenol.

2-NITRO-N-HYDROXYETHYL-p-ANISIDINE • See Azo Dyes.

3-NITRO-p-HYDROXYETHYLAMINOPHENOL • See *o*-Phenylphenol.

2-NITRO-p-PHENYLENEDIAMINE • See *p*-Phenylenediamine.

4-NITRO-m-PHENYLENEDIAMINE • See *p*-Phenylenediamine.

NITROUS OXIDE • **Laughing Gas.** A whipping agent for whipped cosmetic creams and a propellant in pressurized cosmetic containers. Slightly sweetish odor and taste. Colorless. Used in rocket fuel. Less irritating than other nitrogen oxides but narcotic in high concentrations, and it can asphyxiate.

NONANAL • Colorless liquid with an orange-rose odor. Used in perfumery and flavoring. See Aldehyde.

NONANE-1, 3-DIOL MONOACETATE • Colorless to slightly yellow mixture of isomers used in perfumery and flavoring. See Nonanoic Acid and Acetic Acid.

NONANOIC ACID • A colorless, oily liquid that is insoluble in water, it occurs in the oil of pelargonium plants such as the geranium. It is practically insoluble in water and is used in producing salts and in the manufacture of lacquers. Can be very irritating to the skin.

NONCOMEDOGENIC • Does not cause pimples and blackheads by blocking pores.

NONFAT DRY MILK • The solid residue produced by removing the water from defatted cow's milk. See Milk.

NONIONIC • A group of emulsifiers used in hand creams. They resist freezing and shrinkage. Toxicity depends upon specific ingredients.

NONOXYNOL-2 • **Polyoxyethylene (2) Nonyl Phenyl Ether.** Used as a nonionic (*see*) surface-active agent and as a dispersing agent in cosmetics. No known toxicity. See Polyethylene Glycol.

NONOXYNOL-4, -8 • See Nonoxynol-2.

NONOXYNOL-9 IODINE • See Nonoynol-2 and Iodine.

NONOXYNOL-12 IODINE • See Nonoxynol-2 and Iodine.

NONYL ACETATE • Used in perfumery. An ester produced by the reaction of nonyl alcohol and acetic acid (*see*). Pungent odor, suggestive of mushrooms, but when diluted it resembles the odor of gardenias. Insoluble in water. No known toxicity.

NONYL ALCOHOL • **Nonalol**. A synthetic flavoring, colorless to yellow with a citronella oil odor. Occurs in oil of orange. Used in butter, citrus, peach, and pineapple flavorings for beverages, ice cream, ices, candy, and chewing gum. Also used in the manufacture of artificial lemon oil. In experimental animals it has caused central nervous system and liver damage.

y-NONYL LACTONE • Yellowish to almost colorless liquid with a coconutlike odor. Used in perfumery and flavors. See Nonyl Alcohol.

NONYL NONANOATE • **Nonyl Pelargonate.** Liquid with a floral odor used in flavors, perfumes, and organic synthesis. See Nonyl Alcohol.

NONYL NONOXYNOL-10 • See Nonoynol-2.

NONYL NONOXYNOL-49 • See Nonoxynol-2.

NORDIHYDROGUAIARETIC ACID • **NGDA.** An antioxidant used in brilliantines and other fat-based cosmetics. Occurs in resinous exudates of many plants. White or grayish white crystals. Lard containing 0.01 percent NGDA stored at room temperature for 19 months in diffused daylight showed no appreciable rancidity or color change. Canada banned the additive in food in 1967 after it was shown to cause cysts and kidney damage in a large percentage of rats tested. The FDA removed it from the Generally Recognized As Safe list of food additives (GRAS) in 1968. No known toxicity for use in cosmetics.

NORVALINE • A protein amino acid (*see*), soluble in hot water, and insoluble in alcohol. See Valeric Acid.

NOTE • A distinct odor or flavor. "Top note" is the first note normally perceived when a flavor is smelled or tasted; usually volatile and gives "identity." "Middle" or "main note" is the substance of the flavor, the main characteristic. "Bottom note" is what is left when top and middle notes disappear. It is the residue when the aroma or flavoring evaporates.

NTA • Abbreviation for nitriloacetic acid (*see*).

NUTMEG • A natural flavoring extracted from the dried, ripe seed. Used in cola, vermouth, sausage, eggnog, and nutmeg flavorings for beverages, ice cream, ices, baked goods, condiments, meats, and pickles. The oil is used in loganberry, chocolate, lemon, cola, apple, grape, muscatel, rum, sausage, eggnog, pistachio, root beer, cinnamon, dill, ginger, mace, nutmeg, and vanilla flavorings for beverages, ice cream, ices, candy, baked goods, chewing gum, condiments, meats, syrups, and icings. Can cause flushing of the skin, irregular heart rhythm and contact dermatitis.

NYLON • The commonly known synthetic material used as a fiber in eyelash lengtheners and mascaras and as a molding compound to shape cosmetics. Comes in clear or white opaque plastic for use in making resins. Can cause allergic reactions. Resistant to organic chemicals but is dissolved by phenol, cresol (*see both*), and strong acids. No known toxicity.

O

OAK BARK EXTRACT • **Oak Chip Extract.** The extract from the white oak used in bitters, whiskey flavorings for beverages, ice cream, and baked goods. Contains tannic acid (*see*) and is exceedingly astringent. In a wash, the American Indians used it for sore eyes and as a tonic. Used in astringents in herbal cosmetics. No known toxicity.

OAKMOSS • Any one of several lichens that grow on oak trees and yield a resin for use as a fixative (*see*) in perfumery. Stable green liquid with a long-lasting characteristic odor. Soluble in alcohol. No known toxicity but a common allergen in after-shave lotions.

OAT BRAN • The broken coat of oats, *Avena sativa*. See Oat Flour.

OAT EXTRACT • The extract of the seeds of oats, *Avena sativa*. See Oat Flour.

OAT FLOUR • Flour from the cereal grain that is an important crop grown in the temperate regions. Light yellowish or brown to weak greenish or yellow powder. Slight odor; starchy taste. Makes a bland ointment for cosmetic treatments, including soothing baths. No known toxicity.

OAT GUM • A plant extract used as a thickener and stabilizer in foods and cosmetics. Also an antioxidant in butter, creams, and candy. It is used as a thickener and stabilizer in pasteurized cheese spread and cream cheese. In foods, it can cause allergic reactions, including diarrhea and intestinal gas. No known toxicity.

OATMEAL • Meal obtained by grinding oats from which the husks have been removed. Used through the ages by women as a face mask. Here is a modern version: put in blender 4 tablespoons of quick-cooking or regular oatmeal and 1 teaspoon of dried mint leaves; turn to high until the mix is finely ground; add enough hot water to make a spreadable paste; smooth and pat on face gently. When paste is dry, remove with lukewarm water, then rinse well with cool water. Apply chilled witch hazel. Soothing. Nontoxic.

OCOTEA CYMBARUM OIL • An oil obtained by steam distillation from the wood of a Brazilian tree. Used chiefly as a source of safrole (*see*), a natural oil, and as a substitute for sassafras oil (*see*) in cosmetics and in inexpensive soaps. No known toxicity.

1-OCTANOL • **Caprylic Alcohol.** Used in the manufacture of perfumes. Colorless, viscous liquid, soluble in water, insoluble in oil. Occurs naturally in oil of lavender, oil of lemon, oil of lime, oil of lovage, orange peel, and coconut oil. It has a penetrating, aromatic scent. May cause skin rash.

2-OCTANOL • **Caprylic Alcohol.** An oily aromatic liquid, with a somewhat unpleasant odor. For use in the manufacture of perfumes and disinfectant soaps. See 1-Octanol.

OCTOCRYLENE • An absorbent. See Phenol.

OCTODODECANOL • **2-Octyl Dodecanol.** See Stearyl Alcohol.

OCTODODECETH-20, -25 • Polyethylene ethers of octydodecanol and Stearic Acid (*see both*).

OCTODODECYL MYRISTATE • See Myristic Acid.

OCTODODECYL NEODECANOATE • The ester of octyldodecanol and neodecanoic acid (*see both*).

OCTOXYGLYCERYL BEHENATE • An ester of glycerin and behenic acid (*see both*). Used in lipsticks.

OCTOXYNOL-1, -3, -10, -40 • Waxlike emulsifiers, dispersing agents, and detergents used in hand creams, lotions, and lipsticks. Derived from phenol (*see*) and used as a surfactant.

OCTRIZOLE • An absorbent derived from phenol (*see*).

OCTYL ACETOXYSTEARATE • See Stearic Acid.

OCTYL DIMETHYL PABA • Used in sunscreens. See *p*-Aminobenzoic Acid.

OCTYL HYDROXYSTEARATE • See Hexyl Alcohol and Hydroxystearic Acid.

OCTYL ISONONANOATE • See Nonanoic Acid.

OCTYL METHOXYCINNAMATE • Used in sunscreens. See Methyl Cinnamate.

OCTYL PALMITATE • Used in sunscreens. See Palmitate.

OCTYL PELARGONATE • See Pelargonic Acid.

OCTYL SALICYLATE • See Salicylates.

OCTYL STEARATE • See Stearic Acid.

OCTYLACRYLAMIDE/ACRYLATES/BUTYLAMINOETHYL METHACRYLATE COPOLYMERS • See Acrylates.

OCTYLDOCECANOL • See Stearyl Alcohol.

OCTYLDODECETH-20, -25 • Polyethylene ethers of octyldodecanol (*see*).

OCTYLDODECYL STEARATE • The ester of octyldodecanol and stearic acid (*see both*).

OCTYLDODECYL STEAROYL STEARATE • See Stearic Acid.

OLEALKONIUM CHLORIDE • See Quaternary Ammonium Compounds.

OLEAMIDE • **Oleylamide.** See Oleic Acid.

OLEAMIDE DEA • **Oleic Diethanolamide.** See Oleic Acid and Diethanolamide.

OLEAMIDE MIPA • See Oleic Acid and MIPA.

OLEAMIDOPROPYL DIMETHYLAMINE GLYCOLATE • See Quaternary Ammonium Compounds.

OLEAMIDOPROPYL DIMETHYLAMINE HYDROLYZED ANIMAL PROTEIN • See Hydrolyzed Animal Protein.

OLEAMIDOPROPYL ETHYLDIMONIUM ETHOSULFATE • See Quaternary Ammonium Compounds.

OLEAMIDOPROPYL HYDROXYSULTANE • See Quaternary Ammonium Compounds.

OLEAMINE • **Oleyl Amine.** A fatty amine derived from oleic acid (*see*) and used as a stabilizer and plasticizer in creams, lotions, lipsticks, and perfumes. Not as greasy as oil-type stabilizers and plasticizers. No known toxicity.

OLEAMINE OXIDE • See Oleamine.

OLEIC ACID • Obtained from various animal and vegetable fats and oils. Colorless. On exposure to air, it turns a yellow to brown color and develops a rancid odor. Used in preparations of Turkey-red oil (*see*), soft soap, permanent wave solutions, vanishing creams, brushless shave creams, cold creams, brilliantines, nail polish, toilet soaps, and lipsticks. Possesses better skin penetrating properties than vegetable oils. Also employed in liquid makeup, liquid lip rouge, shampoos, and preshave lotions. Low oral toxicity but is mildly irritating to the skin.

OLEOAMPHODIPROPIONATE • See Surfactants.

OLEOAMPHOHYDROXYPROPYLSULFONATE • See Surfactants.

OLEORESIN • A natural plant consisting of essential oil and resin extracted from a substance, such as ginger, by means of alcohol, ether, or acetone. The solvent, alcohol, for example, is percolated through the ginger. Although the oleoresin is very similar to the spice from which it is derived, it is not identical because not all the substances in the spice are extracted. Oleoresins are usually more uniform and more potent than the original product. The normal use range of an oleoresin is from one-fifth to one-twentieth the corresponding amount for the crude spice. Certain spices are extracted as oleoresins for color rather than for flavor. Examples of color-intensifying oleoresins are those from paprika and turmeric.

OLEOSTEARINE • See Tallow and Fatty Acids.

OLEOYL HYDROLYZED ANIMAL PROTEIN • The condensation product after oleic acid chloride and hydrolyzed animal protein have been processed. See Hydrolyzed Animal Protein.

OLEOYL HYDROXYETHYL IMIDAZOLINE • See Imidazoline.

OLEOYL SARCOSINE • The condensation product of Oleic Acid with *N*-methylglycine, widely used in polishing compounds, soaps, and lubricating oils. Can be mildly irritating to the skin.

OLETH-2, AND 3 • See Oleyl Alcohol.

OLETH-3 PHOSPHATE • See Oleth-20.

OLETH-5 AND 10 • See Oleyl Alcohol.

OLETH-10 PHOSPHATE • An emulsifier. See Oleyl Alcohol.

OLETH-20 • An oily liquid derived from fatty alcohols. Used as a surface-active agent (*see*). No known toxicity.

OLETH-20 PHOSPHATE • See Oleth-20.

OLETH-25 AND -50 • See Oleyl Alcohol.

OLEYL ALCOHOL • **Ocenol®.** Found in fish oils. Oily and usually pale yellow. Gives off an offensive burning odor when heated. Chiefly used in the manufacture of detergents and wetting agents and as an antifoam agent; also a plasticizer for softening and lubricating fabrics and as a carrier for medications. No known toxicity.

OLEYL ARACHIDATE • The ester of oleyl alcohol and arachidic acid (*see both*) used as a wax.

OLEYL BETAINE • See Oleamine.

OLEYL IMIDAZOLINE • See Oleyl Alcohol and Imidazoline.
OLEYL LANOLATE • See Lanolin.
OLEYL MYRISTATE • See Myristic Acid.
OLEYL OLEATE • See Oleic Acid.
OLEYL STEARATE • See Oleic Acid and Stearic Acid.
OLIBANUM EXTRACT • **Frankincense Extract.** The extract of various species of *Boswellia carterri*. The volatile, distilled oil from the gum resin of a plant found in Ethiopia, Egypt, and Arabia. It was one of the Gifts of the Magi. It is used in flavorings. No known toxicity.
OLIVE OIL • Superior to mineral oils in penetrating power. Used in brilliantine hair dressings, emollients, eyelash oils, lipstick, nail polish removers, shampoos, soaps, face powders, and hair colorings. Antiwrinkle and massage oils. It is a pale yellow or greenish fixed oil obtained from ripe olives grown around the Mediterranean Sea. May cause allergic reactions.
ONION EXTRACT • Extract of the bulbs of onion, *Allium cepa*. Used in flavorings. No known toxicity.
OPACIFYING AGENTS • Substances such as the fatty alcohols, stearyl and cetyl, (*see both*) that make shampoos and other liquid cosmetics impervious to light.
ORANGE-FLOWER OIL • See Nerol.
ORANGE OIL • **Sweet Orange Oil.** Yellow to deep orange, highly volatile, unstable liquid with a characteristic orange taste and odor expressed from the fresh peel of the ripe fruit of the sweet orange plant species. Once used as an expectorant, it is now employed in perfumery, soaps, and flavorings. Inhalation or frequent contact with oil of orange may cause severe symptoms such as headache, dizziness, and shortness of breath. Perfumes, colognes, and toilet water containing oil of orange may cause allergic reaction in the hypersensitive. Omitted from hypoallergenic cosmetics.
ORGANIC COSMETICS • Cosmetics made from only animal or vegetable products. Used as a gimmick to sell some cosmetics to those who believe "natural" is better, although most cosmetic ingredients are derived from natural sources.
ORIENTAL BLENDS • One of the basic perfume types, this group gives an impression of subtlety and warmth, with an intense note of spices and incense. They usually include amber, musk, and civet. They vary between heavily floral and richly resinous. They are more insistent in their predominating notes than any other type, and usually are worn at night.
ORIZANOL • The ester of ferulic acid and terpene alcohol widely found in plants. Used in flavorings and perfumes. See Cinnamate.

OROTIC ACID • **Pyrimidecarboxylic Acid.** Found in milk and certain molds, it is a growth factor for certain microorganisms.

ORRIS • **Orrisroot Oil. White Flag. Love Root.** Distilled for use in dusting powders, perfumes, dry shampoos, toothpaste, and sachets. Made from the roots of the plant. Yellowish, semisolid, and fragrant oil. Discontinued in the United States because of the frequent allergic reactions to orris, including infantile eczema, hay fever, stuffy nose, red eyes, and asthma. It is, however, used in raspberry, blackberry, strawberry, violet, cherry, nut, and spice flavorings for beverages, ice cream, ices, candy, baked goods, gelatin desserts, chewing gum, and icings.

ORRIS ABSOLUTE • One of the most widely used perfume ingredients, it is the oldest and most expensive of all natural perfume materials. It is twice the price of Rose Otto Bulgaria (*see*) and three times that of French Jasmine (*see* Jasmine). The so-called oil is produced by steam distillation from the underground stems of the iris. The rhizomes are washed, dried, and then stored for three years to acquire their fragrance. Prior to distillation, they are pulverized, and the absolute is distinctly violetlike with a fruity undertone—sweet, floral, warm, and lasting. The bulk of the material is produced in Italy, distillation taking place mostly in France, and sometimes in England and Italy. Can cause allergic reactions. See Orris.

ORRIS ROOT EXTRACT • Obtained from dried orris root. Has an intense odor and is used in perfumery. Used in chocolate, fruit, nut, vanilla, and cream soda flavorings for beverages, ice cream, ices, candy, baked goods, gelatin desserts, and chewing gum. Causes frequent allergic reactions.

OURICURY WAX • The wax exuded from the leaves of the Brazilian palm tree. The hard brown wax has the same properties and uses as carnauba wax (*see*).

OVARIAN EXTRACT • The extract of cow ovaries.

OXALIC ACID • Occurs naturally in many plants and vegetables, particularly in the *Oxalis* family; also in many molds. Used in freckle and bleaching cosmetic preparations. Caustic and corrosive to the skin and mucous membranes; may cause severe intestinal upsets and kidney damage if ingested. Used industrially to remove paint, varnish, rust, and ink stains. Used in dentistry to harden plastic models. Fingernails exposed to it have turned blue, become brittle, and fallen off.

OXAZOLINE • A series of synthetic waxes that are versatile and miscible with most natural waxes and can be applied to the same uses.

OXIDIZED POLYETHYLENE • Polyethylene and oxygen combined. See both.

OXIDIZER • A substance that causes oxygen to combine with another substance. Oxygen and hydrogen peroxide are examples of oxidizers.

OXYQUINOLINE • **8-Hydroxyquinoline.** White crystalline powder, almost insoluble in water. Used as a fungistat and for reddish orange colors when combined with bismuth. Used internally as a disinfectant. Has caused cancer in animals both orally and when injected. See Oxyquinoline Sulfate.

OXYQUINOLINE BENZOATE • **8-Quinolinol Benzoate.** The salt of benzoic acid (*see*) and oxyquinoline (*see*).

OXYQUINOLINE SULFATE • Made from phenols; composed of either white crystals or powder, almost insoluble in water and ether but soluble in alcohol, acetone, and benzene. Used as a preservative in cosmetics for its ability to prevent fungus growth and to disinfect. See Phenol for toxicity.

OZOKERITE • **Ceresin**. A naturally occurring waxlike mineral; a mixture of hydrocarbons. Colorless or white when pure; horrid odor. Upon refining, it yields a hard white microcrystalline wax known as ceresin (*see*). An emulsifier and thickening agent used in lipstick and cream rouge. No known toxicity.

P

PABA • **4-Aminobenzoic Acid. p-Aminobenzoic Acid.** See Para-Aminobenzoic Acid.

PALM-KERNEL ALCOHOL • The mixture of fatty alcohols from palm-kernel oil (*see*).

PALM-KERNEL OIL • **Palm Nut.** The oil from palms, particularly the African palm oil tree. White to yellowish edible fat, it resembles coconut oil more than palm oil. It is used chiefly in making soaps and ointments. No known toxicity.

PALM KERNELAMIDE DEA • A mixture of ethanolamides of the fatty acids derived from palm-kernel oil (*see*).

PALM KERNELAMIDE MEA, MIPA, AND GLYCERIDES • See Palm-Kernel Oil.

PALM OIL • **Palm Butter. Palm Tallow.** Oil used in baby soaps, ordinary soaps, liniments, and ointments. Obtained from the fruit or seed of the palm tree. A reddish-yellow to dark dirty red. A fatty mass with a faint violet odor. Also used to make candles and lubricants. No known toxicity.

PALM OIL GLYCERIDE • See Palm Oil.

PALMAMIDE DEA • A mixture of ethanolamides of the fatty acids derived from palm oil. See Palm Oil.

PALMAMIDE MEA • A mixture of ethanolamides of the fatty acids derived from palm oil (*see*).

PALMAMAMIDE MIPA • A mixture of isopropanolamides of the fatty acids derived from palm oil (*see*).

PALMAMAMIDOPROPYL BETAINE • See Palm Oil and Betaine.

PALMITAMIDE DEA, MEA • See Palmitic Acid.

PALMITAMIDOPROPYL BETAINE • See Palmitic Acid and Surfactants.

PALMITAMINDOPROPYL DIETHYLAMINE • See Palmitic Acid and Surfactants.

PALMITAMINE • See Palmitic Acid.

PALMITAMINE OXIDE • **Palmityl Dimethylamine Oxide.** See Palmitic Acid and Dimethylamine.

PALMITATE • A salt of palmitic acid (*see*) used as an oil in baby oils, bath oils, eye creams, hair conditioners, and cream rouges. Occurs in palm oil, butterfat, and most other fatty oils and fats. See Palmitic Acid for toxicity.

PALMITIC ACID • A mixture of solid organic acids obtained from fats consisting chiefly of palmitic acid with varying amounts of stearic acid (*see*). Used as a texturizer in shampoos, shaving creams, and soaps. It is white or faintly yellow and has a fatty odor and taste. Palmitic acid occurs naturally in allspice, anise, calamus oil, cascarilla bark, celery seed, butter acids, coffee, tea, and many animal fats and plant oils. It forms 40 percent of cow's milk. Obtained from palm oil, Japan wax, or Chinese vegetable tallow. No known toxicity to skin and hair, provided no salts of oleic or lauric acids (*see both*) are present.

PALMITOYL HYDROLYZED ANIMAL PROTEIN • See Hydrolyzed Animal Protein.

PALMITOYL HYDROLYZED MILK PROTEIN • The condensation product of palmitic acid chloride and hydrolyzed milk protein. See Hydrolyzed and Milk.

PANAMA IPECAC • The extract of *Cephaelis acuminata*. See Ipecac.

PANSY EXTRACT • The extract obtained from *Viola tricolor*. Used for colorings. No known toxicity.

PANTHENOL • **Dexpanthenol. Vitamin B-Complex Factor.** Used in hair products and in emollients, and as a supplement in foods. Employed medicinally to aid digestion. It is good for human tissues. No known toxicity.

PANTHENYL ETHYL ETHER • The ethyl ether of the B Vitamin, panthenol (*see*).

PANTHENYL ETHYL ETHERACETATE • The ester of acetic acid and the ethyl ether of the B Vitamin, panthenol (*see*).

PANTOTHENIC ACID • **Vitamin B_5.** A necessity in human diets. It is involved in the metabolism of fats and proteins. Nontoxic.

PAPAIN • An enzyme derived from papaya (*see below*) used in meats as a tenderizer and in cosmetics to remove dead skin. It is also used as a clarifying agent (*see*).

PAPAYA • A base of organic makeup. It is a fruit grown in tropical countries. It contains an enzyme, papain, used as a meat tenderizer and, medicinally, to prevent adhesions. It is deactivated by cooking. Because of its protein-digesting ability, it can dissolve necrotic (dead) material. It may cause allergic reactions.

PARABENS • The parabens, methyl-, propyl-, and parahydroxybenzoate, are the most commonly used preservatives in the United States. In 1977, about 30 percent of the cosmetic products registered with the Food and Drug Administration contained parabens. Water is the only ingredient used more frequently in cosmetics. The parabens have a broad spectrum of antimicrobial activity, are safe to use—relatively nonirritating, nonsensitizing, and nonpoisonous—are stable over the pH (*see*) range in cosmetics, and are sufficiently soluble in water to be effective in liquids. The typical paraben preservative system contains 0.2 percent methyl- and 0.1 percent propylparaben. See Methyl Paraben and Butyl Paraben.

PARAFFIN • Used in solid brilliantines, cold creams, wax depilatories, eyelash creams and oils, eyebrow pencils, lipsticks, liquefying creams, protective creams, and mascaras; also used for extracting perfumes from flowers. Obtained from the distillate of wood, coal, petroleum, or shale oil. Colorless or white, odorless, greasy, and not digestible or absorbable in the intestines. Easily melts over boiling water and is used to cover food products. Pure paraffin is harmless to the skin but the presence of impurities may give rise to irritations and eczema.

PARETH-15-3 • See C11-15 Pareth 9.

PARETH-25-12 • A detergent. See C12-15 Pareth 12.

PARSLEY EXTRACT • See Parsley Oil.

PARSLEY OIL • Used as a preservative, perfume, and flavoring in cosmetics, it is obtained by steam distillation of the ripe seeds of the herb. Yellow to light brown, with a harsh odor. Parsley may cause skin to break out with a rash, redden, and swell when exposed to light. It may also cause an allergic reaction in the sensitive.

PARSLEY SEED OIL • See Parsley Oil.

PASSIONFLOWER EXTRACT • Extract of the various species of *Passiflora carnata.* The American Indians used passionflower for swellings, sore eyes, and to induce vomiting. It has been shown that an extract of the plant depresses the motor nerves of the spinal cord.

PATCHOULI OIL • Used in perfume formulations to impart a long-lasting Oriental aroma in soaps and cosmetics. It is the essential oil obtained from the leaves of an East Indian shrubby mint. Yellowish to greenish-brown liquid, with the pleasant fragrance of summer flowers. May produce allergic reactions.

PAWPAW EXTRACT • **Custard Apple.** The extract of the fruit *Caraya papaya.* The dried and pulverized large brown seeds have been rubbed into the scalp to eradicate head lice. The fruit is rich in vitamins and minerals. No known toxicity for the skin but if taken internally, it can cause vomiting.

PCA • **2-Pyrrolidone-5-Carboxylic Acid.** Employed in the manufacture of polyvinylpyrrolidone (*see*), which goes into hair sprays. Also a high-boiling solvent in petroleum processing, and a plasticizer and coalescing agent for floor polishes. No known skin toxicity.

PEA EXTRACT • The extract of *Pisum sativum.*

PEACH EXTRACT • See Peach Juice Extract.

PEACH JUICE EXTRACT • The liquid obtained from the pulp of the peach, *Prunus persica.* It is used as a natural flavoring and as an emollient. Nontoxic.

PEACH-KERNEL OIL • **Persic Oil.** Used as an oil base in emollients, eyelash creams, and brilliantines. It is a light yellow liquid expressed from a seed. Smells like almonds. Also a flavoring in foods. No known toxicity.

PEANUT OIL • **Arachis Oil.** Used in the manufacturing of soaps, baby preparations, hair-grooming aids, nail dryers, shampoos, and as a solvent for ointments and liniments; also in night creams and emollients. A solvent in salad oil, shortening, mayonnaise, and confections. Also used in conjunction with natural flavorings. Peanut butter is about 50 percent peanut oil suspended in peanut fibers. Greenish-yellow, with a pleasant odor. Prepared by pressing shelled and skinned seeds of the peanut. It is used as a substitute for almond and olive oils in cosmetic creams, brilliantines, antiwrinkle oils, and sunburn preparations. Has been reported to be a mild irritant in soap, but considered harmless to the skin.

PEANUTAMIDE MEA • **Loramine Wax.** See Peanut Oil.

PEANUTAMIDE MIPA • A mixture of isopropanolamides of the fatty acids derived from peanut oil (*see*).

PEARL ESSENCE • **Guanine.** A suspension of crystalline guanine (*see*) in nitrocellulose (*see*) and solvents. Guanine is obtained from fish scales. Used in nail polish to give it a shine. Implants of small amounts of guanine hydrochloride were lethal in mice. No known toxicity to the skin or nails.

PECAN SHELL POWDER • A coloring agent used in cosmetics. Employed medicinally by the American Indians. It is the nut from a hickory of the southern central United States with a rough bark and hard but brittle wood. Edible. No known toxicity.

PECTIN • Emulsifying agent used in place of various gums in toothpastes, hair-setting lotions, and protective creams. The pectins are found in roots, stems, and fruits of plants and form an integral part of such structures. They are used in cosmetics as a gelling and thickening agent. They are soothing and mildly acidic. Also used in foods as a "cementing agent" and as an antidiarrheal medication. No known toxicity to the skin.

PEG • Abbreviation for polyethylene glycol/polyethylene, used in making nonionic surfactants. See Surfactants and Nonionic. The low molecular polyethylene glycols, from 200 to 400, may cause hives and eczema. The higher polyethylenes are not sensitizers.

PEG-4, -6, -8, -9, -10, -12, -14, -16, -18, -32, -40, -150, -200, -350 • Polymers (*see*) of ethylene oxide. Usually, a waxy compound. The number refers to the liquidity: the higher the number, the harder the composition.

PEG-7 BETA-NAPHTHOL • The polyethylene glycol ether of 2-naphthol. See Polyethylene Glycol and Beta-Naphthol.

PEG-8 C12-18 ALKYL ESTER • See C12-18 PEG-8-Ester.

PEG-8 CAPRATE • The polyethylene glycol ester of capric acid. See Capric Acid and Polyethylene Glycol.

PEG-9 CAPRYLATE • The polyethylene glycol ester of caprylic acid (*see*).

PEG-8 CAPRYLATE/CAPRATE • The polyethylene glycol ester of a mixture of caprylic and capric acids (*see all*).

PEG-6 CAPRYLIC/CAPRIC GLYCERIDES • The ethoxylated glycerides of caprylic and capric acid derivatives. See Caprylic and Capric Acid and Glycerides.

PEG-3 TO -200 CASTOR OIL • The polyethylene glycol derivatives of castor oil (*see*). The higher the number after the listing, the more solid the compound. See Polyethylene Glycol.

PEG-3 TO -11 COCAMIDE • The polyethylene glycol amides

of coconut acid. The higher the number, the more solid the compound. Used as emulsifiers. See Polyethylene Glycol and Coconut Oil.

PEG-2 TO -15 COCAMINE • The polyethylene glycol amines of coconut acid. The higher the number, the harder the compound.

PEG-5, -8, OR -15 COCOATE • The polyethylene glycol esters of coconut acid. The lower the number, the more liquid the compound. See Polyethylene Glycol and Coconut Oil.

PEG-2 OR -15 COCOMONIUM CHLORIDE • See Quaternary Ammonium Compounds.

PEG-15 COCOPOLYAMINE • The polyethylene glycol polyamine of coconut acid. See Polyethylene Glycol and Coconut Oil.

PEG-4 THROUGH -150 DILAURATE • The polyethylene glycol diesters of lauric acid (*see*). The higher the number, the more solid the compound. See also Polyethylene Glycol.

PEG-6 TO -150 DIOLEATE • The polyethylene glycol diesters of oleic acid (*see*). The lower the number, the more liquid the compound. See Polyethylene Glycol.

PEG-3 DIPALMITATE • The polyethylene glycol diester of Palmitic Acid (*see*).

PEG-2 THROUGH -175 DISTEARATE • The polyethylene glycol diesters of stearic acid. The higher the number, the more solid the compound. See Stearic Acid and Polyethylene Glycol.

PEG-8 OR -12 DITALLATE • The polyethylene glycol diesters of tall oil (*see*).

PEG-8 DITRIRICONOLEATE • See Ricinoleic Acid and Polyethylene Glycol.

PEG-22 OR -45 DODECYL GLYCOL COPOLYMERS • See Polyethylene Glycol.

PEG-7 OR -30 GLYCERYL COCOATE • The polyethylene glycol ethers of glyceryl cocoate. See Coconut Oil.

PEG-15 OR -20 GLYCERYL RICINOLEATE • The polyethylene glycol ethers of glyceryl ricinoleate. The number signifies the liquidity of the compound. See Polyethylene Glycol and Castor Oil.

PEG-5 THROUGH -120 GLYCERYL STEARATE • See Polyethylene Glycol and Stearic Acid.

PEG-28 GLYCERYL TALLOWATE • See Tallow Glyceride and Polyethylene Glycol.

PEG-25 GLYCERYL TRIOLEATE • See Oleic Acid and Polyethylene Glycol.

PEG-5 THROUGH -200 HYDROGENATED CASTOR OIL • See Polyethylene Glycol and Castor Oil.

PEG-5 HYDROGENATED CORN GLYCERIDES • The polyethylene glycol derivative of mixed glycerides derived from hydrogenated corn oil (*see*).

PEG-8 HYDROGENATED FISH GLYCERIDES • The polyethylene glycol derivative of hydrogenated fish glycerides (*see*).

PEG-5 THROUGH -70 HYDROGENATED LANOLIN • The polyethylene glycol derivatives of hydrogenated lanolin. The higher the number, the more solid the compound. See Polyethylene Glycol and Lanolin.

PEG-13 HYDROGENATED TALLOW AMIDE • See Polyethylene Glycol and Tallow.

PEG-6 THROUGH -10 ISOLAURYL THIOETHER • The polyethylene glycol ethers of dodecyl mercaptan. The number signifies liquidity. See Polyethylene Glycol and Lauryl Alcohol.

PEG-6 OR -12 ISOSTEARATE • The polyethylene glycol esters of isostearic acid. See Polyethylene Glycol and Stearic Acid.

PEG-5 TO -20 LANOLATE • See Lanolin.

PEG-5 THROUGH -100 LANOLIN • The polyethylene glycol derivative of lanolin. The number signifies liquidity. Widely used in cosmetics. See Lanolin.

PEG-75 LANOLIN OIL AND WAX • See Lanolin.

PEG-3 TO -6 LAURAMIDE • The polyethylene glycol amides of lauric acid (*see*).

PEG-3 LAURAMINE OXIDE • See Lauric Acid.

PEG-2 THROUGH -150 LAURATE • The polyethylene glycol esters of lauric acid. The number signifies liquidity. Yellow oily liquid insoluble in water. Widely used in soaps and detergents. Emulsifier in cosmetic creams and lotions. Gives an oil-in-water emulsion. No known toxicity other than allergic reactions in some persons sensitive to laurates. See Lauric Acid.

PEG-6 METHYL ETHER • See Methanol.

PEG-20 METHYL GLUCOSE SESQUISTEARATE • A mixture of polyethylene glycol mono- and diesters of methyl glucose and stearic acid (*see all*).

PEG-2 MILK SOLIDS • See Milk and Polyethylene Glycol.

PEG-4 OCTANOATE • The polyethylene glycol ester of caprylic acid (*see*).

PEG-2 THROUGH -9 OLEAMIDE • The polyethylene glycol amides of oleic acid (*see*). Widely used as a stabilizer and plasticizier.

PEG-2 THROUGH -30 OLEAMINE • The polyethylene glycol amines of oleic acid (*see*). Widely used in vanishing creams, soft soaps, cold creams, and many other cosmetics.

PEG-2 OLEAMONIUM CHLORIDE • See Quaternary Ammonium Compounds.

PEG-12, -20, OR -30 OLEATE • The polyethylene glycol ethers of glyceryl oleate. See Polyethylene Glycol and Glycerin.

PEG-3 THROUGH -150 OLEATE • The polyethylene glycol esters of oleic acid (*see*). Widely used in cosmetic bases and shampoos. Emulsifying agents in creams and lotions. A dark red oil that can be dispersed in water, soluble in alcohol, miscible with cottonseed oil. No known toxicity.

PEG-6 THROUGH -20 PALMITATE • The polyethylene glycol esters of palmitic acid (*see*).

PEG-8 PALMITOYL METHYL DIETHONIUM METHOSULFATE • See Quaternary Ammonium Compounds.

PEG-5 PENTAERYTHRITOL ETHER • The polyethylene glycol ether of pentaerythritol that is used as a plasticizer and synthetic lubricant. See Formaldehyde and Acetaldehyde.

PEG/PPG-17/6 OR 18/4 OR 23/50 OR 35/9 OR 125/30 COPOLYMERS • The copolymers produced by the interaction of ethylene oxide with propylene oxide. Used as plasticizers and bases for cosmetics. See Ethylene Oxide and Propylene Oxide.

PEG-8 PROPYLENE GLYCOL COCOATE • The polyethylene glycol ether of polyethylene glycol cocoate derived from coconut acid (*see*) and used as an emulsifier.

PEG-25 THROUGH -125 PROPYLENE GLYCOL STEARATE • See Stearic Acid.

PEG-2 OR -7 RICINOLEATE • The polyethylene glycol esters of ricinoleic acid (*see*).

PEG-8 SESQUILAURATE • The mixture of polyethylene glycol mono and diesters of lauric acid with ethylene oxide. See Lauric Acid.

PEG-8 SESQUIOLEATE • The mixture of polyethylene glycol mono- and diesters of oleic acid with ethylene oxide. See Oleic Acid.

PEG-6, -8, -20 SORBITAN BEESWAX • The ethoxylated sorbitol derivative of beeswax with ethylene oxide. See Sorbitol and Beeswax.

PEG-5 OR -20 SORBITAN ISOSTEARATE • The ethoxylated sorbitol monoester of isostearic acid and ethylene oxide. See Sorbitol and Stearic Acid.

PEG-40 OR -75 OR -80 SORBITAN LANOLATE • The ethoxylated sorbitol derivative of lanolin and ethylene oxide of 40, 75, or 80 molecules. See Lanolin and Sorbitol.

PEG-3 OR -6 SORBITAN OLEATE • The ethoxylated sorbitan ester of oleic acid. See Oleic Acid and Sorbitan.

PEG-80 SORBITAN PALMITATE • The ethoxylated sorbitol monoester of palmitic acid (*see*).
PEG-40 SORBITAN PEROLEATE • The mixture of oleic acid esters of sorbitol. See Sorbitol and Oleic Acid.
PEG-3 OR -40 SORBITAN STEARATE • See Sorbitol and Stearic Acid.
PEG-30, -40, OR -60 SORBITAN TETRAOLEATE • See Oleic Acid and Sorbitol.
PEG-60 SORBITAN TETRASTEARATE • See Stearic Acid and Sorbitol.
PEG-SOYA STEROLS • See Soybean Oil and Polyethylene Glycol.
PEG-2 TO -15 SOYAMINE • See Polyethylene Glycol and Soya Acid.
PEG-2 THROUGH -150 STEARATE • Widely used emulsifying agents. See Polyethylene Glycol and Stearic Acid.
PEG-2 OR -15 STEARMONIUM CHLORIDE • See Quaternary Ammonium Compounds.
PEG-5 STEARYL AMMONIUM CHLORIDE • See Quaternary Ammonium Compounds.
PEG-12 OR -20 TALLATE • See Polyethylene Glycol and Tall Oil.
PEG-3, -10, OR -15 TALLOW AMINOPROPYLAMINE • See Polyethylene Glycol and Tallow Acid.
PEG-15 TALLOW POLYAMINE • See Tallow Acid.
PEG-20 TALLOWATE • See Polyethylene Glycol and Tallow Acid.
PEG-66 OR -200 TRIHYDROXYSTEARIN • See Surfactants.
PEI • Abbreviation for polyethylenimine.
PEI-7 • **Polyethylenimine 7.** Highly viscous liquid used as an adhesive or anchoring agent for cellophane and as a disinfectant for the skin. Also used in water purification.
PEI-15 THROUGH -2500 • See PEI-7.
PELARGONIC ACID • **Nonanoic Acid.** A synthetic flavoring agent that occurs naturally in cocoa and oil of lavender. Used in berry, fruit, nut, and spice flavorings. A strong irritant.
PELLITORY EXTRACT • **Extract of Pellitory. Parietary Extract.** The extract obtained from the leaves and stem of *Parietaria officinalis*. Used as an emollient, particularly in baby creams and lotions. No known toxicity.
PENNYROYAL EXTRACT • An extract of the flowering herb, *Mentha pulegium*. Used since ancient days as a medicine, scent, flavoring, and food. Obtained from the dried flower tops and leaves, it contains tannin which is soothing to the skin.
PENTADECALACTONE • **Angelica Lactone.** Used as a cosmetic fragrance and in berry, fruit, and liquor flavorings, it is obtained from

the fruit and root of a plant grown in Europe and Asia. No known toxicity.

PENTADESMA BUTTER • **Kanya Butter.** The vegetable fat extracted from the nut of the *Pentadesma butyracea.* See Shea Butter.

PENTAERYTHRITOL • Prepared from acetaldehyde and formaldehyde (*see both*). It is used in synthetic resins.

PENTAERYTHRITOL ROSINATE • The ester of acids derived from rosin (*see*) mixed with pentaerythritol (*see*).

PENTAERYTHRITYL TETRAABIETATE • See Pentaerythritol and Abietic Acid.

PENTAERYTHRITYL TETRAOCTANOATE • See Caprylic Acid.

PENTAERYTHRITYL TETRASTEARATE AND CALCIUM STEARATE • See Stearic Acid.

PENTAHYDROSQUALENE • The end product of hydrogenation (*see*) of squalene (*see*).

PENTANE • The aliphatic hydrocarbon derived from petroleum. Used as a solvent. Narcotic in high doses.

1-PENTANOL • **Pentyl Alcohol. n-Amyl Alcohol.** Liquid, with a mild odor, slightly soluble in water. Used as a solvent. Irritating to the eyes and respiratory passages, and absorption may cause a lack of oxygen in the blood.

PENTAPOTASSIUM TRIPHOSPHATE • See Pentasodium Pentetate.

PENTASODIUM PENTETATE • **Pentasodium Diethylenetriaminepentaacetate. Sodium Tripolyphosphate.** Prepared from dehydration of mono- and disodium phosphates. An inorganic salt used as a water softener, sequestering agent (*see*), emulsifier, and dispersing agent in cosmetic cleansing creams and lotions. Moderately irritating to the skin and mucous membranes. Ingestion can cause violent purging.

PENTETIC ACID • **Penthanil. Diethylenetriaminepentaacetic Acid.** A chelating agent (*see*) to remove iron particles floating in cosmetic solutions. No known toxicity.

PEPPERMINT EXTRACT • See Peppermint Oil.

PEPPERMINT LEAVES • See Peppermint Oil.

PEPPERMINT OIL • Used in toothpaste and tooth powders, eye lotions, shaving lotions, and toilet waters. It is the oil made from the dried leaves and tops of a plant common to Asian, European, and American gardens. Widely used as a food and beverage flavoring. It can cause allergic reactions such as hay fever and skin rash.

PERFUMES • Literally means "through smoke" because the first perfumes were incense. Thereafter, powdered flowers, leaves, wood spices, and aromatic resins were used for fragrances during religious festivals, for the home, and for the body. Some perfumes have as many as 200 ingredients. The essential oils used for today's scents come from leaves, needles, roots, and peels of plants. Floral oils come from petals, whole flowers, gums, and resins. Animal exudates such as musk and ambergris are all used in perfumes. Isolates used in perfumes are made of individual factors in natural oils, which may also be treated chemically. Synthetic chemicals imitate natural aromas and are being used in increasing quantities today. There are three basic scents today: florals, fruits, and modern blends such as woodsy-mossy-leafy, spicy and oriental. Woodsy-mossy-leafy types have a warm aromatic scent with sandalwood, cedarwood, and balsam predominating. Orientals have subtly heavier odors. Fruity perfumes have a clean fresh fragrance. A typical flower perfume (rose) includes phenylethyl alcohol, 35 percent; geraniol, 48 percent; amyl cinnamic aldehyde, 2 percent; benzyl acetate, 4 percent; ionone, 4 percent; eugenol, 2 percent; and terpineol, 5 percent. Perfumes are among the most frequent allergens and are left out of many hypoallergenic products. Complaints to the FDA concerning perfumes include headaches, dizziness, rash, hyperpigmentation (*see* Berloque Dermatitis), violent coughing and vomiting, skin irritation, and the explosion of the perfume container.

PERHYDROSQUALENE • See Squalene.

PERIWINKLE EXTRACT • The extract of *Vinca minor*. See Myrtle.

PERMANENT WAVE NEUTRALIZER • Used to neutralize the acids that curl the hair (*see* Permanent Waves). May contain sodium perborate, bromates, or sodium hexametaphosphate (*see all*). Before 1940, bromate poisoning was rare, but when bromate was put into permanent wave neutralizers for home use, incidents became more common. Many manufacturers then substituted sodium perborate and sodium hexametaphosphate, a product used as a laundry detergent and in water softeners.

PERMANENT WAVES • **Cold Waves.** Chemicals designed to "permanently" bend or curl the hair. Once done only in beauty parlors, kits have been developed for home use. The process in both the beauty parlor and at home consists of applying a waving lotion containing thioglycolic acid, ammonia, and 93 percent water; as well as borax, ethanolamine, or sodium lauryl sulfate (*see all*). Then, after a period of time, depending upon the lotion used and the tightness of the curl desired, a neutralizer is applied. Chemicals in the neutralizer may be sodium or potassium bromate, sodium perborate, or hydrogen peroxide (*see* Permanent Wave Neutralizer). The thioglycolates are toxic and may cause skin irritation and low blood sugar. Among the injuries reported to the FDA were hair damage, swelling of legs and feet, eye irritations, rash in area of ears, neck, scalp, and forehead, and swelling of eyelids.

PEROXIDE • Used in hair bleaches. It is a strong oxidant and can injure the skin and eyes. Chemists are cautioned to wear rubber gloves and goggles when handling it. May cause hair breakage and is an irritant. See Hydrogen Peroxide.

PERSIC OIL • See Apricot and Peach Kernel Oil.

PERSULFATES • A salt derived from persulfuric acid, a strong oxidizer. Persulfates are excellent catalysts that speed hair color changes in hair dye. See Hydrogen Peroxide for toxicity.

PERUVIAN BALSAM • See Balsam Peru.

PETITGRAIN OIL • Used extensively in perfumes. It is the volatile oil obtained from the leaves, twigs, and unripe fruit of the bitter orange tree. Brownish to yellow with a bittersweet odor. Used in food flavorings. Supposedly dissolves in sweat, and under the influence of sunlight becomes an irritant. May cause allergic skin reactions.

PETROLATUM • **Vaseline. Petroleum Jelly. Paraffin Jelly.** Used in cold creams, emollient creams, conditioning creams, wax depilatories, eyebrow pencils, eye shadows, liquefying creams, liquid powders, nail whites, lipsticks, protective creams, baby creams, and rouge. It is a purified mixture of semisolid hydrocarbons from petroleum. Yellowish to light amber or white, semisolid, unctuous mass, practically odorless and tasteless, almost insoluble in water. As a lubricant in lipsticks, it gives them a shine, and in creams, it makes them smoother. Helps to soften and smooth the skin in the same way as any other emollient and is less expensive. The oily film helps prevent evaporation of moisture from the skin and protects the skin from irritation. However, petrolatum does cause allergic skin reactions in the hypersensitive. It is generally nontoxic.

PETROLATUM DISTILLATE • Clear, colorless, highly flammable distillate used as a solvent for fats, oils, and detergents. See Kerosene for toxicity.

pH • The scale used to measure acidity and alkalinity. pH is the hydrogen (h) ion concentration of a solution. The "p" stands for the power factor of the hydrogen ion. The pH of a solution is measured on a scale of 14. A truly neutral solution, neither acidic nor alkaline, such as water, is 7. Acid is less than 7. Alkaline is more than 7. The pH of blood is 7.3; vinegar is 3.1; lemon juice is 2.3; and lye is 13. Skin and hair are naturally acidic. Soap and detergents are alkaline.

PHENACETIN • **Acetophenetidin.** Obtained from phenol and salicylic acid (*see both*). Slightly bitter, crystalline powder, used in sunscreen lotions and soothing creams. Used medicinally as an analgesic and antifever agent. Less toxic than acetanilid (*see*), but may cause kidney damage in prolonged and excessive internal doses. No known toxicity on the skin.

PHENETHYL ALCOHOL • 2-Phenylethanol. Used as a floral scent in rose perfumes and as a preservative in cosmetics. It occurs naturally in oranges, raspberries, and tea. Used in synthetic fruit flavorings. It is a sensitizer.

PHENOL • Carbolic Acid. Used in shaving creams and hand lotions. Obtained from coal tar. Occurs in urine and has the characteristic odor present in coal tar and wood. It is a general disinfectant and anesthetic for the skin. Ingestion of even small amounts may cause nausea, vomiting, and circulatory collapse, paralysis, convulsions, coma, and greenish urine as well as necrosis of the mouth and gastrointestinal tract. Death results from respiratory failure. Fatalities have been reported from ingestion of as little as 1.5 grams (30 grams to the ounce). Fatal poisoning can occur through skin absorption. Although there have been many poisonings from phenolic solutions, it continues to be used in commercial products. Swelling, pimples, hives, and other skin rashes following application to the skin have been widely reported. A concentration of 2 percent causes burning and numbness.

PHENOXYETHANOL • 2-Phenoxyethanol. Oily liquid with a faint aromatic odor and a burning taste derived from treating phenol with ethylene oxide in an alkaline medium. Used as a fixative for perfumes, as a bactericide, insect repellent, and as a topical antiseptic. See Phenol.

PHENOXYISOPROPANOL • 1-Phenoxy-2-Propanol. See Phenol.

PHENYL ANTHRANILATES • See Coal Tar.

PHENYL METHYL PYRAZOLONE • A white powder made from phenylhydrazine with ethylacetoacetate, used as an intermediate in dyes and plastics. See Pyrazole.

N-PHENYL-p-PHENYLENEDIAMINE • 4-Aminodiphenylamine. White crystals, very soluble in alcohol. Used in hair dyes. Intense skin irritation and blisters reported. Similar to other compounds of the group.

N-PHENYL-p-PHENYLENEDIAMINE HCL • White crystals, slightly soluble in water. A constituent of hair dyes. Derived from diphenolic acid (*see*). Probably of moderate toxicity but reports of several skin rashes from its use have been described in the literature. It is thought to be less irritating than its parent compound.

PHENYL TRIMETHICONE • Methyl Phenyl Polysiloxane. Silicone oil used as a skin protectant and to give it gloss. It is treated to make it water-repellent. No known toxicity. See Silicones.

PHENYLACETALDEHYDE • Used in perfumes. An oily colorless liquid with a harsh odor. Upon dilution, emits the fragrance of lilacs and hyacinths. Derived from phenethyl alcohol. Less irritating than formaldehyde (*see*), but a stronger central nervous system depressant. In addition, it sometimes produces fluid in the lungs upon ingestion. Because it is considered an irritant, it is not used in baby cosmetic preparations.

PHENYLACETIC ACID • Used as a starting material in the manufacture of perfumes and soaps. Occurs naturally in Japanese mint, oil of neroli, and black pepper. It has a honeylike odor. Also used as a synthetic flavoring for foods and in the manufacture of penicillin. No known toxicity.

PHENYLALANINE • An amino acid (*see*) considered essential for growth in normal human beings and not synthesized by the body. It is associated with phenylketonuria (PKU), an affliction that, if not detected soon after birth, leads to mental deterioration in children. Restricting phenylalanine in diets results in improvement. Whole egg contains 5.4 percent and skim milk 5.1 percent. Used to improve penetration of emollients. The FDA has asked for further study of this amino acid as a food additive.

PHENYLDIMETHICONE • A mixture of silica gels used in tanning creams. See Dimethicone.

PHENYLENEDIAMINE, m-, o-, p- • Most permanent home and beauty parlor dyes contain this chemical or a related one such as 4-nitro-*o*-phenylenediamine. Also called oxidation dyes, amino dyes, para dyes, or peroxide dyes. PPD was first introduced in 1890 for dyeing furs and feathers. It comes in about 30 shades and is used as an intermediate in coal tar dyes. May produce eczema, bronchial asthma, gastritis, skin rash, and death. Can crossreact with many other chemicals, including azo dyes used for temporary hair colorings. Can also produce photosensitization. Has been found to cause cancer in animals, and Europeans will not allow PPD in their products. In 1979, the National Cancer Institute reported tests showing that coal tar ingredients in some permanent hair dyes caused cancer when fed to laboratory rats. The Food and Drug Administration then announced it was powerless to ban the suspect hair dyes since they were exempted from such action by the 1938 Food, Drug and Cosmetic Act. The FDA tried to make manufacturers put a warning label on the hair dye containers but the cosmetic manufacturers successfully defeated that. The manufacturers, after the publicity, voluntarily removed a commonly used permanent hair coloring, 4-MMPD — 4-methoxy-*m*-phenylenediamine—one of six hair dyes found to cause cancer in animals. The others were 2,4-toluene diamine (used in a few permanent hair colors) 4-amino-2-nitrophenol and 2-nitrophenylenediamine (used in many gold and reddish shade highlighters), Direct Black 38 and Direct Blue 6 (both voluntarily removed from hair dyes). Bruce Ames reported in 1978 that 150 semipermanent hair dyes he tested (see Ames Test) were mutagenic. An estimated 70 to 75 percent of the carcinogens showed up as mutagens in his test. In January 1978 NIOSH reported that a new study of beauticians and cosmetologists showed they have a higher than expected incidence of six kinds of cancer. That study, along with NIC's findings, led NIOSH to recommend that 2, 4-diaminoanisole be treated as a human carcinogen. On April 6, 1978, the FDA issued an order that manufacturers place warnings on the labels of some permanent hair dyes that read: "Warning: contains an ingredient that can penetrate your skin and has been determined to cause cancer in laboratory animals." The FDA also proposed that beauty parlors post notices urging customers to check the labels on products used in salons. The industry representatives successfully fought these suggestions and as of this writing, no signs are posted and the labels do not carry warnings. The FDA still has no power to ban the ingredients in hair dyes or even require manufacturers to demonstrate safety. Not everyone agrees hairdyes are dangerous. Dr. E. Cuyler Hammond of the American Cancer Society, conducted a 13-year test of 5,000 hairdressers and a matched group of non-hairdressers and did not find any difference in the groups. However, the ACS on Feb. 22, 1978, did issue a statement that said: "The results of studies among beauticians and women who use hair dyes have been mixed. But the regulatory agencies feel that in the absence of hard data, they must be cautious. They feel that because of the wide use by the public, even a small potential risk of cancer caused by little exposure could be associated with significant additional cancer cases. While available information does not prove or disprove that hair dyes cause cancer in humans, the ACS advises caution in the use of the substances under question until more definitive evidence is developed."

A preliminary study by New York University researchers suggests that women who have used hair dye for 10 years or more face an increased risk of developing breast cancer. Published in the February 1979 issue of the *Journal of the National Cancer Institute,* the use of hair dye by 129 women with breast cancer was compared to 193 matched controls.

In 1981, F. N. Marzulli and his colleagues at the FDA's Division of Toxicology, reported skin penetration by five substances present in cosmetics. The greatest skin penetration was recorded with 2, 4-

toluenediamine and the least with 2, 4-diaminoanisole when applied to the skin of monkeys and humans. They found 2-nitro-*p*-phenylenediamine and N-nitrosodiethanolamine showed intermediate degrees of skin penetration. Other researchers reported that hair dye containing *p*-toluenediamine sulphate (2, 5-diaminotoluene) resulted in human absorption of about 0.2 percent of the material if the dye were left on for 40 minutes and then rinsed off.

m-PHENYLENEDIAMINE SULFATE • See Phenylenediamine.

p-PHENYLENEDIAMINE SULFATE • See Phenylenediamine.

p-PHENYLEPHRINE HCL • **Hydrochloride.** Same as nasal decongestant Neo-Synephrine HCL®. Used topically to contract blood vessels and as a nasal decongestant; also in eye lotions to "take the red out." Prepared from *m*-hydroxy-*w*-chloroacetophenone and methylamine in water-alcohol solution. Some hypersensitive individuals may experience a mild stinging sensation. Prolonged exposure to air, metal, or strong light will cause oxidation and some loss of potency. Therefore, deeply discolored solutions, while harmless, should be discarded.

PHENYLMERCURIC ACETATE • Made by heating benzene with mercuric acetate. Metal compound; white lustrous prisms. Slightly soluble in water. Used as a germicide. Very toxic internally, and blisters have been reported when it is applied to the skin.

PHENYLMERCURIC BENZOATE • See Benzoic Acid and Mercury.

PHENYLMERCURIC BORATE • Crystalline powder. Soluble in water and alcohol. Local external antiseptic. Much less toxic than most mercury compounds.

o-PHENYLPHENOL • White flaky crystals with a mild characteristic odor. Prepared form phenyl ether. Practically insoluble in water. An intermediate in the manufacture of cosmetic resins. Also a germicide and fungicide in cosmetics. See Phenol for toxicity.

PHENYLTHIOGLYCOLIC ACID • See Thioglycolic Acid Compounds.

PHLOROGLUCINOL • Prepared from various acids for use in hair dyes. Consists of white crystals with a sweet taste. Discolors in the light. The aqueous solution gives a blue violet color. See Pyrogallol for toxicity.

PHOSPHATE • A salt of ester of phosphoric acid (*see*). Used as an emulsifier, texturizer, and sequestrant in cosmetics and foods. No known toxicity.

PHOSPHOLIPIDS • **Phosphatides.** Complex fat substances found in all living cells. Lecithin is an example. It is used in hand creams and lotions. Phospholipids contain phosphoric acid and nitrogen and are soluble in the usual fat solvents, with the exception of acetone (*see*).

They are used in moisturizers because they bind water and hold it in place. No known toxicity.

PHOSPHORIC ACID • An acid, sequestrant, and antioxidant used in hair tonics, nail polishes, and skin fresheners. A colorless, odorless solution made from phosphate rock. Mixes with water and alcohol. No known toxicity in cosmetic use. Concentrated solutions are irritating to the skin.

PHOTOSENSITIVITY • A condition in which the application or ingestion of certain chemicals, such as propylparaben (*see*), causes skin problems—including rash, hyperpigmentation, and swelling—when the skin is exposed to sunlight.

PHTHALIC ACID • Obtained by the oxidation of various benzene derivatives, it can be isolated from the fungus *Gibberella fujikuroi*. When rapidly heated, it forms phthalic anhydride (*see*) and water. It is used chiefly in the manufacture of cosmetic esters, dyes, and nail polishes. Moderately irritating to the skin and the mucous membranes.

PHTHALIC ANHYDRIDE • Prepared from naphthalene by oxidation it consists of lustrous white needles. It is used in the manufacture of cosmetic dyes and artificial resins. It is moderately irritating to the skin and mucous membranes.

PHTHALIC/TRIMELLITIC/GLYCOLS COPOLYMER • See Phthalic Anhydride and Polymer.

PICRAMIC ACID • **4, 6-Dinitro-2-Aminophenol.** A red crystalline acid obtained from phenol (*see*) and used chiefly in making azo dyes (*see*). Highly toxic material. Readily absorbed through intact skin. Vapors absorbed through respiratory tract. Produces marked increase in metabolism and temperature, profuse sweating, collapse, and death. May cause skin rash, cataracts, and weight loss.

PIGMENT BLUE 15 • Classed chemically as a phthalocyanine (copper complex) color. See Chlorophyllin and Colors.

PIGMENT GREEN 7 • Classed chemically as a phthalocyanine (copper complex) color. See Chlorophyllin and Colors.

PIGMENT ORANGE 5 • A monoazo color, the name can be used only when applied to batches of uncertified colors. The CTFA name for certified batches is D & C Orange No. 17 (*see*).

PIGMENT RED 4 • A monoazo color, the name can be used only when applied to batches of uncertified color. The CTFA adopted name for certified batches is D & C Red No. 36 (*see*).

PIGMENT RED 53 • A monoazo color, the name can be used only when applied to batches of uncertified color. The CTFA adopted name for certified batches is D & C Red No. 8.

PIGMENT RED 53:1 • The barium salt of Pigment Red 53. The name can be applied only to uncertified batches of color. The CTFA adopted name for certified color batches is D & C Red No. 9.

PIGMENT RED 57 • A monoazo color, the name can be applied only to uncertified batches of color. The CTFA adopted name for certified batches is D & C Red No. 6.

PIGMENT RED 57:1 • A monazo color, it is the calcium salt of Pigment Red No. 57. The name can be applied only to batches of uncertified color. The CTFA adopted name for certified batches is D & C Red No. 7.

PIGMENT RED 63:1 • A monoazo color, the name can be used only for batches of uncertified color. The CTFA adopted name for certified batches is D & C Red No. 34.

PIGMENT RED 64:1 • A monoazo color, the name can be applied only to uncertified batches. The CTFA adopted name for certified batches is D & C Red No. 31.

PIGMENT RED 112 • A monoazo color. See Azo Dyes.

PIGMENT VIOLET 19 • A quinacridone color. A light-fast pigment derived from coal tar (*see*). It provides a wide range of shades and cosmetic manufacturers are increasing its use.

PIGMENT YELLOW 1 • A monoazo color. See Azo dyes.

PIGMENT YELLOW 3 • A monoazo color. See Azo Dyes.

PIGMENT YELLOW 12 • A diazo color. See Azo Dyes.

PIGMENT YELLOW 13 • A diazo color. See Azo Dyes.

PIGMENT YELLOW 73 • A monoazo color. See Azo Dyes.

PIGSKIN EXTRACT • An extract of the skin of young pigs.

PILEWORT EXTRACT • An extract of *Ranunculs ficuria,* the coarse, hairy, perennial figwort of the eastern and central United States. It was once used to treat tuberculosis. No known toxicity.

PILOCARPINE • Used in hair tonic to stimulate the sweat glands. Derived from a tree grown in Brazil and Paraguay. Soluble in water, alcohol, and chloroform. White, water-absorbing crystals with a bitter taste. Also an antidote for atropine poisoning. Readily absorbed through the skin from the concentrations employed in hair tonics. High concentrations are known to be irritating and toxic, but no available information on toxicity in cosmetics is reported.

PINE CONE EXTRACT • An extract from the cones of *Pinus sylvestris.* See Pine Oil.

PINE NEEDLE EXTRACT • An extract of various species of *Pinus* used to scent bath products and as a natural flavoring in pineapple, citrus, and spice flavorings. Ingestion of larger amounts can cause intestinal hemorrhages.

PINE OIL • The extract from a variety of pine trees. As a pine tar it is used in hair tonics; also a solvent, disinfectant, and deodorant. As an oil from twigs and needles, it is used in pine bath oil emulsions, bath salts, and perfumery. Irritating to the skin and mucous membranes. Bornyl acetate, a substance obtained from various pine needles, has a strong pine odor and is used in bath oils. It can cause nausea, vomiting, convulsions, and dizziness if ingested. In general, pine oil in concentrated form is an irritant to human skin and may cause allergic reactions. In small amounts it is nontoxic.

PINE TAR • A product obtained by distillation of pinewood. A blackish brown viscous liquid, slightly soluble in water. Used as an antiseptic in skin diseases. May be irritating to the skin.

PINE TAR OIL • A synthetic flavoring obtained from pinewood and used in licorice flavorings for ice cream and candy. Used as a solvent, disinfectant, and deodorant in cosmetics. May be irritating to the skin and mucous membranes, and in large ingested doses causes central nervous system depression.

PINEAPPLE EXTRACT • See Pineapple Juice.

PINEAPPLE JUICE • The common juice from the tropical plant. Contains a protein-digesting and milk-clotting enzyme, bromelin (*see*). An antiinflammatory enzyme, it is used in cosmetic treatment creams. It is also used as a texturizer. No known toxicity.

PIPERITONE • A synthetic flavoring agent that occurs naturally in Japanese mint. Used to give dentifrices a minty flavor and to give perfumes their peppermint scent. No known toxicity.

PIPERONAL • **Heliotropin.** A synthetic flavoring and perfume agent that occurs naturally in vanilla and black pepper. White crystalline powder, with a sweet floral odor. Used chiefly in perfumery. Ingestion of large amounts may cause central nervous system depression. Has been reported to cause skin rash. In lipsticks, said to produce smarting of the skin. Not recommended by some cosmetic chemists because of its ability to produce skin irritation.

PLACENTAL ENZYMES, LIPIDS, AND PROTEINS • Derived from bovine placentas, the vascular membrane that nourishes the fetus.

PLACENTAL EXTRACT • Prepared from the placenta, the nourishing lining of the human womb that is expelled after birth. Promoted by cosmetic manufacturers as capable of removing wrinkles. The American Medical Association maintains no such evidence has been presented, nor is it likely. (Newborn babies emerge from the womb with wrinkled skin.) Nontoxic.

PLACENTAL PROTEIN • See Placental Extract.

PLANKTON EXTRACT • An extract of the marine organisms, *Thalassoplankton,* a green micro-algae or seaweed.

PLANTAIN EXTRACT • The extract of various species of *Plantain.* The starchy fruit is a staple item of diet throughout the tropics and is used for bladder infections by herbalists. It is a natural astringent and antiseptic with soothing and cooling effects on blemishes and burns.

PLASTICIZERS • Chemicals added to natural and synthetic resins and rubbers to impart flexibility, workability, or distensibility without changing the chemical nature of the material. Dibutyl phthalate (*see*) is a plasticizer for nitrocellulose used in nail lacquers.

PLUM EXTRACT • The extract of the fruit of the plum tree, *Prunus domestica.* The American Indians boiled the wild plum and gargled with it to cure mouth sores.

PODOPHYLLUM • A bitter, light brown to greenish yellow resin that is irritating to the eyes and mucous membranes. Obtained from an herb, podophyllum, and used as a cathartic. Applied externally in solution in the treatment of venereal disease, warts, and in cell research for its ability to inhibit the division of cancer cells. May be toxic and should not be used over extensive areas, around the mouth, or during pregnancy.

POLISH REMOVER • See Nail Polish Remover.

POLISHING AGENTS • Used in dentifrices to shine teeth. Even after removing debris and stains, teeth may still be dull. Polishing whitens and brightens teeth, and teeth that are polished are less receptive to dental plaque. Substances used to polish teeth are hydrated alumina, sodium metaphosphate, calcium phosphate, and calcium carbonate (*see all*).

POLLEN EXTRACT • An extract of flower pollen.

POLOXAMER 101 THROUGH 407 • See Poloxamer 188.

POLOXAMER 188 • **Poloxalene.** A liquid, nonionic, surfactant polymer. If chain lengths of polyoxyethylene and polyoxypropylene are increased, the product changes from liquid to paste to solid. No known toxicity. See Polymer.

POLOXAMINE 304 TO 1508 • The polyethylene, polyoxypropylene block of polyerm of ethylene diamine. The numbers signify the various properties of the chemicals and whether one is to be used in food, drugs, or cosmetics. In cosmetics, it is used primarily as a surfactant (*see*).

POLYACRYLAMIDE • The polymer of acrylamide monomers, it is white, solid, water-soluble, used as a thickening agent, suspending agent, and as an additive to adhesives. Used in tanning creams. Used in the manufacture of plastics used in nail polishes. Highly toxic and irritating to the skin. Causes central nervous system paralysis. Can be absorbed through unbroken skin.

POLYACRYLIC ACID • See Acrylic Resins.
POLYAMINO SUGAR CONDENSATE • The condensation product of the sugars, fructose, galactose, glucose, lactose, maltose, mannose, rhamnose, ribose, or xylose, with a minute amount of amino acids such as alanine, arginine, aspartic acid, glutamic acid, glycine, histidine, hydroxyproline, isoleucine, leucine, lysine, methionine, phenylalanine, proline, pyroglutamic acid, serine, threonine, tyrosine, or valine. See Amino Acids.
POLYBUTENE • **Indopol. Polybutylene.** A plasticizer. A polymer (*see*) of one or more butylenes obtained from petroleum oils. May asphyxiate.
POLYCHLOROTRIFLUOROETHYLENE • Colorless, impervious to corrosive chemicals, it resists most organic solvents and heat. Nonflammable. Used as a transparent film.
POLYETHYLENE • A polymer (*see*) of ethylene; a product of petroleum gas or dehydration of alcohol. One of a group of lightweight thermoplastics that have a good resistance to chemicals, low moisture absorption, and good insulating properties. Used in hand lotions. No known skin toxicity, but implants of large amounts in rats caused cancer. Ingestion of large oral doses has produced kidney and liver damage.
POLYETHYLENE 6000 OR MORE • Excellent barrier to water vapor and moisture, it resists solvents and corrosive solutions. It is combustible but nontoxic.
POLYETHYLENE GLYCOL • **PEG.** Used in hair straighteners, antiperspirants, baby products, fragrances, polish removers, hair tonics, lipsticks, and protective creams. It is a binder, plasticizing agent, solvent, and softener widely used for cosmetic cream bases and pharmaceutical ointments. Improves resistance to moisture and oxidation. See Polyethylene Glycol for toxicity.
POLYGLYCEROL • Prepared from edible fats, oils, and esters of fatty acids. Derived from corn, cottonseed, palm, peanuts, safflower, sesame and soybean oils, lard, and tallow. Used as an emulsifier in cosmetics. No known toxicity.
POLYGLYCEROL ESTER • One of several partial or complete esters of saturated and unsaturated fatty acids with a variety of derivatives of polyglycerols ranging from diglycerol to triacontaglycerol. Used as lubricants, plasticizers, gelling agents, humectants, surface-active agents, dispersants, and emulsifiers in foods and cosmetic preparations.
POLYGLYCERYL-4 COCOATE • See Coconut Acid and Polyglycerol.

POLYGLYCERYL-10 DECALINOLEATE • See Polyglycerin and Linoleic Acid.

POLYGLYCERYL-10 DECAOLEATE • See Oleic Acid and Polyglycerol.

POLYGLYCERYL-2 DIISOSTEARATE • See Isostearic Acid and Polyglycerol.

POLYGLYCERYL-6 DIOLEATE • See Oleic Acid and Glycerin.

POLYGLYCERYL-6 DISTEARATE • See Stearic Acid and Glycerin.

POLYGLYCERYL-3 HYDROXYLAURYL ETHER • See Lauryl Alcohol and Glycerin.

POLYGLYCERYL-4 ISOSTEARATE • See Isostearic Acid and Glycerin.

POLYGLYCERYL-2 LANOLIN ALCOHOL ETHER • See Lanolin Alcohol and Glycerin.

POLYGLYCERYL-LAURYL ETHER • See Lauryl Alcohol and Glycerin.

POLYGLYCERYL-3 OR -4 OLEATE • Oily liquid prepared by adding alcohol to coconut oil or other triglycerides with a polyglyceryl. Used in foods, drugs, and cosmetics as fat emulsifiers in conjunction with other emulsifiers to prepare creams, lotions, and other emulsion products. In addition, they may also be used as lubricants, plasticizers, gelling agents, and dispersants. No known toxicity.

POLYGLYCERYL-3 OR -4 OR -8 OLEATE • An ester of oleic acid and glycerin (*see both*).

POLYGLYCERYL-2 OR -4 OLEYL ETHER • The ether of oleyl alcohol and glycerin (*see both*) polymer.

POLYGLYCERYL-3-PEG-2 COCOMIDE • See Coconut Oil and Glycerin.

POLYGLYCERYL-2-PEG-4 STEARATE • An ether of PEG-4 stearate (*see*) and glycerin (*see*).

POLYGLYCERYL-2-SESQUIISOSTEARATE • A mixture of esters of isostearic acid and glycerin (*see both*).

POLYGLYCERYL-2-SESQUIOLEATE • A mixture of ester of oleic acid and glycerin (*see both*).

POLYGLYCERYL SORBITOL • A condensation product of glycerin and sorbitol (*see both*).

POLYGLYCERYL-3, -4, OR -8 STEARATE • An ester of stearic acid and glycerin (*see both*).

POLYGLYCERYL-10 TETRAOLEATE • An ester of oleic acid and glycerin (*see both*).

POLYGLYCERYL-2 TETRASTEARATE • See Stearic Acid and Glycerin.

POLYISOBUTENE • See Polybutene.
POLYISOPRENE • The major component of natural rubber but also made synthetically. Nontoxic.
POLYMER • A substance or product formed by combining many small molecules (monomers). The result is, essentially, recurring long-chain structural units that have tensile strength, elasticity, and hardness. Examples of polymers (literally, "having many parts") are plastics, fibers, rubber, and human tissue.
POLYNAPHTHALENE SULFONATE • Used as a solvent in wrinkle creams. See Naphthalene.
POLYOXYETHYLENE COMPOUNDS • The nonionic emulsifiers used in hand creams and lotions. Usually oily or waxy liquids. No known toxicity.
POLYQUARTERNIUM 1 THROUGH 14 • See Quaternary Ammonium Compounds.
POLYSORBATES 1 THROUGH 85 • These are widely used emulsifiers and stabilizers. For example, polysorbate 20 is a viscous, oily liquid derived from lauric acid. It is an emulsifier used in cosmetic creams and lotions and a stabilizer of essential oils in water. It is used as a nonionic surfactant (*see*). Polysorbate 85 is used in tanning lotions.
POLYSORBATE 40 • Is widely used as an emulsifier in cosmetic creams and lotions and as a stabilizer of essential oils in water. All the polysorbates are nontoxic.
POLYSORBATE 60 AND POLYSORBATE 80 • Are both emulsifiers that have been associated with the contaminant 1, 4 dioxane, known to cause cancer in animals. The 60 is a condensate of sorbitol with stearic acid and the 80 a condensate of sorbitol and oleic acid (*see all*). The 60 is waxy and soluble in solvents. The 80 is a viscous liquid with a faint caramel odor and is widely used in baby lotions, cold creams, cream deodorants, antiperspirants, suntan lotions, and in bath oil products.
POLYSTYRENE • Used in the manfacture of cosmetic resins. Colorless to yellowish oily liquid with a penetrating odor. Obtained from ethylbenzene by removing the hydrogen, or by chlorination. Sparingly soluble in water; soluble in alcohol. May be irritating to the eyes, mucous membranes, and, in high concentrations, may be narcotic.
POLYSTYRENE LATEX • A white plastic solid derived from petroleum and used in preparing opaque hair-waving lotions. It has outstanding moisture resistance. No known toxicity.
POLYVINYL ACETATE • See Polyvinylpyrrolidone.
POLYVINYL ALCOHOL • Synthetic resins used in lipstick, setting

lotions, and various creams. A polymer prepared from polyvinyl acetates by replacement of the acetate groups with the hydroxyl groups. Dry, unplasticized polyvinyl alcohol powders are white to cream colored and have different viscosities. Solvent in hot and cold water but certain ones require alcohol-water mixtures. No known toxicity.

POLYVINYL BUTYRAL • The condensation of polyvinyl alcohol and butyraldehyde (*see both*). It is a synthetic flavoring found in coffee and strawberry and used in the manufacture of rubber and synthetic resins and plasticizers. May be an irritant and narcotic.

POLYVINYL CHLORIDE • **PVC. Chloroethylene Polymer.** Derived from vinyl chloride (*see*), it consists of a white powder or colorless granules that are resistant to weather, moisture, acids, fats, petroleum products, and fungus. It is widely used for everything from plumbing to raincoats. It is used in cosmetics and toiletries in containers, nail enamels, and creams. PVC has caused tumors when injected under the skin of rats in doses of 100 milligrams per kilogram of body weight.

POLYVINYL IMIDAZOLINIUM ACETATE • The polymer of vinyl imidazolinium acteta. See Polyvinyl Pyrrolidone.

POLYVINYL METHYL ETHER • See Polyvinyl Alcohol.

POLYVINYLPYRROLIDONE • **PVP.** A faintly yellow, solid, plastic resin resembling albumin. Used to give a softer set in shampoos, hair sprays, and lacquers; also a carrier in emollient creams, liquid lip rouge, and face rouge; and a clarifier in vinegar and a plasma expander in medicine. Ingestion may produce gas and fecal impaction or damage to lungs and kidneys. It may last in the system months to a year. Strong circumstantial evidence indicates thesaurosis—foreign bodies in the lung—may be produced in susceptible individuals from concentrated exposure to PVP in hair sprays. Modest intravenous doses in rats caused them to develop tumors.

POMADES • Almost synonymous with solid brilliantines (*see*) but of older origin. Pomades were originally made with the residual fatty material left from the enfleurage process (*see*) of extracting floral odors. *Poma* (apples) were used, hence giving the hairdressing its name.

PONCEAU SX • A monoazo color, the name can be applied only to uncertified batches of color. The CTFA adopted name for certified batches is FD & C Red No. 4 (*see*).

POPLAR EXTRACT • **Balm of Gilead.** Extract of the leaves and twigs of *Populus nigra*. In ancient times, the buds were mashed to make a soothing salve that was spread on sunburned areas, scalds, scratches, inflamed skin, and wounds. They were also simmered in lard for use as an ointment and for antiseptic purposes. The leaves and bark were steeped by American colonists to make a soothing tea. It supposedly helped allergies and soothed reddened eyes. No known toxicity.

POPPY OIL • A yellow to reddish oil obtained from the seeds of the poppy for use in emulsions and soaps and as a lubricant for fine machinery. Nontoxic.

POTASSIUM ACRYLINOEATE • See Acrylinoleic Acid.

POTASSIUM ALGINATE • See Alginates.

POTASSIUM ALUM • See Alum.

POTASSIUM ALUMINUM POLYACRYLATE • A mixture of potassium and aluminum salts of polyacrylic acid, used as an absorbant. See Acrylates.

POTASSIUM ASPARTATE • The potassium salt of aspartic acid (*see*).

POTASSIUM BICARBONATE • **Carbonic Acid. Monopotassium Salt.** Colorless, odorless, transparent crystals or powder, slightly alkaline, salty taste, used in baking, soft drinks, and in low pH liquid detergents.

POTASSIUM BINOXALATE • **Potassium Acid Oxalate. Salt of Sorrel.** White, odorless crystals, which are poisonous, used in nail bleaches and as a stain remover.

POTASSIUM BIPHTHALATE • **Phthalic Acid Potassium Acid Salt.** A buffer used to affect alkalinity/acidity ratios. See Phthalic Acid.

POTASSIUM BORATE • A crystalline salt used as an oxidizing agent and as a preservative in cosmetics and in flour. See Borates for toxicity.

POTASSIUM BROMATE • Antiseptic and astringent in toothpaste, mouthwashes, and gargles as 3 to 5 percent solution. Colorless or white crystals. Very toxic when taken internally. Burns and skin irritation have been reported from its industrial uses. In toothpaste it has been reported to have caused inflammation and bleeding of gums.

POTASSIUM CARBONATE • **Salt of Tartar. Pearl Ash.** Inorganic salt of potassium. Odorless, white powder, soluble in water but practically insoluble in alcohol. Used in freckle lotions, liquid shampoos, vanishing creams, setting lotions, and permanent wave lotions; also in the manufacture of soap, glass, pottery, and to finish leather. Irritating and caustic to human skin and may cause dermatitis of the scalp, forehead, and hands.

POTASSIUM CASEINATE • The potassium salt of milk proteins. See Casein.

POTASSIUM CASTORATE • The potassium salt of fatty acids derived from castor oil (*see*).

POTASSIUM CHLORATE • Antiseptic, astringent in mouthwashes, toothpaste, and gargles as 2 to 5 percent solution. Used in bleach and freckle lotions and in permanent wave solutions. A colorless or white powder that dissolves slowly in water. Also used in explosives, fireworks, matches, and in printing the dyeing cotton and wool black. May be absorbed through the skin. Irritating to the intestines and the kidney. Can cause dermatitis of the scalp, forehead, and hands. In toothpastes, reported to have caused inflammation of the gums.

POTASSIUM COCO-HYDROLYZED PROTEIN • See Proteins.

POTASSIUM COCOATE • See Coconut Oil.

POTASSIUM CORNATE • The potassium salt of fatty acids derived from corn oil. See Corn Oil.

POTASSIUM DNA • The potassium salt of DNA used in "youth creams" and other creams in which protein is included.

POTASSIUM DODECYLBENZENE SULFONATE • See Quaternary Ammonium Compounds.

POTASSIUM GLYCOL SULFATE • See Polyethylene Glycol.

POTASSIUM GUAIACOL SULFONATE • See Quaternary Ammonium Compounds.

POTASSIUM HYDROXIDE • **Caustic Potash.** Prepared industrially by electrolysis of potassium chloride (*see*). White or slightly yellow lumps. Used as an emulsifier in hand lotions, as a cuticle softener, and as an alkali in liquid soaps, protective creams, shaving preparations, and cream rouges. It may cause irritation of the skin in cuticle removers. Extremely corrosive, and ingestion may cause violent pain, bleeding, collapse, and death. When applied to the skin of mice, moderate dosages cause tumors. May cause skin rash and burning. Concentrations above 5 percent can destroy fingernails as well. Good quality toilet soaps do not contain more than 0.25 percent free alkali.

POTASSIUM IODIDE • **Potassium salt.** A dye remover and an antiseptic. Used in table salt as a source of dietary iodine. It is also in some drinking water. May cause allergic reactions.

POTASSIUM LAURATE • The potassium salt of lauric acid (*see*).

POTASSIUM LAURYL SULFATE • A water softener used in shampoos. See Sodium Lauryl Sulfate.

POTASSIUM OLEATE • **Oleic Acid Potassium Salt.** Used as a detergent. Yellowish or brownish soft mass. Soluble in water or alcohol. No known toxicity.

POTASSIUM METABISULFITE • Potassium Pyrosulfite. White granules or powder with a sharp odor, used as an antiseptic, preservative, antioxidant, and as a developing agent in dyes. Low toxicity.

POTASSIUM MYRISTATE • The potassium salt of myristic acid (*see*).

POTASSIUM OCTOXYNOL-12 PHOSPHATE • The potassium salt of a mixture of esters of phosphoric acid and octogoxynol-12 (*see both*).

POTASSIUM PALMITATE • The potassium salt of palmitic acid (*see*).

POTASSIUM PERSULFATE • Colorless or white odorless crystals. A powerful oxidant. Soluble in water. The solution is acidic and is used in the manufacture of soaps and as a germicidal preparation for the bathroom. Aqueous solutions of 2.5 to 3 percent are not irritating to humans. Twenty-five percent is irritating in animals.

POTASSIUM PHOSPHATE • Monobasic, Dibasic, and Tribasic. Used as a buffering agent in shampoos and in cuticle removers. Colorless to white powder, also used as a yeast food in the production of champagne and other sparkling wines. Has been used medicinally as a urinary acidifier. No known toxicity.

POTASSIUM RICINOLEATE • The potassium salt of ricinoleic acid (*see*).

POTASSIUM SILICATE • Soluble Potash Glass. Colorless or yellowish, translucent to transparent, glasslike particles. Used as a binder in cosmetics and in soap manufacturing. Also used as a detergent, and in the glass and ceramics industries. Usually very slowly soluble in cold water. No known toxicity.

POTASSIUM SODIUM COPPER CHLOROPHYLLIN • Chlorophyllin. Copper Complex. Used in coloring dentifrices in levels not to exceed 0.1 percent. Does not require certification and has been permanently listed for use in coloring dentifrices. See Chlorophyllin for toxicity.

POTASSIUM SODIUM TARTRATE • Rochelle Salt. Used in the manufacture of baking powder and in the silvering of mirrors. Translucent crystals or white crystalline powder with cooling saline taste. Slight efflorescence in warm air. Probably used in mouthwashes, but use not identified in cosmetics. No known toxicity.

POTASSIUM SORBATE • Sorbic Acid Potassium Salt. Used as a mold and yeast inhibitor. May cause mild irritation of the skin.

POTASSIUM STEARATE • Stearic Acid Potassium Salt. White powder with a fatty odor. Strongly alkaline. Used in the manufacture of soap, hand creams, emulsified fragrances, lotions, and shaving creams. Acts as a defoaming agent. No known toxicity.

POTASSIUM SULFATE • Does not occur free in nature but is combined with sodium sulfate. Colorless or white crystalline powder, with a bitter taste. Used as a reagent (*see*) in cosmetics and as a salt substitute; also a water corrective in brewing, a fertilizer, and a cathartic. Large doses can cause severe gastrointestinal bleeding. No known toxicity to the skin.

POTASSIUM SULFITE • White crystals or powder. Slowly oxidizes in air. Used as a preservative. See Sulfur.

POTASSIUM TALLOWATE • The potassium salt of Tallow Acid (*see*).

POTASSIUM THIOGLYCOLATE • See Thioglycolic Acid Compounds.

POTASSIUM TOLUENESULFONATE • A water-soluble powder that may be used in cosmetics as a solubilizing agent (*see*) in conjunction with other detergent materials. This is primarily used in household chemical products and for various industrial purposes. See Toluene for toxicity.

POTASSIUM TROCLOSENE • **Troclosene. Potassium.** Used in solid bleaches and detergents, and as a local antiinfective agent. No known toxicity.

POTASSIUM UNDECYLENATE • Fine, white powder used as a bacteriostat and fungistat in cosmetics and pharmaceuticals. Toxic in high concentrations.

POTASSIUM UNDECYLENOYL HYDROLYZED ANIMAL PROTEIN • See Hydrolyzed Animal Protein.

POTATO STARCH • A flour prepared from potatoes, ground to a pulp and washed of fibers. Swells in hot water to form gel on cooling. A demulcent used in dusting powder, an emollient in dry shampoos and baby powders. With glycerin, forms soothing, protective applications in eczema, skin rash, and chapped skin. May cause allergic skin reactions and stuffy nose in the hypersensitive.

POWDER • **Face, Compact, and Dusting.** Applied to the face with a puff. Usually done at the end of the makeup process. Its objective is to remove the "shine" from the face and to give a healthy subtle glow. Face powders are either loose or compacted. Talc is the principal ingredient (about 50 percent), but face powders also include about 15 percent of the clay, kaolin, and about 10 percent precipitated calcium carbonate, 10 percent zinc oxide, 10 percent zinc stearate, 5 percent magnesium carbonate (*see all*), perfume, and pigments. Also included are fractions of barium sulfate, boric acid, cetyl alcohol, titanium dioxide, rice, or corn starch (*see all*). The absorbing, covering, and adherent properties of the face powder may be changed by varying the amounts of the ingredients or by elimination of some of them. For instance, eliminating titanium dioxide makes the powder more transparent. Various pigments are used for shades of face powder, including yellow ocher, sienna, red ochers, umbers, burnt sienna, and ultramarine blue and violet, all inorganic pigments. Organic pigments used may include D & C Red No. 7 Calcium Lake or D & C Orange No. 4 (*see both*). Problems with face powders are rare. The FDA recorded a concern with rash. Compact powder is similar to face powder but includes binders such as gums (*see*); cake makeup employs a binder such as lecithin. Also used in compact powder to make it keep its shape are glyceryl monostearate glycols or mineral oil (*see all*), and other oils. Dusting powder, usually used after a bath or shower, generally contains talc, perfumes, and zinc stearate (*see*). Toxicity concerns mechanical blocking of pores and subsequent irritation by the powders. See Talc and Starch for toxicity.

PPG • Abbreviation for propylene glycol (*see*).

PPG BUTETH-260 THROUGH 5100 • Emulsifiers. See PPG Buteth-55.

PPG BUTETH ETHER-200 • Emulsifiers. Polymer (*see*) prepared from butyl alcohol with propylene glycol (*see both*).

PPG BUTYL ETHER-300 TO 1715 • Emulsifiers. See PPG Butyl Ether-200.

PPG-4-CETEARETH-12 • Emulsifier. See Cetearyl Alcohol.

PPG-10-CETEARETH-20 • See Cetearyl Alcohol.

PPG-4-CETETH-1 OR -5 OR -10 • See Cetyl Alcohol.

PPG-8-CETETH, -5 OR -10 OR -20 • See Cetyl Alcohol.

PPG-5-CETETH-10-PHOSPHATE • Used in tanning creams. See Cetyl Alcohol and Phosphates.

PPG-10 CETYL ETHER • See Cetyl Alcohol.

PPG-28 CETYL ETHER • See Cetyl Alcohol and Polypropylene.

PPG-30 CETYL ETHER • A liquid nonionic surface-active agent (*see*). No known toxicity. See Cetyl Alcohol.

PPG-20-DECYLTETRADECETH-10 • See Decanoic Acid.

PPG-2 DIBENZOATE • See Dipropylene Glycol Dibenzoate.

PPG-24 OR -66 GLYCERETH-24 OR -12 • See Glycerin.

PPG-27, AND -55 GLYCERYL ETHER • See Glycerin and Propylene Glycol.

PPG-ISOCETYL ETHER • See Cetyl Alcohol.

PPG-3-ISOSTEARETH-9 • See Stearyl Alcohol and Propylene Glycol.

PPG-12-PEG-50 LANOLIN • See Polypropylene and Lanolin.

PPG-2, -5, -10, -20, -30 LANOLIN ALCOHOL ETHERS • See Lanolin Alcohol.

PPG-30 LANOLIN ETHER • Derived from lanolin alcohols (*see*).

PPG-9 LAURATE • See Lauric Acid.
PPG-2 METHYL ETHER • See Methylene Glycol.
PPG-20 METHYL GLUCOSE ETHER • See Propylene Glycol and Glucose.
PPG-3-MYRETH-11 • See Polyethylene Glycol and Myristic Acid.
PPG-4 MYRISTYL ETHER • See Myristyl Alcohol.
PPG-26 OLEATE • **Polyoxypropylene 2000 Monooleate. Carbowax.** A solid polyethylene glycol (*see*). Each PPG is a mixture of several polymers (*see*) with various consistencies. Used as a base or carrier in hand lotions and hair dressings, and various other cosmetic lotions. No known toxicity.
PPG-36 OLEATE • **Polyoxypropylene (36) Monooleate.** See PPG-26 Oleate.
PPG-10 OLEYL ETHER • See PPG-26 Oleate.
PPG-30, -50 OLEYL ETHER • See PPG-26 Oleate.
PPG-6-C12-18 PARETH • A mixture of synthetic alcohols. See Fatty Alcohols.
PPG-2 SALICYLATE • See Dipropylene Glycol Salicylate.
PPG-9-STEARETH-3 • See Stearyl Alcohol.
PPG-11 OR -15 STEARYL ETHER • See Polyproplene Glycol and Stearyl Alcohol.
PPM • Parts per million.
PRECIPITATE • To separate out from solution or suspension. A deposit of solid separated out from a solution or suspension as a result of a chemical or physical change, as by the action of a reagent (*see*).
PREGNENOLONE ACETATE • Derived from the urine of pregnant women. Used topically as an antiinflammatory, antiitch agent. Very slightly soluble in water. A corticosteroid. No known toxicity.
PRESERVATIVES • Because the presence of viable microorganisms in cosmetic products can lead to separation of emulsions, discoloration, the formation of gas and odors, and changes in the general properties, as well as possible infection for the users, a preservative must be effective against a wide range of microorganisms. It must not be toxic internally or externally. It must not alter the character of the product, and it is required to be long-lasting and inexpensive. Many kinds of yeasts, fungi, and bacteria have been identified in cosmetics, including pseudomonas, staphylococcus, and streptococcus. In many instances a product might show no visible evidence of microbial contamination and yet contain actively growing, potentially harmful germs. Esters of *p*-hydroxybenzoic acid (*see*) are the most widely used preservatives.
PRESHAVING LOTIONS • See Shaving Lotions.

PRIMULA EXTRACT • The extract of various species of *Primula* taken from the rhizome and roots of the primrose or cowslip. It has been used as an expectorant, diuretic, and worm medicine. In some sensitive persons, it may cause a rash.
PRISTANE • A liquid hydrocarbon obtained from the liver oil of sharks and from ambergris (*see both*). Used as a lubricant and anticorrosive agent.
PROGESTERONE • A female sex hormone used in face cream for its supposed antiwrinkle properties. There is no proven benefit to the skin and it may be absorbed through the skin and have adverse systemic effects. See Hormone Creams and Lotions.
PROLINE • An amino acid (*see*) used as a food supplement but classified as nonessential. Usually isolated from wheat or gelatin. L-Proline is the naturally occurring form and DL-Proline is the synthetic. GRAS.
PROPANE • A gas heavier than air; odorless wher pure. It is used as a fuel and refrigerant. Cleared for use in a spray propellant and as an aerating agent for cosmetics in aerosols. May be narcotic in high doses.
PROPELLANT • A compressed gas used to expel the contents of containers in the form of aerosols. Chlorofluorocarbons were widely used because of their nonflammability. The strong possibility that they contribute to depletion of the ozone layer of the upper atmosphere has resulted in prohibition of their use for this purpose. Other propellants used are hydrocarbon gases, such as butane and propane, carbon dioxide, and nitrous oxide. The materials dispersed include shaving cream, whipping cream, and cosmetic preparations.
PROPELLANT 11 • **Trichlorofluoromethane. Freon 11®**. A low pressure, odorous propellant used for hair sprays, shaving lathers, and other products with alcohol. Less toxic than carbon dioxide (*see*) but decomposes into harmful materials when exposed to flames or high heat. May be narcotic in high concentrations.
PROPELLANT 12 • **Dichlorodifluoromethane. Freon 12®.** High pressure propellant used in aerosols, particularly for foam products such as hair coloring. Frequently used for perfumes because it has no odor of its own. See Aerosols for toxicity.
PROPELLANT 114 • **Dichlorotetrafluoroethane. Freon 114®.** Most frequently used propellant. It is a low pressure one. See Aerosols for toxicity.
PROPELLANT 142B • **Chlorodifluoroethane. Freon 142®**. A propellant not frequently used because of its high pressure. See Aerosols for toxicity.

PROPELLANT 152A • **Difluoroethane.** Propellant used in glass, plastic, and aluminum containers. See Aerosols for toxicity.

PROPIONIC ACID • Occurs naturally in apples, strawberries, tea, and violet leaves. An oily liquid with a slightly pungent, rancid odor. Can be obtained from wood pulp, waste liquor, and by fermentation. Used in perfume bases and as a mold inhibitor, antioxidant, and preservative in cosmetics. Its salts have been used as antifungal agents to treat skin mold. Large oral dose in rats is lethal. No known toxicity when used externally.

PROPIONIC ANHYDRIDE • Used in perfume oils. It has a more pungent odor than that of propionic acid (*see*). No known toxicity to the skin.

PROPYL ACETATE • Colorless liquid, soluble in water, derived from propane and acetate (*see both*). It has the odor of pears. Used in the manufacture of perfumes and as a solvent for resins. It may be irritating to the skin and mucous membranes.

PROPYL ALCOHOL • Obtained from crude fusel oil. Alcoholic and slightly overpowering odor. Occurs naturally in cognac green oil, cognac white oil, and onion oil. A synthetic fruit flavoring. Used instead of ethyl alcohol as a solvent for shellac, gums, resins, oils; as a denaturant (*see*) for alcohol in perfumery. Not a primary irritant, but because it dissolves fat it has a drying effect on the skin and may lead to cracking, fissuring, and infections. No adverse effects have been reported from local application as a lotion, liniment, mouthwash, gargle, or sponge bath.

PROPYL GALLATE • A fine, white, odorless powder with a bitter taste used as an antioxidant in creams and lotions. No known toxicity.

PROPYLAMINE • **1-Aminopropane.** An alkaline base for cosmetics, it is a colorless liquid with strong ammonia odor. Miscible with water, alcohol, and ether. Strong skin irritant. May cause allergic reactions.

PROPYLENE GLYCOL • **1, 2-Propanediol.** A clear, colorless, viscous liquid, slightly bitter tasting. It is the most common moisture-carrying vehicle other than water itself in cosmetics. It has better permeation through the skin than glycerin and is less expensive although it has been linked to more sensitivity reactions. Absorbs moisture, acts as a solvent and a wetting agent. Used in liquid makeup, foundation makeup, foundation creams, mascaras, spray deodorants, hair straighteners, liquid powders, preshave lotions, after-shave lotions, baby lotions, cold creams, emollients, antiperspirants, lipsticks, mouthwashes, stick perfumes, and suntan lotions. Its use is being reduced, and it is being replaced by safer glycols such as butylene and polyethylene glycol.

PROPYLENE GLYCOL ALGINATE • Kelcoloid®. The propylene glycol ester of alginic acid (*see*) derived from seaweed. Used as a stabilizer and defoaming agent in cosmetics and food. No known toxicity.

PROPYLENE GLYCOL CAPRYLATE • See Polyethylene Glycol and Capric Acid.

PROPYLENE GLYCOL DICAPRYLATE/DICAPRIATE • A gel used in emollients. See Propylene Glycol and Capric Acid.

PROPYLENE GLYCOL DICOCONATE • Mixture of propylene glycol esters of coconut fatty acids. See Propylene Glycol.

PROPYLENE GLYCOL DIPELARGONATE • See Propylene Glycol.

PROPYLENE GLYCOL LAURATE • An ester of propylene glycol and lauric acid. An emulsifying agent for solvents, cosmetic creams, and lotions; also a stabilizer of essential oils in water. Light orange oil, dispersible in water, soluble in alcohol and oils. Nontoxic but can cause allergic reactions in the hypersensitive.

PROPYLENE GLYCOL MYRISTATE • See Propylene Glycol and Myristic Acid.

PROPYLENE GLYCOL RICINOLEATE • Ester of propylene glycol and ricinoleic acid (*see both*).

PROPYLENE GLYCOL STEARATE • Cream-colored wax. Dispenses in water, soluble in hot alcohol. Lubricating agent and emulsifier in cosmetic creams and lotions. Stabilizer of essential oils. No known toxicity.

PROPYLENE GLYCOL STEARATE SE • An emulsifier. See Propylene Glycol.

PROPYLPARABEN • Propyl p-Hydroxybenzoate. Developed in Europe, the esters of *p*-hydroxybenzoic acid are widely used in the cosmetic industry as preservatives, and bacteria and fungus killers. They are active against a variety of organisms, are neutral, low in toxicity, slightly soluble, and active in all solutions, alkaline, neutral, or acidic. Used in shampoos, baby preparations, foundation creams, beauty masks, dentifrices, eye lotions, hair-grooming aids, nail creams, and wave sets. Used medicinally to treat fungus infections. Can cause contract dermatitis. Less toxic than benzoic or salicylic acid (*see both*).

PROTECTIVE CREAMS • Water-repellent or oil-repellent creams designed to act as barrier agents against irritating chemicals, including water. Some products such as the widely used silicones are both water and oil repellent. Among the chemicals used in protective creams are stearic acid, beeswax, glycerin, casein, ammonium hydroxide, zinc stearate, titanium dioxide, butyl stearate, petrolatum, polyethylene glycol, paraffin, potassium hydroxide, magnesium stearate, aluminum compounds, benzoic acid, borates, calamine, ceresin, lanolin, salicylates, sodium silicate, talc, and triethanolamine (*see all*).

PROTEIN FATTY ACID CONDENSATES • See Amides.

PROTEIN PAC • New name for hair moisturizers.

PROTEINS • The chief nitrogen-containing constituents of plants and animals—the essential constituents of every living cell. They are complex but by weight contain about 50 percent carbon, about 20 percent oxygen, about 15 percent nitrogen, about 7 percent hydrogen, and some sulfur. Some also contain iron and phosphorous. Proteins are colorless, odorless, and generally tasteless. They vary in solubility. They readily undergo putrefaction, hydrolysis, and dilution with acids or alkalies. They are regarded as combinations of amino acids (*see*). Cosmetic manufacturers, particularly makers of hair products, claim "protein enrichment" is beneficial to the hair and skin. Hair, of course, is already dead. It does consist of a type of protein, keratin (*see*), but the surface of the hair is cornified tissue that cannot be revitalized. Such products will add body to thin hair and add gloss or luster, but so will other hair conditioners (*see*). As for face creams with protein, the lubricant is more beneficial than the protein. No known toxicity.

PSORALEN® • Named for the Latin *psora,* meaning "itch," and derived from a plant. Used in the treatment of vitiligo (lack of skin pigment), in sunscreen to increase tanning, and in perfumes. It can cause photosensitivity (*see*).

PUMICE • Used in hand-cleansing pastes, skin-cleansing grains, toothpastes, powders, and some soaps for acne treatment. A tooth whitener in Elizabethan times. Used to rub hair from legs and as a nicotine remover paste. Light, hard, rough, porous mass of gritty, gray-colored powder of volcanic origin. Used in cosmetics for removing tough or rough skin. Pumice consists mainly of silicates (*see*) found chiefly in the Lipari Islands and in the Greek Archipelagos. Because of its abrasive action, daily use in dentifrices is not recommended. If used continuously on a dry sensitive skin, it may cause irritation. Reported to be an irritant when used with soapless detergents but is generally considered harmless.

PURCELLINE OIL SYN • A synthetic mixture of fatty esters simulating the natural oil obtained from the preen glands of waterfowl. Used as a fixative in perfumes. No known toxicity.

PURPLE HEATH EXTRACT • Extract of the flowers of *Erice cinerea.*

PVM/MA • Abbreviation for Polyvinyl Methyl Ether/Maleic Anhydride.

PVM/MA COPOLYMER • A copolymer of methyl vinyl ether and maleic anhydride. See Polyvinyl Alcohols.

PVP • **1-Vinyl-2-Pyrrolidone.** Abbreviation for Polyvinyl pyrrolidone.

PVP/DIMETHYLAMINOETHYL-METHYLACRYLATE COPOLYMER • A polymer prepared from vinylpryrrolidone and dimethylaminoethylmethacrylate. See Polyvinyl Pyrrolidone and Acrylates.

PVP/EICOSENE COPOLYMER • A polymer of vinylpyrrolidone and eicosine. See Polyvinyl Pyrrolidone.

PVP/ETHYL METHACRYLATE/METHACRYLIC ACID COPOLYMER • See Polyvinyl pyrrolidone and Acrylate.

PVP/IODINE • Complex of polyvinyl pyrrolidone and iodine (*see both*).

PVP/VA COPOLYMER • A film-former used in hair sprays. See Polyvinyls and Polyvinyl Pyrrolidone.

PVP/VINYL ACETATE/ITACONIOC ACID COPOLYMER • See Polyvinyl Pyrrolidone and Vinyl Polymers.

PYRAZOLE • A crystalline compound used to overcome acidity of aluminum chloride in antiperspirants. Soluble in water, alcohol, ether, and benzene. No known toxicity when used externally. A modest injection into the abdomens of mice is lethal.

PYRIDINE • Occurs naturally in coffee and coal tar. Disagreeable odor; sharp taste. Used as a solvent. Once used to treat asthma, but may cause central nervous system depression and irritation of the skin and respiratory tract. After prolonged administration, kidney and liver damage may result.

PYRIDIUM COMPOUNDS • A toxic, water-soluble, flammable liquid with a disagreeable odor that is obtained by distillation of bone oil or as a by-product of coal tar. Used as a modifier and preservative in shaving creams, soaps, hand creams, and lotions; also a solvent, a denaturant in alcohol, and an industrial waterproofing agent. No known toxicity when used externally. The lethal dose injected into the abdomens of rats is only 3.2 milligrams per kilogram of body weight.

PYRIDOXINE • See Pyridoxine HCL.

PYRIDOXINE DICAPRYLATE • See Pyridoxine Dioctenoate.

PYRIDOXINE DIOCTENOATE • **Vitamin B_6 Hydrochloride.** Texturizer. A colorless or white crystalline powder present in many foodstuffs. A coenzyme that helps in the metabolism of amino acids (*see*) and fats. Also soothing to skin. Nontoxic.

PYROCATECHOL • Used as an antiseptic. Colorless leaflets, soluble in water; prepared by treating salicylaldehyde with hydrogen peroxide. Used in blond-type dyes as an oxidizing agent and for dyeing furs; also in photography. It can cause eczema and systemic effects similar to phenol (*see*).

PYROGALLOL • Antiseptic hair dye for hair restorers. The first synthetic organic dye used in human hair. Discovered in 1786 and suggested for use in hair in 1845. Solution grows darker as it is exposed to air. Consists of white odorless crystals. An aromatic alcohol of pyrogallic acid. Used medicinally as an external antimicrobial and to soothe irritated skin. Ingestion may cause severe gastrointestinal irritation, kidney and liver damage, circulatory collapse, and death. Application to extensive areas of the skin is extremely dangerous. Even with careful use, it can cause a skin rash. Its adverse effects supposedly can be reduced by adding sulfide.

PYROLIGNEOUS ACID • A reddish brown, aqueous liquid obtained by the destructive distillation of hardwood. Contains acetic acid and methanol (*see both*), wood oil, and tars. It is corrosive and may cause epigastric pain, vomiting, circulatory collapse, and death. Used as synthetic flavoring.

PYROPHOSPHATE • **Salt of Pyrophosphoric Acid.** It increases the effectiveness of antioxidants in creams and ointments. In concentrated solutions it can be irritating to the skin and mucous membranes.

PYROPHYLLITE • **Pencil Stone Agalmatolite.** White to yellowish gray mineral consisting predominantly of anhydrous aluminum silicate (*see*) mixed with silica (*see*). Used to color cosmetics and drugs applied to the skin. Permanently listed in 1966 for externally applied cosmetics. No known toxicity.

Q

QUASSIN • Bitter alkaloid obtained from the wood of *Quassia amara*. Chiefly used as a denaturant for ethyl alcohol. Shavings from a plant found in Jamaica and the Caribbean islands. Yellowish white to bright yellow chips. Used to poison flies. Toxic to humans.

QUATERNARY AMMONIUM COMPOUNDS • A wide variety of preservatives, surfactants, germicides, sanitizers, antiseptics, and deodorants used in cosmetics. Benzalkonium chloride (*see*) is one of the most popular. Quaternary ammonium compounds are synthetic derivatives of ammonium chloride (*see*) and are used in aerosol deodorants, after-shave lotions, antidandruff shampoos, antiperspirants, cuticle softeners, hair colorings, hair-grooming aids, hand creams, hair-waving preparations, mouthwashes, and regular shampoos. Diluted solutions are used in medicine to sterilize the skin and mucous membranes. All the quaternary ammonium compounds can be toxic, depending upon the dose and concentration. Concentrated solutions irritate the skin and can cause necrosis of the mucous membranes. Concentrations as low as 0.1 percent are irritating to the eye and mucous membranes except benzalkonium chloride, which is well tolerated at such low concentrations. Ingestion can be fatal.

QUATERNARIUM-1 THROUGH -6 • See Quaternarium-7.

QUATERNARIUM-7 • A surfactant and germicide derived from lauric acid (*see*). Positively charged with a low irritation potential, it is effective against a wide range of organisms.

QUATERNARIUM-8 THROUGH -14 • See Quaternarium-15.

QUATERNARIUM-15 • A water-soluble antimicrobial agent that is active against bacteria but not very active against yeast. It is a formaldehyde (*see*) releaser, and is the number one cause of dermatitis from preservatives, according to the American Academy of Dermatology's Testing Tray results.

QUATERNARIUM-16 THROUGH -29 • See Quaternarium-18.

QUATERNARIUM-18, -19, -20, -23 • Derived from cellulose (*see*), it is a film-former and binding agent used in products to give hair a sheen.

QUATERNARIUM-28 DODECYLBENZYL TRIMETHYLAMMONIUM CHLORIDE • See Quaternary Ammonium Compounds.

QUATERNARIUM-29 DODECYLXYLYL BIS • **Trimethyl Ammonium Chloride.** See Quaternary Ammonium Compounds.

QUATERNARIUM-18 HECTORITE • See Quaternary Ammonium Compounds.

QUERCITIN • The inner bark of a species of oak tree common in North America. Its active ingredient, isoquercitin, is used in dark brown hair dye shades but employed mainly for dyeing artificial hair pieces. Allergic reactions have been reported.

QUILLAJA EXTRACT • **Soap Bark. Quillay Bark. Panama Bark. China Bark.** The extract of the bark of *Quillaja saponaria*. The dried inner bark of a tree grown in South America. Used in fruit, root beer, and spice flavorings for beverages, ice cream, candy. Formerly used to treat bronchitis and externally as a detergent and local irritant. No known toxicity.

QUINCE SEED • The seed of a plant grown in southern Asia and Europe for its fatty acid. Thick jelly is produced by soaking seeds in water. Used in setting lotions, as a suspension in skin creams and lotions, as a thickening agent in depilatories, and as an emulsifier in fragrances, hand creams, lotions, rouges, and wave sets; medicinally as a demulcent. Has been largely replaced by cheaper substitutes. It may cause allergic reactions.

QUININE • The most important alkaloid of the bark of the cinchona tree, which grows wild in South America. White crystalline powder, almost insoluble in water. Used as a local anesthetic in hair tonics and sunscreen preparations. Used in bitters as flavoring for beverages in limited amounts. When taken internally, it reduces fever. It is also used as a flavoring agent in numerous over-the-counter cold and headache remedies as well as "bitter lemon" and tonic water, which may contain as much as 5 milligrams per 100 milliliters. When taken internally, it reduces fever. Cinchonism, which may consist of nausea, vomiting, disturbances of vision, ringing in the ears, and nerve deafness, may occur from an overdose of quinine. If there is a sensitivity to quinine, such symptoms can result after ingesting tonic water. Quinine more commonly causes a rash.

QUINOLINE • A coal tar derivative used in the manufacture of cosmetic dyes. Also a solvent for resins. Made either by the distillation of coal tar, bones, and alkaloids or by the interaction of aniline (*see*) with acetaldehyde and formaldehyde (*see both*). Absorbs water, has a weak base. Soluble in hot water. Also used as a preservative for anatomical specimens. See Coal Tar for toxicity. See also Colors.

QUINOLINE SALTS • A colorless, oily, very hygroscopic liquid with a disagreeable odor. Occurs in coal tar. Used in suntan preparations and perfumes as a preservative and solvent. Also a preservative for anatomical specimens. No known toxicity when used externally.

QUINONES • Potent sensitizers. See Heliotrope.

R

RADISH EXTRACT • Extract of *Raphanus sativus*. The small seeds of the radish remain viable for years. Has been used as a food since ancient times. Used as a counterirritant (*see*) in herbal cosmetics.

RAISIN-SEED OIL • Dried grapes or berries used in lubricating creams. See Grape-Seed Oil.

RAPESEED AMIDOPROPYL BENZYLDIMONIUM CHLORIDE • See Rapeseed Oil and Quaternary Ammonium Compounds.

RAPESEED AMIDOPROPYL ETHYLDIMONIUM ETHOSULFATE • See Rapeseed Oil and Quaternary Ammonium Compounds.

RAPESEED OIL • Brownish-yellow oil from a turniplike annual herb of European origin. Widely grown as a forage crop for sheep in the United States. A distinctly unpleasant odor. Used chiefly as a lubricant, an illuminant, and in rubber substitutes; also used in soft soaps and margarine. Can cause acnelike skin eruptions.

RAPESEED OIL UNSAPONIFIABLES • The fraction of Rapeseed Oil (*see*) which is not changed into a fatty alcohol when it is saponified (heated with an alkali and acid).

RASPBERRY EXTRACT • See Raspberry Juice.

RASPBERRY JUICE • Juice from the fresh ripe fruit grown in Europe, Asia, the United States, and Canada. Used as a flavoring for lipsticks, food, and medicines. It has astringent properties. No known toxicity.

RAYON • Regenerated cellulose. Rayon is man-made textile fibers of cellulose and yarn; produced from wood pulp. Its appearance is similar to silk. Used to give shine and body to face powders and in eyelash extenders in mascaras. No known toxicity.

REAGENT • A chemical that reacts or participates in a reaction; a substance that is used for the detection or determination of another substance by chemical or microscopical means. The various categories of reagents are colorimetric—to produce color-soluble compounds; fluxes—used to lower melting point; oxidizers—used in oxidation; precipitants—to produce insoluble compounds; reducers—used in reduction (*see*); solvents—used to dissolve water-insoluble compounds.

RED PEPPER • **Cayenne Pepper.** A condiment made from the pungent fruit of the plant. Used in sausage and pepper flavorings. Also used as a stimulant in hair tonics but may be an irritant and also cause allergic reactions.

RED PETROLATUM • A minimally refined variety of petrolatum (*see*).

RED RASPBERRY LEAF EXTRACT • An extract of the leaves of the red raspberry (*see*).

REDUCING AGENT • A substance that decreases, deoxidizes, or concentrates the volume of another substance. For instance, a reducing agent is used to convert a metal oxide to the metal itself. It also means a substance that adds hydrogen agents to another, for example, when acetaldehyde is converted to alcohol in the final step of alcoholic fermentation.

REDUCTION • The process of reducing by chemical or electrochemical means. The gain of one or more electrons by an ion or compound. It is the reverse of oxidation.

RESINS • The brittle substance, usually translucent or transparent, formed from the hardened secretions of plants. Among the natural resins are dammar, elemi, and sandarac. Synthetic resins include polyvinyl acetate, various polyester resins, and sulfonamide resins. Resins have many uses in cosmetics. They contribute depth, gloss, flow adhesion, and water resistance. Toxicity depends upon ingredients used.

RESORCINOL • A preservative, antiseptic, antifungal agent, astringent, and antiitching agent, particularly in dandruff shampoos. Also used in hair dyes, lipsticks, and hair tonics. Also used in tanning, explosives, printing textiles, and the manufacture of resins. Obtained from various resins. Resorcinol's white crystals become pink on exposure to air. A sweetish taste. Irritating to the skin and mucous membranes. May cause allergic reactions, particularly of the skin.

RESORCINOL ACETATE • See Resorcinol.

RESTHARROW EXTRACT • A European woody herb, *Onones spinosa,* with pink flowers and long, tough roots used for medicinal purposes and in emollients. No known toxicity.

RETIN-A • A prescription drug to treat acne, it is a Vitamin A derivative. The medication is available in five strengths and in cream, gel, and liquid form. It has a faint medicinal odor, is greaseless and easily absorbed. It reportedly plumps the skin, smooths fine wrinkles and begins to reverse other, less visible signs of sun damage. The drug is believed to increase cell turnover, so dull surface cells are shed more quickly. It thickens the epidermis and improves texture, elasticity, and blood circulation. And it helps normalize uneven cell growth. It is not said to reduce deep wrinkles. It is expected, as of this writing, to eventually be an ingredient in over-the-counter cosmetics. The FDA began a nationwide crack-down on unlicensed manufacturers who have begun to advertise and distribute bogus Retin-A drugs and cosmetics. Some manufacturers are also promoting Vitamin A in products as producing effects similar to Retin-A.

RETINOIDS • Derived from Retinoic Acid, Vitamin A, it is used to treat acne and other skin disorders. See Vitamin A.

RETINOL • Vitamin A (*see*).

RETINYL PALMITATE • The ester of Vitamin A and palmitic acid sometimes mixed with Vitamin D (*see all*).

RHODINOL • Used in perfumes, especially those of the rose type. Isolated from geranium or rose oils. It has the strong odor of rose and consists essentially of geraniol and citronellol (*see both*). Also used in food and beverage flavorings. No known toxicity.

RHODODENDRON EXTRACT • Extract of various species of *Rhododendron.*

RHUBARB • The common plant with large edible leaves. It is combined with henna, black tea, and chamomile for hair dye. Its active principle is chrysophanol, which promotes a desirable blond shade. No known skin toxicity.

RIBOFLAVIN • **Vitamin B_2. Lactoflavin.** Formerly called Vitamin G. Riboflavin is a factor in the Vitamin B-Complex and is used in emollients. Every plant and animal cell contains a minute amount. Good sources are milk, eggs, and organ meats. It is necessary for healthy skin and respiration, protects the eyes from sensitivity to light, and is used for building and maintaining human body tissues. A deficiency leads to lesions at the corner of the mouth and to changes in the cornea.

RIBONUCLEIC ACID • **RNA.** Found in both the nucleus and cytoplasm of the cell, it is the material that contains directions for the genetic code of the cell, DNA.

RICE BRAN OIL • Oil expressed from the broken coat of rice grain.

RICE BRAN WAX • The wax obtained from the broken coat of rice grain.

RICE POWDER • Used in cosmetics and as a drying agent. May cause contact dermatitis. However, rice as a food is hypoallergenic.

RICE STARCH • The finely pulverized grains of the rice plant used in baby powders, face powders, and dusting powders. It is a demulcent and emollient and forms a soothing, protective film when applied. May cause mechanical irritation by blocking the pores and putrefying. May also cause an allergic reaction.

RICINOLEAMIDE • See Ricinoleic Acid.

RICINOLEAMIDE DEA • See Ricinoleic Acid.

RICINOLEATE • Salt of ricinoleic acid found in castor oil. Used in the manufacture of soaps. No known toxicity.

RICINOLEIC ACID • A mixture of fatty oils found in the seeds of castor beans. Castor oil contains 80 to 85 percent ricinoleic acid. The oily liquid is used in soaps, added to Turkey-red oil (*see*), and in contraceptive jellies. It is believed to be the active laxative in castor oil. Also used externally as an emollient. No known toxicity.

RICINOLEOAMPHOGLYCINATE • See Castor Oil.

RICINOLETH-40 • See Castor Oil.

ROCHELLE SALT • **Postassium Sodium Tartrate.** Used in the manufacture of baking powder and in the silvering of mirrors. Translucent crystals or white crystalline powder with cooling saline taste. Slight efflorescence in warm air. Probably used in mouthwashes, but use not identified in cosmetics. No known toxicity.

ROCK SALT CRYSTALS • See Sodium Chloride.

ROCKET EXTRACT • Extract of the leaves of *Eruca sativa.* Used in hair shampoos and skin preparations to cut grease.

ROSE BENGAL • A bluish-red fragrant liquid taken from the rose of the Bengal region of the Asian subcontinent. Used to scent perfumes and as an edible color product to make lipstick dyes. Nontoxic.

ROSE BULGARIAN • **True Otto Oil. Attar of Roses. Rose Otto**

Bulgaria. One of the most widely used perfume ingredients, it is the essential oil, steam-distilled from the flowers of *Rosas Damascena*. The rose flowers are picked early in the morning when they contain the maximum amount of perfume and are distilled quickly after harvesting. Bulgaria is the main source of supply, but it is also grown in the USSR, Turkey, Syria, and Indochina. The liquid is pale yellow and has a warm, deep, floral, slightly spicy, and extremely fragrant, red rose smell. It is used as a flavoring agent in loganberry, raspberry, strawberry, orange, rose, violet, cherry, grape, peach, honey, muscatel, maple, almond, pecan, and ginger ale flavorings for beverages, ice cream, ices, candy, baked goods, gelatin desserts, chewing gym, and jellies. Also used in mucilage, coloring matter, and as a flavoring in pills. May cause allergic reactions.

ROSE EXTRACT • An extract of the various species of rose, it is used in raspberry and cola beverages and fragrances. No known toxicity except for allergic reactions. GRAS.

ROSE GERANIUM • Distilled from any of several South African herbs grown for their fragrant leaves. Used in perfumes, and to scent toothpaste and dusting powders. May cause allergic reactions.

ROSE HIPS EXTRACT • Extract of the fruit of various species of wild roses, it is rich in Vitamin C and is used as a natural flavoring. No known toxicity.

ROSE LEAVES EXTRACT • Derived from the leaves of the species *Rosa*. Used in raspberry and cola beverages.

ROSE OIL • **Attar of Roses.** The fragrant, volatile, essential oil distilled from fresh flowers. Colorless or yellow with a strong fragrant odor and taste of roses. Used in perfumes, toilet waters, and ointments. Nontoxic but may cause allergic reactions.

ROSE OTTO BULGARIA • See Rose Bulgarian.

ROSE WATER • The watery solution of the odoriferous constituents of roses, made by distilling the fresh flowers with water or steam. Used as a perfume in emollients, eye lotions, and freckle lotions. No known toxicity but may cause allergic reactions.

ROSE WATER OINTMENT • See Cold Cream.

ROSEMARY • Used in perfumery. The flowers and leaves of the plant are a symbol of love and loyalty. Rosemary oil is the volatile oil from the fresh flowering tops of rosemary and is used in liniments and hair tonics. Colorless to yellow, with the characteristic odor of rosemary and a warm camphorlike taste. Rosemary has the folk reputation of stimulating the growth of hair and is used in rinse water. It supposedly is also beneficial for the skin. It is used internally as a tonic and astringent and by herbalists as a stimulant for the nerves. No known toxicity when used externally. A teaspoonful may cause illness in an adult, and an ounce may cause death.

ROSEMARY EXTRACT • **Garden Rosemary.** A flavoring and perfume from the fresh aromatic flowering tops of the evergreen shrub grown in the Mediterranean. Light blue flowers and gray green leaves. Used for beverages, condiments, and meat. It is also used in citrus, peach, and ginger flavorings as well as in perfumes. A teaspoonful of the oil may cause illness in an adult, and an ounce may cause death.

ROSIN • Used in soaps, hair lacquers, wax depilatories, and ointments. It is the pale yellow residue left after distilling off the volatile oil from the oleoresin obtained from various species of pine trees. Chiefly produced in the United States. Also used in the manufacture of varnishes and fireworks. It can cause contact dermatitis.

ROUGE • One of the oldest types of makeup. Rouge is applied to the cheeks to give a rosy, healthy look. It is usually a finely divided form of ferric oxide, generally prepared by heating ferrous sulfate. Cake or compact rouge usually contains talc, kaolin, brilliant red lake (certified), zinc oxide, zinc stearate, liquid petrolatum, tragacanth, mucilage (*see all*), and perfume. Liquid rouge usually contains carmine coloring, ammonium hydroxide, glycerin (*see all*), and red coloring pigment. It may also contain polyvinylpyrrolidone or sodium carboxymethyl cellulose, glycerin, color, propylene glycol (*see all*), alcohol, perfume, and water. Rouge paste may contain carmine coloring, ammonium hydroxide, beeswax, cetyl alcohol, stearic acid, cocoa butter, and petrolatum (*see all*). Cream rouge may contain erythrosine as a coloring, stearic acid, cetyl alcohol, potassium hydroxide, glycerin, and water; or sorbitol, lanolin, mineral oil, petrolatum, a color pigment, perfume, and water; or anhydrous or emulisified carnauba wax, ozokerite, isopropyl palmitate, titanium dioxide, talc, certified colors, pigments, and perfume (*see all*). Dry rouge may contain kaolin, talc, precipitated calcium carbonate, magnesium carbonate, titanium dioxide, zinc stearate, certified colors and lakes, inorganic oxides, and perfume (*see all*). A typical formula for an emulsified rouge includes white beeswax, 12 percent; petrolatum, 24 percent; spermaceti, 8 percent; mineral oil, 22 percent; borax, 0.8 percent; water, about 30 percent; pigment, 3.1 percent; *p*-hydroxybenzoic acid, 0.1 percent; perfume (*see all*). Rouge does not figure often in FDA complaints. In recent years there have been complaints of eye irritation and fungus.

ROYAL JELLY • Highly touted as a magic ingredient in cosmetics to restore one's skin to youthfulness. Royal jelly is the very nutritious secretion of the throat glands of the honeybee workers that is fed to the larvae in a colony, and to all queen larvae, and possibly to the adult queen. It is a mixture of proteins plus about 31 percent fats, 15 percent carbohydrates, 15 percent minor growth factors, and 24 percent water and trace elements. If stored, royal jelly loses its capacity to develop queen bees. Even when fresh, there is no proven value in a cosmetic preparation. No known toxicity.

RUBBER • Rubber as well as rubber-based adhesives are common causes of contact dermatitis. The natural gum obtained from the rubber tree is not allergenic; the offenders are the chemicals added to natural rubber gum to make it a useful product. Such chemicals are accelerators, antioxidants, stabilizers, and vulcanizers, many of which can cause allergies. Two of the most frequent, but certainly not the only sensitizers, are mercaptobezothiazole and tetramethylthiuram. Don't forget that the edge of eyelash curlers may have rubber as well as the false eyelashes themselves.

RUBBING ALCOHOLS • Isopropyl alcohol (*see*), probably the most common rubbing alcohol, is used in astringents, skin fresheners, colognes, and perfumes. It can be irritating to the skin. Ethanol (*see*) is used in perfumes and as a solvent for oils. It also can be irritating. Rubbing alcohols are denatured with chemicals to make them poisonous so they will not be ingested as an alcoholic beverage.

RUBEFACIENTS • Help stimulate blood circulation to the scalp and the activity of the oil secreting glands. Pilocarpine (*see*) is an example.

RUE OIL • A spice agent obtained from the fresh, aromatic, blossoming plants grown in Southern Europe and the Orient. It has a fatty odor and is used in baked goods. The oil is obtained by steam distillation and is used in fragrances and in blueberry, raspberry, and other fruit flavorings. Formerly used in medicine to treat disorders and hysteria. It is on the FDA list for study of mutagenic, teratogenic, subacute, and reproductive effects. It may cause photosensitivity.

RYE FLOUR • Used in powders. Flour made from hardy annual cereal grass. Seeds are used for feed and in the manufacture of whiskey and bread. May cause allergic reactions.

S

SACCHARATED LIME • Produced by the action of lime upon sugar. Used as a buffer (*see*) in cosmetics and as a preservative. No known toxicity.

SACCHARIDE HYDROLYSATE • A mixture of sugars derived from using an alkali and water on a mixture of glucose and lactose (*see*).

SACCHARIDE ISOMERATE • See Saccharide Hydrolysate.

SACCHARIN • An artificial sweetener in use since 1879. It is 300 times as sweet as natural sugar. Used as a sweetener for mouthwashes, dentifrices, and lipsticks. It sweetens dentifrices and mouthwashes in 0.05 to 1 percent concentration. On the FDA's top priority list to retest for mutagenic, subacute, and reproductive effects. White crystals or crystalline powder. Odorless or with a faint aromatic odor. It was used with cyclamates in the experiments that led to the ban on cyclamates. The FDA has proposed restricting saccharin to 15 milligrams per day for each kilogram of body weight or 1 gram a day for a 150-pound person.

SAFFLOWER GLYCERIDE • See Safflower Oil.

SAFFLOWER OIL • Used in creams and lotions to soften the skin. Oil is expressed from the seed of an Old World herb that resembles a thistle, with large bright red or orange flowers. Widely cultivated for its oil, which thickens and becomes rancid on exposure to air. No known toxicity.

SAFFRON • Used in perfumery and coloring in cosmetics. It is the dried stigma of the crocus cultivated in Spain, Greece, France, and Iran. Used also in bitters, liquors, and spice flavorings. Formerly used to treat skin diseases. No known toxicity.

SAFROLE • Found in certain natural oils such as star anise, nutmeg, ylang-ylang, it is a stable, colorless to brown liquid with an odor of sassafras and rootbeer. Used in the manufacture of heliotropin (*see*) and in inexpensive soaps and perfumes. Also used as a beverage flavoring. The toxicity of this fragrance ingredient is being questioned by the FDA. It is an animal carcinogen.

SAGE EXTRACT • Used by herbalists to treat sore gums, mouth ulcers, and to remove warts. The oil was used as a meat preservative. No known toxicity.

SAGE OIL • Obtained by steam distillation from the flowering tops of the plant believed by the Arabs to prevent dying. A pale yellow liquid that smells and tastes like camphor. Used to cover gray hair in some rinses and as an astringent in skin fresheners and steam baths. Supposedly has healing power. No known toxicity.

SAGEBRUSH • See Sesquiterpene Lactones.

SALAD OIL • Any edible vegetable oil. Dermatologists advise rubbing salad oils or fats on the skin, particularly on babies and older persons. Vegetable oils are used in commercial baby preparations, cleansers, emollient creams, face powders, hair-grooming preparations, hypoallergenic cosmetics, lipsticks, nail creams, shampoos, shaving creams, and wave sets. Nontoxic.

SALICARIA EXTRACT • **Spiked Loose Strife.** Extract of the flowering herb, *Lythrum salicaria,* that has purple or pink flowers. Used since ancient Greek times as an herb that calms nerves and soothes skin.

SALICYLAMIDE • An analgesic fungicide, and antiinflammatory agent used to soothe the skin. White to slightly pink crystalline bitter powder. Gives a sensation of warmth on the tongue. Soluble in hot water. No known toxicity.

SALICYLANILIDE • Usually made from salicylic acid with aniline. Odorless leaflets, slightly soluble in water, freely soluble in alcohol. Used as a topical antifungal agent, in antibacterial soaps, and topical preparations. In concentrated form may cause irritation of the skin and mucous membranes. When exposed to sunlight, it can cause swelling, reddening, and/or rash of the skin.

SALICYLATES • **Amyl. Phenyl. Benzyl. Menthyl. Glyceryl. Dipropylene Glycol Esters.** Salts of salicylic acid. Those who are sensitive to aspirin may also be hypersensitive to FD & C Yellow No. 5, a salicylate, and to a number of foods that naturally contain salicylate, such as almonds, apples, apple cider, apricots, blackberries, boysenberries, cherries, cloves, cucumbers, currants, gooseberries, grapes, nectarines, oil of wintergreen, oranges, peaches, pickles, plums, prunes, raisins, raspberries, strawberries, and tomatoes. Foods with added salicylates for flavoring may be ice cream, bakery goods (except bread), candy, chewing gum, soft drinks, Jello®, jams, cake mixes, and wintergreen flavors. The salts are used as sunburn preventatives and antiseptics.

SALICYLIC ACID • Occurs naturally in wintergreen leaves, sweet birch, and other plants. Synthetically prepared by heating phenol with carbon dioxide. It has a sweetish taste and is used as a preservative and antimicrobial at 0.1 to 0.5 percent in skin softeners, face masks, hair tonics, deodorants, dandruff preparations, protective creams, hair dye removers, and suntan lotions and oils. It is antipuretic (antiitch) and antiseptic. In fact, in medicine, it is used as an antimicrobial at 2 to 20 percent concentration in lotions, ointments, powders, and plasters. It is also used in making aspirin. It can be absorbed through the skin. Absorption of large amounts may cause vomiting, abdominal pain, increased respiration, acidosis, mental disturbances, and skin rashes in sensitive individuals.

SALICYLIDES • Any of several crystalline derivatives of salicylic acid (*see*) from which the water has been removed.

SALVE • An unctuous adhesive composition or substance applied to wounds or sores; a healing ointment.

SAMBUCUS EXTRACT • See Elder Flowers.

SANDALWOOD OIL • Used in perfume. It is the pale yellow, somewhat viscous, volatile oil obtained by steam distillation from the dried, ground roots and wood of the plant. A strong, warm, persistent odor, soluble in most fixed oils. Used in floral, fruit, honey, and gingerale flavorings for beverages, ice cream, ices, candy, baked goods, and chewing gum. Also used for incense and as a fumigant. May produce skin rash in the hypersensitive, especially if present in high concentrations in expensive perfumes.

SANDARAC GUM • Resin from a plant grown in Morocco. Light yellow, brittle, insoluble in water. Used in tooth cements, varnishes, and for gloss and adhesion in nail lacquers. Also used as an incense. No known toxicity.

SANGUINARIA • **Bloodroot.** Derived from the dried roots and rhizome of the North American herb. The resin is used to soothe the skin, and its reddish juice stanches blood when used in styptic pencils. No known toxicity.

SANTALOL • Alcohol from sandalwood, used in fragrances. See Sandalwood Oil.

SAPONARIA EXTRACT • **Soapwort. Fuller's Herb.** The extract is obtained from *Saponaria officinalis,* a European and Middle Asian herb that has a coarse pink or white flower and foams like soap bubbles when scratched. It is substituted for soap in shampoos. No known toxicity.

SAPONIFICATION • The making of soap, usually by adding alkalies to fat, with glycerol. To saponify is to convert to soap.

SAPONIN • Any of numerous natural glycosides—natural or synthetic compounds derived from sugars—that occur in many plants such as soapbark, soapwort, or sarsaparilla. Characterized by their ability to foam in water. Yellowish to white, acrid, hygroscopic. In powder form they can cause sneezing. Extracted from soapbark or soapwort and used chiefly as a foaming and emulsifying agent and detergent; also to reduce surface tensions, produce fine bubble lather in shaving creams, shampoos, bath oils, and dry shampoos. No known skin toxicity.

SARCOSINES • Found in starfish and sea urchins, and also formed from caffeine. Sweetish, crystalline acids used in dentifrices as an antienzyme to prevent tooth decay. Because of their excellent foaming qualities, they are also used in shampoos. No known toxicity.

SARSAPARILLA EXTRACT • The dried root from tropical American plants. Used in cola, mint, root beer, sarsaparilla, wintergreen, and birch beer flavorings for beverages, ice cream, ices, candy, and baked goods. Still used for psoriasis; formerly used for the treatment of syphilis. No known toxicity.

SASSAFRAS OIL • Used in dentifrices, perfumes, soaps, and powders to correct disagreeable odors. It is the yellow to reddish yellow, volatile oil obtained from the roots of the sassafras. It is 80 percent safrole and has the characteristic odor and taste of sassafras. Applied to insect bites and stings to relieve symptoms; also a topical antiseptic and used medicinally to break up intestinal gas. May produce dermatitis in hypersensitive individuals.

SAVORY EXTRACT • An extract of *Satureia hortensis*, an aromatic mint known as summer or winter savory. Used as a spice, particularly in baked goods.

S-CARBOXY METHYL CYSTEINE • See Cysteine.

SCULPTURED NAILS • Methyl and polymethyl methacrylates are used to form synthetic nails. Methyl methacrylate can be highly sensitizing and polymethylmethacrylate weakly so.

SCURVY GRASS EXTRACT • The extract of the leaves and flower stalks of *Cochlearia officinalis*. The bright green leaves of this northerly herb were collected and eaten in large quantities by European seamen to prevent scurvy. The plant has the strong odor of horseradish to which it is related. No known toxicity.

SD ALCOHOLS 3-A: 23-H; 38-B; 38-F; 39-B; 39-C; 40; 40-A; 40-B; 40-C146. • All ethyl alcohols denatured (*see*) in accordance with government regulations. Used as thickeners, solidifiers, and liquefiers.

SEBACTIC ACID • **Decanedioic Acid**. Colorless leaflets, sparingly soluble in water and soluble in alcohol. Manufactured by heating castor oil with alkalies or by distillation of oleic acid (*see*). The esters of sebacic acid are used as plasticizers in cosmetics. No known toxicity.

SELENIUM SULFIDE • **Selsun®.** Yellow, solid, or brownish powder, insoluble in water. Discovered in 1807 in the earth's crust. Used in antidandruff shampoos. Can severely irritate the eyes if it gets into them while hair is being washed. Occupational exposure causes pallor, nervousness, depression, garlic odor of breath, gastrointestinal disturbances, skin rash. Caused liver injury in experimental animals.

SENSITIVITY • **Hypersensitivity.** An increased reaction to substance that may be quite harmless to nonallergic persons.

SENSITIZE • To administer or expose to an antigen provoking an immune response so that, on later exposure to that antigen, a more vigorous secondary response will occur.

SEQUESTERING AGENT • A preservative which prevents physical or chemical changes affecting color, flavor, texture, or appearance of a product. Ethylenediamine Tetraaceticacid (EDTA) is an example. It prevents adverse effects of metals in shampoos.

SERINE • An amino acid (*see*), nonessential, taken as a dietary supplement. It is a constituent of many proteins. See Proteins.

SERPENTARIA EXTRACT • **Snakeroot. Snakeweed.** Extracted from the roots of *Rauwolfia serpentina*, its yellow rods turn red upon drying. Used in the manufacture of resins, and as a bitter tonic. No known toxicity when applied to the skin but can affect heart and blood pressure when ingested.

SERUM ALBUMIN • The major protein component of blood plasma derived form bovines. Used as a moisturizing ingredient.

SERUM PROTEINS • See Serum Albumin.

SESAME • **Seeds and Oils.** The edible seeds of an East Indian herb, which has a rosy or white flower. The seeds, which flavor bread, crackers, cakes, confectionery, and other products, yield a pale yellow, bland tasting, almost odorless oil used in the manufacture of margarine. The oil has been used as a laxative and skin softener, and contains elements active against lice. May cause allergic reactions, primarily contact dermatitis.

SESQUITERPENE LACTONES • In recent years, more than 600 plants have been identified as containing these substances and more than 50 are known to cause allergic contact dermatitis. Among them are arnica, chamomile, and yarrow (*see all*).

SETTING LOTIONS • Wave-setting lotions, which women apply before rolling their hair in rollers or pins, depend on the hair-swelling ability of the water contained in them and the gum film that dries and holds the hair in place. The natural gums commonly used in such preparations are tragacanth, karaya, acacia, and quince seed, as well as sodium alginate from seaweed. Synthetic gums such as sodium carboxymethyl cellulose and methylcellulose are also used but tend to flake when dry (*see all*). A typical setting lotion may consist of karaya gum dissolved in ethyl alcohol and then mixed with water, glycerin, and perfume. A generally harmless product, but there have been some cases of scalp irritation reported to the FDA.

SHADDOCK EXTRACT • An extract of *Citrus grandis* and named for a 17th-century sea captain who brought the seeds back from the East Indies to Barbados. Shaddock is a very large, thick-rinded, pear-shaped citrus fruit related to and largely replaced by the grapefruit. No known toxicity.

SHAMPOOS • Shampoos are of relatively recent origin because people used to wash their hair with soap. The original products were made of coconut oil and castile soap. In 1930 the liquid detergent shampoos were introduced, followed by the cream type, and then the liquid cream shampoos. Today, shampoos are packaged in plastic tubes or bottles, aerosol cans, jars, and glass. They have various special purposes, such as mending split ends or curing dandruff. They contain a variety of ingredients ranging from eggs to herbs. A soap shampoo today still may contain about 25 percent coconut oil, some olive oil, about 15 percent alcohol, and 50 percent glycerol and water. The soapless shampoo cream may contain 50 percent sodium lauryl sulfate, some sodium stearate (*see both*), and about 40 percent water. The liquid shampoo is the most popular today and usually contains a detergent such as triethanolamine dodecylbenzene sulfonate, ethanolamide of lauric acid (*see both*), perfume, and water. Cream shampoos may have the same ingredients as the liquid in different proportions to obtain a cream, and they usually contain lanolin. Special shampoos contain such things as dehydrated egg powder or herbs. Opacifying agents such as stearyl and cetyl alcohol (*see both*) may be added to the cream lotion types. Various sequestering agents (*see*) may be used to make the water soft to remove the film, and to make the hair shinier. Various finishing agents such as mineral oil and lanolin may be added to make the hair lustrous. Water-absorbing materials such as glycerin and sorbitol (*see*) are used as conditioning agents; these two increase the water absorption of the hair and make it more pliable and less brittle. Preservatives such as *p*-hydroxybenzoic acid and sodium hexametaphosphate (*see both*) may also be used. Ingestion of detergents can cause gastric irritation. Shampoos are among the most frequently cited in complaints to the FDA. Reports include eye irritation, scalp irritation, tangled hair, swelling of hands, face, and arms, and split and fuzzy hair.

SHARK-LIVER OIL • A rich source of Vitamin A believed to be beneficial to the skin. A brown fatty oil obtained from the livers of the large predatory fish. Used in lubricating creams and lotions. No known toxicity.

SHAVING CREAMS • Dry hair is hard and difficult to cut with a razor. The object of a shaving cream is to make the hair softer and easier to shave. Brushless shave creams are emulsions of oil and water, really vanishing creams rather than soaps. Not as efficient as the lathering type, they usually require that the beard (or legs) be washed with soap and water. Shaving creams, which must be applied, are soaps with small but copious bubbles known as lather. They can be applied with a brush or with an aerosol. Aerosol shaving creams produce foam. This foam is applied directly to the beard and is the most popular form used today. Some men still use the older shaving creams offered in a cake or stick. The American Medical Association recommends that men with dry or soap-sensitive skin use brushless shave creams that, because of their emollient properties, soothe the skin and do not dry it out. Men with oily skin, on the other hand, should use the lather-type cream applied by aerosol or brush. The AMA also points out that thorough washing and rinsing of the face in hot water or applying a hot wet towel for a few minutes before shaving will soften a beard as well as any cream.

SHAVING LOTIONS • **Preshave and After-Shave.** Most preshave lotions are designed to be used before shaving with an electric razor. Some are made for a regular razor and usually contain coconut oil, fatty acids, triethanolamine, alkyl arylpolyethylene glycol ether (a dispersant), water and perfume. Preshave preparations temporarily tighten the skin to facilitate cutting the hairs. Electric razor preshave products may contain aluminum phenolsulfonate, menthol, camphor (*see all*), water, and perfume dissolved in alcohol. An oily type of preshave lotion may contain isopropyl myristate or isopropyl palmitate (*see*), 74.5 percent alcohol, and perfume. After-shave lotions are supposed to soothe the skin, which may have been irritated by shaving. The earliest were merely substitutes for water. At the end of the nineteenth century talcum powder appeared among men's shaving products. Then barbershop preparations such as bay rum and witch hazel came into use. By 1916 manufacturers were actively promoting men's toiletries, and today perfume is as common in men's products as it is in women's. After-shave lotions fall into two categories: alcoholic and nonalcoholic. The most common ingredients of the alcoholic type are, in addition to alcohol, glycerin, water, certified color, and perfume. Menthol may be added to give that cool feeling to the skin. Some antiseptics such as hexachlorophene, or quaternary ammonium compounds may also be added (*see all*). Alum may be used for its astringent-styptic effect; also allantoin (*see*) to promote rapid healing of razor nicks. The after-shave nonalcoholic product resembles hand lotion. In fact, hand lotion may be substituted by the consumer. Such products may be prepared from stearic acid, triethanolamine, cetyl alcohol, glycerin (*see all*), distilled water, and very small amounts of lanolin and a preservative such as a *p*-hydroxybenzoic acid (*see*). Many other fats, waxes, and emulsifying agents may be added. Antiseptics and the soothing allantoin, as well as coloring and perfume, may be incorporated into this type of preparation. However, the best beard softener is still water. Reports of problems to the FDA include the product igniting on the face from a lighted cigarette, face irritations, burned skin and peeling, and eye irritation.

SHEA BUTTER • The natural fat obtained from the fruit of the karite tree, *Butyrosperum parkii*. Also called karite butter, it is chiefly used as a food but also used in soap and candles. No known toxicity.

SHEA BUTTER UNSAPONIFIABLES • The fraction of Shea Butter which is not saponified during processing, and is not turned into fatty alcohol.

SHELLAC • A resinous excretion of certain insects feeding on appropriate host trees, usually in India. As processed for marketing, the lacca, which is formed by the insects, may be mixed with small amounts of arsenic trisulfide for color and with rosin. White shellac is free of arsenic. Shellac is used as a candy glaze and polish; in hair lacquer and on jewelry and accessories. May cause allergic contact dermatitis. See Clothing.

SHELLAC WAX • Bleached refined shellac. See Shellac.

SHEPHERD'S PURSE EXTRACT • Extract of the herb, *Capsella bursapastoris*. A member of the mustard family, it is a white-flowered, weedy herb. Its tiny blossoms grow in the form of a cross. Pungent and bitter, it was valued for its astringent properties by early American settlers. Cotton moistened with its juice was used to stop nose bleeds.

SHORTENINGS • See Salad Oils.

SIENNA • Used to color face powder. It is made from any of the various earthy substances that are brownish-yellow when raw, and orange-red to reddish-brown when burnt. They are in general darker in color and more transparent in oils than ochers. No longer authorized for use in cosmetics by the FDA.

SILICA • A white powder, slightly soluble in water, that occurs abundantly in nature and is 12 percent of all rocks. Sand is a silica. Upon drying and heating in a vacuum, hard, transparent, porous granules are formed that are used in absorbent material in toilet preparations, particularly skin protectant creams. Also used as a coloring agent. See Silicones.

SILICATES • Salts or esters derived from silicic acid (*see*). Any of numerous, insoluble, complex metal salts that contain silicon and oxygen and that constitute the largest group of minerals, and with quartz made up of the greater part of the earth's crust (as rocks, soils, and clays). Contained in building materials such as cement, concrete, bricks, and glass. No known toxicity.

SILICEOUS EARTH • Purified silica (*see*) by boiling with diluted acid and washing through a filter. Used in face masks. No known toxicity.

SILICIC ACID • **Silica Gel.** White gelatinous substance obtained by the action of acids on sodium silicate (*see*). Odorless, tasteless, inert, white fluffy powder when dried. Insoluble in water and acids. Absorbs water readily. Used in face powders, dentifrices, creams, and talcum powders as an opacifier. Soothing to skin. No known toxicity.

SILICONES • Any of a large group of fluid oils, rubbers, resins, and compounds derived from silica (*see*), and which are water repellent, skin adherent, and stable over a wide range of temperatures. Used in after-shave preparations, hair-waving preparations, nail driers, hair straighteners, hand lotions, and protective creams. Used commercially in waterproofing and lubrication. No known toxicity when used externally.

SILK AMINO ACIDS • The mixture of amino acids (*see*) resulting in liquefying silk. Used in hair sprays. No known toxicity.

SILK POWDER • Coloring agent in face powders and soaps obtained from the secretion of silkworms. A white solid, which is insoluble in water. Causes severe allergic skin reactions and when inhaled, or ingested, systemic reactions.

SILVER • White metal not attacked by water or atmospheric oxygen. Used as a catalyst (*see*) and as a germicide and coloring in cosmetics. Prolonged absorption of silver compounds can lead to grayish-blue discoloration of the skin. May be irritating to the skin and mucous membranes. Permanently listed for use in nail polish in amounts not to exceed 1 percent.

SILVER BROMIDE • Yellowish, odorless powder; darkens on exposure to light. Used in photography, as a topical antiinfective agent and astringent, and in the production of mirror finishing. May cause contact dermatitis.

SILVER NITRATE • A germicide, antiseptic, and astringent in cosmetics and a coloring agent in metallic hair dyes. Odorless, colorless, transparent, and poisonous. A white crystalline salt, it was used as a nineteenth-century hair dye. It darkens with exposure to light in the presence of organic matter. Silver combines readily with protein and turns brown. Disadvantages are that it may cause unpleasant off-shades and makes the hair stiff. It is also adversely affected by permanent waving. On the skin, it may be caustic and irritating. If swallowed, it causes severe gastronintestinal symptoms and frequently death.

SILVER SULFATE • See Silver Nitrate.

SIMETHICONE • An antifoam compound, a silicone oil, white viscous, liquid. Used as an ointment base ingredient. A topical drug vehicle and skin protectant. Used medicinally to break up intestinal gas. No known toxicity.

SINGLE FLORALS • A basic of perfume that has a definite fragrance of one flower, such as lily of the valley, carnation, or rose. This does not mean that only one note (see Body-Note) is used. Such perfumes require skillful blending to surround the desired single floral with other notes to give it power and beauty without intruding on the single theme.

SISAL • **Agave Lechuguilla.** A wax and intermediate (*see*) obtained from a plant native to the Mexican desert. The dust is irritating to the respiratory tract and may cause allergic asthma. Skin toxicity unknown.

SKATOLE • Used in perfumery as a fixative (*see*). A constituent of beetroot, feces, and coal tar. Gives a violet color when mixed with iron and sulfuric acid. No known toxicity in humans.

SKIN BLEACH • There are a variety of products for removing freckles, age spots (chloasma), flat moles, postinflammatory changes, and even naturally dark skin. The original bleaching creams contained ammoniated mercury (*see*), and many of today's creams still do. Mercury may produce some temporary lightening of the skin by causing sloughing of the outer skin, thus reducing the number of dark pigment cells near the surface. Mercury frequently causes allergic reactions and can have adverse effects internally even though it is only applied to the skin. More efficient bleaching creams today use hydroquinone (*see*), which may cause some lightening of the skin in light- but not in dark-skinned blacks. After treatment is stopped, repigmentation almost always occurs. Some powerful hydroquinone products can produce blotches, allergic reactions, and other undesirable side effects. According to the American Medical Association, bleach products are useful for treating limited areas where excessive pigmentation is the result of an abnormal process. For instance, they may be of limited use in treating melasma, "the mask of pregnancy," that is, the excessive skin pigmentation fairly common in pregnant women and women taking birth control pills. The use of bleach cream is a long-term process and often the only benefit is from the lubricating effect of the cream base, which relieves dryness of the skin. The bases of the creams and ointments are usually petrolatum, mineral oil, lanolin, or vanishing creams of the stearate type (*see all*). Active ingredients, carriers, and scents include acetic acid, alcohol, bismuth compounds, citric acid, potassium carbonate, potassium chlorate, rose water, borate, sugar, benzoin, zinc oxide, and zinc peroxide (*see all*). Among problems reported to the FDA were symptoms of mercury poisoning, swelling of the face and neck, jerking of hands, skin rash, burns, and stomach distress. Mercury was banned from cosmetics in 1973.

SKIN BRACER • There is little difference between shaving lotions (*see*) and skin bracers. A skin bracer may have a high alcohol content and may also be used as a body refresher after a bath or shower. It is made mostly of water, alcohol, and perfume. Toxcity depends upon ingredients.

SKIN FRESHENER • Fresheners are weaker than astringents. They are usually clear liquids designed to make the skin feel cool, tight, and refreshed. May contain about 60 percent witch hazel, about 15 percent camphorated alcohol, 24 percent alcohol, and one percent citric acid. May also contain arnica, bay rum, boric acid, chamomile, floral scents, glycerin, lactic acid, magnesia, menthol, lavender oil, phosphoric acid, talc, benzoin, and aluminum salts (*see all*). Depending upon the ingredients, may cause respiratory or allergic contact dermatitis.

SLIPPERY ELM BARK • Bark from the North American elm. Fragrant and sticky, it contains much mucilage and powder. Mixed with hot water, it forms a fawn-colored mass. Used as a demulcent (*see*). No known toxicity.

SOAP • The oldest cleanser, usually a mixture of sodium salts of various fatty acids. In liquid soaps, potassium instead of sodium salts is used. Bar soaps vary in contents from brand to brand, depending on the fats or oils used. Sodium hydroxide makes a strong soap, fatty acids, a mild soap. So-called ''neutral soaps'' actually are alkaline, with pH around 10 (compared to skin, which is 5 to 6.5 pH) when dissolved in water. Liquid soaps use potassium instead of sodium. Soaps are usually in toothpastes, tooth powder, and shaving creams. Soap is usually made by the saponification of a vegetable oil with caustic soda. Hard soap consists largely of sodium oleate or sodium palmitate and is used medicinally as an antiseptic, detergent, or suppository. Many people are allergic to soaps. They may also be drying to the skin, irritate the eyes and cause rashes, depending upon ingredients.

SOAPWORT • **Fuller's Herb. Saponaria.** A European and Middle Asian perennial herb that has a coarse pink or white flower and foams like soap bubbles when scratched. Substituted for soap in shampoos. No known toxicity.

SODIUM ACETATE • **Sodium Salt of Acetic Acid.** A preservative and alkalizer in cosmetics. Transparent crystals highly soluble in water. In industrial forms, it is used in photography and dyeing processes and in foot warmers because of its heat retention ability. Medicinally, it is used as an alkalizer and as a diuretic to reduce body water. No known toxicity.

SODIUM ACRYLATE/VINYL ALCOHOL • **Acrylic Acid. Polymer with Vinyl Alcohol Sodium Salt.** See Polyvinyls.

SODIUM ALGINATE • An emollient used in baby lotions, hair lacquers, wave sets, and shaving creams. It is the sodium salt of alginic acid extracted from brown seaweed. Occurs as a white to yellowish fibrous or granular powder, nearly odorless, and tasteless. Dissolves in water to form a viscous, colloidal solution and is used in cosmetics as a stabilizer, thickener, and emulsifier. No known toxicity.

SODIUM ALUM • See Alum.

SODIUM ALUMINUM ASCORBATE • See Ascorbic Acid.

SODIUM ALUMINUM CHLOROHYDROXYL LACTATE • The sodium salt of lactic acid and aluminum chlorohydrate (*see both*).

SODIUM ARSENATE • Very poisonous white or grayish powder, it is used in the manufacture of arsenical soap for use on skins, for treating vines against certain scale diseases and as a topical insecticide for animals. May cause contact dermatitis.

SODIUM ASCORBATE • See Ascorbic Acid.

SODIUM BENZOATE • An antiseptic and preservative used in eye creams, vanishing creams, and toothpastes. White odorless powder or crystals with a sweet, antiseptic taste. Once used medicinally for rheumatism and tonsillitis. Now used as a preservative in margarine, codfish, and bottled soft drinks. No known toxicity for external use.

SODIUM BICARBONATE • **Bicarbonate of Soda. Baking Soda.** Used in effervescent bath salts, mouthwashes, and skin-soothing powders. It is an alkali. Its white crystals or powder are used in baking powder as a gastric antacid, as an alkaline wash and to treat burns. Used also as a neutralizer for butter, cream, milk, and ice cream. Essentially harmless to the skin but when used on very dry skin in preparations that evaporate, it leaves an alkaline residue that may cause irritation.

SODIUM BISCHLOROPHENYL SULFAMINE • **Sodium Bischlorophenyl.** See Quaternary Ammonium Compounds.

SODIUM BISULFATE • Colorless or white crystals fused in water. Disinfectant, used in the manufacture of soaps, perfumes, foods, and pickling compounds. See Sodium Bisulfite.

SODIUM BISULFITE • **Sodium Acid Sulfite.** An inorganic salt. It is a white powder with a disagreeable taste. It is used as an antiseptic, an antifermentative in cosmetic creams, mouthwashes, bleaches, perfumes, and hair dyes, to treat parasitic skin diseases, and to remove warts. In its aqueous solution, it is an acid. Concentrated solutions are highly irritating to the skin and mucous membranes. Sodium bisulfite can cause changes in the genetic material of bacteria and is a suspect mutagen. Not permitted in meats and other sources of Vitamin B_1. A strong irritant to the skin and tissue. The Select Committee on GRAS substances found it did not present a hazard at present use levels but that additional data would be needed if higher use occurred.

SODIUM BORATE • Used in freckle lotions, nail whiteners, liquefying (cleansing) creams, and eye lotions as a preservative and emulsifier. Hard, odorless powder insoluble in water, it is a weak antiseptic and astringent for mucous membranes. Used also in bath salts, foot preparations, scalp lotions, permanent wave solutions, and hair-setting lotions. Has a drying effect on the skin and may cause irritation. Continued use of a shampoo containing it will cause the hair to become dry and brittle.

SODIUM BROMATE • An inorganic salt. Colorless, odorless crystals that liberate oxygen. Used as a solvent. See Potassium Bromate for toxicity.

SODIUM BUTYOXYETHOXY ACETATE • See Surfactants.

SODIUM C12-15 ALCOHOL SULFATE • See Sulfonated Oils.

SODIUM C12-18 ALCOHOL SULFATE • The sodium salt of the sulfate of a mixture of synthetic fatty alcohols with 12 to 18 carbons in the alkyl chain. See Sulfonated Oils.

SODIUM C12-15 ALKOXYPROPYL IMINODIPROPIONATE • The sodium salt of propionic acid (*see*).

SODIUM C4-12 OLEFIN/MALEIC ACID COPOLYMER • **Kao Soap.** The sodium salt of a polymer synthesized from C4-12 olefins and maleic anhydride (*see*). Used as a demulcent.

SODIUM C14-16 OLEFIN SULFONATE • See Sulfonated Oils.

SODIUM C11-15 PARETH-7 CARBOXYLATE • The sodium salt of C11-15 Pareth. Used as a gelling agent.

SODIUM C12-13 PARETH SULFATE • The sodium salt of sulfated polyethylene glycol ether of a mixture of synthetic alcohols. See Polyethylene Glycol.

SODIUM C12-15 PARETH-6 CARBOXYLATE • The sodium salt of the organic acid. See Alkanolamines.

SODIUM C12-15 PARETH-7 CARBOXYLATE • The sodium salt of C12-15 Pareth-7 Carboxylic Acid. Used as a gelling agent.

SODIUM C12-15 PARETH SULFATE • The sodium salt of a sulfated polyethylene glycol ether of a mixture of fatty alcohols. See Sulfated Oils.

SODIUM C14-17 SEC ALCOHOL SULFANATE • See Sulfonated Oils.

SODIUM CAPRYL LACTYLATE • See Palm Oil.

SODIUM CAPRYLATE • See Palm Oil.

SODIUM CARBONATE • **Soda Ash.** Small odorless crystals or powder that occurs in nature in ores and is found in lake brines or seawater. Absorbs water from the air. Has an alkaline taste and is used as an antacid and reagent in permanent wave solutions, soaps, mouthwashes, shampoos, foot preparations, bath salts, and vaginal douches. It is the cause of scalp, forehead and hand rash when the hypersensitive use cosmetics containing it.

SODIUM CARBONATE PEROXIDE • See Sodium Carbonate.

SODIUM CARBOXYMETHYL CELLULOSE • Used in setting lotions. It is an artificial gum that dries and leaves a film on the hair. Prepared by treating alkali cellulose with sodium chloroacetate. See Cellulose Gums.

SODIUM CARRAGEENAN • Sodium salt of carrageenan (*see*).

SODIUM CASEINATE • The soluble form of milk protein in which casein is partially neutralized with sodium hydroxide and used as a texturizer. GRAS.

SODIUM CASTORATE • The sodium salt of the fatty acids derived from castor oil (*see*).

SODIUM CETEARYL SULFATE • The sodium salt of a blend of cetyl and stearyl alcohol (*see both*) and sulfuric acid ester. A wax used as a surface-active agent (*see*). No known toxicity.

SODIUM CETYL SULFATE • Marketed in the form of a paste. Contains alcohol, sodium sulfate (*see*), and water. A surface-active agent (*see*). No known toxicity.

SODIUM CHLORIDE • Common table salt. Used as an astringent and antiseptic in mouthwashes, dentifrices, bubble baths, soap, bath salts, and eye lotions. It consists of opaque white crystals. Odorless, with a characteristic salty taste, and absorbs water. Used topically to treat inflamed lesions. Diluted solutions are not considered irritating, but upon drying, water is drawn from the skin and may produce irritation. Salt workers have a great deal of skin rashes. Also reported to irritate the roots of the teeth when used for a long time in dentifrices.

SODIUM CHONDROITIN SULFATE • Present in soft connective tissue, it is abundant in skin, arterial walls, and heart valves. It is used to reduce fats and as a flexible connector between protein molecules. No known toxicity.

SODIUM CITRATE • White odorless crystals, granules, or powder with a cool salty taste. Stable in air. Used as a sequestering agent (*see*) to remove trace metals in solutions and as an alkalizer in cosmetic products. No known skin toxicity.

SODIUM COCAMINOPROPIONATE • See Coconut Oil.

SODIUM COCOATE • See Coconut Oil.

SODIUM COCO-HYDROLYZED ANIMAL PROTEIN • The sodium salt of the condensation product of coconut acid chloride and hydrolyzed animal protein. See Hydrolyzed Animal Protein.

SODIUM COCOMONOGLYCERIDE SULFATE • See Coconut Oil.
SODIUM COCOMONOGLYCERIDE SULFONATE • See Sulfonated Oils.
SODIUM COCOYL GLUTAMATE • A softener. See Glutamate.
SODIUM COCOYL ISETHIONATE • The sodium salt of the coconut fatty acid ester of isethionic acid. See Coconut Oil.
SODIUM COCOYL SARCOSINATE • See Sarcosines.
SODIUM CUMENESULFONATE • A solvent. See Benzene and Phenol.
SODIUM DECETH SULFATE • See Decyl Alcohol.
SODIUM DECYL SULFATE • See Sodium Decylbenzenesulfonate.
SODIUM DECYLBENZENESULFONATE • Used in commercial detergents. May cause skin irritations.
SODIUM DEHYDROACETATE • **Dehydroacetic Acid.** A preservative; white, odorless, powdered, with an acrid taste. Used as a plasticizer, fungicide, and bacteria killer in cosmetics; also an antienzyme ingredient in dentifrices, allegedly to prevent decay, and a kidney tube blocking agent. Can cause impaired kidney function. Large doses can cause vomiting, ataxia, and confusion. There are no apparent allergic skin reactions.
SODIUM DIHYDROXYETHYL GLYCINATE • See Dioctyl Sodium Sulfosuccinate.
SODIUM DNA • The sodium salt of deoxyribonucleic acid. The genetic code of cells used in "youth" creams.
SODIUM DODECYLBENZENESULFONATE • An anionic detergent used in cosmetic bath products, and in creams. It may irritate the skin. Will cause vomiting if swallowed. See Sodium Lauryl Sulfate.
SODIUM ERYTHROBATE • A white odorless powder used as an antioxidant in cosmetics. No known toxicity.
SODIUM-2-ETHYHEXYLSULFOACETATE • Light, cream-colored flakes, water soluble, good foam maker, and good in hard water. Used as a solubilizing agent, particularly for soapless shampoo compositions. See Quaternary Ammonium Compounds.
SODIUM FLUORIDE • Used in toothpastes to prevent tooth decay and as an insecticide, disinfectant, and preservative in cosmetics. Can cause nausea and vomiting when ingested and even death, depending upon the dose. Tooth enamel mottling has also been reported. No known skin toxicity.
SODIUM GLUTAMATE • The monosodium salt of the L-form of glutamic acid. See Glutamic Acid.
SODIUM GLYCERYL OLEATE PHOSPHATE • See Glyceryl Monostearate.

SODIUM HEXYLMETAPHOSPHATE • **Graham's Salt.** Used in bath salts, bubble baths, permanent wave neutralizers, and shampoos. An emulsifier, sequestering agent (*see*), and texturizer. Used in foods and potable water to prevent scale formation and corrosion. Because it keeps calcium, magnesium, and iron salts in solution, it is an excellent water softener and detergent. No known toxicity to the skin.

SODIUM HYALURONATE • The sodium salt of hyaluronic acid. From the fluid in the eye, it is used as a gelling agent. No known toxicity.

SODIUM HYDROGENATED TALLOW GLUTAMATE • See Glutamate and Tallow.

SODIUM HYDROSULFATE • **Sodium Dithionate.** A bacterial inhibitor and antifermentative. Slight odor. White or grayish-white crystalline powder that oxidizes in air. No known toxicity to the skin.

SODIUM HYDROXIDE • **Caustic Soda. Soda Lye.** An alkali and emulsifier in liquid face powders, soaps, shampoos, cuticle removers, hair straighteners, shaving soaps, and creams. White or nearly white pellets, flakes, or sticks. Readily absorbs water. Also a modifier for food starch, a glazing agent for pretzels, and a peeling agent for tubers and fruits. The FDA banned use of more than 10 percent in household liquid drain cleaners. If too much alkali is used, dermatitis of the scalp may occur. Its ingestion causes vomiting, prostration, and collapse. Inhalation causes lung damage.

SODIUM HYDROXYMETHANE SULFONATE • **Sodium Formaldehyde Bisulfite.** See Formaldehyde.

SODIUM HYDROXYMETHYLGLYCINATE • See Glycinate.

SODIUM IODATE • Used in dusting powder and to soothe the skin. White crystalline powder. Antiseptic, particularly to the mucous membranes. No known skin toxicity.

SODIUM IODIDE • White, odorless, water-absorbing crystals. Slowly becomes brown on exposure to air. See Sodium Iodate.

SODIUM ISETHIONATE • See Sodium Hydroxide.

SODIUM ISOSTEARETH-6 CARBOXYLATE • See Isostearic Acid.

SODIUM ISOSTEROYL LACTYLATE • The sodium salt of isostearic acid and lactyl lactate. See Stearic Acid and Lactic Acid.

SODIUM LACTATE • Plasticizer substitute for glycerin. Colorless, thick, odorless liquid miscible with water, alcohol, and glycerin. Solution is neutral. No known toxicity.

SODIUM LANETH SULFATE • See Lanolin.

SODIUM LAURAMINOPROPIONATE • See Propionic Acid.

SODIUM LAURATE • See Sodium Lauryl Sulfate.

SODIUM LAURETH-4 PHOSPHATE • See Sodium Lauryl Sulfate.

SODIUM LAURETH SULFATE • The sodium salt of sulfated ethoxylated lauryl alcohol, widely used as a water softener, and in baby and other nonirritating shampoos as a wetting agent and cleansing agent. See also Surfactants.
SODIUM LAURETH-5, -7, AND -12 SULFATES • See Sodium Laureth Sulfate.
SODIUM LAUROYL GLUTAMATE • A softener. See Glutamate.
SODIUM LAUROYL ISETHIONATE • **Sodium Lauryl Isethionate.** One of the main ingredients in Dove®, it is a mild synthetic soap. See Surfactants.
SODIUM LAUROYL SARCOSINATE • See Sarcosines.
SODIUM LAUROYLISETHIONATE • See Sodium Lauryl Sulfate.
SODIUM LAURYL BENZENE SULFONATE • See Sodium Lauryl Sulfate.
SODIUM LAURYL SULFATE • A detergent, wetting agent, and emulsifier used in bubble baths, emollient creams, cream depilatories, hand lotions, cold permanent waves, soapless shampoos, and toothpastes. Prepared by sulfonation of lauryl alcohol followed by neutralization with sodium carbonate. Faint fatty odor; also emulsifies fats. May cause drying of the skin because of its degreasing ability, and is an irritant to the skin.
SODIUM LAURYL SULFOACETATE • See Sodium Lauryl Sulfate.
SODIUM LIGNOSULFONATE • The sodium salt of polysulfonated lignin derived from wood. It is used as a dispersing agent. A tan, free-flowing powder, it is also used as an emulsifier, stabilizer, and cleaning agent. No known toxicity.
SODIUM MAGNESIUM FLUOROSILICATE • An inorganic salt used in enamel, as an insecticide, and as a rat poison. Used in shampoos to kill lice. See Silicates.
SODIUM MAGNESIUM SILICATES • See Silicates.
SODIUM METABISULFITE • An inorganic salt. A bacterial inhibitor. Used as an antifermentative in sugar, and a preservative for fruit and vegetables. See Bisulfites.
SODIUM METAPHOSPHATE • **Graham's Salts.** Used in dental polishing agents, detergents, water softeners, sequestrants, emulsifiers, food additives, and textile laundering. See Sodium Hexametaphosphate.
SODIUM METASILICATE • An alkali usually prepared from sand and soda ash. Used in detergents. Caustic substance, corrosive to the skin, harmful if swallowed, and cause of severe eye irritations. Preserves eggs in egg shampoos.
SODIUM METHYL NAPHTHALENE SULFONATE • Used in solutions

for peeling fruits and vegetables with a water rinse and in detergents. See Sulfonated Oils.

SODIUM METHYL OLEOYL TAURATE • See Ox Bile.

SODIUM *n*-METHYL-*n*-OLEYL TAURATE • See Ox Bile.

SODIUM MONOFLUOROPHOSPHATE • See Sodium Fluoride.

SODIUM MONOUNDECYLENAMIDO MEA-SULFOSUCCINATE • See Dioctyl Sodium Sulfosuccinate; Sulfonated Oils.

SODIUM MYRETH SULFATE • See Myristyl Alcohol.

SODIUM MYRISTATE • See Myristic Acid.

SODIUM MYRISTOYL ISETHIONATE • See Myristic Acid.

SODIUM MYRISTOYL SARCOSINATE • See Sarcosine.

SODIUM MYRISTYL SULFATE • See Myristyl Alcohol.

SODIUM m-NITROBENZENESULFONATE • See Benzene and Phenol.

SODIUM NONOXYNOL-6 PHOSPHATE OR -9 PHOSPHATE • A complex mixture of esters of phosphoric acid and nonoxynol (*see both*).

SODIUM NONOXYNOL-1 OR -4 SULFATE • See Sulfonated Oils.

SODIUM OCTYL SULFATE • See Sulfonated Oils.

SODIUM OLEATE • **Sodium Salt of Oleic Acid.** White powder, fatty odor, alkaline. Used in soaps. No known toxicity.

SODIUM OLEOYL ISETHIONATE • See Sulfonated Oils.

SODIUM OLETH-7 OR -8 PHOSPHATE • The sodium salts of the phosphate esters of oleth used in mild detergents such as baby shampoos. No known toxicity.

SODIUM OXALATE • **Sodium Salt of Oxalic Acid.** White odorless crystalline powder used as an intermediate (*see*), in hair dyes, and as a texturizer. Toxic when ingested and may be irritating to the skin.

SODIUM OXYNOL-2 ETHANE SULFONATE • See Sulfonated Oils.

SODIUM PALMITATE • Sodium salt of palmitic acid (*see*).

SODIUM PARETH-15-7 OR 25-7 CARBOXYLATE • See Fatty Alcohol.

SODIUM PARETH-23 OR -25 SULFATE • See Fatty Alcohol.

SODIUM PCA • A naturally occurring component of human skin that is believed to be in part responsible for its moisture binding capacity. It is highly water absorbing and at high humidity dissolves in its own water hydration. Application of this compound to the skin as a humectant (*see*) is claimed to increase softness. No known toxicity.

SODIUM PCA METHYSILANOL • See Sodium PCA.

SODIUM PERBORATE • White crystals soluble in water, used as a reagent (*see*), antiseptic, deodorant bleach, and in dentifrices as a tooth whitener; also in foot baths and detergents. Ulcerations of the mouth have been reported in its use in dentifrices. Strong solutions that are very alkaline are irritating if permitted on the skin.

SODIUM PERCARBONATE • Stable, crystalline powder derived from sodium carbonate and hydrogen peroxide (*see both*). Used as a denture cleaner and mild antiseptic. Toxic by ingestion. See Peroxide.

SODIUM PEROXIDE • Yellowish-white powder, absorbs hydrogen and carbon dioxide from air. Derived from carbon dioxide heated in aluminum trays. A strong oxidizing agent and irritant. Used to purify water and germicidal soaps.

SODIUM PERSULFATE • Oxidizing agent that promotes emulsion used in hair-waving solution. An inorganic salt; a crystalline powder which decomposes in moisture and warmth. Can cause allergic reactions in the hypersensitive.

SODIUM PHENATE • See Phenol.

SODIUM PHENOXIDE • See Phenol.

SODIUM o-PHENYL PHENATE • **Sodium Salt of o-Phenylphenol.** Antiseptic, germicide, fungicide, and preservative used in cosmetic creams and lotions. Yellow flakes or powder with a slight soap odor. Soluble in water, alcohol, and acetone. A skin irritant. Regarded as more effective than phenol (*see*) and cresol (*see*) because it has greater germ-killing power, may be used in smaller concentrations, and is less irritating to the skin, although it is often considered toxic by some cosmetic companies for use in products.

SODIUM PHOSPHATE • Buffer and effervescent used in manufacture of nail enamels and detergents. White, crystalline or granular powder, stable in air. Without water, it can be irritating to the skin but has no known skin toxicity.

SODIUM PICRAMATE • **Sodium Salt of Picramic Acid.** See Picramic Acid.

SODIUM POLYMETHACRYLATE • See Acrylates.

SODIUM POLYNAPHTHALENE SULFONATE • See Sulfonated Oils.

SODIUM POLYSTYRENE SULFONATE • See Polystyrene.

SODIUM PROPIONATE • Colorless or transparent, odorless crystals that gather water in moist air. Used as a preservative in cosmetics and foodstuffs to prevent mold and fungus. It has been used to treat fungal infections of the skin, but can cause allergic reactions.

SODIUM PYRITHIONE • **Sodium Omadine®.** Sodium salt of pyrithione zinc derivative. Used as a fungicide and bacteria killer. Used in dandruff shampoos to control dandruff and as an antibacterial in soaps and detergents. No known toxicity.

SODIUM PYROPHOSPHATE PEROXIDE • White powder, water soluble, used as a denture cleanser, in dentifrices, household laundry detergents, and as an antiseptic. See Hydrogen Peroxide.

SODIUM RIBOFLAVIN PHOSPHATE • A B vitamin containing sodium phosphate (*see*).

SODIUM RIBONUCLEIC ACID • **SRNA.** The basic instructions in the cell that tell it how to behave. Since it is believed that the RNA in the cell may make mistakes as we age, it is added to some anti-aging creams.

SODIUM RICINOLEATE • The sodium salt of Ricinoleic Acid (*see*).

SODIUM SACCHARIN • An artificial sweetener in dentifrices, mouthwashes, and lipsticks. In use since 1879. Pound for pound it is 300 times as sweet as natural sugar but leaves a bitter aftertaste. It was used along with cyclamates in the experiments that led to the ban on cyclamates in 1969. The FDA has proposed restricting saccharin to 15 milligrams per day for each kilogram of body weight or one gram a day for a 150-pound person. On the FDA's priority list for further safety testing.

SODIUM SALICYLATE • A white, odorless, crystalline powder used in shaving creams and in sunscreen lotions. Becomes pinkish upon long exposure to light; also used to lower fever and kill pain in animals. Mild antiseptic, analgesic, and preservative. May cause nasal allergy. See Salicylates.

SODIUM SARCOSINATE • The sodium salt of sarcosine. See Sarcosines.

SODIUM SEQUICARBONATE • White crystals, flakes, or powder produced from sodium carbonate. Soluble in water. Used as an alkalizer in bath salts, shampoos, tooth powders, and soaps. Irritating to the skin and mucous membranes. May cause allergic reaction in the hypersensitive.

SODIUM SILICATE • **Water Glass.** An anticaking agent preserving eggs, detergents in soaps, depilatories, and protective creams. Consists of colorless to white or grayish-white crystallike pieces or lumps. These silicates are almost insoluble in cold water. Strongly alkaline. As a topical antiseptic can be irritating and caustic to the skin and mucous membranes. If swallowed it causes vomiting and diarrhea.

SODIUM SILICOALUMINATE • See Silicates.

SODIUM SOAP • See Sodium Stearate.

SODIUM SOYA HYDROLYZED ANIMAL PROTEIN • The sodium salt of the condensation product of soya acid chloride and hydrolyzed animal protein. See Hydrolyzed Animal Protein.

SODIUM STANNATE • An inorganic salt. White or colorless crystals. Absorbs water from air. Used in hair dyes. No known toxicity.

SODIUM STEARATE • 92.82 percent stearic acid (*see*). A fatty acid used in deodorant sticks, stick perfumes, toothpastes, soapless shampoos, and shaving lather. A white powder with a soapy feel and a slight tallowlike odor. Slowly soluble in cold water or cold alcohol. Also a waterlike odor. Also a waterproofing agent and has been used to treat skin diseases and in suppositories. One of the least allergy causing of the sodium salts of fatty acids. Nonirritating to the skin.

SODIUM STEAROYL LACTYLATE • See Lactic Acid.

SODIUM STYRENE/ACRYLATES/PEG-10 DIMALEATE COPOLYMER • An opacifier. See Styrenes and Acrylates.

SODIUM STYRENE/ACRYLATES/DIVINYLBENZENE COPOLYMER • An opacifier. See Styrenes, Benzene, and Acrylates.

SODIUM STYRENE/PEG-10 MALEATE/NONOXYNOL-10 MALEATE/ACRYLATE • An opacifier. See Styrenes and Acrylates.

SODIUM SULFATE • **Salt Cake.** Occurs in nature as the minerals mirabilite and thenardite. Used chiefly in the manufacture of dyes, soaps, and detergents. Also used as a chewing gum base and, medicinally, to reduce body water. It is a reagent (*see*) and a precipitant; mildly saline in taste. Usually harmless when applied in toilet preparations. May prove irritating in concentrated solutions if applied to the skin, permitted to dry and then remain. May also enhance the irritant action of certain detergents.

SODIUM SULFITE • An antiseptic, preservative, and antioxidant used in hair dyes. White to tan or pink, odorless or nearly odorless powder having a cooling, salty, sulfurlike taste. It has been used medicinally as a topical antifungal agent. It is also used as a bacterial inhibitor in wine brewing and distilled-beverage industries. Also an antifermentative in the sugar and syrup industries and an anti-browning agent in cut fruits, and is used in frozen apples, prepared fruit pie mix, peeled potatoes, maraschino cherries, dried fruits, and glaced fruits. Used to bleach straw, silk and wool; and as a developer in photography; products containing sulfites may release sulfur dioxide. If this is inhaled by people who suffer from asthma it can trigger an asthmatic attack. Sulfites are known to cause stomach irritation, nausea, diarrhea, skin rash, or swelling in sulfite-sensitive people. People whose kidneys or livers are impaired may not be able to produce the enzymes which break down sulfites in the body. Sulfites may destroy thiamine and consequently are not added to foods which are sources of this B vitamin.

SODIUM SULFONATE • A bubble bath clarifying agent and a dispersing agent used to make shampoos clear. See Sulfonated Oils.

SODIUM TALLOW SULFATE • A defoamer, emollient, intermediate (*see*), and surface-active agent. A mixture of sodium alkyl sulfates. See Tallow.

SODIUM TALLOWATE • The sodium salt of tallow (*see*). Used in soaps and detergents.

SODIUM TARTRATE • A laxative, sequestrant, chemical reactant, and stabilizer. See Tartaric Acid.

SODIUM/TEA-LAUROYL HYDROLYZED ANIMAL PROTEIN • A mixture of sodium and triethanolamine salts of the condensation product of undecylenic acid chloride and hydrolyzed animal protein. See Hydrolyzed Animal Protein.

SODIUM/TEA-UNDECYLENOYL HYDROLYZED ANIMAL PROTEIN • A mixture of sodium and triethanolamine salts of the condensation product of undecylenic acid chloride and hydrolyzed animal protein. See Hydrolyzed Animal Protein.

SODIUM THIOGLYCOLATE • The sodium salt of mercaptoacetic acid. See Thioglycolic Acid Compounds.

SODIUM TOLUENESULFONATE • **Methylbenzenesulfonic Acid. Sodium Salt.** An aromatic compound that is used as a solvent. See Benzene.

SODIUM TRIDECETH-7 CARBOXYLATE • The sodium salt of trideceth-7 carboxylic acid. See Tridecyl Alcohol.

SODIUM TRIDECETH SULFATE • The sodium salt of sulfated ethoxylated tridecyl alcohol (*see*).

SODIUM TRIDECYL SULFATE • See Sulfonated Oils.

SODIUM TRIDECYLBENZENESULFONATE • A mixture of alkyl benzene sulfonates used as a synthetic detergent. See Sodium Dodecylbenzene Sulfonate.

SODIUM TRIMETAPHOSPHATE • See Sodium Metaphosphate.

SODIUM TRIPOLYPHOSPHATE • **STPP.** Used in bubble baths and as a texturizer in soaps. It is a crystalline salt, moderately irritating to the skin and mucous membranes. Ingestion can cause violent purging. See Sodium Phosphate.

SODIUM UNDECYLENATE • A sodium salt of undecylenic acid. Occurs in sweat. A topical fungicide. Liquid or crystals with a sweaty odor prepared from castor oil. No known toxicity.

SODIUM UROCANATE • The sodium salt of urocanic acid. See Histadine.

SODIUM XYLENESULFONATE • Used as a solubilizer. An isolate from wood and coal tar. No known toxicity. See Xylene.

SOLUBILIZATION • The process of dissolving in water such substances as fats and liquids that are not readily soluble under standard conditions by the action of a detergent or similar agent. Technically, a solubilized product is clear because the particle side of an emulsion is so small that light is not bounced off the particle. Solubilization is used in colognes and clear lotions. Sodium sulfonates (*see*) are common solubilizing agents.

SOLUBILIZED VAT BLUE 5 • A vat dye (*see*) in the form of a soluble sodium salt of a sulfuric acid monoester. Vat dyes are more expensive than ordinary dyes and are used in pastels. See Vat Dyes for toxicity.

SOLUBILIZED VAT DYES • These are the sodium salts of vat dyes. They are comparatively expensive but give excellent penetration and fastness. See Vat Dyes.

SOLUBLE (ANIMAL) COLLAGEN • The protein derived from the connective tissues of young animals. See Soluble and Collagen.

SOLVENT • A liquid capable of dissolving or dispensing one or more substances. Methyl ethyl ketone is an example of a solvent.

SOLVENT BLACK 3 • A diazo color. See Solvent Dye.

SOLVENT BLUE 16 • Classed chemically as an anthraquinone color (*see*). See Solvent Dye.

SOLVENT BLUE 35 • Classed chemically as an anthraquinone color (*see*). See Solvent Dye.

SOLVENT DYE • Generally insoluble in water, but dissolves in varying degrees in different organic media in liquid, molten, and solid forms. These include alcohols, oils, fats, and waxes. The use of a solvent dye depends upon fastness to light and adequate solubility, in powders, resins, and plastic. Can be irritating to the skin.

SOLVENT GREEN 3 • An anthraquinone color (*see*). The name can be used only when applied to uncertified batches of this color. The CTFA adopted name for certified (*see*) batches is D & C Green No. 6 (*see*).

SOLVENT GREEN 7 • A pyrene color, the name can be used only for batches of uncertified color. The CTFA adopted name for certified (*see*) batches is D & C Green No. 8 (*see*). Pyrene is a cancer-causing agent.

SOLVENT RED 3 • A monoazo color (*see*). See also Solvent Dye.

SOLVENT RED 23 • A diazo color (*see*). The name can be used only for uncertified batches of this color. The CTFA adopted name for certified (*see*) batches is D & C Red No. 17 (*see*).

SOLVENT RED 24 • **Calico Oil Red.** A diazo color (*see*). See also Solvent Dyes.

SOLVENT RED 43 • A fluoran color. The sodium salt of this is Acid Red 87. The Solvent Red 43 name can be used only when applied to uncertified batches of color. The CTFA adopted name for certified (*see*) batches is D & C Red No. 21.

SOLVENT RED 48 • A fluoran color. The sodium salt is Acid Red 92. The name Solvent Red 48 can be used only for uncertified batches. The CTFA adopted name for certified (*see*) batches is D & C Red No. 27.

SOLVENT RED 49:1 • A xanthene color (*see*). It is the stearic acid salt of Basic Violet 10. The name Solvent Red 49:1 can be applied only to batches of uncertified color. The CTFA adopted name for certified (*see*) batches is D & C Red No. 37 (*see*). Banned in 1988.

SOLVENT RED 72 • A fluoran color. The name can be applied only to uncertified batches. The CTFA adopted name for certified (*see*) batches is D & C Orange No. 5 (*see*).

SOLVENT RED 73 • A fluoran color. The sodium salt is Acid Red 95. The name Solvent Red 73 can be applied only to uncertified batches of color. The CTFA adopted name for certified (*see*) batches is D & C Orange No. 10 (*see*).

SOLVENT VIOLET 13 • An anthraquinone color. The name is applied only to uncertified batches of this color. The CTFA adopted name for certified (*see*) batches is D & C Violet No. 2 (*see*).

SOLVENT YELLOW 13 • A quinoline color. The name can be applied only to uncertified batches of this color. The CTFA adopted name for certified (*see*) batches is D & C Yellow No. 11 (*see*).

SORBETH-20 • See Sorbitol.

SORBETH-6 HEXASTEARATE • See Sorbitol and Stearic Acid.

SORBIC ACID • A white free-flowing powder obtained from the berries of the mountain ash. Also made from chemicals in the factory. Used in cosmetics as a preservative and humectant. A mold and yeast inhibitor, it is also used in foods and beverages. Used as a replacement for glycerin in emulsions, ointments, embalming fluids, mouthwashes, dental creams, and various cosmetic creams. A binder for toilet preparations and plasticizers. Producers a velvetlike feel when rubbed on skin. In large amounts sticky. Practically nontoxic but may cause skin irritation in susceptible people. When injected under the skin in 2,600-milligram doses per kilogram of body weight, it caused cancer in rodents.

SORBITAN DIISOSEATE • The diester of isostearic acid (*see*) and hexitol.

SORBITAN DIOLEATE • The diester of oleic acid and hexitol anhydrides derived from sorbitol. See Sorbitan Fatty Acid Esters.

SORBITAN FATTY ACID ESTERS • Mixture of fatty acids (*see*) and esters of sorbitol (*see*) and sorbitol with the water removed. Widely used in the cosmetics industry as an emulsifier and stabilizer. Also used to prevent irritation from other cosmetic ingredients.

SORBITAN ISOSTEARATE • See Sorbitan Fatty Acid Esters.

SORBITAN LAURATE • **Span 20®.** Oily liquid, insoluble in water, soluble in alcohol and oils. An emulsifier in cosmetic creams and lotions; a stabilizer of essential oils in water. No known toxicity.

SORBITAN OLEATE • **Sorbitan Monooleate.** An emulsifying agent, defoaming agent, and plasticizer. No known toxicity.

SORBITAN PALMITATE • **Span 40®.** Derived from sorbitol (*see*). An emulsifier in cosmetic creams and lotions; a solubilizer of essential oils in water. Light yellow wax, insoluble in water, soluble in solvents. No known toxicity.

SORBITAN SESQUIOLEATE • An emulsifier. See Sorbitol and Oleic Acid.

SORBITAN SEQUISTEARATE • See Sorbitan Stearate.

SORBITAN STEARATE • **Sorbitan Monostearate.** An emulsifier in cosmetic creams and lotions, a solubilizer of essential oils in water. Used in antiperspirants, cake makeup, hand creams, hair tonics, rouge, and suntan creams. Manufactured by reacting edible commercial stearic acid with sorbitol (*see both*). Light cream to tan colored, hard, waxy, solid, with a bland odor and taste. Soluble in temperatures above its melting point in toluene, ethanol, methanol, and ether. No known toxicity.

SORBITAN TRIISOSTEARATE • See Stearic Acid.

SORBITAN TRIOLEATE • See Sorbitol.

SORBITAN TRISTEARATE • An emulsifier and alternate for sorbitan stearate (*see*). No known toxicity.

SORBITOL • A humectant. Gives a velvety feel to skin. Used as a replacement for glycerin in emulsions, ointments, embalming fluid, mouthwashes, dental creams, and various cosmetic creams. A binder for toilet preparations and a plasticizer. Also used in hair sprays, beauty masks, cuticle removers, foundation cake makeup, hand lotions, liquid powders, dentifrices, after-shave lotions, deodorants, antiperspirants, shampoos, and rouge. First found in the ripe berries of the mountain ash; it also occurs in other berries (except grapes), and in cherries, plums, pears, apples, seaweed, and algae. Consists of white hygroscopic powder, flakes, or granules, with a sweet taste. It is a texturizing agent and a sequestrant. Also used in antifreeze, in foods as a sugar substitute, in writing inks to ensure a smooth flow from the point of the pen, and to increase the absorption of vitamins in pharmaceutical preparations. Medicinally used to reduce body water and for intravenous feedings. No known toxicity if taken externally. However, if ingested in excess, it can cause diarrhea and gastrointestinal disturbances; also it may alter the absorption of other drugs making them less effective or more toxic.

SORBUS EXTRACT • **Service Tree Extract**. The extract of *Sorbus domestica*. An extract that was used by the American Indians to make a wash for eyes sore and blurred from the sun and dust.

SORREL EXTRACT • **Rumex Extract.** An extract of the various species of *Rumex*. The Europeans imported this to the Americas and the Indians adopted it. Originally the root was used as a laxative and as a mild astringent. It was also used for scabs on the skin and as a dentifrice. It was widely used by American medical circles in this century to treat skin diseases.

SOY EXTRACT • See Soybean Oil.

SOY FLOUR • See Soybean Oil.

SOY STEROL • See Soybean Oil.

SOY STEROL ACETATE • See Soybean Oil and Acetate.

SOYA ACID • See Soybean Oil.

SOYA HYDROXYETHYL IMIDAZOLINE • See Ethylenediamine and Urea.

SOYAETHYL MORPHOLINIUM ETHOSULFATE • See Soybean Oil and Quaternary Ammonium Compounds.

SOYAMIDE DEA • See Soybean Oil.

SOYAMIDOPROPYL BENZYLDIMONIUM CHLORIDE • See Quaternary Ammonium Compounds.

SOYAMIDOPROPYL DIMETHYLAMINE • See Amides.

SOYAMIDOPROPYL ETHYLDIMONIUM ETHOSULFATE • See Quaternary Ammonium Compounds.

SOYAMINE • See Soybean Oil.

SOYAMINOPROPYLAMINE • See Quaternary Ammonium Compounds.

SOYATRIMONIUM CHLORIDE • **Soya Trimethyl Ammonium Chloride.** See Ammonium Chloride and Soybean Oil.

SOYBEAN OIL • Extracted from the seeds of plants grown in eastern Asia, especially Manchuria, and the midwestern United States. Used in the manufacture of soaps, shampoos, and bath oils. Pale yellow to brownish-yellow. Also used in the manufacture of margarine. Debittered soybean flour contains practically no starch and is widely used in dietetic foods. Soybean oil is used in defoamers in the production of beet sugar and yeast, in the manufacture of margarine, shortenings, candy, and soap. Soybean is used in many products including MSG, dough mixes, Lea & Perrins Sauce, Heinz Worcestershire Sauce, La Choy Oriental Shoyu Sauce, soy sauce, salad dressings, pork link sausages, luncheon meats, hard candies, nut candies, milk, and coffee substitutes. It is made into soybean milk, soybean curd, and soybean cheese. About 300 million bushels of soybean are grown yearly in the U.S.A., one third more than in China. May cause allergic reactions, including hair damage and acnelike pimples.

SOYBEAN OIL UNSAPONIFIABLES • The fraction of Soybean Oil which is not saponified (turned into fatty alcohol) in the refining of soybean oil fatty acids.

SPEARMINT OIL • Used in perfumes, perfumed cosmetics, and toothpaste. It is the essential volatile oil obtained by steam distillation from the fresh, above ground parts of the flowering plant grown in the United States, Europe, and Asia. It is colorless, yellow or yellow-green with the characteristic taste and odor of spearmint. Also used as a flavoring agent in food. May cause allergic reactions such as skin rash.

SPEEDWELL • Used in shampoos. It is an herb, a common hairy perennial grown in Europe, with pale blue or lilac flowers. It has a reputation among herbalists of inducing sweating and restoring healthy body functions; also an expectorant tonic, a treatment for hemorrhages, and a medication for skin diseases. No known toxicity.

SPERMACETI • **Cetyl Palmitate.** Used as a base for ointments and creams, and as an emollient in cleansing creams. Also in shampoos, cold creams, and other creams to improve their gloss and increase their viscosity. Derived as a wax from the head of the sperm whale. Generally nontoxic but may become rancid and cause irritations.

SPICY BOUQUETS • One of the basic perfume types, they derive their characteristics from spice-giving ingredients, such as cinnamon, clove, vanilla, and ginger, but they may also be characterized by spiciness inherent in the flower notes of the perfume composition.

SPIKE LAVENDER OIL • **French Lavender.** Used in perfumes. A pale yellow, stable oil obtained from a flower grown in the Mediterranean region. A lavenderlike odor. Used in cologne, toilet water, blended with lavender oil, soaps, and varnishes. Used also for fumigating to keep moths from clothes, and in food and beverage flavorings. No known toxicity.

SPINACH EXTRACT • An extract of the leaves of spinach, *Spinacea oleracea.*

SPIRAEA EXTRACT • **Queen Meadow.** An extract from the flowers of *Spiraea ulmaria.* Contains an oil similar to wintergreen (*see*). The roots are rich in tannic acid (*see*).

SPLEEN EXTRACT • The extract of bovine spleen used in "youth creams."

SPRAY DEODORANT • With antiperspirant action. Usually contains aluminum phenol sulfonate, 10 percent; propylene glycol, 5 percent; alcohol, 85 percent; and perfume. May seriously irritate the eyes, especially if you wear contact lenses. Caution is advised, especially since aerosol is a highly efficient way of delivering materials to the lungs. Dispenses by aerosols (*see*). See Deodorants.

SQUALENE • Obtained from shark-liver oil. Occurs in smaller amounts in olive oil, wheat germ oil, and rice bran oil. Human sebum is 25 percent squalene. It has a faint agreeable odor, is tasteless, and mixes with vegetable and mineral oils, organic solvents, and fatty substances. Insoluble in water. It is used as a fixative (*see*) in perfumes, as a bactericide, and in surfactants (*see*). It is very expensive, so today hydrogenated polyisobutane (*see*) is often used as a substitute because it is half the cost. No known toxicity.

STABILIZER • A substance added to a product to give it body and to maintain a desired texture, for instance, the stabilizer alginic acid, which is added to cosmetics.

STANNIC CHLORIDE • **Tin Tetrachloride.** A thin, colorless, fuming, caustic liquid, soluble in water, used as a mordant (*see*) in metallic hair dye and as a reagent (*see*) in perfumes and soaps. May be highly irritating to the eyes and mucous membranes.

STANNOUS CHLORIDE • **Tin Dichloride.** An antioxidant, soluble in water, and a powerful reducing agent, particularly in the manufacture of dyes. May be irritating to the skin and mucous membranes.

STANNOUS FLUORIDE • **Tin Difluoride. Fluoristan.** Prepared by dissolving tin in hydrofluoric acid. Used in dentifrices as a decay preventative. No know toxicity.

STANNOUS PYROPHOSPHATE • **Salt of Tin.** It is relatively nontoxic and poorly absorbed from the gastrointestinal tract. Used as a mordant (*see*). No known toxicity when used externally. See Phosphate.

STARCH • **Acid Modified. Pregelatinized and Unmodified.** Starch is stored by plants and is taken from grains of wheat, potatoes, rice, corn, beans, and many other vegetable foods. Insoluble in cold water or alcohol but soluble in boiling water. Comparatively resistant to naturally occurring enzymes, which is why processors modify starch to make it more digestible. Used in dusting powders, dentifrices, hair colorings, rouge, dry shampoos, baby powders, emollients, and bath salts. Soothing to the skin and used to treat rashes. Used internally as a gruel for diarrhea. Allergic reaction to starch in toilet goods includes stuffy nose and other symptoms due to inhalation. Absorbs moisture and swells, causing blocking and distension of the pores and leading to mechanical irritation. Particles remain in pores and putrefy, accelerated by sweat.

STARCH/ACRYLATES/ACRYLAMIDE COPOLYMER • See Starch and Acrylic Acid.

STARCH DIETHYLAMINOETHYL ETHER • See Starch.

STEARALKONIUM BENTONITE • See Quaternary Ammonium Compounds.

STEARALKONIUM CHLORIDE • Improves the ability to comb the hair and adds shine. See Quaternary Ammonium Compounds.

STEARALKONIUM HECTORITE • See Quaternary Ammonium Compounds.

STEARAMIDE • An emulsifier. Colorless leaflets, insoluble in water. No known toxicity. See Stearic Acid.

STEARAMIDE DEA • **Stearic Acid Diethanolamide.** See Stearamide.

STEARAMIDE DIBA STEARATE • An emulsifier. See Stearamide.

STEARAMIDE MEA STEARATE • See Stearamide.

STEARAMIDE MIPA • See Stearamide.

STEARAMIDE OXIDE • A hair conditioner. See Stearamide.

STEARMIDOPROPALKONIUM CHLORIDE • See Quaternary Ammonium Compounds.

STEARAMIDOPROPYL DIMETHYLAMINE • See Dimethylamine.

STEARAMINE • See Stearic Acid.

STEARAMINE OXIDE • See Stearyl Alcohol.

STEARATES • See Stearic Acid.

STEARETH-2 • A polyoxyethyle (*see*) ether of fatty alcohol. The oily liquid is used as a surfactant (*see*) and emulsifier (*see*). No known toxicity.

STEARETH-4 THROUGH -100 • The polyethylene glycol ethers of stearyl alcohol. The number indicates the degree of liquidity; the higher, the more solid. See Steareth-2.

STEARIC ACID • Used in deodorants and antiperspirants, liquid powders, foundation creams, hand creams, hand lotions, liquefying creams, hair straighteners, protective creams, shaving creams, and soap. Occurs naturally in butter acids, tallow, cascarilla bark, and other animal fats and oils. A white, waxy, natural fatty acid, it is the major ingredient used in making bar soap and lubricants. A large percentage of all cosmetic creams on the market contains it. It gives pearliness to hand creams. It is also used as a softener in chewing gum base, for suppositories, and as a food flavoring. It is a possible sensitizer for allergic people. See Fatty Acids.

STEARIC HYDRAZIDE • See Stearic Acid.

STEARMIDOETHYL DIETHYLAMINE • See Stearic Acid and Diethylamine.

STEAROAMPHOACETATE • See Quaternary Ammonium Compounds.

STEAROAMPHOCARBOXYGLYCINATE • See Surfactants.

STEAROAMPHODIACETATE • See Quaternary Ammonium Compounds.

STEAROAMPHOHYDROXYPROPYLSULFONATE • See Quaternary Ammonium Compounds.

STEAROAMPHOPROPIONATE • See Stearic Acid and Propionic Acid.

STEARONE • Derived from stearic acid. It is insoluble in water and is used as an antiblocking agent. See Stearic Acid.

STEAROXY DIMETHICONE • See Stearic Acid and Dimethicone.

STEAROXYTRIMETHYLSILANE • See Stearic Acid and Silicones.

STEAROYL LACTYLIC ACID • See Stearic Acid and Lactyl Lactate.

STEAROYL SARCOSINE • See Sarcosines.

STEARTRIMONIUM CHLORIDE • See Quaternary Ammonium Compounds.

STEARTRIMONIUM HYDROLYZED ANIMAL PROTEIN • See Quaternary Ammonium Compounds.

STEARYL ACETATE • The ester of stearyl alcohol and acetic acid (*see both*).

STEARYL ALCOHOL • **Stenol.** A mixture of solid alcohols prepared from sperm whale oil. Unctuous white flakes, insoluble in water, soluble in alcohol and ether. A substitute for cetyl alcohol (*see*) to obtain a firmer product at ordinary temperatures. Used in pharmaceutical, cosmetic creams, for emulsions, and as an antifoam agent and lubricant; also in depilatories, hair rinses, and shampoos. No known toxicity.

STEARYL BETAINE • See Surfactants and Stearic Acid.

STEARYL CAPRYLATE • The ester of stearyl alcohol and citric acid (*see both*).

STEARYL CITRATE • The ester of stearyl alcohol and citric acid (*see both*).

STEARYL ERUCAMIDE • See Quaternary Ammonium Compounds.

STEARYL ERUCATE • See Stearyl Alcohol and Erucic Acid.

STEARYL GLYCYRRHETINATE • The ester of stearyl alcohol and glycyrrhetinate (*see both*).

STEARYL HEPTANOATE • The ester of stearyl alcohol and heptanoic acid. Used as a wax. See Stearyl Alcohol and Heptanoic Acid.

STEARYL HYDROXYETHYL IMIDAZOLINE • See Quaternary Ammonium Compounds.

STEARYL LACTATE • An emulsifier that occurs in tallow and other animal fats as well as vegetable oils. No known toxicity.

STEARYL OCTANOATE • The ester of stearyl alcohol and 2-ethylhexanoic acid. See Stearyl Alcohol.
STEARYL STEARATE • The ester of stearyl alcohol and stearic acid (*see both*).
STEARYL STEAROYL STEARATE • See Stearyl Alcohol.
STEARYLDIMETHYL AMINE • See Stearyl Alcohol.
STEARYLVINYL ETHER/MALEIC ANHYDRIDE COPOLYMER • A polymer of stearylvinyl ether and maleic anhydride (*see both*).
STEROIDS • Class of compounds that includes certain drugs of hormonal origin, such as cortisone, and is used to treat the inflammations caused by allergies.
STEROL • Any class of solid complex alcohols from animals and plants. Cholesterol is a sterol and is used in hand creams. Sterols are lubricants in baby preparations, emollient creams, and lotions, emulsified fragrances, hair conditioners, hand creams, and hand lotions. No known toxicity.
STIFFENING AGENT • An ingredient to add body to shaving soaps and creams. Many of the gums, such as karaya and carrageenan (*see*), are used for this purpose.
STILLINGIA • **Chinese Tallow Tree. Queen's Root. Yaw Root.** Dried roots of a southeastern United States plant. An acrid resin; fixed and volatile oils. Used as a drying oil in cosmetics. Formerly used medicinally to induce vomiting. No known toxicity in cosmetics.
STONEROOT • **Horse Balm.** Used for its constituents of resin, saponin, and tannic acid (*see all*). An erect smooth perennial; a strong-scented herb of eastern North America with pointed leaves. It produces a chocolate-colored powder with a peculiar odor and bitter astringent taste. Soluble in alcohol. No known toxicity.
STORAX • **Styrax. Sweet Oriental Gum.** Used in perfumes. It is the resin obtained from the bark of an Asiatic tree. Grayish-brown, fragrant semiliquid, containing styrene and cinnamic acid (*see both*). Once used in medicine as a weak antiseptic and as an expectorant. Also used in food and beverage flavorings. Moderately toxic when ingested. Can cause urinary problems when absorbed through the skin. Can cause skin irritation, welts, and discomfort when applied topically. A common allergen.
STPP • See Sodium Tripolyphosphate.
STRAMONIUM • **Thorn Apple. Jimsonweed. Stinkweed.** Used in antiperspirants for its antiperspirant properties. Obtained from the dried leaves and flowering tops of a plant grown in Europe, Asia, and the United States. Leaves contain 0.25 to 0.45 percent alkaloids consisting of atropine, hyoseyamine, and scopolamine. It is used

medicinally to treat intestinal spasms, asthma, and Parkinson's disease. No known toxicity.

STRAWBERRY EXTRACT • See Strawberry Juice.

STRAWBERRY JUICE • Fresh ripe strawberries are reputed to contain ingredients that soften and nourish the skin. Widely used in natural cosmetics today. No scientific evidence of benefit or harm.

STRAWFLOWER EXTRACT • The extract of *Helichrysum italicum*, grown for its bright yellow strawlike flowers. Used in coloring.

STRONTIUM DIOXIDE • **Strontium Peroxide.** A white odorless and tasteless powder derived by passing oxygen over hot strontium. Used as a bleaching agent and antiseptic. It is highly flammable and explosive.

STRONTIUM HYDROXIDE • Used chiefly in making soaps and greases in cosmetics. Colorless, water-absorbing crystals or white powder. Absorbs carbon dioxide from the air. Very alkaline in solution. Also used in refining beet sugar and separating sugar from molasses. Irritating when applied to the skin.

STRONTIUM SULFIDE • Used in depilatories, it is less irritating than sodium sulfide and more efficient than calcium sulfide. It is a sulfur compound that occurs free or in combination, such as gypsum; found most often in volcanic areas. It is a gray powder with the odor of hydrogen sulfide and is slightly soluble in water. May cause skin rash, irritation, and hair breakage.

STYPTIC PENCIL • A cylindrical stick comprised of potassium aluminum sulfate, glycerin, and talc. It has an astringent effect, tending to contract or bind. Designed to check blood flow, primarily from razor nicks. May sting but nontoxic.

STYRAX • See Storax.

STYRENE • Obtained from ethylbenzene by taking out the hydrogen. Colorless to yellowish oily liquid with a penetrating odor. Used in the manufacture of cosmetic resins and in plastics. May be irritating to the eyes and mucous membranes, and in high concentrations it is narcotic.

STYRENE/ACRYLAMIDE COPOLYMER • An opacifier. See Acrylates.

STYRENE/ACRYLATE/AMMONIUM METHACRYLATE COPOLYMER • A polymer (*see*) of styrene and a monomer of acrylic acid, methacrylic acid, or one of their esters. Used in liquid eyeliners. See Styrenes and Acrylates.

STYRENE/ACRYLATE COPOLYMER • An opacifier. See Acrylates.

STYRENE/ACRYLIC ACID COPOLYMER • See Styrene and Acrylates.

STYRENE/PVP/COPOLYMER • Prepared from vinylpyrrolidone and styrene monomers, it is used in liquid eyeliners as a carrier for color. See Styrene and Polyvinyl Pyrrolidone.

SUCCINIC ACID • Occurs in fossils, fungi, lichens, etc. Prepared from acetic acid (*see*). Odorless; very acid taste. The acid is used as a plant growth retardant. A germicide and mouthwash and used in perfumes and lacquers; also a buffer and neutralizing agent. Has been employed medicinally as a laxative. No known toxicity in cosmetic use. Large amounts injected under the skin of frogs kills them.

SUCCINIC ANHYDRIDE • A starch modifier. See Succinic Acid.

SUCROSE • **Sugar. Cane Sugar. Saccharose.** A sweetening agent and food, a starting agent in fermentation production, a preservative and antioxidant in pharmacy, a demulcent, and a substitute for glycerin (*see*). Workers who handle raw sugar often develop rashes and other skin problems. Sugar when it oxidizes with sweat draws water from the skin and causes chapping and cracking. Infections, erosions, and fissures around the nails can occur. No known toxicity in cosmetics.

SUCROSE ACETATE ISOBUTYRATE • A denaturant for rubbing alcohols (*see both*).

SUCROSE BENZOATE • See Benzoic Acid.

SUCROSE BENZOATE/SUCROSE ACETATE ISOBUTYRATE/BUTYL BENZYL PHTHALATE COPOLYMER • The condensation polymer of sucrose benzoate, sucrose acetate, isobutyrate, and butyl benzyl phthalate monomers. Used as a film.

SUCROSE BENZOATE/SUCROSE ACETATE ISOBUTYRATE/BUTYL BENZYL PHTHALATE/METHACRYLATE COPOLYMER • The condensation product of sucrose benzoate, sucrose acetate isobutyrate, butyl benzyl phthalate, and methyl methacrylate monomers. Used as a film. See Acrylates.

SUCROSE DISTEARATE • A mixture of sucrose and stearic acid (*see both*).

SUCROSE LAURATE • A mixture of sucrose and lauric acid (*see both*).

SUCROSE OCTAACETATE • A preparation from sucrose (*see*). A synthetic flavoring. Used in adhesives and nail lacquers; a denaturant for alcohol. No known toxicity.

SUCROSE STEARATE • A mixture of sucrose and stearic acid (*see both*).

SUDAN III. • **Oil Red. Oil Scarlet. Solvent Red 23.** A reddish-brown powder used in coloring for waxes, oils, stains, dyes, and resins. May cause contact dermatitis.

SUGAR • See Sucrose.

SULFAMIC ACID • A cleaning agent in cosmetics and used in the manufacture of hair dyes and lakes (*see*). A strong white crystalline acid used chiefly as a weed killer, in cleaning metals, and as a flameproofing and softening agent. Moderately irritating to the skin and mucous membranes.

SULFATED CASTOR OIL • See Turkey-Red Oil.

SULFATED GLYCERYL OLEATE • Produced by adding sulfuric acid to glyceryl oleate. See Sulfonated Oils.

SULFATED OIL • **Sulphated Oil.** A compound to which a salt of sulfuric acid has been added to help control the acid/alkali balance.

SULFIDES • Inorganic sulfur compounds that occur free or in combination with minerals. They are salts of weak acid and are used as hair dissolving agents in depilatories. They are skin irritants and may cause hair breakage.

SULFONAMIDE FORMALDEHYDE • A solvent in nail polish and the most frequent cause of nail polish dermatitis, which generally affects the neck and eyelids. Sulfonamide is the amide of sulfonic acid. See Formaldehyde and Sulfonamide Resins.

SULFONAMIDE RESINS • **Sulfanilamide.** The use of sulfonamides dates back to 1934 when the dye, prontosil, was shown to cure certain infections caused by bacteria. Sulfonamides are bacteria killers and are used to inhibit germ growth in cosmetics. They are also used to contribute depth, gloss, flow adhesion, and water resistance to films in nail lacquers. They may cause allergic reactions.

SULFONATED OILS • **Sulfated.** Prepared by reacting oils with sulfuric acid. Used in soapless shampoos and hair sprays as an emulsifier and wetting agent. Shampoos containing sulfonated oils were first manufactured in 1880 and were effective in hard or soft water. Sulfonated oils strip color from both natural and colored hair and can bring out streaks. Sulfated castor oil has been used to remove all types of dye. Applied to hair and heated, it is used as a hair treatment. Sulfonated oils are used in hair tonics that remain on the hair as hairdressings. May cause drying of the skin.

SULFUR • **Brimstone.** A mild antiseptic in antidandruff shampoos, dusting powders, ointments, and permanent wave solutions. Occurs in the earth's crust in the free state and in combination. Used in hair tonic to stimulate the scalp and in acne creams and lotions. Also a stimulant to healing when used on skin rashes; derivatives are used in depilatories. May cause irritation of the skin. A case of death was reported following absorption through the scalp of cold wave solution containing free sulfur. Death was attributed to acute hydrogen sulfide poisoning.

SULFUR TAR COMPLEX • **Tricosulfan®.** The product obtained from the distillation of wood of various species of fir, and treated with sulfur.

SULFURIC ACID • **Oil of Vitriol.** A clear, colorless, odorless, oily acid used to modify starch and to regulate acidity/alkalinity. It is very corrosive and produces severe burns on contact with the skin and other body tissues. Diluted sulfuric acid has been used to stimulate appetite. It is used as a topical caustic in cosmetic products. If ingested undiluted, it can be fatal.

SULFURIZED JOJOBA OIL • A mixture of sulfur and jojoba oil (*see both*).

SUNBURN LOTION • **Includes Creams and Sprays.** Serious sunburn requires medical attention and the use of oils, including butter, is not recommended. However, there are a number of soothing lotions, creams, and sprays for mild sunburn on the market. A common formula includes mineral oil, 10 percent; lanolin, 2.5 percent; propylene glycol, 2.5 percent; triethanolamine, 5.0 percent (*see all*); and water, distilled, 80 percent.

SUNFLOWER SEED OIL • Oil obtained by milling the seeds of the large flower produced in the USSR, India, Egypt, and Argentina. A bland, pale yellow oil, it contains amounts of Vitamin E (*see* Tocopherols) and forms a "skin" after drying. Used in food and salad oils, and in resin and soap manufacturing. No known toxicity.

SUNFLOWER SEED OIL GLYCERIDE • See Sunflower Seed Oil and Glycerides.

SUNSCREEN PREPARATIONS • See Suntan Preparations.

SUNSET YELLOW • A monoazo color. The name can be used only when applied to batches of uncertified color. The CTFA adopted name for certified (*see*) batches is FD & C Yellow No. 6 (*see*).

SUNTAN PREPARATIONS • Preparations to prevent painful sunburn that encourage a change in pigmentation (a tan) have a large market. Suntan creams (emulsions) may contain para-aminobenzoic acid, mineral oil, sorbitan stearate, poloxamers (*see all*), and 62 percent water. A suntan ointment may contain petrolatum, stearyl alcohol, mineral oil, sesame oil, and calcium stearate (*see all*). A suntan lotion may contain methyl anthranilate, propylene glycol, ricinoleate, glycerin (*see all*), and about 65 percent alcohol and 10 percent water. A suntan oil may contain salicylates, about 40 percent sesame oil (*see both*), and 55 percent mineral oil. Suntan preparations may also contain alcohol, *p*-aminobenzoic acid and derivatives, benzyl salicylate, cinnamic acid derivatives, and coumarin (*see all*). A common suntan oil formula includes 2-ethyl hexyl salicylate, 5 percent; sesame oil, 40 percent; mineral oil, about 55 percent perfume; color; and an antioxidant. Complaints to the FDA concerning sunscreen preparations include rash, blisters, burns, yellowed skin, and even death. The newer brands of sunscreens available protect against UVA rays of the sun, which tan, and UVB rays which burn. They are called broad spectrum sunscreens and they list the UVA blocker, oxybenzone, among their ingredients. A few new sunscreens also block the infrared heat rays, which, according to Dr. Albert Kligman of the University of Pennsylvania Medical School, may also damage the skin. The maximum protection means choosing an SPF 15 broad spectrum product that's also formulated to block infrared heat rays. Some sunscreens also claim water resistance that lasts for up to 50 minutes.

SURFACE-ACTIVE AGENTS • See Surfactants.

SURFACTANTS • These are wetting agents. They lower water's surface tension, permitting water to spread out and penetrate more easily. These surface-active agents are classified by whether or not they ionize in solution and by the nature of their electrical charges. There are four major categories—anionic, nonionic, cationic, and amphoteric. Anionic surfactants, which carry a negative charge, have excellent cleaning properties. They are stain and dirt removers in household detergents, both powders and liquids, and toilet soaps. Nonionic surfactants have no electrical charge. Since they are resistant to hard water and dissolve in oil and grease, they are especially effective in spray-on oven cleaners. Cationic surfactants have a positive charge. These are primarily ammonia derivatives and are antistatic and sanitizing agents used as friction reducers in hair rinses and fabric softeners. Amphoteric surfactants may be either negatively charged or positively charged, depending on the activity or alkalinity of the water. They are used for cosmetics where mildness is important such as in shampoos and lotions.

SWEET ALMOND OIL • Used in perfumes and in the manufacture of fine soaps and emollients. Expressed from the seeds of a plant. Colorless or pale yellow, oily liquid, almost odorless, with a bland taste. Insoluble in water. No known skin toxicity. See Bitter Almond Oil.

SWEET BAY OIL • Used in perfumes. It is the yellow-green volatile oil from the leaves of the laurel. No known toxicity.

SWEET BIRCH • See Methyl Salicylate.

SWEET CLOVER EXTRACT • The extract of various species of *Melilotus*, grown for hay and soil improvement. It contains coumarin (*see*) and is used as a scent to disguise bad odors.

SWEET MARJORAM OIL • **Marjoram Pot.** Used in perfumery and hair preparations. The natural extract of the flowers and leaves of two varieties of the fragrant marjoram. Also a food flavoring. No known toxicity.

SWEET VIOLET EXTRACT • The extract of the flowers of *Viola odorata* of Eurasia and North Africa that is the source of many of the commercially developed violets. Used in perfumery.

SYLVIC ACID • See Abietic Acid.

SYNTHETIC BEESWAX • A mixture of alcohol esters.

SYNTHETIC JOJOBA OIL • See Jojoba Oil.

SYNTHETIC SPERMACETI • See Spermaceti.

SYNTHETIC WAX • A hydrocarbon wax derived from various oils.

T

TALC • **French Chalk.** The main ingredient of baby and bath powders, face powders, eye shadows, liquid powders, protective creams, dry rouges, face masks, foundation cake makeups, skin fresheners, foot powders, and face creams. Gives a slippery sensation to powders and creams. Talc is finely powdered native magnesium silicate, a mineral. It usually has small amounts of other powders such as boric acid or zinc oxide added as a coloring agent. Prolonged inhalation can cause lung problems because it is similar in chemical composition to asbestos, a known lung irritant and cancer-causing agent.

TALCUM POWDER • Talc-based powders have been linked to ovarian cancer. In Boston's Brigham and Women's Hospital, of 215 women with ovarian cancer, 32 had used talcum powder on their genitals and sanitary napkins. Talc easily works it way up the reproductive tract. Eventually, a few particles reach the ovaries and may set the stage for cancer. All factors considered in the study, the risk of ovarian cancer was raised to 3.28 times greater for women who use talc than for women who don't. Daniel Cramer, M.D., the obstetrician-gynecologist who wrote of the findings in the journal, *Cancer*, said further studies are needed before doctors could recommend that women should not use talc, but said that he, himself, advises patients to use other products such as cornstarch-based powders or creams. Talcum powder has been reported to cause coughing, vomiting, or even pneumonia when it is used carelessly and inhaled by babies. See Talc.

TALL OIL • **Liquid Rosin.** A by-product of the pine wood pulp industry and used to scent shampoos, soaps, varnishes, and fruit sprays. "Tall" is Swedish for "pine." Dark brown liquid; acrid odor.

A fungicide and cutting oil. It may be a mild irritant and sensitizer.

TALL OIL BENZYL HYDROXYETHYL IMIDAZOLINIUM CHLORIDE • See Quaternary Ammonium Compounds and Tall Oil.

TALLAMIDE DEA • See Tall Oil.

TALLAMPHOPROPIONATE • See Tall Oil.

TALLOW • The fat from the fatty tissue of cattle and sheep in North America. Used in shaving creams, lipsticks, shampoos, and soaps. White, almost tasteless when pure, and generally harder than grease. May cause eczema and blackheads.

TALLOW ACID • See Tallow.

TALLOW AMIDE • See Tallow.

TALLOW AMIDOPROPYLAMINE OXIDE • See Tallow Acid.

TALLOW AMINE • See Tallow.

TALLOW AMINE OXIDE • See Tallow.

TALLOW GLYCERIDES • A mixture of triglycerides (fats) derived from Tallow.

TALLOW HYDROXYETHYL IMIDAZOLINE • See Tallow and Imidazoline.

TALLOW IMIDAZOLINE • See Tallow.

TALLOWAMIDE DEA AND MEA • See Tallow Acid.

TALLOWAMIDOPROPYL HYDROXYSULTAINE • See Quaternary Ammonium Compounds.

TALLOWAMINOPROPYLAMINE • See Quaternary Ammonium Compounds.

TALLOWAMPHOACETATE • See Quaternary Ammonium Compounds.

TALLOWETH-6 • See Tallow.

TALLOW TRIMONIUM CHLORIDE • **Tallow.** Trimethyl Ammonium Chloride. See Quaternary Ammonium Compounds.

TAMARIND EXTRACT • The extract of *Tamarindus indica*, a large tropical tree grown in the East Indies and Africa. Preserved in sugar or syrup, it is used as a natural fruit flavoring. The pulp contains about 10 percent tartaric acid. No known toxicity.

TANNIC ACID • Used in sunscreen preparations, eye lotions, and antiperspirants. It occurs in the bark and fruit of many plants, notably in the bark of the oak and sumac, and in cherry, coffee, and tea. Used medicinally as a mild astringent and when applied it may turn the skin brown. Also used in food flavorings. Tea contains tannic acid, and this explains its folk use as an eye lotion. Excessive use in creams or lotions in hypersensitive persons may lead to irritation, blistering, and increased pigmentation.

TAR OIL • The volatile oil distilled from wood tar, generally from the family *Pinaceae*. Used externally to treat skin diseases, the principle toxic ingredients are phenols and naphthalenes. Toxicity estimates are hard to make because even the U.S. Pharmacopoeia does not specify the phenol content of official preparations. However, if ingested, it is estimated that one ounce would kill. See Pine Tar Oil, which is a rectified tar oil used as a licorice flavoring.

TARRAGON • Used in perfumery to improve the note (*see*) of chypre-type perfumes (*see*). Derived from the dried leaves of a small European perennial herb, wormwood. Pale yellow oil; grown for its aromatic, pungent foliage. Also used in making pickles and vinegar. No known toxicity.

TARS • An antiseptic, deodorant, and bug killer. Any of the various dark brown or black, bituminous, usually odorous, viscous liquids or semiliquids obtained by the destructive distillation of wood, coal, peat, shale, and other organic materials. Used in hair tonics and shampoos and as a licorice food flavoring. May cause allergic reactions.

TARTARIC ACID • Effervescent acid used in bath salts, denture powders, nail bleaches, hair-grooming aids, hair rinses, depilatories, and hair coloring. Widely distributed in nature in many fruits but usually obtained as a by-product of winemaking. Consists of colorless or translucent crystals, or a white, fine-to-granular crystalline powder, which is odorless and has an acid taste. In strong solutions it may be mildly irritating to the skin.

TARTRAZINE • **FD & C Yellow No. 5.** Bright orange yellow powder used in foods, drugs, and cosmetics and as a dye for wool and silk. Those allergic to aspirin are often allergic to tartrazine. Allergies have been reported in persons eating sweet corn, soft drinks, and cheese crackers—all colored with Yellow No. 5. It is derived from coal tar.

TBS • See Tribromsalan.

TCC • See Triclocarban.

TEA- • The abbreviation for triethanolamine.

TEA • The leaves, leaf buds, and internodes of plants having leaves and fragrant white flowers, prepared and cured to make an aromatic beverage. Cultivated principally in China, Japan, Ceylon, and other Asian countries. Tea is a mild stimulant and its tonic properties are due to the alkaloid caffeine; tannic acid (*see*) makes it astringent. Used by natural cosmeticians to reduce the puffiness around the eyes. A cotton or gauze pad is dampened with a weak solution of tea and placed on the eyelids. One then lies down for five or ten minutes. No known toxicity.

TEA-ABIETOYL HYDROLYZED ANIMAL PROTEIN • The salt of the condensation product of abietic acid chloride and hydrolyzed animal protein (*see both*).

TEA-C12-15 ALCOHOLS SULFATE • See Triethanolamine, Alcohols, and Sulfate.

TEA-COCO HYDROLYZED ANIMAL PROTEIN • See Hydrolyzed Animal Protein and Surfactants, Anionic.

TEA-COCO HYDROLYZED PROTEIN • See Proteins.

TEA-COCOATE • The treithanolamine (*see*) soap derived from coconut fatty acids (*see*). No known toxicity.

TEA-COCYL GLUTAMATE • A softener. See Glutamate.

TEA-COCYL SARCOSINATE • See Cocoyl Sarcosine.

TEA-DODECYLBENZENESULFONATE • See Sulfonated Oils.

TEA-EDTA • See Ethylenediamine Tetraacetic Acid.

TEA-HYDROGENATED TALLOW GLUTAMATE • A softener. See Glutamate.

TEA-LAURETH SULFATE • See Surfactants, Anionic.

TEA-LAUROYL ANIMAL COLLAGEN AMINO ACIDS • Protein enhancer for cosmetic creams. See Hydrolyzed Animal Proteins.

TEA-LAUROYL ANIMAL KERATIN AMINO ACIDS • See Keratin Amino Acids.

TEA-LAUROYL GLUTAMATE • A softener. See Glutamate.

TEA-LAUROYL SARCOSINATE • See Sarcosines.

TEA-LAURYL BENZENE SULFONATE • See Surfactants.

TEA-LAURYL SULFATE • See Sodium Lauryl Sulfate.

TEA-MYRISTAMINOPROPIONATE • See Surfactants.

TEA-MYRISTATE • See Myristic Acid and Surfactants.

TEA-MYRISTOL HYDROLYZED ANIMAL PROTEIN • See Hydrolyzed Animal Protein and Surfactants.

TEA-OLEAMIDO PEG-2 SULFOSUCCINATE • Triethanolamine and succinic acid (*see both*).

TEA-OLEATE • **Triethanolamine Oleate.** See Oleic Acid and Ethanolamines.

TEA-PALM-KERNEL SARCOSINATE • See Sarcosines.

TEA-PCA • See Ethanolamines.

TEA SORBATE • See Triethanolamine and Sorbic Acid.

TEA-STEARATE • See Triethanolamine and Stearic Acid.

TEA-SULFATE • See Triethanolamine and Sulfuric Acid.

TEA-TREE OIL • The essential oil obtained from the leaves of an Australian tree. Light yellow. Used as a germicide in cosmetics. Eleven to thirteen times as powerful as carbolic acid. Penetrates the skin quickly and accelerates the healing of skin disorders. No known toxicity.

TEA-UNDECYLENOYL HYDROLYZED ANIMAL PROTEIN • See Hydrolyzed Animal Protein.

TERPENES • A class of unsaturated hydrocarbons (*see*). Its removal from products improves their flavor and gives them a more stable, stronger odor. However, some perfumers feel that the removal of terpenes destroys some of the original odor. Has been used as an antiseptic. No known toxicity.

TERPINEOL • A colorless, viscous liquid with a lilaclike odor, insoluble in mineral oil, and slightly soluble in water. It is primarily used as a flavoring agent but is also employed as a denaturant to make alcohol undrinkable. It has been used as an antiseptic. It can be a sensitizer.

TERPINYL ACETATE • Colorless liquid, odor suggestive of bergamot and lavender. Slightly soluble in water and glycerol. Derived by heating terpineol with acetic acid (*see both*). Used as a perfume and flavoring agent. No known toxicity.

TERTIARY BUTYLHYDROQUINONE TBHQ • This antioxidant was put on the market after years of pushing by food manufacturers to get it approved. It contains the petroleum-derived butane and is used either alone or in combination with the preservative-antioxidant butylated hydroxyanisole (BHA) and/or butylatedhydroxytoluene (BHT). Application to the skin may cause allergic reactions.

TESTICULAR EXTRACT • Extract of bovine testicular tissue.

TETRABROMOFLUORESCEIN • **Eosine Yellow.** A red color with a yellowish or brownish tinge prepared by adding bromine fluorescein (*see*). Used to make lipstick indelible and to color nail polish. It may be a photosensitizer (*see*), causing inflamed lips and respiratory and gastrointestinal symptoms. Tetrabromofluorescein is also used to dye wool and silk and paper.

TETRACHLOROETHYLENE • **Perchloroethylene.** A colorless, nonflammable liquid with a pleasant odor, made from acetylene and chlorine. Used as a solvent in cosmetics. Used medicinally against hookworms. Narcotic in high doses. Has a drying action on the skin and can lead to adverse skin reactions.

TETRAHYDROFURFURYL ACETATE • See Furfural.

TETRAHYDROFURFURYL ALCOHOL • A liquid that absorbs water and is flammable in air. A solvent for cosmetic fats, waxes, and resins. Mixes with water, ether, and acetone. Mildly irritating to the skin and mucous membranes. See Furfural.

TETRAHYDROGERANYL HYDROXYL STEARATE • See Stearic Acid and Hydroxylation.

TETRAHYDROXYPROPYL ETHYLENEDIAMINE • Clear, colorless,

thick liquid, a component of the bacteria-killing substance in sugar cane. It is strongly alkaline and is used as a solvent and preservative. It may be irritating to the skin and mucous membranes and may cause skin sensitization.

TETRAMETHYL DECYNEDIOL • See Fatty Alcohols.

TETRAMETHYLAMMONIUM CHLORIDE • See Quaternary Ammonium Compounds.

TETRAMETHYLTHIURAM DISULFIDE • **Thiram.** An agriculture chemical found to be a germicide when incorporated in soap. A disinfectant, insecticide, fungicide, and bacteria killer. May cause irritation of nose, throat, and skin. Also, it may be harmful if swallowed or inhaled. One should not breathe the spray or mist and should avoid contact with eyes, skin, or clothing. Causes allergic skin reactions.

TETRAPOTASSIUM PHOSPHATE • **TKPP.** An emulsifier. See Tetrasodium Pyrophosphate.

TETRASODIUM EDTA • **Sodium Edetate.** Powdered sodium salt that reacts with metals. A sequestering agent and chelating agent (*see both*) used in cosmetic solutions. Can deplete the body of calcium if taken internally. See Ethylenediamine Tetraacetic Acid. No known toxicity on the skin.

TETRASODIUM PYROPHOSPHATE • **TSPP.** A sequestering agent, claryifying agent, and buffering agent for shampoos. Produced by removing water from dibasic sodium phosphate. Insoluble in alcohol. A water softener in bath preparations. No known toxicity.

TEXTURIZER • A chemical used to improve the texture of various cosmetics. For instance, in creams that tend to become lumpy, calcium chloride (*see*) is added to keep them smooth.

TFC • **Tricloflucarban.** A disinfectant used in cosmetics. No known toxicity.

THEOBROMA OIL • **Cocoa Butter.** Yellowish-white solid with chocolatelike taste and odor. Derived from the cacao bean. Widely used in confections, suppositories, pharmaceuticals, soaps, and cosmetics. No known toxicity but may cause allergic reactions in the sensitive.

THEOPHYLLINE • A white powder, soluble in water. Occurs in tea. Its current use in cosmetics has not been revealed. However, it is a smooth muscle relaxant, heart stimulant, and diuretic (reduces body water). It can cause nausea and vomiting if ingested. The toxic dose in humans is only 2.9 milligrams per kilogram of body weight.

THIAMINE HCL • **Vitamin B_1.** A white crystalline powder used in emollients and as a dietary supplement in prepared breakfast foods, peanut butter, milk, and noodle products. Acts as a helper in important energy-yielding reactions in the body. Practically all commercial Vitamin B_1 is synthetic. The vitamin is destroyed by alkalies and alkaline drugs. No known toxicity.

THIAMINE NITRATE • A B-vitamin. A white crystalline powder used as a diet supplement and to enrich flour. No known toxicity. GRAS.

THICKENING AGENTS • Substances to add body to lotions and creams. Those usually employed include such natural gums as sodium alginate and pectins.

THIMEROSAL • **Mercurochrome.** The metallo-organic compound also called Merthiolate. Used as a bacteriostat and fungistat in eye preparations. May cause allergic reaction from either the mercury or the salicylates in the compound.

THIODIGLYCOL • See Thioglycolic Acid Compounds.

THIODIPROPIONIC ACID • An acid freely soluble in hot water, alcohol, and acetone. Used as an antioxidant for soap products and polymers (*see*) of ethylene. No known toxicity.

THIOGLYCEROL • Used in soothing skin lotions. Prepared by heating glycerin (*see*) and alcohol. Yellowish, very viscous liquid, with a slight sulfur odor. Used to promote wound healing. No known toxicity.

THIOGLYCOLIC ACID COMPOUNDS • Prepared by the action of sodium sulfohydrate on sodium chloroacetate. A liquid with a strong unpleasant odor; mixes with water and alcohol. The ammonium and sodium salts are used in permanent wave solutions and as a hair straightener. The calcium salts are used in depilatories, hair-waving solutions, and lotions. Thioglycolates can cause hair breakage, skin irritations, severe allergic reactions, and pustular reactions.

THIOINDIGOID DYE • See Vat Dyes and Indigo.

THIOKOL® • One of the first synthetic elastomers (*see*), it is used in face masks, nail enamels, and in the manufacture of rubbers and resins. No known toxicity.

THIOLACTIC ACID • Used in depilatories and hair-waving preparations. See Thioglycolic Acid.

THIOLANEDIOL • An antibacterial. See Phenol.

THIOSALICYLIC ACID • Sulfur yellow flakes, slightly soluble in hot water. Used in the manufacture of cosmetic dyes. No known toxicity.

THREONINE • An essential amino acid (*see*); the last to be discovered (1935). Prevents the buildup of fat on the liver. Occurs in whole eggs, skim milk, casein, and gelatin.

THUJA OIL • See White Cedar Leaf Oil.

THYME • Used to flavor toothpaste, mouthwashes, and to scent perfumes, after-shave lotions, and soap. It is a seasoning from the dried leaves and flowering tops of the wild creeping thyme grown in Eurasia and throughout the United States. Used as a flavoring in cough medicines. May cause contact dermatitis and hayfever.

THYMOL • Used in mouthwashes, and to scent perfumes, after-shave lotions, and soap. Obtained from the essential oil of lavender, origanum oil, and other volatile oils. It destroys mold, preserves anatomical specimens, and is a topical antifungal agent with a pleasant aromatic odor. It is omitted from hypoallergenic cosmetics because it can cause allergic reactions.

TIN OXIDE • A coloring agent in cosmetics. A brownish black powder insoluble in water. No known toxicity.

TINCTURE OF BENZOIN • See Benzoin.

TIPA • The abbreviation for triisopropanolamine.

TIPA-STEARATE • See Stearic Acid.

TITANIUM DIOXIDE • The greatest covering and tinting power of any white pigment, used in bath powders, nail whites, depilatories, eye liners, white eye shadows, antiperspirants, face powders, protective creams, liquid powders, lipsticks, hand lotions, and nail polish. Occurs naturally in three different crystal forms. Used chiefly as a white pigment and as an opacifier; also a white pigment for candy, gum, and marking ink. No known toxicity when used externally. In high concentrations the dust may cause lung damage. Permanently listed for general cosmetic coloring in 1973.

TITANIUM HYDROXIDE • See Titanium Dioxide.

TOCOPHEROLS • **Vitamin E.** An antioxidant in baby preparations, deodorants, and hair-grooming aids. Obtained by the vacuum distillation of edible vegetable oils. Used as a dietary supplement and as an antioxidant for essential oils, rendered animal fats, or a combination of such fats with vegetable oils. Helps form normal red blood cells, muscle, and other tissues. Protects fat in the body's tissues from abnormal breakdown. Experimental evidence shows Vitamin E may protect the heart and blood vessels and retard aging.

TOCOPHERYL SUCCINATE • **Vitamin E Succinate.** Obtained by the distillation of edible vegetable oils and used as a dietary supplement and as an antioxidant for fats and oils. No known toxicity.

TOILET SOAP • A mild, mostly pure soap made from fatty materials of high quality, usually by milling and molding to form cakes. Usually contains an emollient (*see*), perfume, color, and a stabilizer with preservatives. More pleasant to use and less drying to the skin.

TOILET WATER • The scent is similar to that of perfume, but it does not last as long and is not as strong or as expensive. Usually made by adding a large amount of alcohol to the perfume formula. In Europe it is called "lotion"—8 ounces of perfume oil per gallon as compared to 20 to 24 ounces per gallon for perfumes. Considered moderately toxic if swallowed. Skin reactions depend upon ingredients.

TOLERANCE • The ability to live with an allergen.

TOLUENE • Used in nail polish. Obtained from petroleum or by distilling balsam Tolu. Used chiefly as a solvent. Resembles benzene but is less volatile, flammable, or toxic. May cause mild anemia if ingested, and it is narcotic in high concentrations. Being tested at the U.S. Frederick Cancer Research Center for possible cancer-causing effects. It can cause liver damage and is irritating to the skin and respiratory tract. While halogenated hydrocarbons like toluene are assumed responsible for health risks, long-term effects of low-level exposure to them have been found in at least 20 cities where toluene is present in the drinking water.

TOLUENE-2, 5-DIAMINE • See Toluene.

TOLUENE-3, 4-DIAMINOTOLUENE • An intermediate chemical in the manufacture of polyurethanes, dyes for textiles, fur and leather, varnishes, pigments, and hair dyes. In a National Cancer Institute study, it caused liver cancer when fed to rats and mice as well as breast cancer in female rats. In tests, a closely related compound, 2,4-toluenediamine, had the greatest absorption through the scalp of the hair dyes tested. See Phenylenediamine.

TOLUENE SULFONAMIDE/FORMALDEHYDE RESIN • It is used as a "nail strengthener" or hardener, and to improve adhesion and gloss. There is supposed to be no free formaldehyde in this widely used formula. Large cosmetic manufacturers stopped producing nail hardeners with free formaldehyde in the 1960s because of the frequent adverse reactions reported. This compound is a strong sensitizer while in the liquid state but not when solidified, therefore, if it doesn't touch the skin while being applied, even a person sensitive to the ingredients may not have a reaction.

o-TOLYL BIGUANIDE • See Toluene.

TOMATO EXTRACT • **Tomatine.** Extract from the fruit of the tomato, *Solanum esculentum*. Used as a fungicide and as a precipitating agent. Nontoxic.

TONER • In cosmetics, an organic pigment that is used in full strength. For example, D & C Red No. 7 (*see*).

TONKA • **Tonka Bean. Coumarouna Bean.** Brownish black seeds with a wrinkled surface and brittle shiny, or fatty, skins. A vanillalike odor and a bitter taste. Used in the production of natural coumarin (*see*), flavoring extracts, and toilet powders.

TOOTHPASTE • See Dentifrices.

TOP COAT • Same ingredients as in base coat (*see*) so as to give the nail enamel a greater floss and to help prevent chipping.

TOP-NOTE • The first impression of a fragrance upon the sense of smell. The most volatile part of the perfume. It is one of the most important factors in the success of the perfume, but does not persist after the first sniff.

TORMENTIL EXTRACT • The extract of the roots of *Potentilla erecta*.

TRAGACANTH • See Gum Tragacanth.

TRANSLUCENT POWDER • Because they contain more titanium dioxide (*see*) than other face powders, translucent makeups are actually more opaque. But other than that, they contain the same ingredients.

TRIACETIN • **Glyceryl Triacetate.** Primarily a solvent for hair dyes. Also a fixative in perfume and used in toothpaste. A colorless, somewhat oily liquid with a slight fatty odor and a bitter taste. Obtained from adding acetate to glycerin (*see both*). Soluble in water and miscible with alcohol. No known toxicity in above use. Large subcutaneous injections are lethal to rats.

TRIBROMSALAN • **TBS. 3, 4′, 5-Tribromosalicylanilide.** Used in medicated cosmetics; an antiseptic and fungicide. Irritating to the skin and may cause allergic reaction when skin is exposed to the sun. Salicylanilide is an antifungal compound used to treat ringworm. TBS is in the most popular soaps to kill skin bacteria. Used as a germicide frequently replacing hexachlorophene (*see*).

TRIBUTYL CITRATE • The triester of butyl alcohol and citric acid (*see both*), it is a pale yellow, odorless liquid used as a plasticizer, antifoam agent, and solvent for nitrocellulose. Low toxicity.

TRI (BUTYLCRESYL) BUTANE • Used as a stabilizer. See Phenol.

TRICALCIUM PHOSPHATE • The calcium salt of phosphate (*see*). A polishing agent in dentifrices; also an anticaking agent in table salt and vanilla powder, and a dietary supplement. No known toxicity. See Calcium Phosphate.

TRICETETH-5 PHOSPHATE • See Phosphoric Acid and Ceteth-5.

TRICLOCARBAN • **Trichlorocarbanilide. TCC.** A bacteria killer and antiseptic in soaps, medicated cosmetics, deodorants, and cleansing creams. Prepared from aniline (*see*). In May 1983, it was revealed that tests for this soap ingredient were falsified and that rat deaths were not reported. The reasons for the deaths were not confirmed.

TRICHLOROETHANE • Used in cosmetics as a solvent and degreasing agent. Nonflammable liquid. Insoluble in, and absorbs some water. Less toxic than carbon tetrachloride, which is used in fire extinguishers. Trichloroethane solutions are irritating to the eyes and mucous membranes, and in high concentrations can be narcotic. Can be absorbed through the skin. Inhalation and ingestion produce serious symptoms ranging from vomiting to death.

TRICLOSAN • A broad spectrum antibacterial agent that is active primarily against some types of bacteria. It is used in deodorant soaps, vaginal deodorant sprays, and other cosmetic products as well as in drugs and household products. Its deodorant properties are due to the inhibition of bacterial growth. Can cause allergy contact dermatitis, particularly when used in products for the feet.

TRICRESYL PHOSPHATE • **TCP.** A plasticizer in nail polishes and a strengthener in lubricants. Colorless or pale yellow liquid. Can cause paralysis many days after exposure. For instance, in 1960, approximately 10,000 Moroccans became ill after ingesting cooking oil adulterated with turbojet engine oil containing 3 percent TCP. Can be absorbed through the skin and mucous membranes, causing poisoning. Persons sensitive to the plasticizer in eyeglass frames may develop a skin rash from tricresyl. Toxic dose in humans is only 6 milligrams per kilogram of body weight.

TRIDECETH-3 (PEG-3 TRIDECYL ETHER) • See Polyethylene Glycols.

TRIDECYL ALCOHOL • Derived from tridecane, a paraffin hydrocarbon obtained from petroleum. Used as an emulsifier in cosmetic creams, lotions, and lipsticks. No known toxicity.

TRIDECYL SALICYLATE • See Salicylates.

TRIDECYL STEARATE • See Stearic Acid.

TRIDECYLBENZENE SULFONIC ACID • See Sulfonamide Formaldehyde.

TRIDETH-3 • See Tridecyl Alcohol.

TRIDETH-6, -10, -12 • See Tridecyl Alcohol.

TRIETHANOLAMINE • A coating agent for fresh fruits and vegetables and widely used in surfactants (*see*), and as a dispersing agent and detergent in hand and body lotions, shaving creams, soaps, shampoos, and bath powders. Its principal toxic effect in animals has been attributed to overalkalinity. Gross pathology has been found in the gastrointestinal tract in fatally poisoned guinea pigs. It is an irritant.

TRIETHANOLAMINE DODECYLBENZENE SULFONATE • **Linear.** Made from ethylene oxide and used in bubble baths and soapless shampoos. May be mildly irritating to the skin. See Ethanolamines.

TRIETHANOLAMINE-d-1-2-PYRROLIDONE-5-CARBOXYMETHYLATE • **Triethanolamines.** A colorless liquid, soluble in water, and used as a soap base and oil emulsifier. See Ethanolamines.

TRIETHANOLAMINE STEARATE • Made from ethylene oxide. Used in brilliantines, cleansing creams, foundation creams, hair lacquers, liquid makeups, fragrances, liquid powders, mascara, protective creams, baby preparations, shaving creams, lathers, and preshave lotions. A moisture absorber, viscous, used in making emulsions. Cream colored; turns brown on exposure to air. May be irritating to the skin and mucous membranes, but less so than many other amines (*see*).

TRIETHANOLAMINE TRISODIUM PHOSPHATE • Made from ethylene oxide and used in cuticle softeners. May be mildly irritating to the skin. See Ethanolamines.

TRIETHONIUM HYDROLYZED ANIMAL PROTEIN ETHOSULFATE • See Hydrolyzed Animal Protein and Quaternary Ammonium Compounds.

TRIETHYL CITRATE • **Citric Acid. Ethyl Citrate.** A plasticizer in nail polish. Odorless, practically colorless, bitter; also used in dried egg as a sequestering agent (*see*), and to prevent rancidity. Citrates may interfere with laboratory tests for blood, liver, and pancreatic function, but no known skin toxicity.

TRIETHYLENE GLYCOL • Used in stick perfume. Prepared from ethylene oxide and ethylene gycol (*see both*). Used as a solvent. See Polyethylene Glycol for toxicity.

TRIHYDROXY STEARIN • Isolated from cork and used as a thickener. No known toxicity.

TRILAURYL CITRATE • See Lauryl Alcohol and Citric Acid.

TRIIODOTHYRONINE • Possesses 5 times the activity of the thyroid drug L-thyroxine used in thyroid replacement therapy. It increases the metabolic rate and oxygen consumption of animal tissues.

TRIISOPROPANOLAMINE • A crystalline, white solid. A mild base used as an emulsifying agent. No known toxicity.

TRIISOSTEARIN • See Glycerin and Isostearic Acid.

TRILANETH-4 PHOSPHATE • See Lanolin Alcohols.

TRILAURIN • See Lauric Acid.

TRILAURYLAMINE • See Lauryl Alcohol.

TRILINOLEIC ACID • **Trimer Acid.** See Linoleic Acid.

TRILINOLEIN • The triester of glycerin and linoleic acid (*see both*).

TRIMAGNESIUM PHOSPHATE • **Magnesium Phosphate, Tribasic.** Occurs in nature as the mineral, bobierite. A white crystalline powder, it absorbs water and is used in cosmetics as an alkali. No known toxicity.

TRIMETHYLHEXANOL • See Hexanol.
TRIMETHYLOLPROPANE TRIISOSTEARATE • See Propane and Isostearic Acid.
TRIMETHYLOLPROPANE TRIOCTANOATE • See Propane and Octanoic Acid.
TRIMETHYLSILOXYSILICATE • See Silicates.
TRIMYRISTIN • **Glyceryl Trimyristate.** Solid triglyceride of myristic acid that occurs in many vegetable fats and oils, particularly in coconut oil and nutmeg butter. White to yellowish-gray, it is used as an emollient in cold creams and for shampoos. No known toxicity.
TRIOLEIN • **Glyceryl Trioleate.** From the Palestine olive and one of the chief constituents of nondrying oils and fats used in cosmetics. Colorless to yellowish, tasteless, odorless. Used in cosmetic creams and oils. No known toxicity.
TRIOLETH-8 PHOSPHATE • Derived from phosphoric acid and oleyl alcohol (*see both*).
TRIOLEYL PHOSPHATE • Used as an emulsifier. No known toxicity. See Oleyl Alcohol.
TRIPABA PANTHENOL • See Panthenol and PABA.
TRIPALMITIN • Occurs in fats and is prepared from glycerol and palmitic acid (*see both*). Insoluble in water. See Palmitic Acid for toxicity.
TRIPHENYL PHOSPHATE • A noncombustible substitute for camphor in celluloid. Colorless; insoluble in water. Stable, fireproof, and used as a plasticizer in nail polish. Causes paralysis if ingested, and skin rash in hypersensitive people. Inhalation of only 3.5 milligrams per kilogram of body weight is toxic to humans.
TRIPHENYLMETHANE GROUP • **Tritan.** Certified dyes made from the reduction (*see*) of carbon tetrachloride and benezene with aluminum chloride. Very soluble in water, affected by light and alkalies. Among the triphenylmethane group are FD & C Blue No. 1 and FD & C Green Nos. 1, 2, and 3. See Colors for toxicity.
TRIPOLYPHOSPHATE • A buffering agent in shampoos. A phosphorus salt. Used to soften water, as an emulsifier, and a dispersing agent. Can be irritating because of its alkalinity. May cause esophageal stricture if swallowed. Moderately irritating to the skin and mucous membranes. Ingestion can cause violent vomiting.
TRIS (HYDROXYMETHYL) NITROMETHANE • Crystals from ethyl acetate and benzene (*see both*). Soluble in alcohol. Inhibits bacterial growth in water systems, cutting oils, nonprotein glues, and sizings. Irritating to the skin and mucous membranes. May release formaldehyde (*see*).

TRIS (NONYLPHENYL) PHOSPHITE • See Phenol.
TRISODIUM EDTA • See Terasodium EDTA.
TRISODIUM HEDTA • Mineral suspending agents. See Sequestrants.
TRISODIUM HYDROXY EDTA • See Tetrasodium EDTA.
TRISODIUM HYDROXYETHYL ETHLENEDIAMINETRIACETATE • See Tetrasodium EDTA.
TRISODIUM NTA • See Sequestrants.
TRISODIUM PHOSPHATE • Obtained from phosphate rock. Highly alkaline. Used in shampoos, cuticle softeners, bubble baths, and bathsalts for its water-softening and cleaning actions. Phosphorous was formerly used to treat rickets and degenerative disorders and is now used as a mineral supplement for foods; also in incendiary bombs and tracer bullets. Can cause skin irritation from alkalinity.
TRISTEARIN • Present in many animal and vegetable fats, especially hard ones like tallow and cocoa butter, it is used in surfactants, quaternary ammonium compounds, and emollients. No known toxicity.
TRISTEARYL CITRATE • The triester of stearyl alcohol and citric acid (*see both*).
TROMETHAMINE • Made by the reduction (*see*) of nitro compounds, it is a crystalline mass used in the manufacture of surface-active agents (*see*). Used as an emulsifying agent for cosmetic creams and lotions, mineral oil, and paraffin wax emulsions. Used medicinally to correct an overabundance of acid in the body. No known toxicity.
TRUE FIXATIVE • This holds back the evaporation of the other materials. Benzoin is an example. See Fixatives.
TRYPTOPHAN • A tremendous amount of research is now in progress with this amino acid (*see*). First isolated in milk in 1901, it is now being studied as a means to calm hyperactive children, induce sleep, and fight depression and pain. Although it is sold over the counter, it is not believed to be completely harmless and has been suspected of being a co-carcinogen and to affect the liver when taken in high doses. In cosmetics, it is used to increase the protein content of creams and lotions. No known toxicity in cosmetics.
TUBEROSE OIL • Derived from a Mexican bulbous herb commonly cultivated for its spike of fragrant white single or double flowers that resemble small lilies. Tuberose oil is used in perfumes. Can cause allergic reactions.
TURKEY-RED OIL • One of the first surface-active agents (*see*). Used in shampoos. Contains sulfated castor oil. It has been used to obtain bright clear colors in dyeing fabrics. See Sulfonated Oils.

TURPENTINE GUM • A solvent in hair lotions, waxes, perfume soaps, and to soothe skin. It is the oleoresin from a species of pines. Also a food flavoring. Readily absorbed through the skin. Irritating to the skin and mucous membranes. In addition to being a local skin irritant, it can cause allergic reactions.

TYROSINE • Widely distributed amino acid (*see*), termed nonessential because it does not seem to be necessary for growth. It is used as a dietary supplement. It is a building block of protein and is used in cosmetics to help creams penetrate the skin. No known toxicity.

U

ULTRAMARINE, BLUE, GREEN, PINK, RED, AND VIOLET • Colorings permanently listed for external use only, including in the area of the eye, in 1976. See Colors.

2, 3-UNDECADIONE • A synthetic butter flavoring agent for beverages, ice cream, ices, candy, and baked goods. No known toxicity.

γ-UNDECALACTONE • **Peach Aldehyde.** Colorless to light yellow liquid with a peachy odor. Derived from undecylenic acid with sulfuric acid. A synthetic fruit flavoring, colorless or yellow, with a strong peach odor. Used for beverages, ice cream, ices, candy, baked goods, gelatin desserts, and chewing gum. Used also in perfumery. No known toxicity.

UNDECANAL • A synthetic flavoring agent. Colorless to slightly yellow, with a sweet, fatty odor. Used in lemon, orange, rose, fruit, and honey flavorings for beverages, ice cream, ices, candy, baked goods, and chewing gum. No known toxicity.

9-UNDECANAL • A synthetic citrus and fruit flavoring for beverages, ice cream, ices, candy, baked goods, and chewing gum. No known toxicity.

10-UNDECANAL • A synthetic citrus, floral, and fruit flavoring agent for beverages, ice cream, ices, and candy. No known toxicity.

1-UNDECANOL • Colorless liquid with a citrus odor used in perfumery and as a flavoring. See Undecylenic Acid.

2-UNDECANOL • Antifoaming agent, perfume fixative, and plasticizer. See Undecylenic Acid.

2-UNDECANONE • A synthetic flavoring agent that occurs naturally in rue and hops oil. Used in citrus, coconut, peach, and cheese flavorings for beverages, ice cream, ices, candy, baked goods, and puddings. No known toxicity.

10-UNDECEN-1-YL ACETATE • A synthetic citrus and fruit flavoring agent for beverages, ice cream, ices, candy, and baked goods. No known toxicity.

UNDECYL ALCOHOL • A synthetic lemon, lime, orange, and rose flavoring agent for beverages, ice cream, ices, candy, and baked goods. No known toxicity.

UNDECYLENIC ACID • Occurs in sweat. Obtained from ricinoleic acid (*see*). A liquid or crystalline powder, with an odor suggestive of perspiration or citrus. Used as a fungicide, in perfumes, as a flavoring, and as a lubricant additive in cosmetics. Has been given orally but it causes dizziness, headaches, and stomach upset. No known toxicity for the skin.

UNDECYLENYL ALCOHOL • Colorless liquid with a citrus odor. Used in perfumes. It is combustible but has a low toxicity.

UNDECYLIC ACID • See Undecylenic Acid.

UNDECYLPENTADECANOL • See Fatty Alcohols.

UNSAPONIFIABLE OLIVE OIL • The oil fraction that is not broken down in the refining of olive fatty acids.

UNSAPONIFIABLE RAPESEED OIL • The oil that is not broken down in the refining of rapeseed oil fatty acids.

UNSAPONFIABLE SHEA BUTTER • The fraction of shea butter that is not broken down during processing.

UNSAPONIFIABLE SOYBEAN OIL • The fraction of soybean oil that is not broken down in the refining recovery of soybean oil fatty acids.

UREA • **Carbamide.** A product of protein metabolism excreted in human urine. Derived from ammonia and liquid carbon dioxide. Used in yeast food and wine production up to 2 pounds per gallon. It is used to "brown" baked goods such as pretzels, and consists of colorless or white odorless crystals that have a cool salty taste. An antiseptic and deodorizer used in liquid antiperspirants, ammoniated dentifrices, roll-on deodorants, mouthwashes, hair colorings, hand creams, lotions, and shampoos. Medicinally, urea is used as a topical antiseptic and as a diuretic to reduce body water. Its largest use, however, is a fertilizer, and only a small part of its production goes into the manufacture of other urea products. No known toxicity. The final report to the FDA of the Select Committee on GRAS Substances stated in 1980 that it should continue its GRAS status with no limitations other than good manufacturing practices.

UREASE • An enzyme that hydrolyzes urea (*see*) to ammonium carbonate (*see*).

UROCANIC ACID • Prepared from L-histidine.

USNIC ACID • Antibacterial compound found in lichens. Pale yellow, slightly soluble in water. No known toxicity.

V

VA • Abbreviation for Vinyl Acetate.

VAGINAL DEODORANTS • **Feminine Hygiene Sprays.** Introduced in 1966, vaginal deodorant sprays have grown very popular. Marketed as mists or powders in aerosol sprays and widely advertised as products to keep women feeling "feminine," they are designed to prevent "feminine odor" and to give that "clean feeling." Classified as cosmetics, these deodorants did not need clearance for the ingredients. Reports to the FDA of irritations and other problems from the sprays within the last two years include bladder infections, burning, itching, swelling, rash, boils in the vaginal area, and blood in the urine. Physicians recommend soap and water as more beneficial than the sprays, and that concentrating chemicals, including perfumes, in one area is not wise because of the possibility of allergic reactions and irritations. Ingredients of vaginal deodorants include emollients such as glycerides, myristate, polyoxyethylene derivatives, perfumes, and propellants. Some sprays, in addition, contain an antibacterial. The allergies and skin reactions may not only occur in the women who use these products, but in their male partners who are exposed to the ingredients during sexual relations. Among some of the problem spray ingredients identified were benzalkonium chloride, chlorhexidine, isopropyl myristate, and perfume.

VALERIAN • See Valeric Acid.

VALERIC ACID • Used in the manufacture of perfumes. Occurs naturally in apples, cocoa, coffee, oil of lavender, peaches, and strawberries. Colorless, with an unpleasant odor. Usually distilled form valerian root. It is used also as a synthetic flavoring, and some of its salts are used in medicine. No known toxicity.

VALINE • An essential amino acid (*see*). Occurs in the largest quantities in fibrous protein. It is indispensable for growth and nitrogen balance. Used in suntan lotions. No known toxicity in cosmetics but the FDA has asked for further study of this ingredient as a food additive.

VANCIDE FP • See Captan.

VANILLA EXTRACT • Used in perfumes and flavorings. Extracted from the full-grown unripe fruit of the vanilla plant of Mexico and the West Indies. Also a food flavoring and scent made synthetically from eugenol (*see*); also from the waste of the wood pulp industry. One part vanillin equals 400 parts vanilla pods. The lethal dose in mice is 3 grams (30 grams to the ounce) per kilogram of body weight. A skin irritant that produces a burning sensation and eczema. May also cause pigmentation of the skin.

VANILLIN • Used in perfumes. Occurs naturally in vanilla and potato parings but is an artificial flavoring and scent made synthetically from eugenol (*see*); also from the waste of the wood pulp industry. One part vanillin equals 400 parts vanilla pods. The lethal dose in mice is 3 grams (30 grams to the ounce) per kilogram of body weight. A skin irritant that produces a burning sensation and eczema. May also cause pigmentation of the skin.

VANISHING CREAM • An emollient cream that creates the feeling of vanishing when rubbed on the skin. See Emollients.

VASELINE® • **Petroleum Jelly. Petrolatum. Paraffin Jelly.** Used in cold creams, emollient creams, conditioning creams, wax depilatories, eyebrow pencils, eyeshadows, liquefying creams, liquid powders, nail whites, lipsticks, protective creams, baby creams, and rouge. While usually soothing to the skin, it may cause allergic reactions, particularly in creams and hair dressings, because it is a derivative of petroleum.

VAT DYES • Water-soluble aromatic organic compounds. They dissolve in water when vatted with an alkaline solution of the reducing (*see*) agent sodium hydrosulfite. Good fastness. Considered low in toxicity.

VEGETABLE GUMS • Includes derivatives from quince seed, karaya, acacia, tragacanth, Irish moss, guar, sodium alginate, potassium alginate, ammonium alginate, and propylene glycol alginate. All are subject to deterioration and always need a preservative. The gums function as liquid emulsions, that is, they thicken cosmetic products and make them creamy. No known toxicity other than allergic reactions in hypersensitive persons.

VEGETABLE OILS • Peanut, sesame, olive, and cottonseed oil obtained from plants and used in baby preparations, cleansing creams, emollient creams, face powders, hair-grooming aids, hypoallergenic cosmetics, lipsticks, nail creams, shampoos, shaving creams, and wave sets. No known toxicity.

VERBENA EXTRACT • Has a characteristic odor, insoluble in water. Used as a perfume ingredient. See Terpenes.

VERONICA EXTRACT • Extract of the flowering herb, *Veronica*, a small herb of wide distribution that has pink or white flowers. Used in perfumery.

VETIVER OIL • **Vetiverol. Khus-Khus.** Stable, brown to reddish-brown oil from the roots of a fragrant grass. Used in soaps and perfumes, it has an aromatic to harsh woodsy odor. No known toxicity.

VETIVER RECTIFIED • Perfume ingredient. See Vetiver Oil.

VIBURNUM EXTRACT • **Haw Bark. Black Extract.** Extract of the fruit of a hawthorn shrub or tree. Used in fragrances and in butter, caramel, cola, maple, and walnut flavorings for beverages. Has been used as a uterine antispasmodic. No known toxicity.

VINEGAR • Used for hundreds of years to remove lime soap after shampooing. It is a solvent for cosmetic oils and resins. Vinegar is about 4 to 6 percent acetic acid. Acetic acid occurs naturally in apples, cheese, grapes, milk, and other foods. No known toxicity but may cause an allergic reaction in those allergic to corn.

VINYL CHLORIDE • Banned in aerosol cans for hair sprays and deodorants in 1974. It is a proven cause of liver cancer in workers who work with the compound.

VINYL POLYMERS • Includes resins used in false nails and nail lacquer preparations. A major class of polymer (*see*) material widely used in the plastics, synthetic fibers, and surface coatings. Such materials are derived from the polymerization of vinyl groups, which include vinyl acetate and vinyl chloride. Vinyls are made from the reaction between acetylene and certain compounds such as alcohol, phenol, and amines. Inhalation of 300 parts per million is toxic in humans.

VINYL PYRROLIDONE • See Polyvinyl Pyrrolidone.

VINYLDIMETHICONE • See Siloxane and Vinyl Polymers.

VIOLET EXTRACT • **Flowers and Leaves.** Green liquid with typical odor of violet. It is taken from the plant widely grown in the United States. Used in perfumes, face powders, and for coloring inorganic pigments. May produce skin rash in the allergic.

VITAMIN A • A yellow viscous liquid insoluble in water. Used in lubricating creams and oils for its alleged skin-healing properties. Can be absorbed through the skin. Its absence from the diet leads to a loss in weight, retarded growth, and eye diseases. Too high a level can cause the skin to turn yellow, birth defects, and pressure on the brain. See also Retinoids and Retın-A.

VITAMIN C • See Ascorbic Acid.

VITAMIN D^2 • **Calciferol.** A pale yellow, oily liquid, odorless, tasteless, insoluble in water. Used for its alleged skin-healing properties in lubricating creams and lotions. The absence of Vitamin D in the food of young animals can lead to rickets, a bone-affecting condition. It is soluble in fats, and fat solvents and is present in animal fats. Absorbed through the skin. Its value in cosmetics has not been proven. No known toxicity to the skin.

VITAMIN E • See Tocopherols.

VITAMIN E ACETATE • See Tocopherols.

VITAMIN E SUCCINATE • See Tocopherols.

W

WALNUT EXTRACT • An extract of the husk of the nut of *Juglans spp.*, used in walnut flavorings and for brown coloring. No known toxicity.

WALNUT LEAVES • Used in hair products for "split ends." See Walnut Extract.

WALNUT OIL • See Walnut Extract.

WALNUT SHELL POWDER • The ground shell of English Walnuts, *Juglans regia*. See Walnut Extract.

WATER • The major constituent of all living matter and the ingredient used most in the cosmetics industry. Because of this fact, the industry fought labeling that required listing ingredients in descending order because water would be first most of the time. However, listing in descending order is now required. It is important that water used in cosmetics be sterile to avoid contamination of the product. Manufacturers may also have to soften water in some areas because of the high mineral content that may affect the texture and appearance of the finished product.

WATERCRESS EXTRACT • Extract obtained from *Nasturtium officinalis*.

WAVE SET • See Setting Lotions.

WAXES • Obtained from insects, animals, and plants. Waxes have a wide application in the manufacture of cosmetics. Beeswax, for instance, is a substance secreted by the bee's special glands on the underside of its abdomen. The wax is glossy and hard but plastic when warm. Insoluble in water but partially soluble in boiling alcohol. Used in hair-grooming preparations, hair straighteners, as an epilatory to remove unwanted hair, and as the traditional stiffening agent (*see*) in lipsticks. Wax esters such as lanolin or spermaceti (*see both*) differ from fats in being less greasy, harder, and more brittle. Waxes are generally nontoxic to the skin but may cause allergic reactions in the hypersensitive depending upon the source of the wax.

WETTING AGENT • Any of numerous water-soluble agents that promote spreading of a liquid on a surface or penetration into a material such as skin. It lowers surface tension for better contact and absorption.

WHEAT BRAN • The broken coat of *Triticum aestivum*. See Wheat Germ.

WHEAT BRAN LIPIDS • An extract of the coat of wheat. See Wheat Germ.

WHEAT FLOUR • Milled from the kernels of wheat, *Tricticum aestivum*. See Wheat Starch.

WHEAT GERM • The golden germ of the wheat is high in Vitamin E. See Tocopherols. It is used by organic cosmeticians to make a face mask to counteract dry skin. Here is the formula: crush ¼ cup wheat germ plus 1 tablespoon sesame seeds with a mortar and pestle or with the back of a spoon. Add 2 tablespoons of fresh olive oil and mix well. Spread on face and neck. Leave on for 10 minutes. Remove with lukewarm water. Then rinse with cold water. Apply a rinse of chilled witch hazel (*see*).
WHEAT GERM EXTRACT • See Tocopherols.
WHEAT GERM GLYCERIDES • See Tocopherols.
WHEAT GERM OIL • See Tocopherols.
WHEAT GERMAMIDOPROPYL BETAINE • See Surfactants.
WHEAT GERMAMIDOPROPYL DIMETHYLAMINE LACTATE • See Tocopherols.
WHEAT GERMAMIDOPROPYLAMINE • See Tocopherols.
WHEAT GLUTEN • Used in powders and creams as a base. A mixture of proteins present in wheat flour and obtained as an extremely sticky yellowish gray mass by making a dough and then washing out the starch. It consists almost entirely of two proteins, gliadin and glutenin. It contributes to the porous and spongy structure of bread. No known toxicity.
WHEAT STARCH • A product of cereal grain. It swells when water is added. Used as a demulcent, emollient, and in dusting and face powders. May cause allergic reactions such as red eyes and stuffy nose.
WHEY PROTEIN • Obtained from the thin, watery part of milk separated from the curds, it is used in emollients. No known toxicity.
WHITE • Inorganic pigments are widely used to "color" cosmetics white. The most widely used are zinc oxide and titanium dioxide to whiten face powders. Also used are gloss white (aluminum hydrate), barium sulfate (blanc fixe) and alumina (*see all*).
WHITE CEDAR LEAF OIL • **Oil of Arborvitae.** Stable, pale yellow volatile oil obtained by steam distillation from the fresh leaves and branch ends of the eastern arborvitae. Has a strong camphoraceous and sagelike scent. Used as a perfume and scent for soaps and room sprays. Also used as a flavoring agent. Soluble in most fixed oils. See Cedar for toxicity.
WHITE LILY EXTRACT • Extract of the bulbs of *Lilium candidum*. Edible bulbs that were made into soup by the American Indians, the lily is used in perfumery.
WHITE NETTLE EXTRACT • Obtained from the flowers of *Lamium album*. See Nettles.

WILD AGRIMONY EXTRACT • **Extract of Wild Pansy.** The extract of the herb, *Potentilla anserina*. The American Indians used to crush the leaves to treat boils and swellings. By the late 1800s, the wild pansy was being ground up and used to treat many skin diseases including impetigo, skin ulcers, and scabies.

WILD CHERRY • **Wild Black Cherry Bark.** The dried stem bark collected in autumn in North America. Used in lipsticks and cherry flavorings for food and medicines. Also used as a sedative and expectorant medicinally. No known toxicity.

WILD INDIGO ROOT • **Baptisia. Bastard Indigo.** A wild uncultivated plant of North America with showy yellow or blue flowers. Used as a coloring. No known toxicity.

WILD MARJORAM EXTRACT • Extract of the flowering ends of *Origanum vulgare*. Yellow or greenish-yellow liquid containing about 40 percent terpenes (*see*). Used in perfumery. See Marjoram Oil.

WILD MINT EXTRACT • Extract of the leaves and tender twigs of *Mentha arvensis*. The Cheyenne Indians prepared a decoction of the ground leaves and stems of wild mint and drank the liquid to check nausea. Pulegone and thymol (*see*) are derived from an oil of wild mint. Its odor resembles peppermint.

WILD PANSY • See Agrimony Extract.

WILD THYME EXTRACT • The flowering tops of the plant grown in Eurasia and throughout the United States. The dried leaves are used in emollients and fragrances and as a seasoning in foods. Has also been used as a muscle relaxant. No known toxicity.

WILLOW LEAF EXTRACT • The extract of the leaves of the willow tree species, *Salix*. The willow has been used for pain-relieving and fever-lowering properties since ancient Greece. The American Indians used willow baths to cool fevers, and indeed, the extract of willows contain salicylic acid, a close cousin of aspirin.

WINTERGREEN OIL • **Menthyl Salicylate.** Used in toothpaste, tooth powder, and perfumes. Obtained naturally from betula, sweet birch, or teaberry oil. Present in certain leaves and bark but usually prepared by treating salicylic acid with methanol (*see both*). Also used as a food and beverage flavoring. Wintergreen is a strong irritant. Ingestion of relatively small amounts may cause severe poisoning and death. Average lethal dose in children is 10 milliliters and in adults 30 milliliters. It is very irritating to the mucous membranes and skin and can be absorbed rapidly through the skin.

WISTERIA • Used in perfumes. The extract from the Asiatic, mostly woody vines, of the family that produces showy blue, white, purple, and rose flowers. No known toxicity.

WITCH HAZEL • A skin freshener, local anesthetic, and astringent made from the leaves and/or twigs of *Hamamelis virginiana*. Collected in the autumn. Witch hazel has an ethanol content of 70 to 80 percent and a tannin content of 2 to 9 percent. Witch hazel water, which is what you buy at the store, contains 15 percent ethanol. See Ethanol for toxicity.
WOOD FAT • Crude Lanolin (*see*).
WOODRUFF • **Master of the Woods.** Used in perfumes and sachets. Made of the leaves of an herb grown in Europe, Siberia, North Africa, and Australia. It is a symbol of spring, and has a clean fresh smell. No known toxicity.
WOOL WAX ALCOHOLS • **Wool Fat.** Chemically more like a fat than a wax, it is the deposit sheep make on their wool. Used as emollients. See Lanolin Alcohols.
WRINKLE REMOVERS • Periodically, the cosmetics industry comes up with a magic ingredient that will prevent or cure wrinkles. Among such ingredients in recent years was serum albumin (from bulls), and estrogen. Another wrinkle remover contained some unidentified ingredients that irritated the skin so that it "puffed up" and the wrinkles "filled out." Turtle oil, natural proteins, and polyunsaturates, among many others, were supposed to feed aging skin, but there is no apparent biochemical or physiological activity in any of them. The companies really went wild in the mid-80s when Christiaan Barnard, M.D., the pioneer South African heart surgeon, lent his name to a Swiss product with "glycel" and mysterious ingredients that reversed the aging process in the skin. Other competitors came out with similar claims. Ironically, around the same time, physicians reported that Retin-A, a Vitamin A derivative, actually did have some wrinkle-reducing effects. It is difficult for the Federal Trade Commission and the FDA to get after promoters of wrinkle creams. By the time the agencies bring the manufacturers to court, it has taken several years and a great deal of money and manpower. Then all the manufacturers have to do is open up under different names or change the names of their products and start selling wrinkle creams all over again. The constant advertising that wrinkles are bad also has its deleterious effects on the psyche of people who may have them.

X

XANTHAN GUM • A gum produced by a pure culture fermentation of a carbohydrate with *Xanthomonas campestris*. Also called "corn sugar gum." It is used as a thickener, an emulsifier, and a stabilizer. No known toxicity.

XANTHENE • Colorants are divided into acid and basic groups. They are the second largest category of certified colors. The acids are derived from fluorescein. The quinoid acid type is represented by FD & C Red No. 3, erythrosine, used frequently in lipsticks. The phenolic formulations, often called "bromo acids" is represented by D & C Red. 2, used to "stain" lips. The only basic type certified is D & C Red 19, also called Rhodamine B.

XANTHOPHYLL • **Vegetable Lutein.** A yellow coloring originally isolated from egg yolk, now isolated from petals of flowers. Occurs also in colored feathers of birds. One of the most widespread carotenoid alcohols (a group of red and yellow pigments) in nature. Provisionally listed for use in food. Although carotenoids can usually be turned into Vitamin A, xanthophyll has no Vitamin A activity.

XANTHOXYLUM AMERICANUM • See Zanthoxylum.

XYLENE • Since xylene is an aromatic hydrocarbon as is chlorine, it warrants further investigation as a cancer-causing agent. There has been no definite association but it is toxic by inhalation or ingestion. Used as a solvent.

XYLENE SULFONIC ACID • A mixture of aromatic acids. See Surfactants.

XYLITOL • Formerly made from birchwood, but now made from waste products from the pulp industry. Xylitol has been reported to have diuretic effects, but this has not been substantiated. It is used in chewing gum and as an artificial sweetener. It has been reported to sharply reduce cavities in teeth but costs more than sugar. FDA preliminary reports cited it as a possible cancer-causing agent.

XYLOCAINE® • **Lidocaine.** Used in after-shave lotions. A local anesthetic that interferes with the transmission of nerve impulses, thereby effecting local anesthetic action. Recommended by manufacturers for topical use on mucous membranes only. Can cause allergic reactions. Not permitted in cosmetics in Switzerland.

Y

YARROW • A strong scented, spicy, wild herb used in astringents and shampoos. Its astringent qualities have caused it to be recommended by herbalists for greasy skins. According to old herbal recipes, it prevents baldness when the hair is washed regularly with it. Used medicinally as an astringent, tonic, and stimulant. May cause a sensitivity to sunlight and artificial light, in which the skin breaks out and swells.

YEAST • A fungi that is a dietary source of folic acid. It produces enzymes that will convert sugar to alcohol and carbon dioxide. No known toxicity.

YEAST EXTRACT • See Yeast.

YELLOW NO. 5 • All foods containing this coloring, which is the most widely used color additive in food, drugs and cosmetics, are supposed to identify it on the label. The FDA ordered this so that those allergic to it could avoid it. See also Tartrazine and Salicylates.

YLANG-YLANG OIL • A light yellow very fragrant liquid obtained in the Philippines from flowers. Used for perfumes and as a food and beverage flavoring. May cause allergic reactions.

YOGURT • A dairy product produced by the action of bacteria or yeast in milk. No known toxicity. Supposedly has emollient properties.

YUCCA EXTRACT • **Mohave Extract. Joshua Tree. Adam's Needle.** Derived from a southwestern United States plant and used as a base for organic cosmetics and a root beer flavoring for beverages and ice cream. No known toxicity.

Z

ZANTHOXYLUM • **Xanthoxylum. Ash Bark. Toothache Tree. Angelica Tree.** The dried bark or berries of this tree, which grows in Canada and south of Virginia and Missouri, is used to ease the pain of toothaches, to soothe stomachaches, and as an antidiarrheal medicine. No known toxicity. A member of the rue family.

ZEIN • Used in face masks, nail polishes, and as a plasticizer. It is the principal protein in corn. Obtained as a yellowish powder by extracting corn gluten with an alcohol; also used to make textile fibers plastics, printing inks, varnishes, and other coatings and adhesives. No known toxicity.

ZINC • A white brittle metal insoluble in water and soluble in acids or hot solutions of alkalies. Widely used as an astringent for mouthwashes and as a reducing agent (*see*) and reagent (*see*). Ingestion of the salts can cause nausea and vomiting. It can cause contact dermatitis.

ZINC ACETATE • The zinc salt of acetic acid (*see*). Used in medicine as a dietary supplement and as a cross-linking agent for polymers (*see*). For toxicity, see Zinc Salts.

ZINC BORATE • The inorganic salt of zinc oxide and boric oxide, it is used as a fungistat and mildew inhibitor. See Zinc Salts.

ZINC CARBONATE • A cosmetic coloring agent, it is a crystalline salt of zinc occurring in nature as smithsonite. See Zinc for toxicity.

ZINC CHLORIDE • **Butter of Zinc.** A zinc salt used as an antiseptic and astringent in shaving creams, dentifrices, and mouthwashes. Odorless and water absorbing; also a deodorant and disinfectant. Can cause contact dermatitis and is mildly irritating to the skin. Can be absorbed through the skin.

ZINC GLUTAMATE • The zinc salt of glutamic acid (*see*).

ZINC HYDROLYZED ANIMAL PROTEIN • See Hydrolyzed Animal Protein.

ZINC MYRISTATE • The zinc salt of myristic acid (*see*).

ZINC NEODECANOATE • The zinc salt of neodecanoic acid (*see*).

ZINC OLEATE-STEARATE • A white, dry, greasy powder, insoluble in water, soluble in alcohol. An antiseptic and astringent in cosmetic creams. Used medicinally to treat eczema and other skin rashes. No known toxicity.

ZINC OXIDE • **Flowers of Zinc.** Used to impart opacity to face powders, foundation creams, and dusting powders. A creamy white ointment used medicinally as an astringent, antiseptic, and protectant in skin diseases. Zinc is believed to encourage healing of skin disorders. It is insoluble in water. In cosmetics it is also used in baby powder, bleach and freckle creams, depilatories, face packs, antiperspirants, foundation cake makeup, nail whiteners, protective creams, rouge, shaving creams, and white eye shadow. Workers suffer skin eruptions called "zinc pox" under the arm and in the groin when working with zinc. Zinc pox is believed to be caused by the blocking of the hair follicles. Because of its astringent qualities, zinc oxide may be unsuitable for dry skins. Generally harmless, however, when used in cosmetics. Permanently listed as a coloring in 1977.

ZINC PEROXIDE • **Zinc Superoxide.** Disinfectant, antiseptic, deodorant, and astringent applied as a dusting powder alone or with talc or starch. White to yellowish white powder. Liberates hydrogen peroxide, a bleach. It is used in bleach and freckle creams and medicinally as a deodorant for festering wounds and skin diseases. No known toxicity.

ZINC PHENOLSULFONATE • A phenol that is used as a topical astringent when mucous membranes are inflamed. Also used in deodorants. See Phenols.

ZINC PYRIDINETHIONE • **Zinc Pyrithione.** An antidandruff ingredient that is reportedly damaging to nerves. A bactericide and fungicide used in antidandruff products. A rare sensitizer but may crossreact with ethylene diamine, piperazine, or hydrochloride derivatives (*see all*).

ZINC RESINATE • Made by fusing zinc oxide and rosin (*see*).

ZINC RICINOLEATE • The zinc salt of ricinoleate (*see*). Used as a fungicide, emulsifier, and stabilizer.

ZINC ROSINATE • The zinc salt of rosin (*see*).

ZINC SALICYLATE • A zinc salt used as an antiseptic and astringent in dusting powders and antiperspirants. White odorless needles or crystalline powder. It is omitted from hypoallergenic cosmetics. Causes both skin irritations and allergic reactions.

ZINC STEARATE • **Zinc Soap.** A mixture of the zinc salts of stearic and palmitic acids (*see both*). Widely used in cosmetic preparations because it contributes to adhesive properties. Also used as a coloring agent. Baby powders of 3 to 5 percent zinc are water repellent and prevent urine irritations. Zinc soap is also used in bath preparations, deodorants, face powders, hair-grooming preparations, hand creams, lotions, and ointments. It is used in tablet manufacture and in pharmaceutical powders and ointments. Inhalation of the powder may cause lung problems and produce death in infants from pneumonitis, with lesions resembling those caused by talc but more severe. No known toxicity on the skin.

ZINC SULFATE • **White Vitriol.** The reaction of sulfuric acid with zinc. Mild crystalline zinc salt used in shaving cream, eye lotions, astringents, styptic, as a gargle spray, skin tonic, and after-shave lotion. Used medicinally as an emetic. Irritating to the skin and mucous membranes. May cause an allergic reaction. Injection under the skin of 2.5 milligrams per kilogram of body weight caused tumors in rabbits.

ZINC SULFIDE • An inorganic zinc salt used as a white pigment and as a fungicide. See Zinc Salts.

ZINC SULFOCARBOLATE • See Zinc Sulfate.

ZINC UNDECYLENATE • A zinc salt. Occurs in sweat. Used to combat fungus in cosmetics and on the skin. Made by dissolving zinc oxide (*see*) in diluted undecylenic acid (*see*). Has an odor suggestive of perspiration. No known toxicity. See Antiperspirants.

ZIRCONIUM • Discovered in 1789. Bluish-black powder or grayish-white flakes used as a bonding agent and abrasive; also in the preparation of dyes. High quality zirconium is used as a pigment toner and solvent. Mildly acidic, it has been used in body deodorants and antiperspirants. Zirconium hydroxide is used in nail whiteners. Low systemic toxicity, but a disease of the skin has been reported in users of a deodorant containing sodium zirconium lactate. Manufacturers voluntarily removed zirconium from spray antiperspirants in 1976 because the element was found harmful to monkey lungs. The FDA has said that zirconium is safe in formulations other than sprays. Zirconium oxide and zirconium silicate are no longer authorized for use as colorings.

ZIRCONIUM SILICATE • See Zirconium.

ZIRCONYL CHLORIDE • **Zirconium Oxychloride.** Used to make other zirconium compounds and to precipitate acid dyes. Acts as a solvent. Mildly acidic. It has been used in deodorants and antiperspirants but because of skin bumps, particularly under the arm, it has been discontinued.

ZIRCONYL HYDROXYCHLORIDE • Colorless powder that absorbs moisture. See Zirconium.

BIBLIOGRAPHY

Allen, Linda, *The Look You Like*. Chicago: Committee on Cutaneous Health and Cosmetics, American Medical Association, 1971.

The Condensed Chemical Dictionary. llth ed. Revised by N. Irving Sax and Richard J. Lewis, Sr. New York: Van Nostrand Reinhold, 1987.

CTFA Cosmetic Ingredient Dictionary. 3rd ed. Edited by Norman Estrin, Ph.D., Patricia Crosly, Charles Haynes. Washington, D.C.: Cosmetic, Toiletry and Fragrances Association, Inc., 1982.

CFTA Cosmetic Ingredient Dictionary. 3rd ed. Supplement. Edited by Joanne M. Whelan. Washington, D.C.: Cosmetic, Toiletry and Fragrances Association, Inc., 1985.

Done, Alan, *Toxic Reactions to Common Household Products*. Paper read at the Symposium on Adverse Reactions sponsored by the Drug Service Center for Disease Control, December 1976, San Francisco.

Fisher, Alexander A., *Contact Dermatitis*. 3rd ed. Philadelphia: Lea & Febiger, 1986.

Gleason, Marion N., et al., *Clinical Toxicology of Commercial Products*. Baltimore: The Williams & Wilkins Co., 1969.

Gordon, Lesley, *A Country Herbal*. New York: Mayflower Books, 1980.

Greenberg, Leon A., and David Lester, *The Handbook of Cosmetic Materials*. New York: Interscience Publishers, 1954.

Kahn, Julius, "Hypo-Allergenic Cosmetics," *NARD Journal* (February 20, 1967).

Kibbe, Constance V., *Standard Textbook of Cosmetology*. Rev. ed. Bronx, N.Y.: Milady Publishing Corp., 1981.

March, Cyril, M.D., and Alexander Fisher, M.D., *Cutaneous Reactions to Cosmetics*. Chicago: American Medical Association, 1965.

Martin, Eric W., et al., *Hazards of Medications*. Philadelphia: J.B. Lippincott Co., 1971.

The Merck Index. 8th, 9th, and 10th eds. Rahway, N.J.: Merck, Sharp and Dohme Research Laboratories, 1983.

The Merck Manual. 15th ed. Edited by Robert Berkow, M.D. Rahway, N.J.: Merck, Sharp and Dohme Research Laboratories, 1987.

Miall, L. Mackenzie, and D. W. A. Sharp. *A New Dictionary of Chemistry*. 4th ed. New York: John Wiley & Sons, Inc., 1968.

Physicians' Desk Reference. Oradell, N.J.: Medical Economics, 1988.

Principles of Cosmetics for Dermatologists. St. Louis: C.V. Mosby Co., 1982.

Prospective Study of Cosmetic Reactions, 1977–1980. North American Contact Dermatitis Group, *Journal of the American Academy of Dermatology*, Vol. 6, No. 5 (May 1982).

Steadman's Medical Dictionary. 24th ed. Baltimore: The Williams & Wilkins Co., 1982.

Suspected Carcinogens: A Subfile of the NIOSH Toxic Substance List. Rockville, Md.: Tracor Jitco, Inc., U.S. Department of Health, Education and Welfare, 1975.

Suspected Carcinogens: A Subfile of The Registry of Toxic Effects of Chemical Substances. Cincinnati: U.S. Department of Health, Education and Welfare, Public Health Services, Center for Disease Control, 1976.

Toxicity Testing: Strategies to Determine Needs and Priorities. Washington, D.C.: National Research Council, National Academy Press, 1984.

White, John Henry, *A Reference Book of Chemistry*. 3rd ed. New York: Philosophical Library, 1965.

Winter, Ruth, *Cancer-Causing Agents: A Preventive Guide*. New York: Crown Publishers Inc., 1979.